Germany since Unification

Also by Klaus Larres

POLITICS OF ILLUSION: Churchill, Eisenhower and the German Question, 1945–1955 (*in German*)

THE FEDERAL REPUBLIC OF GERMANY SINCE 1949: Politics, Society and Economy Before and After Unification (*co-editor with P. Panayi*)

GERMANY AND THE UNITED STATES IN THE 20th CENTURY: A Political History (*in German, co-editor with T. Oppelland*)

A HISTORY OF THE FEDERAL REPUBLIC OF GERMANY, 1949–1989 (*in German, co-author with T. Oppelland*)

UNEASY ALLIES: British–German Relations and European Integration since 1945 (*editor*)

Germany since Unification

The Development of the Berlin Republic

Edited by

Klaus Larres
Reader in Politics
The Queen's University of Belfast
Northern Ireland

Second Edition

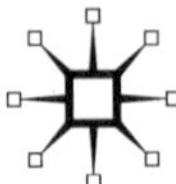

First edition, *Germany since Unification: The Domestic and External Consequences*, published 1998 by Macmillan Press Ltd

Published 2001 by
PALGRAVE
Houndmills, Basingstoke, Hampshire RG21 6XS and
175 Fifth Avenue, New York, N. Y. 10010
Companies and representatives throughout the world

PALGRAVE is the new global academic imprint of St. Martin's Press LLC Scholarly and Reference Division and Palgrave Publishers Ltd (formerly Macmillan Press Ltd).

ISBN 0–333–91829–0 hardback
ISBN 0–333–91999–8 paperback

This book is printed on paper suitable for recycling and made from fully managed and sustained forest sources.

A catalogue record for this book is available from the British Library.

Library of Congress Cataloging-in-Publication Data
Germany since unification : the development of the Berlin republic / edited by Klaus Larres.—2nd ed.
p. cm.
Includes bibliographical references and index.
ISBN 0–333–91829–0 — ISBN 0–333–91999–8 (pbk.)
1. Germany—Politics and government—1990– 2. Germany—Economic conditions—1990– 3. Germany—Social conditions—1990– 4. Germany—History—Unification, 1990. I. Larres, Klaus.

JN3971.A91 G464 2000
943.089'9—dc21

00–062709

10 9 8 7 6 5 4 3 2 1
10 09 08 07 06 05 04 03 02 01

Printed and bound in Great Britain by
Antony Rowe Ltd, Chippenham, Wiltshire

Contents

List of Tables

Notes on the Contributors

Professor William M. Chandler is Professor of Political Science at the University of California, San Diego. Previously he taught at McMaster University in Hamilton, Ontario, Canada. His recent publications include *Public Policy and Provincial Politics*, with M.A. Chandler (1979); *Federalism and the Role of the State*, edited with H. Bakvis (1987); *Challenges to Federalism: Policy-making in Canada and the Federal Republic of Germany*, edited with C.W. Zöllner (1989).

Professor Michael Cox is Professor of International History in the Department of International Politics in the University of Wales, Aberystwyth; he is also editor of the *Review of International Studies*. His recent publications include *US Foreign Foreign Policy after the Cold War: Superpower Without a Mission?* (1995); *The Ideas of Leon Trotsky*, edited with H. Ticktin (1995); *Rethinking the Soviet Collapse: Sovietology, the Death of Communism and the New Russia*, (ed.) (1998); *The Eighty Years' Crisis: International Relations, 1919–1999*, edited with T. Dunne and K. Booth (1998).

Professor Christopher Flockton teaches in the Department of Linguistic and International Studies at the University of Surrey in Guildford, England. His recent publications include 'The Federal German Economy', in D. Dyker (ed.), *The European Economy*, vol. 2 (1992); 'Labour Market Problems and Labour Market Policy', with J. Esser, in G. Smith et al., *Developments in German Politics* (1992); 'Economic Management and the Challenge of Reunification', in G. Smith et al., *Developments in German Politics 2* (1996).

Dr Till Geiger is a Lecturer in European Studies at The Queen's University of Belfast, Northern Ireland. His recent publications include 'Like a Phoenix from the Ashes!? Western Germany's return to the European market, 1945–58', *European Contemporary History* 3 (1994); *Regional Trade Blocs, Multilateralism and the GATT*, edited with D. Kennedy (1996); 'National defense policies and the failure of military integration in NATO: American military assistance and Western European rearmament, 1949–1954', with L. Sebesta, in F. Heller and J. Gillingham (eds), *The United States and the Integration of Europe* (1996).

Steven Hurst is a Lecturer in Politics at the Manchester Metropolitan University, UK. He is the author of *The Carter Administration and Vietnam* (1996); and *US foreign policy between 1989 and 1992: The Foreign Policy of the Bush Administration: In Search of the New World Order* (1999).

Dr Adrian Hyde-Price is a Senior Lecturer at the Institute for German Studies of the University of Birmingham, England. His recent publications include *European Security Beyond the Cold: Five Scenarios for the Year 2010* (1991); '"Of Dragons and Snakes": Contemporary German Security Policy', in G. Smith et al., *Developments in German Politics 2* (1996); *The International Politics of East Central Europe* (1996).

Dr Charlie Jeffery is Deputy Director of the Institute for German Studies at the University of Birmingham, England. His recent publications include *German Federalism Today*, edited with P. Savigear (1991); *Federalism, Unification and European Integration*, edited with R. Sturm (1993); *The Regional Dimension of the European Union*, edited volume (1996).

Dr Klaus Larres is a Reader in Politics and a Jean Monnet Professor for European Foreign and Security Policy at The Queen's University of Belfast, Northern Ireland. His recent publications include *Politik der Illusionen: Churchill, Eisenhower und die deutsche Frage 1945–1955* (1995); *The Federal Republic of Germany since 1949: Politics, Economy and Society before and after Unification*, edited with P. Panayi (1996); *Deutschland und die USA im 20. Jahrhundert: Eine Geschichte der politischen Beziehungen*, edited with T. Oppelland (1997); *Geschichte der Bundesrepublik Deutschland 1949–1989,* co-authored with T. Oppelland (1999); *Uneasy Allies: British-German Relations and European Integration since 1945*, ed. (2000).

Dr Eric Owen Smith is a Senior Lecturer in Economics at Loughborough University, England. His recent publications include *Third Party Involvement in Industrial Disputes: A Comparative Study of West Germany and Britain*, with B. Frick and T. Griffiths (1989); *The German Economy* (1994); 'Incentives for Growth and Development', in S.F. Frowen and J. Hölscher (eds), *The German Currency Union of 1990 – A Critical Assessment* (1996).

Dr Panikos Panayi is a Principal Lecturer in History at De Montfort University in Leicester, England. His recent publications include *The* *enemy in our midst: Germans in Britain during the First World War* (1991); *German Immigrants in Britain during the Nineteenth Century, 1815–1914* (1995); *The Federal Republic of Germany since 1949: Politics, Society and Economy before and after Unification*, edited with K. Larres (1996).

Professor Rolf Steininger is Professor of Modern History and Director of the Institute of Contemporary History at the University of Innsbruck, Austria. His recent publications include *The German Question. The Stalin Note of 1952 and the Problem of Reunification* (1990); *Die doppelte Eindämmung: europäische Sicherheit und deutsche Frage in den Fünfzigern*, edited (1993); *Deutsche Geschichte 1945–1990: Darstellung und Dokumente*, 4 vols (1996).

Glossary and Abbreviations

ABS-Gesellschaften	Employment Enterprises
AFG	Job Creation Law (Arbeitsförderungsgesetz)
AGMs	General meetings of shareholders
Ampelkoalition	See traffic-light coalition
Amt für Verfassungsschutz (AVS)	Office for the protection of the constitution (MI5/FBI equivalent)
Aufschwung Ost/West	Economic upswing east/west
Auslandsdeutsche	German citizens living abroad
Aussiedler	Ethnic Germans
AWAC	Airborne Warning and Control System (US radar system for early detection of enemy forces)
Basic Law	West German and then all-German constitution
BBk	Bundesbank (German Central Bank)
BdL	Bank of the German Länder (Bank deutscher Länder)
Benelux countries	Belgium, the Netherlands, Luxembourg
BFD	Union of Free Germans (Bund Freier Deutscher)
BMF	Federal Finance ministry (Bundesministerium der Finanzen)
BMI	Federal Interior Ministry (Bundesministerium des Inneren)
BRD	Bundesrepublik Deutschland (= FRG)
Bundesbank (BBk)	Federal Central Bank
Bundespost	Federal Post Office

Bundesrat	Upper house of federal Parliament
Bundesregierung	Federal government
Bundestag	Lower house of federal Parliament
Bundeswehr	Federal armed forces
Bündnis 90 (B90)	Umbrella organisation of the East German citizens' movements
CAP	Common agricultural policy
CDU	Christian Democratic Union
CFE	Conventional Forces in Europe
CFM	Council of Foreign Ministers
CFSP	(EU) Common Foreign and Security Policy
CJTF	Combined Joint Task Forces (between NATO and WEU)
Comecon	Council for Mutual Economic Assistance
CSCE	Conference on Security and Cooperation in Europe
CSSR	former Czechoslovakia
CSU	Christian Social Union (only in Bavaria)
DA	Demokratischer Aufbruch (Democratic Awakening)
DDR	Deutsche Demokratische Republik (= GDR)
Demokratie Jetzt	Democracy Now
Demokratische Freiheit	Democratic Freedom
Demokratischer Aufbruch	Democratic Awakening (DA)
Deutsche Alternative (DA)	German Alternative (DA)
Deutsche Bahn AG	Federal railways
Deutsche Reichs Partei (DRP)	German Empire Party
Deutschland	Germany
Deutschlandpolitik	Inner-German policy
DFOR	NATO Deterrence Force for Bosnia Herzegovina (successor to SFOR)
DFP	German Free Democratic Party (Deutsche

	Freidemokratische Partei)
DFP	German Forum Party (Deutsche Forums Partei)
Die Grünen	West German Green Party
DIW	Deutsches Institut für Wirtschaft
DM	Deutsche Mark (West German and then all-German currency)
DP	German Party (Deutsche Partei)
DSU	German Social Union (Deutsche Soziale Union)
DVU	German People's Union (Deutsche Volksunion)
EC	European Community
ECB	European Central Bank
ECJ	European Court of Justice
ECSC	European Coal and Steel Community (Schuman Plan)
ECU	European Currency Unit
EDC	European Defence Community
EEC	European Economic Community
EFTA	European Free Trade Association
EMS	European Monetary System
EMU	European Economic and Monetary Union
EPU	European Political Union
ERM	Exchange Rate Mechanism
EU	European Union
Euro	Common European currency
Europäische Friedensordnung	European peace order
Europapolitik	European politics
FAP	Free Workers Party (Freiheitliche Deutsche Arbeiterpartei)
FAZ	Frankfurter Allgemeine Zeitung (conservative daily paper)

FDI	Foreign Direct Investment
FDP	Free Democratic Party, the Liberals (Freidemokratische Partei)
FOTL	Follow on to the Lance missile system
FRG	Federal Republic of Germany
FRUS	Foreign Relations of the United States
Gastarbeiter	Guestworkers
GDP	Gross Domestic Product
GDR	German Democratic Republic (East Germany)
Gemeinsame Verfassungskommission	Joint constitutional commission
Gemeinschaftswerk Aufschwung Ost	The common effort for achieving an economic upswing in the east
GEMSU	German Economic, Monetary and Social Union (July 1990)
Glasnost	Openness, policy of more open consultative government
GNP	Gross National Product
Grand coalition	CDU/CSU-SPD
Grundgesetz	Basic Law
Ifo	Institute for industrial research (Institut für Wirtschaftsforschung)
IFOR	NATO Implementation Force for Bosnia Herzegovina
IGC	Intergovernmental Conference of 1996 to review the Maastricht Treaty
CJTF	Combined Joint Task Forces between NATO and WEU
INF	Intermediate-Range Nuclear Missiles
Innere Führung	Inner democratic leadership
Kartellamt	Monopolies Commission
Kombinat	East German state monopoly
KPD	German Communist Party

Kreditabwicklungsfond	State Credit Agency
Laissez-faire	Free Market philosophy
Land (plural: Länder)	German federal state
LDP	East German Liberal Party (Liberal-demokratische Partei)
LDPD	East German Liberal Democratic Party (Liberal-demokratische Partei Deutschlands)
Lufthansa AG	Federal airways
M3	Money supply, coins and notes in circulation (usually including currency deposits)
Magdeburger Modell	SPD-Green minority government tolerated by the PDS (developed in Saxony-Anhalt in June 1994)
MBO	Management buy-out
Mittellage	Central location
Mittelstand	Medium-sized enterprises
MRDB	Monthly Report of the German Bundesbank
NATO	North Atlantic Treaty Organisation
NDPD	East German National Democratic Party (National-demokratische Partei Deutschlands)
NPD	National Democratic Party (Nationaldemokratische Partei Deutschlands)
Oder-Neisse line	Border between Poland and Germany
OECD	Organisation for Economic Cooperation and Development
OM	Ostmark (East German currency)
OSCE	Organisation for Security and Cooperation in Europe
Ossies	East Germans

Ost-CDU	East German CDU
Ostpolitik	Eastern policy, policy towards the East
PDS	Party of Democratic Socialism (successor to SED)
Perestroika	Restructuring, domestic economic and political reform policy
Pfennig	Penny
Politbüro	Political body consisting of the ruling élites in former communist countries
Postbank	Federal post office bank
Postdienst	Federal postal services
Presse- und Informationsamt	Federal Press and Information Office
PRO	Public Record Office, London
R&D	Research and Development
Rabattgesetz	Law limiting the pricing freedom of retailers
RAF	Red Army Faction (West German terrorist organisation)
Rapallo Treaty	German–Russian friendship treaty of 1922
Realpolitik	The strategy of pursuing policies oriented on 'realistic' power politics
Reich	Empire
Reichsbahn	East German railways
Reps	Republican Party (die Republikaner)
Ruhrgebiet	(West) Germany's industrial heartland
Sachverständigenkommission	Committee of experts
Sanierungsfähig	Feasible economic restructuring
SDI	Strategic Defence Initiative
SDP	East German Social Democratic Party
SED	Socialist Unity Party (the ruling communist party in the GDR)

SEA	Single European Act
SFOR	NATO Stabilization Force for Bosnia Herzegovina (successor to IFOR)
Sicherheitspolitik	Security policy
SME	Social Market Economy
SNF	Short-range nuclear weapons
Sonderweg	Special path
Soziale Marktwirtschaft	Social Market Economy (SME)
Sozialistische Reichs Partei (SRP)	Socialist Empire Party
SPD	Social Democratic Party
Standortfrage	International competitiveness of a given industrial location
Standortsicherungsgesetz	Law to ensure the competitiveness of Germany as an industrial location
Stasi	East German State Security Police
Stromvertrag	Electricity Contract
THA	Treuhandanstalt
Traffic-light coalition	SPD-FDP-Bündnis-90/Green coalition (red-yellow-green)
Treuhandanstalt	Public trustee institution (THA)
UN	United Nations
USSR	Union of the Soviet Socialist Republics
VAT	Value Added Tax
Verflechtung	Network
Volkskammer (VK)	People's assembly, East German parliament
Volkspartei	People's Party
Waffen SS	Schutzstaffel, particularly cruel paramilitary security organ during the 'Third Reich'
Wende	Turning point, change
Wessies	West Germans
Westbindung	Attachment to the West
Westintegration	Integration with the West

Westpolitik	Western policy, policy towards the West
WEU	Western European Union
Wirtschaftswunder	West German economic miracle
Zonenrandgebiet	West German territory bordering on the GDR

Introduction to the Second Edition

I am pleased that the publisher expressed the wish to proceed with a second revised and expanded edition of *Germany since Unification* with the new subtitle *The Development of the Berlin Republic*. The publication of the second edition appears to be particularly appropriate in view of the change of government from the CDU/CSU-FDP coalition, led by Helmut Kohl for almost 18 years, to Gerhard Schröder's new Red–Green coalition which came to power in October 1998 (Weidenfeld, 1999). In September 1999 the Social Democratic/Green government, the German *Bundestag* and most of the important ministries moved to Berlin. Despite some scepticism as to whether the relocation of Germany's seat of government to its capital Berlin will result in the development of a different Republic, and a more strident and less willing state to accept integration in the western world in general and the European Union in particular, the German government has always rejected such suspicions as groundless.

Indeed, there seems to be little reason to expect the emergence of a more powerful and less integrated Germany. Instead, with respect to the unified country's still unresolved economic, financial and social problems, there was talk of Germany as the new 'sick man' of Europe in 1999. While this seems to have been an exaggeration (after all, in 1999 the German economy grew by 1.4 per cent) during its first eighteen months in office the domestic performance of the Schröder/Fischer government has been less than impressive. In areas such as social, economic and nuclear affairs the government disappointed, and was generally unable to embark upon a different or more successful political course than the previous Kohl governments. In view of Germany's continuing economic problems, and the resignation of Finance Minister Oskar Lafontaine in March 1999, the government's efforts increasingly have been directed at cautiously reforming Germany's economic structure in a neo-liberal sense. After all, with Lafontaine's departure the traditional 'socialist' wing of the SPD was substantially weakened (Lafontaine and Müller, 1998; Lafontaine, 1999) in favour of Schröder's much more trendy neo-liberal 'champagne socialism' (Herres and Waller, 1998).

Moreover since early 1999 the Schröder government's agenda has become increasingly dominated by a modernising pro-business agenda. It envisages substantial reductions in state intervention and state spending on the welfare state, and Germany's social-safety net (including pensions and the health service) in favour of general economic deregulation and greater individual responsibility. These are of course mere euphemisms for indicating that the individual German citizen will in future have to pay for many services formerly provided or at least subsidised by the German state. The Schröder government appears to be in the process of attempting to realise all three of the major commandments of monetarism (tight control of the money supply, low public expenditure and low taxation, and the liberalisation of the labour market) (Pulzer, 1995: 147). Indeed, Chancellor Schröder is busy implementing Anglo-Saxon economic doctrines (Ross, 2000). This also explains the Chancellor's great interest in a social democratic 'third way' promulgated above all by British Prime Minister Tony Blair's 'New Labour' policies (Giddens, 1998; Hombach, 1998; Meyer, 1998; Unger *et al.*, 1998; Misik, 1998). Thus, in June 1999 the two politicians' agreement on important economic and social–political positions led to the publication of the so-called Schröder/Blair paper. This paper, symbolising both politicians' attempt to find a *neue Mitte* (a new middle), was most controversial among some traditionalist sections of the SPD. It was difficult to envisage that Schröder (or for that matter Blair) would have been able to agree on such a paper with the much more traditional–socialist French Prime Minister Jospin. In March 2000, when speaking at a conference in Oxford Blair announced that Anglo-German relations 'had never been warmer than they are today' (Larres, 2000).

However, in contrast to developments in the USA and to a more limited extent in Britain, Schröder's efforts on behalf of a neo-liberal economic policy did not lead to an economic upturn and a reduction of Germany's mass unemployment in 1999. Despite the economic benefits expected from the introduction of the euro on 1 January 1999, by mid 1999 the average unemployment rate in all 11 euro-zone countries was still a depressing 10.3 per cent, which compared very badly with a rate of 4.3 per cent in the booming USA. Indeed, in July and August 1999 Germany's unemployment rate also stood at 10.3 per cent; the average unemployment rate for 1999 was 10.5 per cent. Although this meant that compared with the year before unemployment in July and August had dropped by 100 000, just over four million Germans were still registered as searching for work (and this figure excluded those supported by state subsidised work schemes, people on short-time work and the large number of involuntary students, pensioners, housewives and so on not registered as unemployed and looking for work). On average, just under 4.1 million Germans were unemployed in 1999. The situation continued to remain much more serious in the new *Länder* in the east than in the old *Länder* in western Germany (in the east in 1999 unemployment was 17.6 per cent compared to 8.8 per cent in the west). The new red–green coalition's inability to improve Germany's economic performance contributed decisively to the six consecutive regional election defeats which the SPD and the Greens suffered between February and October 1999 (for details, see Chandler/Larres below).

It was only in spring 2000 that Schröder's economic policy appeared to show some slow results. However, the development of a generally more favourable economic climate also deserves some credit; after all, by early 2000 an economic upturn of on average four per cent (ranging from Germany's and Italy's 2.5 per cent to Finland's 4.9 per cent and Ireland's 7.5 per cent economic growth) and a reduction of unemployment could be observed in most EU countries. In April 2000 the rate of unemployment in the whole of Germany dropped to 9.8 per cent. The country had 3.99 million people out of work. Compared to the year before unemployment had decreased by 159 000; it was the lowest unemployment figure in April for four years and it meant that unemployment had fallen below the psychologically important four million threshold. This slow reduction of unemployment continued in May and Chancellor Schröder expected optimistically that by late 2000 the German economy would grow by at least 2.5 per cent and perhaps even by up to 3.0 per cent. Inflation did not appear to be a problem. In April 2000 the German rate of inflation even fell to 1.5 per cent from 1.9 per cent in March. This was slightly less than the average rate of inflation of 2.1 per cent in the euro area (this meant that inflation in the euro zone was just 0.1 per cent over the target rate set by the European Central Bank in Frankfurt). Yet, if the euroland economies grow further rising inflation may well cause headaches again.

Schröder and his Finance Minister Hans Eichel urgently need to demonstrate that they are capable of producing the policies which will lead to a much improved performance of the German economy. After all, in the general election in late 2002 and in the various regional elections in the meantime, the German voters will measure the success or failure of the Schröder government in the Chancellor's ability to increase substantially Germany's economic performance and decrease unemployment – as he repeatedly promised during the 1998 election campaign. Thus Schröder is under great pressure to enhance drastically his domestic political achievements if he wishes to be re-elected in 2002. The Chancellor therefore hopes that by 2002 the number of people unemployed in Germany will have dropped below 3.5 million.

In spring 2000, however, German voters still expressed dissatisfaction with the red–green government in Berlin. The modest improvement of the German economy did not seem to have impressed them. Schröder and the SPD should also have benefitted more than they did from one of the most serious crises in the history of the Federal Republic. This was the revelation of the CDU's party-funding scandal in November and December 1999. Former Chancellor Kohl admitted to accepting considerable amounts of secret cash donations from wealthy businesspeople throughout the 1990s, and possibly the 1980s, which he deposited in secret accounts for his personal political use. The German party financing laws, introduced by the Kohl government itself in the mid 1980s after a previous donation scandal, specifies that the receipt of funds above 20 000 deutschmarks need to be declared and are not allowed to remain anonymous. Kohl channelled the anonymous money, for example, to local and regional CDU organisations to build up a huge system of patronage and ensure the obedience of as many CDU politicians as possible. He may also have used the donations for other still unknown political activities. It had never happened before in the history of the Federal Republic that a German chancellor had become deliberately and knowingly involved in illegal financial activities (Pflüger, 2000; Scheuch and Scheuch, 2000). Therefore, at least two questions need to be asked.

Was Kohl only able to remain CDU party leader (and thus in the last resort chancellor) due to his ability to generously provide considerable sums of money to regional and local party organisations? It certainly must be assumed that the secret cash donations helped Kohl to maintain his personal influence within the CDU party at all political levels (the so-called 'system Kohl'). This was important in view of his many inner-party rivals throughout his reign. However, according to the former chancellor the money was only used to bolster the cash starved CDU party organisations in the former GDR. Even more importantly, the question arises if and what kind of political favours the secret donors received in return. Was the Kohl government corrupt? Were the donations, for example, linked to the sale of tank components to Saudi Arabia as has been alleged and was the purchase of the East German oil refinery Leuna by the then state-owned French group Elf Aquitaine facilitated in that way? The suspicion has been expressed that the Mitterrand government in Paris was behind the latter. Perhaps the French purchase of a bankrupt East German company which would give Kohl credit for having saved the survival of an important regional employer was President's Mitterrand's way of ensuring that the chancellor would remain committed to embarking on the deepening of European integration and the establishment of monetary union which both politicians had agreed upon as the other side of the coin of German unification. This 'deal' later led to the Maastricht Treaty. It would appear that many of the relevant secret documents, which could have shed light on these issues, were illegally shredded after the Kohl government had lost the 1998 general election.

While Kohl does not appear to have enriched himself personally, these are serious accusations which go to the heart of German democracy and the role of the chancellor in German politics. Moreover, similar illegal financial dealings in some of the CDU's regional organisations (above all in Hesse) were revealed, indicating that the corruption of German politics had spread beyond the CDU headquarters. A parliamentary commission has been established to shed light onto the entire affair and its findings may well lead to the commencement of criminal investigations and perhaps indictments of senior German politicians. Above all, Kohl still adamantly refuses to name any of his donors and this has led to speculation about the unsavoury nature of some of these people. Instead, the former chancellor has collected eight million deutschmarks which he has given to the CDU to compensate his party for the high fines levied on it by the President of the national parliament for the activities of Kohl and other senior CDU politicians (including former treasurer Walther Leisler Kiep) for the submission of manipulated annual financial accounts throughout the 1990s (and perhaps during the 1980s as well) to keep the anonymous and illegal donations secret.

The CDU itself has already borne some consequences. Kohl was asked to give up his honorary chairmanship of the party. Since early 2000, the CDU's former hero has been increasingly shunned by most of the party's senior politicians. Moreover, in April 2000 Angela Merkel replaced Wolfgang Schäuble, Kohl's handpicked successor as party leader, who had also become embroiled in the scandal. Merkel promised a new beginning. After all, she was the first woman and the first politician from the former GDR to head one of Germany's major parties. Although Merkel served as a minister in the last Kohl government and subsequently became the party's general manager, Merkel has only been in politics since 1990. She is generally regarded as an honest and straightforward politician. However, her more liberal outlook and relative inexperience has already been criticized by the CDU's arch-conservative Bavarian sister party, the CSU, and its formidable leader, Bavarian Prime Minister Edmund Stoiber, who may himself wish to become the CDU/CSU's chancellor candidate in 2002.

Although due to the CDU's funding scandal, the SPD and the Greens won the regional election in Schleswig Holstein in February 2000, many Germans are still disappointed about the achievements of the coalition government in Berlin. This may have contributed to the SPD's and the Greens' poor performance in the regional election in North Rhine Westfalia in May 2000 (for details see Chandler/Larres below). Moreover, the early stages of the red–green government's three tier tax reform of 1999/2000, with its aim to modernise the German tax and pension system for the years until 2005, has failed to meet with a positive response from the German consumers, German industry and the parliamentary opposition parties CDU/CSU, FPD and the PDS. The reform envisages the lowering of income and corporation taxes which are to be financed by closing tax loops. However, in the mind of many Germans the tax reform was identified with substantially higher taxes on petrol, gas and oil for heating purposes which were introduced in the context of the controversial new 'ecological tax reform' which took effect on 1 April 1999. Moreover, social security tax (to be paid by both employees and employers) was levied on income from part-time or low paid employment (the so-called 630-mark jobs); hitherto this income had been entirely tax free. The imposition of the new tax led to many people giving up their low paid jobs as their take home pay proved to be so low that holding a 630-mark job was not financially rewarding anymore. In particular this development led to claims that the government's tax reform effectively introduced new taxes on the weaker sections of society and helped to destroy jobs, instead of contributing to the creation of new sources of employment. Although, the monthly contribution of employees' to their pension funds were simultaneously reduced by 0.8 per cent, most voters failed to see the personal advantages they might obtain from the red–green tax reform. The business community, which is to benefit from much lower corporation taxes, was also doubtful whether the entire reform programme was sufficiently substantial to have an impact on Germany's economic development. Similarly, Finance Minister Eichel's promise to reduce the federal debt and decrease the government's annual new borrowing requirement from approximately 50 million deutschmarks to zero by 2005–6 was regarded with scepticism. However, despite much opposition, in July 2000 the government managed to steer a somewhat revised, major income tax reform for the years 2001–05 through the CDU demurated *Bundesrat*. This was a considerable victory for Schröder and Eichel and a devastating defeat for the new CDU leadership. (see also Flockton below).

Furthermore, the government's support for initiatives to strengthen Germany's role in the financial world were not rewarded with success. The attempted merger between the Deutsche Bank and the Dresdner Bank to create the world's largest bank collapsed in April 2000. The government had been much in favour of this merger as it would have challenged the global dominance of American banks.

The Schröder government also failed with its clumsily executed plan to have Caio Koch-Weser, a state secretary in the Finance Ministry, appointed as the next head of the International Monetary Fund (IMF), which lends money to financially troubled countries while in return insisting on the fulfilment of certain economic conditions. Despite early indications from Washington that Koch-Weser was unacceptable, the Schröder government persisted with his nomination and persuaded the EU to accept Koch-Weser as the European candidate. However, after months of wrangling he was formally rejected by the United States which holds a blocking minority vote. It was felt by President Clinton and Treasury Secretary Larry Summers that Koch-Weser was too open-minded about the concerns of the developing world and would thus be unlikely to embark on the required restructuring of the IMF in a neo-liberal way. Yet, Schröder continued to insist on a German candidate as head of the IMF; after all Germany had never headed this organisation and the Chancellor wished to demonstrate Germany's increased international financial importance. Eventually, the German Chancellor proposed Horst Kohler, the director of the European Bank for Reconstruction and Development in London, and managed to obtain his endorsement as the EU's candidate. Köhler, a member of the CDU is internationally best known for his role in contributing to the successful negotiations of European Economic and Monetary Union (EMU); he also participated in G7 summits as a member of Helmut Kohl's government. Köhler was acceptable to Washington and was voted in as head of the 182-nation IMF in late March 2000. The entire episode did little to enhance the Schröder government's international credibility; it had indeed been handled with an extraordinary lack of skill and diplomatic acumen.

However, with regard to the payment of compensation to Holocaust victims of foreign nationality (including many from Eastern Europe), the Schröder government and its main negotiator, former economics minister Otto Graf Lambsdorff, showed much greater skill. Collective court cases against companies such as Ford, Volkswagen, BMW, Daimler-Chrysler, Siemens, Krupp and others had been instigated on behalf of the victims by American lawyers in spring 1998. Despite many months of complicated negotiations between the legal associations representing the Holocaust victims and German industry, which pays half of the amount of compensation (the government and thus the German tax payer funds the other half), a deal was eventually reached in mid December 1999. However, many details still needed to be clarified. It was agreed subsequently that Germany will pay 10 billion marks into a fund which would then be distributed among the surviving 240 000 former slave-workers and the surviving 1 million people who were compelled to work as forced labourers by the Nazis. The final settlement was signed in Berlin in mid July 2000. The first payments, on average DM 15 000 were, to be made later in the year. While the deal offers the ageing generation of Holocaust victims some last minute compensation for their great suffering during the Nazi era, the German government expects that the agreement ensures that no further legal demands for compensation from German companies (or foreign companies based in Germany during the Nazi era) which collaborated with Hitler can be made in countries such as the United States. Thus, despite a good deal of justified criticism about the hesitation of German industry to agree to pay half of the amount of compensation and the unfortunate prolonged legal wrangling, it appeared that ultimately both sides, the ageing victims as well as German business and the German government, benefited from the settlement.

In summer 2000 the government's envisaged reform legislation concentrated on the further overhaul of the German tax and pension systems, the continued deregulation of German industry, the attempt to bring about the end of the use of atomic energy in the Federal Republic and on the restructuring of the *Bundeswehr* (on the latter, see Hyde-Price below). Moreover, Berlin still intended to progress with the long overdue reforms of the German transport system and the country's rather outmoded and unnecessarily inflexible higher education system. It was also envisaged to loosen Germany's labour and competition laws further to make them less restrictive and improve the German economy's ability to compete internationally.

However, Chancellor Schröder's so-called 'green card' proposal which he launched in March 2000 to enable up to 20 000 foreign information technology experts from outside the EU to come to Germany on a temporary five-year basis met with fierce criticism. Nevertheless, the

Bundestag passed it in July 2000. While most employers welcomed the Chancellor's initiative as they shared his view that German industry was falling behind in competing in the new knowledge based global economy due to a serious lack of computer expertise in the Federal Republic, the CDU/CSU emphasized the importance of educating German students instead of attracting foreigners. During the election campaign in North Rhine Westfalia in April and May 2000 this heated debate about Germany's ability to compete in the internet economy culminated in the nasty slogan coined by Jürgen Rütgers, the regional CDU leader, 'Kinder statt Inder'. He advocated the production of the required expertise from within the Federal Republic as quickly as possible instead of allowing Indians and other foreigners to obtain special work permits to take up employment in Germany. The European Monitoring Centre on Racism and Xenophobia in Vienna expressed great concern about the slogan. Chancellor Schröder viewed the phrase as 'indecent' and economically counterproductive. Even without Rüttger's harmful slogan it can be expected that, in view of the competition of the United States and other countries for information technology experts, the government will find it difficult to attract this expertise to Germany.

Schröder's green coalition partner has so far hardly been able to put its stamp on the policy of the red–green coalition. Most of their proposals have come to nothing. Suggestions such as introducing more severe speed limits on cars to prevent accidents and save petrol and thus preserve the environment, the speedy termination of the use of atomic energy, as well as a greater general emphasis on environmental legislation, have largely met with little enthusiasm in the ranks of its senior coalition partner. However, the Greens are not prepared to accept the SPD proposal that most atomic energy plants should continue operating for another 30 years (and thus almost until the end of their technological lives) before they are shut down. Not surprisingly the atomic energy industry has indicated that they could live with such a scheme. There is also the question whether the government will need the agreement of the *Bundesrat* which is dominated by the opposition CDU/CSU, for the contemplated exit from atomic energy. Green Health Minister Andrea Fischer's attempt throughout 1999 to introduce a major reform of Germany's expensive public health system failed when the *Bundesrat* vetoed it. Even many supporters of the government were relieved as they had become disenchanted with the entire complicated and highly controversial enterprise which would have put a much greater financial burden on individual patients. Yet, the general confusion and lack of direction which reigns among the Greens and is complemented by the party's weakening position due to its poor performance in almost all the regional elections in 1999–2000 makes life easier for the Chancellor. Occasionally Schröder is inclined to hint at the possibility of entering into a coalition with the small FDP if the Greens become too critical of the governmental policy favoured by the SPD. The Greens do not have this choice; for the time being a CDU/CSU–Green government is still not imaginable.

The declining strength of the euro increasingly worried the government during the spring of 2000. Above all, due to the still spectacularly booming American economy, by late April 2000 the European currency had lost 22 per cent of its initial value against the dollar since its launch in January 1999. Replacing the deutschmark – which for decades had been one of the world's strongest currencies – with the weak euro appeared to undermine the confidence of many Germans in the European Union and the entire European integration process. However, the weakness of the euro may have helped the German (and European) export industry and contributed to the gradual upturn in the EU's economic performance. According to *The Economist* 'one of the reasons for the euro's weakness was 'the markets' reluctance to believe that Europe has the political will for structural reform'. The magazine was convinced that neither Germany nor any other eurozone country could be selected 'as a model of structural reform of the sort required to sustain the [European economic] recovery' which emerged slowly in the spring and summer of 2000. What *The Economist* believes needs to be achieved is that 'magic mix of deregulation, tax reform and a looser labour market' which neo-liberal economic policy in Britain and the United States managed to introduce (29 April 2000, 45–7). Indeed, the red–green government in Berlin has made only very slow progress with the realisation of the cautious economic restructing of Germany which Chancellor Schröder said he wished to pursue to improve the German economy and reduce unemployment when he came to power in October 1998 (Prantl, 2000).

However, against all expectations, the Schröder government appears to have been much more successful in the foreign policy field than in domestic affairs. During the German EU presidency and in the course of the important European summit meetings in Berlin and Cologne in the first half of 1999 the new government succeeded in instigating moderate changes in the policy and institutional structure of the European Union and was able to make progress with the realisation of the EU's ambitious *Agenda 2000* programme. It was agreed to consider the reform of the EU's common agricultural policy (CAP), its regional policy and its complicated financial system. This was important as there was an urgent need to prepare the EU for its eastern expansion, which is expected to occur in approximately 2003/04, when in all probability Poland, Hungary, the Czech Republic, Estonia and perhaps a few other countries will be admitted to membership of the European Union. Moreover, during the German EU presidency decisive moves towards the development of a European foreign policy and a more integrated European defence structure were taken (see below; and Kirchner, 2000). However, the Schröder government did not achieve all of its aims. The Chancellor had talked about representing 'German interests' and had expressed his desire to lower Germany's significant financial contribution to the EU. In the end this only happened to a rather limited extent; Schröder only obtained a largely cosmetic concession in this matter. Moreover, France succeeded in opposing any dramatic change to CAP, Spain managed to continue receiving large European subsidies for regional development purposes and Britain defended its rebate to a large extent.

Furthermore, Schröder managed to prevent a paralysis of the EU by overcoming the deep European crisis which had been provoked by the resignation of the EU Commission led by Jacques Santer. Schröder and his colleagues succeeded in persuading Romano Prodi to be available as the new President of the EU Commission; the Secretary General of NATO, Xavier Solana, agreed to become the EU's new and first special representative for foreign affairs with effect from October 1999. Thus, on the whole Chancellor Schröder and Foreign Minister Joschka Fischer successfully coped with a major political test shortly after their election victory.

The same applied to a much more challenging event in the spring of 1999. The German government's active military participation in, and skilful domestic management of, the Kosovo war in the former Yugoslavia between 24 March and 10 June 1999 surprised many (Scharping, 2000). The Schröder/Fischer government not only survived despite strong domestic opposition to the war in many quarters in Germany (and in particular among Green party activists and voters). It was also able to demonstrate to the outside world unified Germany's international reliability and loyalty to the western alliance. Domestically, however, this led to a most controversial debate about how to reform the German conscript army, the *Bundeswehr* and Germany's general defence structure. After all, it can be expected that due to Germany's full reintegration into the international community since 1991, NATO, as well as the United Nations and other organisations, will expect the country to contribute to similar emergency situations in the future; and they will expect the German government to do so effectively and speedily. Thus, Germany will need to cope with the financial strains resulting from such activities (see also Hyde-Price below).

During the European summit meeting in Cologne in June 1999 Germany signed up to the development of a European Defence Organisation and managed to incorporate all fifteen EU member states into this process. Hitherto, European defence matters had largely been dominated by France and Britain; their defence co-operation was based on the December 1998 agreement at St Malo. At the Helsinki summit in December 1999 Germany agreed to participate in the creation of a European Rapid Reaction Force. This force is meant to be ready as early as 2003 to enable the EU to fulfil its conflict management and conflict intervention obligations as agreed in the so-called 'Petersberg tasks': peace preservation, humanitarian intervention, and peace making (Heisbourg, 2000). Yet, in view of the continuing reduction in financial resources for the German armed forces and with regard to the heated discussion over the future structure of the *Bundeswehr*, it is obvious that the red–green government, like its predecessor, does not feel any desire to transform the Federal Republic into the European continent's leading military force or into a new great power. Although, occasionally some authors advocate such a course (Schöllgen, 1999: 201–7; Schwarz, 1994), this appears to be mere wishful thinking on the part of a minority of conservative authors. It has very little in common with the much more common sense policy of the red–green coalition government in Berlin. In this, as in many other respects, the policy of the Schröder administration is not all that different from the main features of the Kohl government's foreign policy.

In view of the great continuity which characterises Germany's foreign policy and with respect to the government's great difficulties of improving Germany's economic situation, the red–green coalition's first two years in office have made it clear that Chancellor Schröder has not embarked on a radical departure in German politics. Instead, his approach is of a piecemeal and cautiously reformist nature. Thus, to a large extent the political and economic developments in Germany since unification are still dominated by the agenda and the legacy of the Kohl years (Clay and Paterson, 1998). The latter is perhaps most aptly characterised with the help of the words *Stillstand* and *Reformstau* – the terms which aptly describe the Kohl government's inability to overcome Germany's political and economic stagnation by embarking on and realizing a substantial reform programme. The accusation of 'muddling through' which the SPD and the Greens levied against the Kohl government throughout the 1980s and 1990s, when they were in opposition, appears to be a policy which has been adopted by the SPD–Green coalition partners. The financial and economic–structural legacies of the immediate unification years which the Kohl administration failed to tackle are a burden which the Schröder/Fischer government also appears to be unable to shake off. It is hoped that the chapters in this book will contribute to an understanding of the nature of this legacy which will need to be overcome if the Schröder government is to succeed with its aim of improving Germany's economic performance and of fully integrating eastern Germany's new *Länder* economically and socially into a truly unified state.

For the second edition of this book the original contributions have largely remained unaltered, although any typesetting and occasional other mistakes have been corrected. Instead of asking the individual contributors to rewrite their chapters, the publisher proposed that the authors should be asked to update their contributions by means of a brief account of the developments which have occurred since the publication of the first edition in January 1998. These accounts can be found below. In addition Mick Cox and Steven Hurst have contributed a new chapter based on recently made available new sources, which analyses the important topic of the role of the United States in German unification and concludes with a section on German–American relations in the 1990s.

CHRISTOPHER FLOCKTON: THE GERMAN ECONOMY

Hesitant recovery after mid-decade recession, slow structural reforms and a change of government

Germany suffered a mild recession in 1995–96, which was occasioned by a 5 per cent appreciation in the external value of the Deutschmark as well as by abnormal wage inflation following the engineering industry settlement of 5.5 per cent. This then acted as the pacesetter for wage settlements more generally. Net exports fell and companies responded to cost increases by a renewed and concerted attack on labour costs, leading to heavy labour shedding in manufacturing. The recession was short-lived but the slow, hesitant upturn, confirmed in 1997, was then undermined by the emerging markets crises of 1998. The growth has then done almost nothing to offset the historic record unemployment of a seasonally-unadjusted 4.66 millions in January 1997. This all-German unemployment level at the rate of 12.2 per cent exceeded the 1933 figure for the first time, reawakening older fears of the political consequences of mass unemployment. (Deutsche Bundesbank, *Monatsberichte*).

Of particular concern was the marked slowing of growth in the new *Bundesländer*, leading to a further divergence with the west. In 1997, 1998 and continuing in 1999, the eastern GDP growth rates fell far below those of the west and confirmed once more the view that the catch-up between east and west would be a matter of decades, with the severe political and public finance consequences this would entail. The slowdown in the east was prompted primarily by the ending of the very generous tax allowances (amounting to DM33 billion) for construction projects in the new *Länder* which had led to a huge excess supply of office and retailing space in eastern German cities as well as to inappropriate housing developments. Construction had led the upturn in the east, kick-starting growth, and by 1996 represented 16 per cent of eastern GDP compared with 14.6 per cent for manufacturing, whereas construction represents only 6 per cent of western GDP. Eastern manufacturing grew at rates of 18 per cent per annum from late 1992 to the end of 1995 but has since slowed very markedly to approximately 8 per cent per annum. GDP growth has been well below that of the west in recent years at 1.6 per cent in 1997 and 1.9 per cent in 1999 (*Wirtschaft und Statistik*, various issues). This very heavy dependency on federal tax breaks and western demand demonstrates once more how far eastern Germany is from reaching self-sustained growth. Only large-scale second labour market measures such as the 500 000 beneficiaries at the end of 1995, have prevented registered unemployment from rising far above the 16–18 per cent experienced in recent years (Deutsche Bundesbank, *Monatsberichte*).

Fiscal difficulties and the introduction of the euro

The scale of financial transfers to the east has been the prime cause of the heavy deficits in the federal budget and the marked rise in debt. Net transfers of the order of DM10 billion annually have been typical for the 1990s and future transfers of DM95 billion annually were programmed in the last Kohl government's medium-term financial plan through to the early years of the next decade. A recasting of regional assistance, but no effective scaling back, has been agreed until 2004, when further restructuring of the *Länder* financial equalisation mechanism will be needed. Of course, the scale of the deficits and debt led to some doubts in 1996/97 whether Germany would meet the Maastricht Treaty fiscal convergence criteria, which Germany itself had insisted upon as tests for participation in the single currency. In the event, by emergency expenditure freezes, the bringing forward of privatisation sales, tax increases (such as the Solidarity surcharge and the increases in petrol tax), Germany managed to meet these criteria, achieving a deficit in 1997 of 2.8 per cent of GDP and a debt/GDP ratio of 62 per cent (slightly in excess of the 60 per cent criterion).

The transition to the single currency tended to dominate macroeconomic policy discussion during the period 1995–98, once it became clear that Mediterranean EU members (with the exception of Greece) were making every effort to meet the Maastricht commitments and so be eligible for entry. In Germany, there was not only considerable popular opposition to the replacement of the DM by the euro whose price stability was uncertain. Politicians, economists and commentators alike favoured a narrow, core membership in the first round, from January 1999 onwards, to include only those countries whose nominal convergence on German conditions had already been well-established. Tensions were marked both among the CDU–CSU/FDP coalition but also within the SPD. In response to such concern, Kohl's Finance Minister Theo Waigel first proposed in December 1995 that a 'Stability Pact' be created to ensure that there was no fiscal backsliding among participants once the single currency had been created. This led to serious disagreement with the incoming French government in May 1997, as did the question of nomination to the position of president of the European Central Bank (ECB). Three constitutional court submissions sought without success to have the abolition of the DM ruled unconstitutional. In late March 1998, the Bundesbank approved, in what appeared to be a very political judgement, that there should be a broad EMU membership of eleven countries and this was confirmed by the Bundestag which voted for the euro in early April 1998 (*Handelsblatt*, various). Thus, the euro was introduced on 1 January 1999 with German participation.

Structural and labour market policies

This relatively tight macro stance dictated by the Maastricht conditions rendered structural reform even more pressing, since supply-side sources of growth would have to be stimulated and given that welfare state reforms were also necessary. The SPD and Green opposition favoured a looser macroeconomic policy and, together with the DGB Trade Union Confederation, supported a labour market policy of cuts in working time and abolition of overtime to share the available work. Attempts at creating an 'Alliance for Jobs', a tripartite agreement which sought to trade job stability for wage moderation, were twice made by the Kohl government, the second time occurring in 1996. Even if this failed at national level, because of the Kohl government's pursuance of structural reforms such as the sick pay changes, nevertheless, at the level of the firm, such alliances became commonplace as ways of managing labour-shedding or maintaining employment. Reforms to collective bargaining, in the form of much more workplace negotiation, have been a key feature of labour market adjustment in the recent period. In eastern Germany, however, a more radical approach has been adopted by employers, by their departure from the employers' federations, and therefore their leaving the formal collective bargaining machinery. Some commentators ask if eastern Germany, with its much less regulated labour market, is the future path for the western Länder.

In its Fifty Point Plan of January 1996 and its Programme for Growth and Jobs of April 1996, the Kohl government set out its medium-term economic policy and particularly its structural reform agenda. It itemised a broad spread of changes with fairly radical reforms proposed in the tax, pensions and health systems, changes in shop opening hours, in sick pay provision, in employment assistance and in the employment protection offered to employees in small firms. This approach appeared to rejuvenate the supply-side agenda, first instituted in 1982, but which had become mired in the compromises and delays required by coalition government and a federal system. In the event, the SPD dominance of the *Bundesrat*, which has to approve almost all important federal legislation (particularly if it has financial implications), meant that only minor reforms were passed.

Advent of a red–green coalition government

Following the decisive defeat of the CDU–CSU/FDP coalition at the September elections in 1998, the arrival of the SPD–Green coalition with Chancellor Gerhard Schröder and Finance Minister Oskar Lafontaine in an uneasy alliance brought a marked shift in economic policy. The supply-side reforms of the Kohl government in the 1990s were almost all reversed and the new government appeared to espouse a neo-Keynesian demand-side orientation at domestic and EU levels.

Finance Minister Lafontaine appeared determined to challenge the orthodoxy of the previous 16 years, when he demanded lower central bank interest rates, currency target zones for the euro, and a formal co-ordination of financial, tax and labour market policy among the eurozone countries, so as to stimulate employment through a more coherent budgetary policy stance and labour market support. His espousal of the notion of 'European economic governance', shared by French Finance Minister Strauss-Kahn, recognized the change of policy framework which the euro introduced, including the need to adopt fiscal coherence among the eleven, in the face of a transfer of monetary policy responsibility to the independent ECB. The fractious red–green government in Bonn/Berlin managed rapidly to institute a tax reform which favoured wage earners and their families, at the expense of the corporate sector, and it agreed (after internal acrimony) on the institution of an energy tax whose proceeds would lead directly to an abatement of social security charges on labour. It also worked to bring about the end of nuclear power (*Handelsblatt*, various). On pension reform, its ideas would only lead to higher charges and this was symptomatic of a programme which was redistributive, rather than attacking rigidities and costs in the productive economy and welfare systems.

After Lafontaine's departure as finance minister in March 1999 and his replacement by Hans Eichel, the red–green government's economic policy began to follow a more business friendly course. However, Eichel's tax reform is meant to benefit both German business and the ordinary consumer. The tax reform envisages that, on the whole, tax payers will have to pay 75 billion deutschmarks less tax in 2005 than in 1998. This includes a reduction of the tax burden on Germany's medium-sized companies (the so-called *Mittelstand*) of approximately DM20 billion. Part of Eichel's tax reform has already been realized by the new tax laws which came into effect in April 1999. The government's controversial intention to levy a tax on retirement pensions, however, has been challenged in the constitutional court. Until 2005 the German consumer is to benefit by a further tax saving of 45 billion deutschmarks. By means of clever manoeuvring, readiness to enter into uneasy compromises and backroom financial deals, Finance Minister Eichel managed to obtain the support of several CDU-led regional governments for his tax reform. Thus, to the utter consternation and great embarrassment of the new CDU leadership – party leader Angela Merkel and the rather aggressive parliamentary leader Friedrich Merz – the Schröder government's reform programme for the years 2001–05 was successfully passed by the *Bundesrat* in July 2000.

The reform will proceed in five major stages. Initially, beginning in January 2001, income tax for lower income groups will be reduced to 19.9 per cent and to 48.5 per cent, from the current 51.0 per cent for higher income groups (in 1999 it had already been reduced from 53 per cent). By January 2003 this will decrease to 17 and 47 per cent and by January 2005 to 15 and 42 per cent respectively. Moreover, from 2002 corporation tax will decrease from currently 40 per cent to 25 per cent; this means that including other commercial and trading taxes most companies will face a total tax burden of approximately 39 per cent. After January 2002 capital gains tax on the sale of companies' cross shareholdings in other corporations will be abolished. It is expected that this will lead to a major wave of restructuring of Germany's corporate landscape. Furthermore, some of the tax cuts available to big corporations will also be extended to Germany's many non-incorporated companies (the *Mittelstand*) and to the large number of small businesses. On the whole, the tax reform was welcomed by many national and international observers as a step in the right direction to reverse Germany's reputation 'as a high-tax, low-growth and institutionally rigid society' which it had obtained in the 1990s (*Financial Times*, 15/16 July 2000).

The Schröder government also plans to reform Germany's expensive pension system by stabilizing the individual contributions to the system until 2030. The government and the opposition agree that contributions ought not to consist of much more than 20 per cent of an employee's gross monthly salary. However, there appears to be a consensus that the quality of the system will need to be lowered to ensure that the system can continue to be financed without imposing too much of a financial burden on both employers and employees. Moreover, both the SPD and the CDU/CSU are in favour of employees complementing their state pension by taking out private retirement insurance. In the future employees may well be expected to spend up to 2.5 per cent of their gross salary on such a scheme but it is still uncertain whether this will be a voluntary or a compulsory requirement. The government has however indicated that there will be governmental support available for lower income groups (up to an annual salary of DM 60 000) to enable them to buy into additional private pension schemes. It is clear however that while taxes will come down, the state pension schemes and other provisions of the German welfare state, which Germans have been long accustomed to, will be considerably reduced in the years ahead. Paradoxically it is a red–green coalition in Germany that has embarked on turning the country towards a much more market orientated and individualistic economic course which, for example, in Britain was begun as early as the 1980s when Margaret Thatcher was prime minister.

WILLIAM M. CHANDLER AND KLAUS LARRES: THE GERMAN GENERAL ELECTION OF SEPTEMBER 1998 AND THE EUROPEAN AND REGIONAL ELECTIONS IN GERMANY, 1999–2000

The September 1998 election constitutes a watershed event that clarifies the changing shape of the party system in the post-unity era (Padgett and Saalfeld, 1999). In 1994, the Kohl government found itself running behind the opposition SPD then led by Rudolf Scharping (who became defence minister in October 1999). However, as the campaign unfolded the Christian Democrats recovered to jump ahead, with Kohl going on to capture a narrow but decisive re-election victory. In 1998 the Kohl campaign never really found sufficient momentum and on election day the chancellor was rejected by the voters. The Christian Democrats dramatically tumbled to a level of support unknown to them since 1949.

The SPD's remarkable recovery (compared to its low point in 1990) brought it back to levels of popularity enjoyed governments led by Willy Brandt and Helmut Schmidt in the 1970s. This stunning victory and corresponding debacle for the CDU/CSU meant that for the first time since 1972 the Social Democrats could claim the status of strongest party in the Bundestag. They now found themselves in the happy position of being able to choose their coalition partner. SPD gains (+4.5 per cent) occurred across the board with the most significant gains coming directly from the CDU/CSU (−6.3 per cent). This happened not merely because Gerhard Schröder proved more telegenic than Kohl but also because voters saw him as more competent to deal with the persisting problem of high unemployment. In terms of social bases the SPD maintained and reinforced its traditional core but also made gains in occupational and social sectors where traditionally it has not been the strongest party. Gains among older voters, especially women and among white collar employees, civil servants and the self-employed, reflected the success of the SPD's 'new middle' appeal.

As in the two preceding elections, 1998 produced sharp differences in voting behaviour between the old and the new *Länder*. Eastern voters again played a critical role in reshaping the political complexion of German politics. Disillusionment with federal government policy towards

Table I.1 Results of the German General Elections (Bundestagswahlen) of 1990, 1994 and 1998:

	1990			1994			1998		
	FRG	West	East	FRG	West	East	FRG	West	East
Turnout	77.8%	78.4	75.5	79.1	80.7	73.4	82.2	82.8	80.0
CDU/CSU	43.8	44.2	42.6	41.5	42.2	38.5	35.1	37.0	27.3
	(319 seats)			(294 seats)			(245 seats)		
SPD	33.5	35.9	25.0	36.4	37.6	31.8	40.9	43.3	35.1
	(239 seats)			(252 seats)			(298 seats)		
FDP	11.0	10.6	12.5	6.9	7.7	4.0	6.2	7.0	3.3
	(79 seats)			(47 seats)			(43 seats)		
Bündnis 90/ Greens	5.1	4.7	6.2	7.3	7.8	5.3	6.7	7.3	4.1
	(8 seats)			(49 seats)			(47 seats)		
PDS	2.4	0.3	9.9	4.4	0.9	17.6	5.1	1.2	21.6
	(17 seats)			(30 seats)			(36 seats)		
Others	4.2	4.3	3.5	3.5	3.9	2.7	6.0	5.2	8.6
	(—)			(—)			(—)		

Source: Statistisches Bundesamt

the east produced a disastrous drop in support (of about 11 per cent) for the CDU in the new *Länder* in the east. In an important sense, a normalisation occurred as eastern working class voters (who in 1990 and 1994 had voted disproportionately for the CDU) now turned to the SPD allowing the SPD for the first time to claim to be the strongest party across eastern Germany with 35.1 per cent of the vote.

Minor party developments also reflect essential aspects of party system transformation, because the life and death of five-per cent parties can decisively shape governing majorities in German politics. By early 1998, the fate of these smaller parties still appeared uncertain. Primary attention was directed to the question of the FDP retaining its representation in the *Bundestag*. However, by surviving as a viable party with over 6 per cent in September 1998, the FDP had mixed feelings about losing its share of power but hoped for a chance to revive its fortunes during a spell in opposition. The PDS moved from survival to solidification by holding on to its four direct mandates (all in the former East Berlin) and surpassing the 5 per cent barrier which many had mistakenly claimed could not be done without substantial gains in the west. The election of 1998 also confirmed the failure of extremism: all far-right parties remained fringe players and were non-factors in the outcome.

Although the Greens stagnated, dropping slightly from their 1994 level to 6.7 per cent, they held their essential core electorate. More importantly, because the Greens had committed themselves to participating in a government with the SPD, even in losing votes, they remained clear winners and benefited from the SPD surge which culminated in a red–green majority. A difficult fusion of the eastern *Bündnis 90* and the western Greens had been achieved in 1993. Sixteen years after entering the Bundestag, the *Bündnis 90*/Green party of protest entered the mainstream by gaining a share of power at the federal level. The 1994 and 1998 results signalled an ageing process among both Green activists and voters. By 1999, the fading of the Green's youth appeal was painfully exposed in the February 1999 regional election in Hesse, where the Greens lost 4 per cent of their electorate (dropping from 11.2 per cent to 7.2 per cent). This was the fifth consecutive regional election in which the Green vote dropped. They also lost 4 seats (and 4.2 per cent of the vote) in the subsequent regional election in Bremen in June 1999 where the SPD and the CDU gained 10 and 5 seats (9.2 per cent and 4.5 per cent) respectively with the FDP again being unable to re-enter the regional parliament in Bremen (in fact the party lost another 0.9 per cent and only gained 2.5 per cent of the vote). Hower, SPD leader Henning Scherf remained in office as mayor of Bremen and continued the grand coalition with the CDU.

The red–green exercise of power at the national level rather quickly exposed internal tensions, and not only during the war in Kosovo between late March and mid June 1999. The priorities laid out in the red–green governing agenda (including demand-side economic management, redistributive tax reform, rapid exit from nuclear energy, higher energy taxes and reform of citizenship laws) evoked a mix of popular ambivalence and strong hostility. Electoral setbacks in the Hessian Landtag election in February 1999 provided the first direct test of popular disillusionment with the new majority in Bonn. Although the SPD actually obtained 39.4 per cent of the vote (1.4 per cent more than in 1995) and gained 46 seats – two seats more than four years ago – as indicated above the Greens lost substantially. The Greens only gained a mere eight seats compared to 13 seats in 1995. This enabled the CDU, who increased its share of the vote in Hesse by 4.2 per cent to 43.4 per cent, to form a new coalition government. Although the FDP had lost 2.3 per cent of the vote (and two seats) and only just managed to obtain enough votes (5.1 per cent and 6 seats) to pass the 5 per cent hurdle, both parties had a majority of two seats to replace Hesse's red–green government. Thus, the CDU was the clear winner of the regional election in Hesse and the party soon formed a coalition government with the FDP under new Minister President Roland Koch. Subsequently, in the course of the dramatic revelations of the party funding scandal which rocked the Federal Republic in late 1999 and early 2000, it was revealed that the CDU's victory in Hesse had at least been partially financed by means of illegally obtained donations and other revenues. This money had helped to support the CDU's controversial campaign against the new nationality laws which may well have swayed a number of voters to support the CDU. Still, this loss of power in Hesse was a severe blow to the SPD and the Greens. For both parties Hesse had always been a traditional bastion of support. Moreover, it was in Hesse where the first albeit short-lived red–green coalition government had been created in October 1985. The outcome of the elections in Hesse also resulted in the fact that only a few months after coming to power the Schröder government lost its majority in the 69-vote *Bundesrat*. This would make the passing of controversial legislation (for example the new nationality laws and the reform of the tax and pension systems) much more difficult than anticipated.

Thus, the unexpected defeat of the red–green coalition in Hesse led to an immediate reaction by the Schröder government. The Chancellor began to backtrack on the goals of tax reform, dual citizenship and a quick exit from nuclear energy. After only half a year in power, this also led to the surprise resignation of Schröder's principal rival for power within the SPD, finance minister Oskar Lafontaine, who held very different views on economic policy than the Chancellor. Lafontaine cited the lack of co-operation within the government as his main reason for leaving politics (he also resigned his parliamentary seat and his position as SPD chairman which was taken over by Schröder) (Lafontaine, 1999). Lafontaine was replaced as finance minister by the former Hessian Minister President Hans Eichel.

Subsequently, the Schröder government also suffered in the European election of June 1999 (Helms, 1999) which showed a very low turnout across the entire continent (in Germany a mere 45.2 per cent). While the SPD vote dropped from 32.2 per cent five years ago to 30.7 per cent (and from 40 to 33 seats), and the Green vote from 10.1 per cent to 6.4 per cent (and from 12 to seven seats), the CDU/CSU under their new chairmen Wolfgang Schäuble/Edmund Stoiber gained a dramatic victory. The CDU/CSU obtained 48.7 per cent of the vote (consisting of the CDU's 39.3 per cent (up from 38.8 per cent) and the Bavarian CSU's 9.4 per cent) and 53 seats, an increase of six seats (43 for the CDU and 10 for the CSU). The low priority given to European

Table I.2 Results of the European elections in Germany in 1994 and 1999: total seats for the Federal Republic in the European Parliament: 99

	1994			1999		
	FRG	West	East	FRG	West	East
Turnout	60.0%			45.2%		
CDU/CSU	38.8 (47 seats)	40.3	32.9	48.7 (53 seats)	50.7	40.6
SPD	32.3 (40 seats)	33.9	25.3	30.7 (33 seats)	32.6	23.6
FDP	4.1 (—)	4.2	3.6	3.0 (—)	2.2	0.0
Bündnis 90/ Greens	10.1 (12 seats)	11.2	5.8	6.4 (7 seats)	7.4	2.9
PDS	4.7 (—)	0.6	20.6	5.8 (6 seats)	1.3	23.0
Others	10.2 (—)	9.8	11.8	5.4 (—)	4.7	7.7

Source: *Statistisches Bundesamt*, Commission of the European Communities

elections in general and the final dramatic phase of the war in Kosovo may have influenced many SPD and Green supporters not to bother voting in the European election. However, the CDU/CSU's impressive victory indicated that almost nine months after Schröder's election as Chancellor the majority of Germans were very unhappy with the performance of the red–green government.

The perception of the Schröder government's deep unpopularity was reinforced by the subsequent four regional elections in September 1999 and the local elections in North Rhine Westfalia (NRW) in the same month as well as by the election in the city of Berlin in October. All of these elections proved to be disastrous for the red–green coalition. The poor performance of the SPD and the Greens was largely blamed on Chancellor Schröder's inability to impress the voters with his social and economic policy on the national level. The Greens were particularly affected. They did not manage (neither did the FDP) to obtain parliamentary seats in either of the five regional elections in September and October 1999.

While the PDS, the former East German communists, were not able to receive any noticeable electoral support in the western German states, the party remained strong in eastern Germany and particularly in the former East Berlin. However, extreme right-wing parties (like the DVU, the Republikaner or the NPD) had relatively little success; the DVU only did relatively well in Brandenburg where the party gained 5.3 per cent of the vote (the right won 3.9 per cent in Thuringia and 2.7 per cent in Berlin; it had already gained 3.3 per cent in Bremen and 2.7 per cent in Hesse earlier in the year). A noticeable development was, however, that in all of the seven regional elections in 1999 as well as in the local elections in NRW the voter turnout declined considerably (the exceptions were the unaltered turnout in Hesse and the slightly increased turnout in Saxony).

In the election in Brandenburg the controversial but locally much admired SPD Prime Minister (*Ministerpräsident*) Manfred Stolpe, who is alleged to have collaborated with the Stasi during GDR times, managed to remain in office. However, he lost his absolute majority and entered into a SPD–CDU grand coalition government with the PDS and the right-wing DVU, the only parliamentary opposition parties (the latter received 5 seats, the PDS 22 seats). However, Stolpe's share of the vote dropped by almost 15 per cent (from 54.1 per cent to 39.3 per cent) and the CDU was able to increase its vote by almost 8 per cent (from 18.7 in 1994 to 26.5 per cent). The PDS also increased its vote considerably, it gained 23.3 per cent as compared to 18.7 per cent five years ago. Once again, neither the FDP nor the Greens managed to obtain parliamentary seats in Brandenburg.

In the Saarland, Lafontaine's successor as regional Prime Minister, Reinhard Klimmt, was less lucky. The SPD's vote dropped by 5 per cent and neither the Green party nor the FDP managed to get over the 5 per cent hurdle. The CDU, however, increased its vote by almost 7 per cent from 38.6 per cent to 45.5 per cent and its leader Peter Müller became new regional Prime Minister with a very slim absolute majority. After he had lost the election and thus his post as Prime Minister of the Saarland, Klimmt was asked by Chancellor Schröder to become national transport minister; his acceptance and thus his refusal to become leader of the opposition in the regional parliament in Saarbrücken was much criticised.

In the third election in September 1999 in the eastern German state of Thuringia with its capital Erfurt the locally much admired CDU Prime Minister Bernhard Vogel (prior to 1990 he had been a long-serving Prime Minister of Rhineland Palatinate) had no difficulty remaining in power. This time, however, he enjoyed an absolute majority and therefore did not need to continue the grand coalition with the SPD. The SPD's regional and national unpopularity was made clear by Vogel's ability to increase the CDU vote from 42.6 per cent to 51 per cent. Consequently, the SPD's share of the vote dropped to 18.5 per cent (from 29.6 per cent in 1994) and the Green vote declined from 4.5 per cent to a mere 1.9 per cent. The FDP languished at 1.1 per cent of the vote, a drop of almost 2 percentage points.

The local elections in North Rhine Westfalia, which took place on the same day as the election in Thuringia, proved to be an even greater disaster for both the SPD and the Greens. Moreover, NRW is the Federal Republic's industrial heartland and the state's many industrial cities have been traditionally dominated by the Social Democrats. While the CDU managed to increase its share of the vote by 10 per cent (from 40.3 per cent to 50.3 per cent), the SPD vote fell by more than 8 percentage points (from 42.3 per cent to 33.9 per cent). The Green vote dropped by almost 3 per cent (from 10.2 per cent to 7.3 per cent). The FDP's share of the vote increased but by only 0.5 per cent to 4.8 per cent. While the low turnout of only 55 per cent (a drop from 81.7 per cent in 1994) might explain some of the SPD's losses, it was clear that the voters used the local elections in NRW to express their great dissatisfaction with the work of the red–green governments in both Düsseldorf and Berlin.

In view of the electoral trend throughout 1999, the election in the eastern state of Saxony in October produced no great surprises. As expected, former West German politician Kurt Biedenkopf was confirmed as Prime Minister with his seat of government in the regional capital Dresden. Although his share of the vote fell slightly by 1.2 per cent, the CDU result of 56.9 per cent was still most impressive. Biedenkopf had successfully defended his absolute majority. The SPD vote, however, dropped to a very meagre 10.7 per cent. This was a loss of almost 6 per cent and the party's worst electoral result in any regional election since the end of the Second World War. While the Greens and the FDP once again remained much below the 5 per cent hurdle, the PDS increased its share of the vote by almost 6 per cent to 22.2 per cent.

A month later the election in Berlin on 10 October 1999 confirmed the general trend. However, the SPD managed to halt its rapid loss of unpopularity though it could not yet reverse its declining vote. The SPD's share of the vote in the national capital only dropped by 1.2 per cent (from 23.6 per cent in 1995 to 22.4 per cent). But CDU candidate Eberhard Diepgen had no difficulty remaining in power as mayor of Berlin and head of a CDU–SPD grand coalition government. Diepgen even increased his party's vote by 3.4 per cent (from 37.4 per cent to

40.8 per cent). While the FDP vote remained largely unchanged (2.2 per cent compared to 2.5 per cent four years ago), the Green party suffered a heavy loss in this traditionally left–liberal city. The Green vote fell from 13.2 per cent to 9.9 per cent. On the whole, the still continuing unpopularity of the Schröder/Fischer government had more devastating consequences for the Greens than for the SPD.

Then, in November 1999, the CDU party funding scandal with former Chancellor Kohl at its centre came to light. Chancellor Schröder greatly benefited from this situation. Yet, a scandal surrounding the potentially illegal but certainly immoral use of corporate jets for the private and complimentary use by SPD politicians in Düsseldorf, the capital of North Rhine Westfalia, prevented the Berlin government from being able to fully exploit the considerably more serious Kohl scandal as much as they otherwise would have been able to do.

However, the SPD won the regional election in Schleswig Holstein in late February 2000 and SPD Prime Minister Heide Simonis was able to remain in office as head of the red–green coalition government. The SPD even managed to increase its share of the vote by 3.4 per cent (from 39.8 per cent in 1996 to 43.2 per cent). Still, the vigorous election campaign of the CDU candidate Volker Rühe, the former defence minister, who was largely seen as untainted by the funding scandal, ensured that the CDU vote only fell by 2.0 per cent (from 37.2 per cent to 35.2 per cent). This constituted a considerable relative success for Rühe. Moreover, the liberal FDP managed to increase its share from 5.7 per cent to 7.6 per cent of the vote. The Greens, however, suffered yet another devastating defeat; their vote fell by almost 2 per cent (from 8.1 per cent to 6.2 per cent).

On 14 May 2000 the regional election in North Rhine Westfalia confirmed the SPD and Prime Minister Wolfgang Clement in power as head of a red–green coalition government. However, both the SPD and the Greens lost almost approximately 3 per cent of the vote each obtaining 42.8 per cent and 7.1 per cent respectively. This was a sobering result for the ruling coalition. Clement's homemade scandal involving the use of corporate jets by SPD politicians may have had a negative impact. However, in view of the CDU funding scandal involving former Chancellor Kohl, which still dominated the political landscape, and the controversial racist utterances by CDU candidate Ruttgers about 'Kinder statt Inder' in the context of Chancellor Schröder's green card proposal (for details, see Larres above) the SPD might have expected a much better election result. Yet, the disappointing economic performance of the regional as well as the national red–green government

Table I.3 Results of the German Regional Elections (Landtagswahlen) in 1999–2000

	Turn-out	SPD	CDU	FDP	Greens	PDS	DVU/ Rep./NPD
Hesse	66.4						
7/2/99 (19/2/95)	(66.3)	39.4 (38.0)	43.4 (39.2)	5.1 (7.4)	7.2 (11.2)	– (–)	2.7 (–)
Bremen	60.1						
6/6/99 (14/5/95)	(68.6)	42.6 (33.4)	37.1 (32.6)	2.5 (3.4)	8.9 (13.1)	2.9 (–)	3.3 (2.5)
Brandenburg	54.4						
5/9/99 (11/9/94)	(56.3)	39.3 (54.1)	26.6 (18.7)	1.9 (2.2)	1.9 (2.9)	23.3 (18.7)	5.3 (1.1)
Saarland	68.7						
5/9/99 (16/10/94)	(83.5)	44.4 (49.4)	45.5 (38.6)	2.6 (2.1)	3.2 (5.5)	0.8 (–)	1.3 (1.4)
Thuringia	59.9						
12/9/99 (16/10/94)	(74.8)	18.5 (29.6)	51.0 (42.6)	1.1 (3.2)	1.9 (4.5)	21.4 (16.6)	3.9 (1.3)
Saxony	61.1						
19/9/99 (11/9/94)	(58.4)	10.7 (16.6)	56.9 (58.1)	1.1 (1.7)	2.6 (4.1)	22.2 (16.5)	2.9 (1.3)
Berlin	65.9						
10/10/99 (22/10/95)	(68.6)	22.4 (23.6)	40.8 (37.4)	2.2 (2.5)	9.9 (13.2)	17.7 (14.6)	2.7 (2.7)
Schleswig Holstein	69.5						
27/2/00 (24/3/96)	(71.8)	43.2 (39.8)	35.2 (37.2)	7.6 (5.7)	6.2 (8.1)	– (–)	2.7 (4.3)
NRW	56.7						
14/5/00 (14/5/1995)	(64.0)	42.8 (46.0)	37.0 (37.7)	9.8 (4.0)	7.1 (10.0)	1.1 (–)	1.1 (0.8)

Sources: Statistische Landesämter, Statistisches Bundesamt, Fischer Weltalmanach

over the last few years influenced voters decisively to either stay at home (with 56.7 per cent the turnout was exceptionally low) or to vote for the opposition. Moreover, the SPD has been governing North Rhine Westfalia since 1958. This is a rather long period of time in office which is bound to be unhealthy for the development of any party. The real winner of the election in North Rhine Westfalia was the FDP. Under its leader Jürgen Möllemann the party managed to increase its share of the vote by almost 10 per cent and was thus again able to obtain seats in the regional parliament in Düsseldorf. The FDP had not been able to overcome the 5 per cent hurdle in 1995. Like in other western German states, with only 1.1 per cent of the vote the PDS failed to perform well.

The election result in North Rhine Westfalia was perhaps a reflection of the relatively speedy recovery of the CDU from the funding scandal under its new national leader Angela Merkel. While on account of this scandal the CDU was largely paralysed during the first four months of the year 2000, in May 2000 the CDU once again began to perform more effectively as the major opposition party in Berlin. In all likelihood this means that until the general election in late 2002 Chancellor Schröder will be faced with an ever better organised and a more effective opposition. It can be expected that his political life will become increasingly difficult; at the point of writing it was by no means clear whether or not Schröder will manage to remain in office for a second term.

On the whole it can be said that the collapse of the GDR in late 1989, followed by unification a year later, provided a shock to the entire German political system, but revolutionary transformations were confined to the citizens of the eastern *Länder*. For party politics, unification introduced a substantial new electorate without any firm ties to the established parties. The political fallout is still in process and by the year 2000 it became clear that this change had brought some significant adaptations in party competition. In Bundestag elections a five party system has emerged (SPD, CDU/CSU, FDP, Greens, PDS). Within the *Länder* two distinct patterns have crystallised. In the new Länder a relatively balanced three-way competition among CDU, SPD and PDS can be observed. Other minor parties like the FDP and the Greens retain only marginal presence and, usually, are no longer factors in government formation in eastern Germany. In the old Federal Republic, however, we find a persisting pattern of two large parties with one or two small parties playing critical coalition roles. Here the PDS has made no significant inroads and practically plays no important role. The change of leadership and the retirement of the popular leaders Gregor Gysi and Lothar Bisky will hardly be able to give the PDS a more prominent role in the old *Länder*. While the influence of the Green party as a major political force in the *Länder* appears to be weakening, the election in North Rhine Westfalia points to the fact that the FDP may well have benefited from a process of rejuvenation in opposition. Only the election to the Bundestag in 2002, however, will demonstrate whether this will be reflected on the national level.

PANIKOS PANAYI: RACIAL EXCLUSIONISM IN GERMANY

The 'racial crisis' of the early 1990s had resolved itself by the middle of the decade due to two main factors. First, the decline of the euphoric nationalism and the inevitable xenophobia attached to it in the immediate aftermath of reunification. Second, the decrease in the numbers of visible immigrants and refugees as a result of the change in asylum law regulations in 1992. However, illegal immigrants continue to move into Germany across the Polish border. Consequently, the potent manifestations of xenophobia which characterised the years between 1991 and 1993 have lessened but not disappeared. Racial attacks continue to take place but large-scale riots now seem a thing of the past. Similarly, while the NPD, the DVU and the Republikaner together with countless other smaller neo-Nazi groupings continue to exist, by 1998/99 they had declined to the low levels of support of the 1970s and 1980s. In the September 1998 federal election the DVU only obtained 1.2 per cent of the vote while the Republikaner attracted a mere 1.8 per cent.

The decline of extreme racism does not mean it has disappeared: rather, it has simply returned to the level which characterised the Federal Republic before the unification crisis. Foreigners continue to face social and economic discrimination while the changes in the Nationality Laws of 1991 and 1993 have not solved the problem of excluding immigrants and their offspring from the rights enjoyed by German citizens. However, the numbers of foreigners who become naturalised German citizens have increased.

In one sense the Federal Republic has become rather like the USA in terms of attitudes towards race. There is a fairly advanced western half in which minorities can succeed economically, which contrasts with the eastern part of the country where relatively few foreigners live. As a liberal nation state, Germany still differs little from other western European democracies in the late twentieth century, practising peaceful racial exclusionism, especially through its immigration and nationality laws.

Nevertheless, at the start of 1999 new dramatic developments occurred as the new SPD–Green Coalition decided to introduce a new nationality law allowing dual citizenship for people living in Germany with foreign nationality. The government proposed not to insist anymore on the requirement that the holder of a German passport could not be in possession of another passport at the same time. The necessity to give up the passports of their native country in order to obtain German citizenship had put off many of the 7.3 million foreigners (almost 10 per cent of the population), including 2 million Turks more or less permanently living in Germany, from considering applying for German citizenship. However, in response to the new government's initiative, the opposition CDU launched a much publicised and most controversial but surprisingly popular petition against the envisaged new nationality law. It was alleged that 'dual nationality' would lead to split loyalties; people with two or more nationalities would not consider themselves German and therefore would not be prepared to integrate themselves fully into German society. Moreover, under the impact of the lost regional elections in Hesse (see above) Schröder soon changed his mind and, despite much opposition within the ranks of the SPD's

Green coalition partner, announced an uneasy compromise. After all, the loss of the government's majority in the *Bundesrat* meant that Chancellor Schröder needed the agreement of the opposition for the successful reform of Germany's outdated citizenship laws. The new law was eventually passed in spring 1999 and took effect on 1 January 2000. It specifies that children born in Germany of foreign residents will automatically be considered German citizens; in addition they will be able to enjoy the citizenship of their parents' country of origin if the state in question does not object. However, this will only be considered a temporary solution. At the age of 18 these children will have to decide which nationality they wish to have for the rest of their lives. Consequently, they will have to give up one of their two passports and one of their two nationalities by the time they reach adulthood. If they have not taken this decision by the age of 23, their German citizenship will cease. The German state still will not tolerate that a person is a German national as well as a citizen of another country.

TILL GEIGER: THE ECONOMIC TRANSITION PROCESS IN GERMANY AND EAST-CENTRAL EUROPE

By the mid 1990s the euphoria following the collapse of communism in East Germany and East-Central Europe had largely evaporated and given way to growing cynicism about the emerging social structures in the new democracies. This development led to a renewed questioning of the key decisions taken by policy-makers after the fall of the Berlin Wall. The continued scepticism about the progress of transition begs the question why policy-makers opted for a leap to democracy and a market economy rather than staged transition over time. In 1989 there was the widespread presumption that the introduction of the capitalist system in East-Central Europe would lead to prosperity within the foreseeable future. It was assumed that the fall of state socialism and the (re-)turn to liberal democracy represented a complete break with the past. However, this explanation overlooked the reality of an outmoded industrial structure and uncompetitiveness of the transition economies. At the same time, policy-makers confronted a historically unique situation for which no contingency plans existed. Therefore, policy-makers reinterpreted the discursive structures, which had shaped the cold war world, to formulate a response to the momentous chain of events triggered by the fall of the Berlin wall.

The sudden collapse of communism in Eastern Europe occurred much more rapidly than most analysts had thought possible. In the late 1980s, few observers had dared to predict the imminent demise of state socialism partly because the west had invested heavily in Gorbachev's leadership, the reform process and disarmament. The catacyclism of the events of 1989 catapulted the leading figures of the Eastern European opposition into power all over East-Central Europe. These new policy-makers faced the daunting tasks of establishing a liberal democracy and a market economy largely unprepared. Under pressure from the velvet revolutionaries on the streets the fledgling democratic governments tried to expedite the transition process by implementing economic reforms while establishing new democratic structures. The new political leaders found it difficult to meet the demonstrators' demands for instantaneous prosperity, continued social security and political freedom. Caught unaware, western policy-makers implored the new Eastern European elite to adopt capitalism and liberal democracy but at the same time offered only very limited financial and economic assistance to the emerging democracies in East-Central Europe. In the case of the GDR demonstrators undermined the attempts by the Modrow government and the opposition to reform the East German state.

The pressure from the streets forced the new governments to take incisive decisions rapidly without developing an overall strategy for political and economic transition. As a consequence some initial decisions induced undesired outcomes. For example, privatisation of the state sector has been slow and bedevilled by problems throughout Eastern Europe. The Czech government recently announced that it would renationalise some firms in order to prevent their collapse and further increases in unemployment. In the unified Germany, the restoration of old property rights has prevented the early repair of the capital and housing stock. At the same time, the restructuring of the economy has led to massive increases in unemployment in the former state socialist countries. The growing inequalities are testing the solidarity among the citizens of fledgling democracies as well as in the new *Bundesländer*. A decade after the fall of the Berlin wall many eastern Germans (Ossies) continue to feel that they are second class citizens, excluded from German society. Given the continued problems of transition, it may well be the best prospect for continued peace in Europe to renegotiate the institutional arrangements governing intergovernmental (economic, political and security) co-operation in Europe. In such a process, western countries ought to accept the fledgling democracies in East-Central Europe as full and equal partners rather than supplicants.

To some extent, western policy-makers perceived themselves as victors in the cold war, but at the same time clung to existing institutional arrangements in response to the uncertainty regarding the outcome of the transition process in the Soviet Union and East-Central Europe. Despite the rhetoric of a 'common European house', western policy-makers have been rather reluctant to incorporate the new democracies into the (western/European/Atlantic) community of states. The European Union has been extremely reluctant to grant the emerging East-Central European market economies preferential access to the single European market. On balance, western European governments seem at times more concerned to protect their own national interest than to show solidarity with the fledgling democracies of East-Central Europe. At the same time, the tenth anniversary of the fall of the Berlin wall led to renewed calls for a 'Marshall Plan' for Russia and East-Central Europe; in particular this was the case in the aftermath of the 1999 war in Kosovo. Given the continued problems of transition in the former state socialist countries, a comprehensive western aid programme might greatly assist the development of the political and economic infrastructure needed for the long-term stability of the new European democracies. The eastern enlargement of the EU, now expected to occur in 2003/04, will be of immense importance for the economic, and also political, stabilisation of East-Central Europe.

ADRIAN HYDE-PRICE: GERMANY'S SECURITY POLICY DILEMMAS

The late 1990s have seen a steady recalibration of German security policy as the Federal Republic adjusts to the new demands and responsibilities it faces. Germany remains essentially a *Zivilmacht* (Maull, 1997), although it has shed most of the political and constitutional restraints (many of them self-imposed) which characterised the semi-sovereign West Germany of the cold war years. The Berlin Republic thus promises to be a 'normalised' *Zivilmacht*, more comparable to other civilian powers like Sweden or Holland, rather than to traditional nation-states like France or the UK. The key change in German security policy and strategic culture in the 1990s has been in respect to the use of military force. The key catalyst for this change has been Bosnia and then the 1999 war in Kosovo.

The deployment of Bundeswehr troops abroad

Throughout the early 1990s, the conservative–liberal government of Kohl – and most notably the gifted CDU Defence Minister, Volker Rühe – sought to build a broad public and political consensus for the deployment of Bundeswehr troops for UN-mandated peace-support operations abroad. This involved sending German troops to Somalia; German participation in AWAC flights over Bosnia; and a German contingent in IFOR/SFOR. A particularly significant step was the May 1997 Bundeswehr operation in Albania. German troops were sent to Albania to assist in the evacuation of embassy staff and other civilians. This was the first ever unilateral deployment of the Bundeswehr in an out-of-area operation and took place without a formal UN mandate. It thus constituted a significant landmark in terms of the 'normalisation' of German security policy. Of significance too was the public reaction to this event, which was broadly supportive. This widening public acceptance of new Bundeswehr missions reflects an important political shift among opinion formers on the centre-left. In the early and mid 1990s, out-of-area deployment of German troops had been opposed by many Greens and some Social Democrats. However, in the face of mounting evidence of atrocities and ethnic cleansing in Bosnia, Foreign Minister Joschka Fischer posed the question, 'What is to be done?' His answer was clear: in the face of widespread violation of basic human rights, it was the moral and political duty of the Greens to support a multilateral military intervention, including the use of German troops (Markovits and Reich, 1998: 242). As Fischer noted, 'it took a foreign army to free Auschwitz' (quoted in *The Economist*, 24 October 1998, 60). Fischer's intervention in the debate was crucial and helped shift broader sections of German public opinion in favour of an expanded mission for the Bundeswehr. Yet this broad consensus has its limits: public support for the use of Bundeswehr troops in peace keeping and peace-support operations involves two conditions: the operation must have a clear mandate under international law (primarily expressed through a UN Security Council or OSCE resolution) and must be multilateral (the Albania operation was an exceptional event). In this sense again, the Berlin Republic has become a 'normal' civilian power. Another interesting development in German security policy is the increasing use of what has been called 'minilateralism'.

Minilateralism (NATO, WEU, OSCE) and trilateralism

Traditionally, the Federal Republic has focused its foreign and security policy on multilateral frameworks (primarily NATO and the EU/WEU, but also the OSCE), underpinned by strategic partnerships (with the USA, France and Russia). However, the 1990s have witnessed the emergence of smaller diplomatic groupings which fall into an 'institutional grey zone' between unilateralism and multilateralism. The prime example of this is the Contact Group, consisting of Germany, France, Britain, Russia and the USA (Italy joined later). It was established in April 1994 to co-ordinate the response of the international community to events in the Balkans and represents a reaction to the perceived failure of the EU (and CFSP), the UN and OSCE.

Germany has also become involved in a series of triangular diplomatic initiatives: the 'Weimar triangle' (with Poland and France); Danish–German–Polish co-operation in building a trilateral military corps; and the triangle with Russia and France. These trilateral and minilateral initiatives are likely to become a more important aspect of the Berlin Republic's evolving foreign and security policy. As Reinhardt Rummel has noted, Germany will follow a 'double strategy', first seeking to 'launch activity via the EU, but if this leads to no tangible success in a decent timespan, it will co-operate with a smaller group or with partners from outside the Union' (Rummel 1996, 60). The formation of a red–green coalition government in October 1998 had significant implications for the evolution of German security policy. The result of the elections constituted both a decisive political change and a significant generational change. The key individuals involved in the formation of German security policy are Chancellor Gerhard Schröder, Foreign Minister Joschka Fischer and Defence Minister Rudolph Scharping. Despite the previously radical stance of both SPD and Greens on security policy, the coalition has promised continuity in German foreign and security policy and reaffirmed Germany's international commitments to its partners and allies. Despite this emphasis on continuity, three new themes have become apparent.

The Schröder Government's new security policy

The first is to do with the old bug-bear of German security policy, nuclear weapons. The SPD–Green Coalition Accord of October 1998 included a commitment to work for a 'No-First-Use' of nuclear weapons by NATO. When Joschka Fischer raised the issue in a series of newspaper interviews, US Defence Secretary William Cohen responded by insisting that the US would resist any attempt to depart from NATO's existing policy. Defence Minister Scharping, on a visit to the USA at the time, was quoted by his US colleague as promising that Germany had no intention of questioning core elements of NATO's strategy. Nonetheless, Scharping himself underlined that the new government cherished 'the vision of a nuclear-weapons free world', and stressed that nuclear weapons should only play a political role. Joschka Fischer subsequently raised the issue at a NATO meeting in Brussels. Although there is little chance that NATO will abandon its first use policy, this incident demonstrates three things: continuing German sensitivity on the issue of nuclear weapons; the potential for open disagreements within the red–green coalition; and the likelihood that the new German government will resist US efforts to redefine and expand NATO's role within the wider international system.

The second new theme concerns the use of military force. The new SPD–Green government has accepted that military force is sometimes necessary in order to prevent genocide and aggression. However, the employment of military power will remain a sensitive political issue for the Berlin Republic (Hoffmann and Longhurst, 1999). Joschka Fischer stressed that the military is a blunt instrument and has little utility unless it is part of a clear political strategy. This was the lesson he drew from the four-day US–UK bombing campaign against Iraq in December 1998: whether or not the campaign was a 'military' success, it failed to resolve any of the underlying problems and was not part of a coherent political strategy. For the Berlin Republic, therefore, the use of military power for political purposes will only be accepted if diplomatic efforts to find a political settlement have been exhausted. At the same time, the new government has placed heavy emphasis on further arms reductions and controls, particularly in the framework of the CFE (Conventional Forces in Europe) Treaty.

The third theme of the new SPD–Green government follows from the second: the emphasis on conflict prevention, preventive diplomacy and the peaceful resolution of disputes. This has always been a strong element of German security policy and diplomatic practice, and is one of the features which defines Germany as a civilian power. Under the new government, it has received renewed emphasis. This is evident in two regards. First, the commitment to offer Bundeswehr troops for UN-Standby Forces which was included in the Coalition Accord. Second, Joschka Fischer's commitment to work for an upgrading of the role of the OSCE in European security. For example, in his speech to the

OSCE Ministerial Council in Oslo on 3 December 1998, Fischer underlined the desire of the German government to see the OSCE play an even stronger role in Europe, and called for the creation of an OSCE Training Centre which would prepare members of OSCE Missions with the necessary skills of conflict prevention and resolution.

Plans ventilated throughout 1999 to reduce the number of soldiers serving in the *Bundeswehr* (currently approximately 340 000) by more than 100 000 and thus effectively to less than half of the number of the West German troops prior to 1990 found the cautious approval of Defence Minister Scharping. In late May 2000 the conclusions of the strategic review of the commission of 21 experts, chaired by former federal president Richard von Weizsäcker, on the future of the Bundeswehr were published. The report proposed a radical restructuring of the German forces. It was suggested that the *Bundeswehr* should be reduced to 240 000 soldiers and turned into a largely professional force capable of intervening in international emergency situations in the euro–atlantic area. The commission also proposed that 130 000 soldiers instead of the hitherto contemplated 50 000 should serve as intervention forces. Yet, as the weekly *Die Zeit* emphasized, due to the necessity of rotating troops and maintaining a security margin in case of the simultaneous emergence of a second crisis, only 10 per cent of this number would actually be available as active intervention forces at any time. Following a decision by the European Court in the Hague in January 2000 that not to allow women to handle arms in the *Bundeswehr* (as forbidden under article 12a of the Basic Law) was discriminatory, the report also recommended that women ought to have the same rights as their male colleagues within the armed forces. The Weizsäcker commission also advised that the command hierarchy of the *Bundeswehr* should be reorganised.

Furthermore, the review on the restructuring of the *Bundeswehr* concluded that in the years to come only 30 000 soldiers instead of currently 130 000 should be conscripts. Thus, it was contemplated to dilute (though not end) male and perhaps soon female conscription. In the post-cold war world, not large armies with heavy armour and a great number of tanks are required, but small units of flexible and high quality rapid reaction forces which can be used to respond effectively to global (or at least euro–atlantic) emergency situations. However, there are also financial reasons for the Schröder government's interest in overhauling the structure of the country's armed forces. The Weizsäcker report, however, recommended that the 10-month period young men will have to serve in the Bundeswehr should be maintained. This corresponds with the view of the ministry of defence.

The government's interest in maintaining a conscript army lies in the bad experiences with a professional army during the time of the Weimar Republic. The regular intake of conscripts and the concept of the 'citizen in uniform' as developed in the 1960s and 1970s was very helpful in ensuring that a close link between the army and society at large was maintained; the separate development of the army as 'a state within a state' did not occur. Yet, after the cold war large reserve forces such as provided by a conscript army are not needed anymore. Moreover, if merely 30 000 conscripts are drafted annually as suggested this means that only approximately eight per cent of Germany's young men would have to serve in the *Bundeswehr* (or to do community service as conscientious objectors). This would lead to great injustice between the young people who will have joined and the majority who will not have to join the armed forces. Critics pointed out that the suggested reform might be cheaper but it would be unwise to undermine the *Bundeswehr* as a conscript force. The proposed reduction of the German forces' civilian employees from 130 000 to 80 000 was meant to save up to DM3 billion annually.

While there was much criticism in SPD and CDU circles about the proposed reduction of the strength of the German forces and the dilution of male conscription which, it was claimed, would endanger the *Bundeswehr's* stability and effectiveness, only the Greens expressed themselves wholeheartedly in favour of the reforms. They believed, however, that the envisaged restructuring should go even further and that the *Bundeswehr* ought to be reduced to no more than 200 000 troops.

The proposals of May 2000 certainly indicate that the Berlin Republic does not intend to develop large military forces and become a European superpower as feared by Mrs Thatcher and others in 1990. On the contrary, increasing dissatisfaction about the combat readiness, the morale of the German soldiers and the antiquated technical and hardware equipment of the *Bundeswehr* is increasingly being voiced from within German political and military circles and, perhaps more importantly, by spokespersons for NATO and the American government. It was argued in mid 2000 that an emergency such as the war in Kosovo was increasingly less likely to be met successfully by Germany and most other EU countries. Yet, Finance Minister Eichel's drive to cut expenditure on the military, as well as elsewhere, for budgetary reasons appears to enjoy the undiminished support of Chancellor Schröder.

Outlook

German security policy since unification has witnessed some significant shifts. In particular, Germany is now politically willing and constitutionally able to participate in multilateral peace support operations. The Berlin Republic will bc a 'normal' Zivilmacht, committed to multilateral co-operation where possible and 'minilateralism' when necessary. As before, the central aim of German foreign and security policy remains the building of a stable peace order in Europe, primarily by extending the transatlantic security community steadily eastwards. With Joschka Fischer in charge of the Federal Republic's *Auswärtige Amt*, Germany has a foreign minister of considerable intellect, vision and charisma. Thus united Germany enters the third millennium as a mature and stable democracy, aware of its responsibilities as Europe's central power, and committed to strengthening both European integration and international co-operation. Whatever mistakes the Berlin Republic might make in its foreign and security policy in the future, no-one should doubt the historic transformation that has occurred in Germany's role in Europe: after the horrors of total war and the Holocaust, modern Germany has emerged as a central bastion of the Kantian 'Pacific Union' which has developed among the democracies of the transatlantic security community.

MICHAEL COX AND STEVEN HURST: THE USA, GERMAN UNIFICATION AND AMERICAN–GERMAN RELATIONS IN THE 1990S

The United States was essential for the realisation and the successful management of the process of German unification. After an initial period of caution, the Bush administration seized the initiative in superpower relations by pressing Mikhail Gorbachev to make good his pledge to accept self-determination for Eastern Europe, including the two Germanys. President Bush's confidence in the stability of West German democracy then enabled him swiftly to embrace the possibility of German unification in the aftermath of the collapse of communist regimes in Eastern Europe in late 1989. The US also felt the need to support and manage the unification process in order to ensure that a united Germany would remain firmly within the structures of NATO. The chief obstacle to the achievement of Bush's twin goals was the opposition of the USSR. The initial opposition of Thatcher's Britain and Mitterrand's France was much less important. Together with the Kohl government in Bonn, Washington therefore devised a number of initiatives designed to secure Moscow's acceptance of German unification inside NATO. Chief among these were the so-called '2+4' process for negotiating the details of unification and reform of NATO structures and missions. After several months of negotiations these initiatives, plus a number of economic and financial 'sweeteners' offered to Moscow by Bonn, eventually secured Russian acceptance of German unification inside NATO. The diplomacy of the Bush administration was vital to the success of German unification and laid the basis for strong German–American relations in the post-cold war world.

It is hoped that the articles contained in the second edition of this book as well as the new introduction will contribute to the interest in the nature of the German state since unification. Although the contributors to this book differ in their interpretation of many aspects of German domestic and foreign policy, there is little controversy regarding the view that with German unification neither an economic or political superpower nor a particularly dangerous or unreliable state has come into being. Instead, together with France, Britain and Italy united Germany is merely one of the top four players in the European concert of states and in the process of European integration.

The united German state has perhaps become a more 'normal' state (Nagengast, 1999; also Ross, 1999). The relocation of Germany's seat of government from Bonn to Berlin in 1999 has not changed this. The Schröder government, like the governments which preceded it from Adenauer to Kohl, continues to view Germany's national interest to be its close integration with the European Union and the maintenance of good relations with the USA but also with other important powers, such as Russia (Larres, 1999). It does not appear that the move of the seat of government to Berlin will alter these fundamental tenets of German policy as they have developed since the establishment of the FRG in 1949.

Still, in the summer of 2000 there were clear signs of a decisive largely export-driven improvement in Germany's economic performance. This has resulted in a somewhat more confident outlook among government ministers and the German people regarding the internal employment situation and the international competitiveness of their country. These positive developments, however, were seriously tarnished by deeply disconcerting indications of ever more widespread anti-foreigner and anti-Semitic sentiments in many parts of Germany. It is a particularly virulent problem among young men in eastern Germany. It has led to calls for a ban of the right-wing NPD, which appears to be active in recruiting young neo-Nazis, and for greater efforts in educating young people in the former GDR about the criminal nature of the Hitler regime. Yet, so far the authorities appear to be rather helpless about how to react to this serious crisis, which is not only greatly damaging to Germany's internal health and stability, but also to the united country's international reputation.

REFERENCES

Blair, Tony (1998), *The Third Way: New Politics for the New Century* (London: Fabian Society).

Clay, Clemens and William E. Paterson eds (1998), *The Kohl Chancellorship* (London: Frank Cass).

Deutsche Bundesbank, *Monatsberichte* (1997–1999).

Giddens, Anthony (1998), *The Third Way: The Renewal of Social Democracy* (Oxford: Polity Press).

Heisbourg, Francois (2000), 'Trittbrettfahrer? Keine europäische Zukunft ohne Deutschland', *Internationale Politik*, No. 4, 35–42.

Helms, Ludger (1999), 'Turning Indifference into a Minor Landslide: The 1999 European Elections in Germany', *German Politics*, Vol. 8, No. 3, December, 161–6.

Herres, Volker and Klaus Waller (1998), *Der Weg nach oben. Gerhard Schröder. Eine politische Biographie* (Munich: Econ).

Hoffmann, Arthur, and Kerry Longhurst (1999), 'German Strategic Culture and the Changing Role of the Bundeswehr', *WeltTrends*, 22 (Spring), 145-62.

Hombach, Bodo (1998), *Aufbruch: Die Politik der neuen Mitte* (Düsseldorf: Econ).

Kirchner, Emil J. (2000), 'NATO or WEU? Security Policy since 1990', in K. Larres (ed.), *Uneasy Allies: British–German Relations and European Integration since 1945* (Oxford: Oxford University Press).

Lafontaine, Oskar (1999), *Das Herz schlägt Links* (Munich: Econ).

Lafontaine, Oskar and Christa Müller, (1998) *Keine Angst vor der Globalisierung. Wohlstand und Arbeit für alle* (Bonn: Dietz).

Larres, Klaus, 'Deutschland in Europa. Nationale Interessen und internationale Ordnung im 20. Jahrhundert' [review article], *Bulletin of the German Historical Institute London*, 21/1 (May 1999), 83–8.

Larres, Klaus (2000), 'Introduction: Uneasy Allies or Genuine Partners? Britain, Germany, and European Integration', in Klaus Larres (ed. with E. Meehan), *Uneasy Allies: British-German Relations and European Integration since 1945* (Oxford: Oxford University Press), 1–24.

Markovits, Andrei and Simon Reich (1998), *Das Deutsche Dilemma. Die Berliner Republik zwischen Macht und Machtverzicht* (Berlin: Alexander Fest Verlag).

Maull, Hans (1997), 'Zivilmacht Deutschlands. Vierzehn Thesen fuer eine neue deutsche Aussenpolitik', in Dieter Senghaas, ed., *Frieden Machen* (Frankfurt am Main: Suhrkamp), 63–76.

Meyer, Thomas (1998), *Die Transformation der Sozialdemokratie. Eine Partei auf dem Weg ins 21. Jahrhundert* (Bonn: Dietz).

Misik, Robert (1998), *Die Suche nach dem Blair-Effekt: Schröder, Klima und Genossen zwischen Tradition und Pragmatismus* (Berlin: Aufbau Verlag).

Nagengast, Emil (1999), 'Europapolitik and National Interest: Are the Germans Normal Yet?', *Debatte*, 7/1 (1999), 9–23.

Padgett, Stephen and Saalfeld, Thomas (eds) (1999), *Bundestagswahl'98: The End of an Era?*, Special Issue of *German Politics*, Vol. 8, No. 2 (August).

Pflüger, Friedrich (2000), *Ehrenwort. System Kohl und der Neubeginn* (Stuttgart: Deutsche Verlags-Anstalt).

Prantl, Heribert, *Rot-Grün. Eine erste Bilanz* (Hamburg: Campe Paperback, 2000).

Pulzer, Peter (1995), *German Politics, 1945–1995* (Oxford: Oxford University Press).
Ross, Jan (1998), *Die neuen Staatsfeinde. Was für eine Republik wollen Schröder, Henkel, Westerwelle und Co.?* (Berlin: Alexander Fest Verlag).
Ross, Jan, 'Vorspiele der Berliner Republik. Ein politisches Stimmungsbild', *Merkur*, 599 (February 1999), 108–19.
Rummel, Reinhardt (1996), 'Germany's Role in the CFSP: "Normalität" or "Sonderweg"?', in Christopher Hill, ed., *The Actors in Europe's Foreign Policy* (London: Routledge), 40–67.
Scharping, Rudolf (1999), *Wir dürfen nicht wegsehen. Der Kosovo-Krieg und Europa* (Weinheim: Beltz Quadriga).
Scheuch, Erwin K. and Scheuch, Ute (2000), *Die Spendenkrise. Parteien außer Kontrolle* (Reinbek bei Hamburg: Rowohlt Taschenbuch).
Schöllgen, Gregor (1999), *Die Aussenpolitik der Bundesrepublik Deutschland. Von den Anfängen bis zur Gegenwart* (Munich: C.H. Beck).
Schwarz, Hans-Peter (1994), 'Germany's National and European Interests', Daedalus 123/2 (1994), 81–106; also in Arnulf Baring (ed.), *Germany's New Position in Europe: Problems and Perspectives* (Oxford: Berg), 107–30.
Thiele, Hans-Guenter, ed. (1997), *Die Wehrmachtsausstellung. Dokumentation einer Kontroverse* (Bremen: Edition Temmen).
Unger, Frank, Andreas Wehr and Karen Schönwälder (1998), *New Democrats, New Labour, Neue Sozialdemokraten* (Berlin: Elefanten Press).
Weidenfeld, Werner (1999), *Zeitenwechsel: von Kohl zu Schröder, die Lage* (Stuttgart: Deutsche Verlags-Anstalt).

Introduction to the First Edition

The breaching of the Berlin Wall, the collapse of the GDR, the unification of West and East Germany and the end of the Cold War dominated world events in 1989–90. Since then united Germany has begun to cope with the political, economic, social and external challenges unification has posed to its institutions and way of life in both the western and eastern part of the once divided country. While the country has successfully tackled some of the problems unification has presented, like the threat to the stability of the state from right-wing groups and parties, other issues, as for example the high rate of unemployment and the Stasi legacy, still remain unresolved.

The nine contributors to the book, all experts in their field, analyse the way united Germany has tackled the many expected as well as entirely unforeseen problems caused by unification and highlight the gradually emerging short- and long-term patterns in Germany's gradual adjustment to new realities. The country has not only become more populous and territorially bigger but is also burdened with many underestimated problems, particularly economic and social ones. The emergence of a new economic, political and perhaps military superstate, as feared by many in 1990, has however not materialised. Instead Germany today is only just coping with the domestic and external challenges of unification. The economic and social integration of the former East Germany into the Federal Republic however has still not been completed and may yet take another decade or two.

The first seven years after unification constitute an appropriate period of time to evaluate the progress the united country has made towards digesting the financial, economic, social and external challenges unification has posed. Although it is much too early to arrive at a definitive assessment of this continuing process, a certain historical distance has already developed since unification in 1990 and its immediate aftermath. As the individual contributions in the book will show, the attempt to arrive at a first assessment of the situation in united Germany during the first seven years of the growing together of the old Federal Republic and the former GDR is a challenging but also very interesting task.

The book has been divided into three parts. The first part deals with the historical dimension of contemporary German history and with the events of 1989–90. The first contribution, by Rolf Steininger, gives an overview of the German question throughout the post-World War II era. The author looks at the attempt to create a unified but neutral Germany in the 1950s, reviews the consequences of Ostpolitik in the 1970s and 1980s, and analyses the process of German unification and the changed mood in post-unification Germany.

In the following article Klaus Larres analyses the German revolution of 1989–90. He particularly concentrates on the direct and indirect causes of these events and the role the East German people played in bringing down the government of a well-fortified police state. He concludes that internal and particularly external stimuli were important for the revolutionary uprising of 1989 but that most credit must be given to the courage and determination of the East German people.

Part II looks at the domestic consequences of German unification. Christopher Flockton analyses the problems and prospects of the German economy since 1989–90. He concludes that it will probably take 15 or 20 years for the former GDR to catch up economically with the western part of the united state. The catastrophic fall in output and the fundamental restructuring of the eastern German economy since economic and monetary unification in July 1990 had dire short- and middle-term consequences. At the time many people warned of a so-called 'Mezzogiorno effect' but these voices were ignored for largely political reasons. Flockton looks at the terms and conditions of economic and monetary union, the role of the subsequent privatisations overseen by the Treuhandanstalt and other strategies by the Bonn government to restructure the eastern German economy. Flockton comes to the conclusion that greater economic dynamism is not only required in the former GDR but also in western Germany if the country is to cope with the challenges of unification, high unemployment and the global competition from the south-east Asian economies.

In the chapter that follows William Chandler writes about the development of the German party system since 1990. He analyses the organisational adaptation of the party system in the former GDR to the new circumstances and looks at the development within the right- and left-wing sectors of German party politics during the first six years since unification. He ends his article with an analysis of coalitional politics since the all-German election of December 1990. Chandler comes to the conclusion that despite a certain dealignment tendency so far no fundamental restructuring of the German party system and its electoral support has taken place. The old West German party system shows a surprising endurance.

The next contribution, by Charlie Jeffery, looks at German federalism in the 1990s. The author analyses the structure of cooperative federalism in the old Federal Republic and then concentrates on the challenges of unification and European integration for German federalism and the role of the German Länder. He comes to a pessimistic conclusion. The economic and political east–west divide which unification has been unable to overcome so far has undermined the ability of the Länder to act collectively against the power of the federal authorities. It has also made it more difficult for the Länder to assume a greater role in European politics independent of the federal state. Jeffery concludes that Germany seems indeed to be on the road to a divided polity.

The final chapter of Part II by Panikos Panayi deals with the role of racism and neo-nationalism in united Germany. Panayi concludes that every modern state tends to exclude the ethnic groups and individuals who do not conform to its citizenship rules. Germany is no exception. He looks at German attitudes towards immigrants in historical perspective, analysing the sudden rise in racist attacks in the first few years after unification and the role of the extreme Right in united Germany. He concludes that the great influx of refugees and ethnic Germans immediately after unification was curbed by the controversial change of Article 16 of the Basic Law (the right to asylum) which came into effect in July 1993 and led to a more restricted asylum policy. This caused a reduction in the number of immigrants coming to Germany which in turn resulted in fewer physical attacks on immigrants. It also appeased many right-wing voters with Chancellor Kohl's CDU/CSU and reintegrated them into the party just in time for the general election of October 1994.

Part III concentrates on the external consequences of unification. Eric Owen Smith looks at the German model and its impact on European integration and concludes that many elements of German economic and financial practices have already been incorporated within the EU structures. He proves this by looking at the EU's monetary and fiscal policy as well as Germany's and the EU's social and antitrust policies. In this context Owen Smith also analyses in detail the terms and consequences of German economic, monetary and social union in mid-1990. The author concludes that without at least a partial adoption of Germany's social and fiscal policies it will be very difficult to make stable and viable progress with European integration. EMU will only be possible if many features of the German model are accepted at the European level.

The contribution by Till Geiger concentrates on the economic transition process in Germany and east-central Europe. The end of the Cold War and its ideological conflict started the overdue re-evaluation of the discursive interpretations of the institutional arrangements which emerged in the post-World War II era. However, many myths and assumptions of the Cold War still influence the transformation to the post-Cold War world in east-central Europe. Geiger analyses and exposes these myths and offers a different way forward. He concludes that only more flexible institutional arrangements and an open dialogue of all European states can find new ways towards a new European order. Further and wider economic integration may well offer the best solution to obtaining political and economic stability in Germany and east-central Europe.

The final chapter of the book, by Adrian Hyde-Price, deals with Germany's security policy dilemmas since unification. The author looks at German security policy in the light of the changes since 1990 but also as far as Germany's history and geopolitical situation is concerned. Hyde-Price attempts to assess the major trends and dynamics of German security policy since 1990. He seeks to identify the implications of this policy on the European Union and on world politics in general. The author sees Germany's security policy revolving around three capitals (Washington, Moscow, Paris) and three international organisations (NATO, WEU, OSCE). Hyde-Price concludes that united Germany's security policy situation must be understood as a series of policy dilemmas, not as clear choices and strategies. He is convinced that these dilemmas cannot be resolved, they can only be managed. In the foreseeable future it will be one of united Germany's major tasks to manage its security dilemmas so well that it is able to contribute to overcoming the continuing divides on the European continent and therefore add to Europe's stability.

On the whole, the book offers the reader an attempt at evaluating Germany's performance to date. Taken together, the nine chapters enable the reader to obtain a comprehensive picture of the most important domestic and external consequences of unification without overlooking the historical dimension.

The initial idea for the book was born at a conference on German Unification at The Queen's University of Belfast. Although subsequently the structure of the enterprise changed considerably, I wish to thank the Queen's University as well as the Department of Politics and its head Professor Robert Eccleshall for their generous support. I am of course also very grateful to the individual authors for their willingness to contribute to this volume. As almost all of the contributors used different wordprocessing packages, I depended on the valuable computer assistance rendered by Eileen McGuire. Much needed moral and also some very helpful editorial support was given by my wife Patricia McCourt Larres and a very special thanks must therefore go to her.

Klaus Larres
Belfast, August 1996

Part I
The German Question and the Revolution of 1989–90

1 The German Question, 1945–95

Rolf Steininger

THE PERIOD OF OCCUPATION (1945–49)

The future of Germany was the most important of all European questions after the war. Germany posed an infinitely complex problem. What had seemed common to Anglo-Soviet interests during the war – the need to contain Germany and to devise the best means of preventing the revival of a strong, aggressive Germany – became rapidly overshadowed by what divided them: all the Cold War issues. In Germany and among the western allies divergent interpretations of the Potsdam agreement – which the Soviets regarded as 'holy writ' – were put down to Soviet deception. Whatever faith British Foreign Office officials had had in Soviet good will, they had abandoned almost entirely by early 1946. British Foreign Secretary Ernest Bevin sent Prime Minister Clement Attlee a note on 10 April 1946 in which he gave his view of Moscow's intentions: 'The Russians', he wrote,

> have decided upon an aggressive policy based upon militant Communism and Russian chauvinism . . . and seem determined to stick at nothing, short of war, to obtain [their] objectives. At the present time [Russia's] aggressive policy is clearly directed to challenging this country everywhere.[1]

This conclusion had a great effect on the German policy of the British government. Up to that time the British had thought of the German problem solely in terms of Germany itself and their purpose had been to devise the best means of preventing the revival of a strong, aggressive Germany. At times, the emphasis had been on re-education but more often on controls and security measures (Steininger, 1996). This desire to prevent a German revival clearly could not be discarded, since it was a goal which they still had in common with the Russians. But, as Bevin wrote in a top secret Cabinet paper on 3 May 1946:

> It can no longer be regarded as our sole purpose, or indeed, perhaps our primary one. For the danger of Russia has become certainly as great as, and possibly even greater than that of a revived Germany. The worst situation of all would be a revived Germany in league with or dominated by Russia.[2]

This, of course, greatly complicated an already complex problem. It involved avoiding measures which would permanently alienate the Germans and drive them into the arms of the Soviet Union. It also meant not giving the impression that the USSR always got its way in four-power discussions about Germany. It involved the British being no less constructive in their approach to the problems in their Occupation Zone in Germany than the Soviets loudly proclaimed themselves to be in theirs. It meant maintaining a sufficiently high standard of living in western Germany to prevent the communists from exploiting the economic hardships suffered by the population. And, above all, it involved accepting the partitioning of Germany at the Elbe and the integration of the western part into an anti-Soviet bloc to act as a bulwark against Communism. If a decision were to be made in favour of partition, then it was 'most important to ensure that responsibility for the break was put squarely on the Russians'.[3] At the same time, it was realised that full US support would be essential and that some Americans were not ready for this. However, their leading representatives in Germany, especially General Lucius D. Clay, would oppose it vehemently (Smith, 1990).

The British were certainly right in their estimation of the attitude of the Americans in Germany; yet, they often misjudged the view of the officials in the State Department in Washington. Fearing collaboration between Russia and a new *Reich*, Freeman Matthew, Director of the Office of European Affairs, informed Dean Acheson, Acting Secretary of State, in early April 1946: 'It is high time we made some top level decisions with regard to Germany.' And George F. Kennan, who had assumed a year before that the Russians had a well-worked-out reparations plan designed to achieve political goals in Germany and western Europe, now warned of a 'Soviet political program' for taking over all Germany. Therefore, Kennan advocated that partition be carried 'to its logical conclusion' with the development of a West German State. US Ambassador Smith in Moscow supported Kennan's view in April:

> I have held for many months that our immediate objectives should be integration of the western zones of Germany into a political unit oriented towards western Europe and western democracy. (Yergin, 1977: 226–7)

The question was whether the Russians really had a 'political programme' for taking over Germany and whether Russian policy was based on a desire for security or expansion. When Secretary of State

James Byrnes posed this question to his French colleague Georges Bidault in April 1946 in Paris, he had in mind a device to test Russian intentions: the famous twenty-five-year four-power treaty guaranteeing German demilitarisation. At the July 1946 Council of Foreign Ministers' meeting in Paris, Soviet foreign minister Molotov emphatically refused to support this proposal – even when the US were prepared to extend it to forty years. Therefore, Byrnes as well as Bevin became convinced that the Russians were bent on further westward expansion and, for this reason, wanted to encourage economic paralysis and political disintegration in Germany (Yergin, 1977: 230). At the end of the conference, after Bevin had put forward his ultimatum to separate the British zone economically from the other three zones, Byrnes offered to operate the American zone together with any or all of the other occupying powers as a single unit. When a few weeks later this offer was put on the agenda of the Allied Control Council the Russians wanted to know what the French position was. As the French made clear their intention not to accept Byrnes' proposal, the Russians apparently dropped it too. Perhaps they let the French kill what they wanted to kill anyway (Kessel, 1989: 101 ff.).

Thus, there was no four-power treaty and no economic unity let alone political unity for Germany; but soon (from January 1947) an economic unit that became known by the name of 'Bizonia'. But the creation of this Bizone was more than just the economic fusion of the British and American zones; in fact it was the turning-point in post-war Germany. It marked the end of four-power cooperation, and the beginning of Anglo-American collaboration in Germany. It was now looked upon as a safeguard against the much-feared American retreat into isolationism. With all this, Bizonia was the beginning of the end of German unity. There could be no political unity if there was no economic unity. In the words of a Foreign Office official (A.A.E. Franklin) in July 1946:

> If Germany is to be divided economically, political division will almost certainly follow, though it need not necessarily do so immediately.[4]

The partition of Germany along the Elbe was well under way in 1946. The British were the first who – as early as February 1946 – started talking about that strategy as one way of solving the German question and of keeping communism to the east of the Elbe (Steininger, 1988; Steininger, 1992). The Americans did not accept this immediately, but when the idea of keeping Germany united failed they followed suit. It is well known what happened next: the open outbreak of the Cold War, the announcement of the Truman Doctrine and the Marshall Plan, and two more futile conferences about Germany in Moscow and London in 1947. In the wake of the communist coup in Czechoslovakia, Bevin became finally convinced that Russia represented a 'threat to western civilisation'.[5] A western Six Power Conference (US, UK, France, Benelux) was held in London between February and June 1948. Here the formal decision was taken to set up a West German State.

ATTEMPTS TO CREATE A UNIFIED BUT NEUTRAL GERMANY (1952–55)

The first West German government (a coalition between the Christian Democrats [CDU/CSU], the Free Democrats [FDP] and the Deutsche Partei [DP]) was established in September 1949 with Konrad Adenauer as chancellor. His prime political objective was the integration of the new Federal Republic of Germany into western Europe, including rearmament but not unification (Köhler, 1994). The SPD on the other hand feared that this policy would irrevocably slam the door on unification (Lösche and Walter, 1992). This controversy reached its first climax in 1952 when on 10 March the Soviet government took the initiative and presented a new note to the western governments (the following is based on Steininger, 1990).

The Russians offered a united Germany (without the territories east of the Oder-Neisse line) including a small national army for its self-defence.[6] There were no political or economic strings attached. The only precondition was that a unified Germany should not become a member of any kind of military alliance which involved the USA. Many Germans thought this proposal should be investigated at all costs and the details examined. But in his first public comment on 16 March 1952, Chancellor Adenauer simply said: 'There is nothing new in this note.' It was, he suggested, merely intended to isolate the Federal Republic by neutralizing the country and preventing its integration with western Europe. Adenauer firmly believed that it was up to West Germany to prove its loyalty to the West by rejecting Stalin's offer flatly and expediting the conclusion of the contractual agreements for the rearmament and simultaneous integration of the Bonn Republic with the West which were close to completion (Herbst et al., 1990).

Adenauer was, however, constrained by the fact that an outright rejection would give the appearance of forsaking West Germany's own national interests in the interests of western Europe or, as Jakob Kaiser, the minister for all-German affairs, put it in a Cabinet meeting, of being 'more American that the Americans'. Coalition elements which were less wedded to European integration as an end in itself, more sensitive to charges of 'Quislingism' and more susceptible to nationalist slogans opposed the rejection of Stalin's proposal and urged further exploration of the Russian offer before any final commitment to the West. This group recommended a slowing down rather than speeding up of the treaty negotiations regarding the FRG's integration with the West. 'Thus far', the US High Commissioner John McCloy reported to Washington on 29 March 1952, this coalition group was 'not – repeat not – very strong, comprising chiefly a few soft-headed nationalists like [vice-chancellor Franz] Blücher, and some left-wing CDU [members of parliament] including Kaiser [whom McCloy regarded as "starry-eyed"] and [Heinrich von] Brentano', the leader of the CDU parliamentary group (Schwartz, 1991).

At this stage Britain and France were more afraid of a rearmed and reunited Germany than of Stalin's Russia. Particularly, Russian–German collaboration was regarded as the ultimate nightmare among western policymakers. The 'Rapallo-Komplex' was still very much alive (Larres, 1996). 'Indeed', as Lord Salisbury, Under-Secretary of State, wrote to Prime Minister Churchill a year later, in August 1953, 'the main purpose of the EDC [European Defence Community] and Bonn arrangements was to prevent, so far as humanly possible, a Soviet–German alignment'.[7] The western powers all acted on the basis of what would best serve their long-term interests: to prevent the development of a neutral as well as of a too powerful Germany (Steininger, 1989). The French Quai d'Orsay was convinced that the Soviet proposals were a serious but very dangereous attempt to settle the German question. The British Foreign Secretary Anthony Eden also noted at this point: '[this] has been my view all along, i. e. that the Soviets are sincere in these proposals.' In the State Department, attitudes varied. Some people worried that if occupation troops were to be withdrawn, the Soviet troops would halt at the Oder-Neisse rivers, in other words just beyond the border, while the western troops would have to retreat to uncertain bridgeheads in France, or even to return to the United States. On the other hand, 'unity plus national army plus peace' seemed hard to beat, as the American Embassy in Moscow observed.

When the Soviets in their second note of 9 April accepted in principle for the first time ever the idea of holding free all-German elections under the supervision of the four Allied powers, the opposition in West

Germany vigorously demanded that Adenauer investigate all avenues – including four-power talks – for unification. The atmosphere in West Germany and France became 'volatile and even hysterical', as Ivone Kirkpatrick, the British High Commissioner in West Germany, reported to London. US Secretary of State Acheson decided – as a tactical move – that talks with the Russians should take place, though admittedly at the level of high commissioners and not foreign secretaries. After all, he thought that 'many Germans tend to feel we are forcing them down a path of *our* choosing'. He cabled his High Commissioner McCloy:

> if the Soviets are really prepared to open up the Eastern Zone, we should force their hand. We *cannot* allow our plans to be thwarted merely by *speculation* that Soviets may be ready actually to pay a high price.

Adenauer needed one day and 'half the night' to make up his mind. Then he said 'no' to Acheson's proposal. He doubted that the Cabinet would authorise him to sign the contractual agreements with the West if there existed the prospect of talks with Moscow which might lead to German unification on a neutral basis.

Thus, no talks with the Soviet Union were entered into. Instead, in May 1952, Adenauer signed the treaties for the Federal Republic's rearmament and integration with the West, thus firmly anchoring his state in the western camp. The western powers had won the 'battle of the notes', as Eden put it (Eden, 1960: 45).

Although the treaties were signed, but not yet ratified – in fact they were never ratified by all the countries concerned – there was still a German question: 'We must face the fact there will always be a "German question" and a "Prussian danger"', Churchill wrote in a secret memorandum in July 1953.[8] After Stalin's death in March 1953 it was British Prime Minister Churchill who wanted to go to Moscow, if necessary, on a 'solitary pilgrimage' to try to settle the German question and to defuse the Cold War (Larres, 1995: 67 ff.). In a cable to US President Eisenhower the British prime minister wrote:

> I have the feeling that we might both of us together or separately be called to account if no attempt was made to turn over a leaf so that a new page would be started with something more coherent on it than a series of casual and dangerous incidents at the many points of contact between the two divisions of the world. (Boyle, 1990: 31)[9]

His mind was not closed to the possibility of a united and neutralised

Germany as part of a settlement with the Russians. He was of the opinion that a united, independent Germany would not become an ally of Soviet Russia or abandon its moral association with the free powers of Europe and America. To him three facts stood out:

> 1. The character of the German people rises superior to the servile conditions of the Communist world.
>
> 2. They have a potent object lesson in the fate of the eastern zone and millions of witnesses will exist for many years to testify to the horrors of Communist rule, even exercised by Germans over Germans.
>
> 3. The hatred which Hitler focused against Bolshevism is strong in German hearts. The eyes of Germany are turned against Soviet Russia in fear, hate and intellectual antagonism. (Larres, 1995: 187–8)[10]

This was Churchill's last gambit (Glees, 1985), but it was nipped in the bud. The ageing prime minister had a stroke in late June 1953. Moreover, his own officials in the British Foreign Office were against him, the Americans and the French were opposed to his ideas and, above all, Adenauer was aghast at Churchill's intentions (Larres, 1995: 147 ff.; Larres, 1997); and, as Churchill had put it, 'our honour would prevent us letting Adenauer down'.[11]

Adenauer did not want this kind of Germany. What then did he want? Perhaps a top-secret document in the Public Record Office in London gives the answer. Entitled 'German Unity' it was written on 16 December 1955 by Ivone Kirkpatrick, then Permanent Under-Secretary of State in the Foreign Office, and runs as follows:

> 1. The German Ambassador told me yesterday that he wished to make a particularly confidential communication to me on this subject. I would recollect that I had told him on my return from Geneva that I had come to the conclusion that we might eventually have to be more elastic than the Americans were prepared to be and that we might have to move to a position in which we declared that provided Germany was unified by means of free elections and provided the unified German Government had freedom in domestic and foreign affairs, we should sign any reasonable security treaty with the Russians.
>
> 2. The Ambassador told me that he had discussed this possibility very confidentially with the Chancellor. Dr Adenauer wished me to know that he would deprecate reaching this position. The bald reason was that Dr Adenauer had no confidence in the German people. He

> was terrified that when he disappeared from the scene a future German Government might do a deal with Russia at the German expense. Consequently he felt that the integration of Western Germany with the West was more important than the unification of Germany. He wished us to know that he would bend all his energies towards achieving this in the time which was left to him, and he hoped that we would do all in our power to sustain him in this task.
>
> 3. In making this communication to me the Ambassador naturally emphasized that the Chancellor wished me to know his mind, but that it would of course be quite disastrous to his political position if the views which he had expressed to me with such frankness ever became known in Germany.

Foreign Secretary Harold Macmillan noted: 'I think he is right.' (Foschepoth, 1990: 289–90).[12]

In August 1961 the building of the Berlin Wall finally sealed the partition of Germany. President Kennedy privately was sceptical regarding the possibility and even the desirability of German unification. As Frank Cash, an official in the German Office of the State Department, later recalled: the Kennedy White House decided very early that the phrase 'German unification' should 'no longer be included in drafts for use by the President'. As a result, the State Department was compelled to adopt such 'circumlocutions as "self-determination for the German people" or "freedom of choice for the German people"' (Catudal, 1980: 61; Mayer, 1996; Arenth, 1997).

OSTPOLITIK AND ITS CONSEQUENCES (1969–1980S)

It was Willy Brandt, foreign minister and vice chancellor from 1966–69, and then chancellor between 1969 and 1974, who initiated West Germany's *Ostpolitik* in the late 1960s. This policy remained a major pillar of West German foreign policy throughout the 1970s and 1980s. Brandt and his Social Democratic Party (SPD) realised that the establishment of closer contacts between the two German states required an improvement of relations with eastern Europe and Bonn's territorial recognition of the *status quo* of Europe's postwar borders. Egon Bahr, Willy Brandt's chief adviser (Lutz, 1992), had already suggested in 1963 a strategy of 'change through rapprochement', a policy which in Bahr's opinion would enhance relations between the two German governments *and* the German people (Griffith, 1978; Whetten, 1971; Bark and Gress, 1989; Garton Ash, 1993).

When elected chancellor in 1969, Brandt intensified his *Ostpolitik* (Baring, 1982; Larres, 1996: 301–19). The chancellor's eastern policy hinged, however, on a major axiom: continuation of the Federal Republic's *Westpolitik*, i.e. West Germany's commitment to a firm anchoring in the Atlantic alliance. Importantly, Bonn's objective to improve relations with the East was facilitated by a global *détente* process. After the 1962 Cuban missile crisis, the United States and the Soviet Union had recognised the necessity of defusing tensions. Consequently, they commenced a *détente* process which eventually led to the signing of the Salt I treaty in 1972 (Brandt, 1989: 168 ff., 185 ff.; Kissinger, 1994: 733 ff.; Garthoff, 1994: 123 ff.; Nelson, 1995).

Brandt's vigorous pursuit of *Ostpolitik* contributed to the signing of a host of bilateral treaties between the Federal Republic of Germany and the eastern European nations with breath-taking speed (Ehmke, 1994: 125 ff.; Bender, 1989: 158 ff.). Rapprochement between West and East Germany necessitated improved relations with the Soviet Union. Negotiations between Bonn and Moscow culminated in the signing of a treaty in December 1970. This accord stipulated the mutual renunciation of force, the acceptance by West Germany of the Oder-Neisse line, the border between Poland and East Germany, and the existing border between the FRG and the German Democratic Republic – all on the condition that a permanent settlement of the border questions was reserved for an eventual peace treaty for the whole of Germany. To underscore West Germany's commitment to unification of the two German states, the Brandt government informed the Soviet Union in writing that this treaty would not preclude West Germany's attempt to work toward German unity (Borowsky, 1983: 19–22; Koch, 1992: 408–29; Gromyko, 1989: 197–201). In December 1970, Bonn signed a treaty with Poland which restated West Germany's pledge to recognise the postwar border between Poland and Germany. Both countries also renounced the use of force and agreed to establish diplomatic relations. Chancellor Brandt, who went to Poland to sign this treaty, received worldwide attention when he knelt in front of Warsaw's Ghetto memorial recognising Germany's terrible crime against humanity during World War II (Borowsky, 1983: 22–4; Koch, 1992: 428–9).

Ratification of these treaties, as well as the signing of an agreement between the two German states, hinged on a four-power agreement on West Berlin. In September 1971, the four former allied powers signed the quadripartite agreement, which guaranteed unimpeded access between West Berlin and West Germany. Whereas the western allies reaffirmed West Berlin's special status, the Soviet Union permitted West

Berlin to maintain its ties with West Germany. Subsequent agreements between the Federal Republic of Germany and the German Democratic Republic largely referred to the regulation of the transit traffic of persons and goods, telephone services, as well as cultural and commercial cooperation between the two states (Keithly, 1986; Bender, 1989: 233 ff.; Koch, 1992, 429–35).

Brandt's major objective in opening relations with eastern Europe was to pursue *Deutschlandpolitik*. This was Bonn's attempt to improve relations with East Germany which he hoped would enhance the lot of the East Germans who had been cut off from the West since the construction of the Berlin Wall in 1961. The chancellor justified his rapprochement with the GDR by emphasising that there were 'two German states, but only one German nation'. Brandt and his East German counterpart Willi Stoph met twice in 1970, first in Erfurt, then in Kassel (Brandt, 1989: 225–9). However, progress towards an understanding between the two German governments could not be made unless Bonn recognised the GDR as a sovereign state. Difficult and protracted negotiations finally resulted in the signing of the Basic Treaty in December 1972, according to which West Germany agreed to recognise the GDR *de facto* and accept the exchange of permanent representatives (though not ambassadors) between the two states. Again, as was the case after the completion of the German-Soviet treaty of 1970, Bonn made it clear in a separate letter that the Basic Treaty would not preclude Bonn's attempt to pursue unification. Brandt's motto – 'two German states, one German nation' – left the door open for possible unification though, at the time, it seemed to be as remote as ever (Borowsky, 1983: 25–6, 35–44; Bender, 1989: 247–9).

In West Germany, the Christian Democrats (CDU) adamantly denounced the signing of the treaties with the Soviet Union and Poland as well as Brandt's recognition of the East German republic. They argued that those treaties violated the commitment to unification as stated in the Basic Law, the West German constitution. However, in 1972 the CDU's attempt to unseat the Brandt coalition government consisting of the Social Democrats and the Free Democrats (SPD-FDP) failed, and *Ostpolitik* and *Deutschlandpolitik* would soon become an integral part of the foreign policy programme of all West German political parties (Clemens, 1989; Siekmeier and Larres, 1996).

Instead of maintaining the illusion of unification the SPD-FDP coalition government intended to improve the human contacts between the people in both parts of Germany. This, they believed, could be achieved by fully recognising the GDR as a sovereign state and seeking cooperation with the SED regime on practical matters. They were at least partially successful. In the 1970s, the GDR government relaxed its stringent policies and permitted a limited number of its citizens to visit the FRG in case of a family emergency (Larres, 1995b; Craig, 1994).

In 1973, the FRG also negotiated a treaty with Czechoslovakia according to which Bonn agreed to nullify the Munich agreement of September 1938 and recognise the territorial *status quo* between the two states. The two nations also agreed to establish diplomatic relations with each other. Subsequently, the FRG established diplomatic relations with Hungary and Bulgaria (Borowsky, 1983: 126–9).

Bonn's *détente* policy with eastern Europe, especially the Basic Treaty, was a necessary prerequisite for the 1975 Helsinki agreement. This treaty, signed by the heads of 33 European nations and those of the United States and Canada, recognised the post-war *status quo* in Europe, and thus the division of Europe and Germany (Heraclides, 1993; Bloed, 1994).

During the FRG's negotiations with the East, the United States emphasised the importance of West Germany in American foreign policy while chancellor Helmut Schmidt, who had succeeded Brandt in 1974, reiterated Europe's and West Germany's close partnership with Washington (Dittgen, 1997). Moreover, Schmidt was determined to strengthen the security of the Atlantic partnership by demanding the deployment of intermediate-range nuclear missiles (INF) in western Europe to offset the Soviet missile build-up in eastern Europe. Schmidt's party, the Social Democrats, eventually opposed their own chancellor on the INF deployment issue (Jäger, 1987: 193ff., 225–6; Dittgen, 1991). The internal disagreement within the SPD and differences on economic issues between the SPD and the Free Democrats with whom the SPD had formed a coalition government since 1969, caused the collapse of the centre-left government in 1982 and resulted in a *Wende*, a change of government in Bonn (Balfour, 1992: 218–19; Turner, 1992: 174–95; Bölling, 1982).

The Christian Democrats, who earlier had strongly opposed the *détente* policy of the SPD-led government, formed a coalition with the Free Democrats (FDP) under Helmut Kohl. Although a shift from a centre-left to a centre-right coalition government had taken place in 1982, Hans-Dietrich Genscher, foreign minister since 1974, remained in post and pursued with vigour the *Ostpolitik* of the two previous administrations in both of which he had served. It was Genscher, in particular, who asked the western allies to take Gorbachev and his reforms seriously and who called for stronger economic and technological cooperation between East and West (Genscher, 1995: 489 ff.). Chancellor Kohl and a large segment of his CDU were convinced of the practical necessity of continuing *Ostpolitik*. His party and he also occasionally reiterated their wish to see Germany united again. But more importantly, *Deutschlandpolitik* had improved relations with the GDR and had dramatically enhanced direct contacts between millions of West Germans and their East German counterparts (Turner, 1992: 187–8, 208 ff.; Balfour, 1992: 221 ff.). Realising that continued opposition to *Ostpolitik* and *Deutschlandpolitik* would be politically unwise, the Kohl government began to improve relations with the Soviet Union and its satellite states. In 1987, it even hosted East German party chief Erich Honecker, thus elevating the international status of the GDR and providing it with a greater degree of legitimacy (Turner, 1989: 214–17; McCauley, 1992: 214; Clemens, 1992).

GERMAN UNIFICATION

In 1987 unification of the two Germanys seemed to be as remote as ever. Confident of the permanence of the division of Germany, particularly since the 1975 Helsinki agreement, the Honecker regime had dismantled the automatic machine guns mounted on the German–German border. It also permitted a greater number of its citizens to travel to West Germany. Whereas 1.2 million citizens below retirement age were able to visit the West in 1987, three million could do so in 1988. Not too long before the collapse of the Berlin Wall, Honecker even predicted that the Wall would still exist in fifty or a hundred years (Garton Ash, 1993: 356).

Both East and West regarded the division of Germany as a prerequisite for stability in Europe. As late as 1989, analysts such as George F. Kennan argued against German unity (Kennan, 1995: 171–2). Moreover, the Social Democrats and the West German Greens viewed the division of Germany as permanent. The SPD had established close contacts with the SED and even signed a joint declaration with the East German Communist Party in 1987 (Lehmbruch, 1993: 23).

However, reforms in the Soviet Union initiated by Gorbachev contributed to demands for political and economic changes in eastern Europe, particularly in Poland and Hungary. In the GDR, an increasing number of dissidents and East German citizens became more outspoken in their criticism of the repressive SED regime (Gorbachev, 1995: 700 ff., 928 ff.).

Though Honecker released between 2000 and 3000 dissidents, political activists and undesirable citizens to West Germany annually for hard cash of between $30 000 and $50 000 per person, opposition to the Honecker regime mounted during the latter part of the 1980s (Weber, 1988: 98–104; Gransow and Jarausch, 1991: 52 ff.). The SED, however, rejected the introduction of reforms, either political or economic. Reacting to the spread of *glasnost*, it even banned *Sputnik*, a Soviet magazine published in German, from distribution in the GDR. In an action regarded as reprehensible by many East German citizens, the Party openly commended Communist China for having used brutal force to suppress the mass demonstration in Tiananmen Square in Beijing in 1989. The SED seemed oblivious to dramatic changes taking place in the Soviet Union and in the neighbouring eastern European countries, as well as to the improvement of relations between Moscow and West Germany (Gorbachev, 1995: 930–6; Glaeßner, 1992: 215; Lehmbruch, 1993; Fulbrook, 1995: 201 ff.).

In June 1989, during Mikhail Gorbachev's official state visit to the Federal Republic of Germany, the two governments emphasised the central importance of German–Soviet relations and signed a host of bilateral agreements. Influenced by Gorbachev's *perestroika* and *glasnost* and the Soviet leader's determination to reduce the military confrontation in Europe, NATO agreed to support greater cooperation with the East and introduced a new security strategy which took into account the radical changes of the Cold War framework in Europe (Gorbachev, 1995: 706–10).

While Gorbachev's reforms contributed to the erosion of the communist regimes in eastern Europe, peaceful revolutions in most of these countries, including the GDR, eventually caused their collapse. In the case of East Germany, *Deutschlandpolitik* initiated by the centre-left Brandt administration and continued by the Schmidt-Genscher government, and after 1982, by the centre-right Kohl-Genscher administrations, contributed to the improvement of relations between the two German states.

This led to a dramatic increase of personal contacts by millions of Germans on both sides. Moreover, these closer contacts between the two Germanys and their populations prevented the East German state from developing its own national identity. The vast majority of East Germans saw in the West German democratic state and its economic wealth the model they wished to imitate (Anderson et al., 1993: 2–4; Lehmbruch, 1993: 22).

Amidst the massive flight of East Germans to West Germany in the summer and autumn of 1989, triggered by the opening of the Hungarian border to Austria on 2 May 1989, the GDR celebrated its fortieth anniversary on 7 October 1989. Gorbachev, in his speech commemorating the anniversary, alluded to the vulnerability of the East German Communist regime when he cautioned GDR leaders that 'life punishes those who come too late'. Only two days later, almost 100 000 people in Leipzig staged a demonstration requesting major reforms. Large-scale demonstrations followed in other cities, the largest being held in East Berlin with almost a million people participating. On 18 October, SED party chief Erich Honecker was forced to resign. On 9 November, the SED decided to open the border crossings to West Berlin and West Germany, which triggered the collapse of the Berlin Wall. While the demonstrators, before the disintegration of the Wall, expressed their desire for democratic reforms by chanting 'we are the people', they would soon clamour for unification by shouting 'we are one people' (Gorbachev, 1995: 711–12, 933–6; Garton Ash, 1993: 344–7).

Less than three weeks after the sudden and unexpected collapse of the Berlin Wall on 9 November 1989, Chancellor Helmut Kohl presented a ten-point proposal to the Bundestag suggesting the creation of 'confederate structures' with the goal of creating a 'federal state order' which would end the division of Germany. Kohl, realising the East Germans' desire for unity, became the driving force toward German unification (Szabo, 1992: 38 ff.; Genscher, 1995: 669 ff.).

However, the possibility of German unification raised the spectre of the resurrection of a 'Greater Reich' or the creation of a 'Fourth Reich'. Initially, the Soviet Union rejected unification, and British and French politicians and officials expressed their reservations. Of all the countries, Poland was particularly nervous about the prospect of German unity, especially since Chancellor Kohl was reluctant to acknowledge the Oder-Neisse line as the final border between Germany and Poland. With the exception of the Polish people, public opinion in the West – though not generally among the leading intellectuals (Glaeßner, 1992: 222 ff.) – generally supported unification. Still, Europeans were concerned that Germany once again was about to become the predominant power in Europe. Also, the British and French feared the economic consequences of unification and both countries were apprehensive about a revival of fascism, the British more so than the French (James and Stone, 1992: 221 ff.; Verheyen and Soe, 1993: 35 ff.; Thatcher, 1995: 792 ff.).

To reduce Poland's anxiety over the restoration of a powerful unified Germany, West German President Richard von Weizsäcker demanded the recognition of the Oder-Neisse line by the Federal Republic of Germany, a demand which Chancellor Kohl initially attempted to postpone for political reasons. After immense pressure by Poland, the Kohl administration, just two weeks before the all-German elections on 2 December 1990, agreed to sign a treaty with Warsaw guaranteeing permanent recognition of the Oder-Neisse rivers as the final border between Poland and the recently united Germany (Garton Ash, 1993: 353–6; Neckermann, 1991: 34–5, 40).

Germany's closest ally, the United States, strongly supported unity without much hesitation. President George Bush and Chancellor Kohl, as well as foreign ministers Genscher and James Baker cooperated closely to realise German unification against the initial opposition from Britain, France and, of course, the USSR (Zelikow and Rice, 1995; Bortfeldt, 1997). Among the American public, only 16 per cent believed that a unified Germany would attempt to dominate the world, 73 per cent thought it would not (Merkl, 1993: 5–6, 315–18; Treverton, 1992: 180–3).

Without Soviet approval, German unity could not have been accomplished. Obviously, opposition to any German aggrandisement was prevalent among Soviet citizens and members of the Communist Party, many of whom still remembered the brutal consequences of the Nazi aggression during World War II. However, President Gorbachev, who initially had not hesitated to voice his strong reservations, agreed to unification in principle in January 1990 (McCauley, 1992: 180; Gorbachev, 1995: 714).

The public in both German states supported unity in general although the East Germans were much more enthusiastic than their western counterparts. However, there was also widespread scepticism in both parts of Germany. In East Germany, citizens' movements founded in the late 1980s such as the 'New Forum' and 'Democracy Now', rejected unification. Instead, they preferred a 'third way' between capitalism and communism. The citizens' groups were in a minority, however. The vast majority of the East Germans, who by late 1989 chanted 'Germany united Fatherland', had opted for West German democracy and prosperity rather than the 'humane socialism' offered by the citizens' movements (Merkl, 1993: 77 ff.; Neckermann, 1991: 12–13, 29–30; Fulbrook, 1995: 201 ff.).

In West Germany, a small number of intellectuals, such as Jürgen Habermas and Günter Grass opposed unification (Gransow and Jarausch, 1991: 125–8, 148–52). Also, the West German Greens initially perceived the GDR as a separate state, a 'society beyond capitalism and state socialism'. However, the Greens, confronted by the rapidly evolving unification process and the results of the March 1990 elections in East Germany, shifted their attitude from opposition to support of unity. The West German Social Democrats also found it difficult to react to the rapidly unfolding events. In fact the party became badly split on the unification issue. Oskar Lafontaine, whom the SPD had selected as their candidate for chancellor, was initially reserved toward German unity and wanted to slow down the unification process. He warned the West Germans of the consequences of hasty unification. He foresaw increased inflation, high unemployment, higher taxes, and generally enormous costs for the West German state and its citizens (Lafontaine, 1990: 174 ff.). On the other hand, then SPD chairman Hans-Jochen Vogel and elder statesman Willy Brandt supported rapid unification, the latter proclaiming already in November 1989 'what belongs together will grow together again'. (Brandt, 1989: 501–12; Merkl, 1993: 119 ff.; Gransow and Jarausch, 1991: 143–4).

Though Lafontaine, who eventually began to support unification during the 1990 election campaign, was ultimately correct in his pessimistic predictions, Chancellor Kohl recognised the yearning of the vast majority of East Germans (and to a lesser degree of many West Germans) for immediate unification. They certainly rejected a 'third road' as recommended by East German intellectuals. Moreover, they did not want to wait five years to obtain a share in the West German prosperity. The East Germans desired immediate unification. Their determination to unite with the West was reflected in the March 1990 elections in the GDR. Forty-eight per cent of the citizens voted for the pro-unity 'Alliance for Germany' consisting of the Christian Democrats and the German Social Union, both modelled on their West German counterparts. The SPD received barely 22 per cent and the 'Alliance 90' consisting of the citizens' movements which rejected unification, received a mere 2.9 per cent of the vote (Merkl, 1993: 131–4; Gransow and Jarausch, 1991: 148).

Some critics have alleged that the East German desire for unification was primarily motivated by 'deutschmark nationalism', the wish of the majority of East Germans to participate in the prosperity of the western world. Though prosperity and West German consumerism were important motives, the East Germans had no desire after forty years of communism to experiment with any form of socialism, nor did they trust reform movements inside the GDR. Instead, they opted for unification with West Germany which at the time provided them with a much more attractive model (Lehmbruch, 1993).

The March elections, in which the Christian Democrats and their political allies won a stunning victory, accelerated the unification process. In May, the newly established democratic East German government and its West German counterpart signed a treaty on the economic and social union between the two countries which came into effect on 2 July 1990. It permitted the East Germans to exchange their valueless East German marks for West German marks on the basis of largely a one-to-one rate. The suggestion by Lafontaine that integration should be a gradual process was unrealistic in view of the near collapse of the East German economy and the desire of the East German citizens for immediate unification. The Kohl administration hoped that economic union and the favourable currency exchange would alleviate the mounting economic problems in the East. However, as soon became evident, the short-term beneficiary of the economic fusion was West Germany, rather than the East as intended. Its economic production increased due to the soaring demand of western goods in eastern Germany, whereas the East German economy experienced almost a total collapse during the first year after the economic union had been initiated (see Chapters 5 and 7).

Actual unification and attainment of full German sovereignty, however, required official consent by the Soviet Union and the three western powers. During Kohl's visit to the Soviet Union in July 1990, the chancellor proposed to limit the German armed forces to 370 000. President Gorbachev in turn granted unified Germany full sovereignty and permitted Germany to stay in the NATO alliance. In September, the two countries reached agreements on the conditions for withdrawal of Soviet troops from East Germany by the end of 1994. Chancellor Kohl promised to finance the gradual removal of Soviet troops to the tune of eight billion dollars. Finally in November 1990, during Gorbachev's state visit to the already unified Germany, the two governments signed far-reaching agreements concerning cooperation in the economic, scientific, political and cultural spheres. They also pledged never to engage in armed aggression against each other or against other states (Gorbachev, 1995: 708–27).

Earlier, the four allied powers and the two German states had agreed to negotiate an agreement detailing provisions for German unity. After a series of meetings, the 'Two-Plus-Four' powers signed a treaty in Moscow on 12 September 1990 which guaranteed full sovereignty to unified Germany. This treaty was a prerequisite for the actual unification of the two German states on 3 October 1990 (Gorbachev, 1995: 708–27; Ludlow, 1991). At the end of November 1990, thirty-two

European nations and the United States and Canada reconfirmed German unity and the termination of the division of Europe at the CSCE Conference in Paris (Gorbachev, 1995: 740–41). All-German elections, scheduled for 2 December, returned the existing centre-right Kohl-Genscher government. Unification of the two German states had been accomplished in just over a year.

AFTER UNIFICATION

The initial euphoria generated by German unification soon gave way to anxiety and bitterness in both parts of the recently unified country (see in detail Parts II and III). In spring 1991, almost three million eastern Germans, one-third of the former GDR's work force, were either unemployed or on reduced working hours. Growing dissatisfaction among the workers spilled over into the streets when tens of thousands of citizens demonstrated in Leipzig and other eastern German cities. This time their protest was directed against the Kohl government which had promised the Germans in the East a share in the prosperity of West Germany. The people protested against rising unemployment and the fact that their wages were generally only 40 per cent of those in the western part of Germany.

In the West, Kohl, during the election campaign in autumn 1990, had pledged that unification could be accomplished without raising taxes. Only a few months after unification, the chancellor was forced to submit wide-ranging tax proposals to the Bundestag. New taxes were levied with effect from July 1991. Ever since, the price of unification has continued to rise rapidly, and by one estimate could already have reached 200 billion dollars. General dissatisfaction about government policies and broken promises has caused a decline in the popularity of both Kohl and his party. Still, the Kohl government was able to win the 1994 general election, albeit with a much reduced majority (Larres, 1995); subsequently the German Bundestag re-elected Kohl as chancellor by a majority of only one vote. Not so much Kohl's achievements as chancellor since unification but the opposition SPD's inability to offer an attractive alternative to the government have ensured the survival of the Kohl government.

Once Germany's unity was accomplished, its allies expected the new Germany to shoulder greater responsibilities. Despite the fact that the German constitution was widely interpreted as prohibiting military activities outside the NATO area, the allies criticised Germany's refusal to send troops in support of the Gulf war in 1991. However, Kohl did not have the necessary majority in the Bundestag to change the constitution and enable the united country to become militarily active out of area. There was, however, no political will to get involved militarily either. Instead united Germany continued the West German tradition of supporting the western alliance financially (Gutjahr, 1994; Janning, 1996).

Another major problem almost immediately faced by united Germany was the location of its government. Although with unification Berlin had become the capital of the united country, it was necessary to determine whether the seat of the government was to remain in Bonn or should move to Berlin. After heated debates in parliament and throughout Germany, the Bundestag voted on 20 June 1991 by a narrow majority of 17 to move both the Bundestag and the government to Berlin. The Bundesrat, the upper house, decided to stay temporarily in Bonn; however, in all likelihood it also will move to Berlin in the near future. Among those arguing on behalf of Berlin as the seat of government were Chancellor Kohl and Wolfgang Schäuble, the then minister of the interior, Willy Brandt and then foreign minister Hans-Dietrich Genscher. Those supporting the retention of Bonn as the seat of government were the president of the Bundestag Rita Süssmuth and labour minister Norbert Blüm from the CDU as well as Johannes Rau, SPD minister-president of North-Rhine Westphalia.

So far unification has not produced a fusion of the two Germanys; no real feeling of togetherness has emerged. The initial optimism expressed by politicians who predicted a smooth merger has given way to a more pessimistic outlook. An opinion poll taken in the summer of 1991 dramatically revealed the alienation between the two Germanys caused by the 45-year division. Large majorities on both sides were of the opinion that 'only since unification has it become evident how different eastern and western Germans are'. Drastic differences were also reflected in the sentiment voiced by 84 per cent of eastern Germans who regarded themselves as second-class citizens. Even Chancellor Kohl admitted:

> As far as inner unity goes, the economic and social challenges will admittedly take longer and cost more than most, including myself, had originally assumed.

He added: 'What I hoped to achieve in three to five years will perhaps need twice that time.' Even that timetable appears optimistic (Saxony's minister-president Kurt Biedenkopf speaks of '10 to 15 years'). To a surprising degree, the fallen Wall continues to divide the Germans – the 64 million in the West from the 16 million in the East. Before the Wall came down politicians talked of two states but one nation. More than half a decade after unification it is one state but still two societies. Biedenkopf was brutally honest when he told western Germans what unification would cost them – around 1400 billion DM (*c.* 600 billion pounds sterling) – and how they should pay: up front.

> It's not solidarity or the warmth of togetherness that makes you want to divide your income with someone else over a longer period of time. It's basic interest. West Germany's basic interest is getting rid of this burden as soon as possible.

Unfortunately, the unexpected social divide has contributed to business' scepticism about investing in the east. Many companies have discovered that production in Poland or the Czech Republic, just a few miles further east, is considerably cheaper than setting up factories in eastern Germany. The insecurity and fears surrounding a transition that has included the systematic dismantling of everything from day-care centres to state-provided burials have also had a devastating social effect on the former GDR citizens: since 1989, the eastern birthrate has dropped by half. The number of marriages was down 38 per cent in 1993. In a society in which women formerly made up half of the work force, seven in ten women were jobless, most of them against their will. Bärbel Bohley, a political activist who played a prominent role in the 1989 revolt, put it this way in 1993:

> There's a terrible lethargy here now. People sit back and say 'Do it for us.' We have freedom now, and that is worth something. But we look at the Wessies and they seem so tall. They rule us, and we take it.

The process of 'growing together' is still arduous and still requires patience on both sides. With contrasting political and socio-economic structures in place for forty-five years, a speedy merger cannot be expected. The prosperous Germans in the western part need to exercise tolerance towards their brethren in the east who have lived under an authoritarian communist regime for almost half a century. Likewise, the eastern Germans have to adapt to an open, pluralistic and multicultural society which necessitates tolerance and recognition of minorities and non-Germans. Genuine union and an amalgamation of the two parts of Germany still seem to be years away. Serious efforts to overcome the differences will be required by both the government and the German people in East and West. The situation in post-unification Germany is unique, there are hardly any precedents in history. Perhaps it can be compared with the situation in the United States at the end of the Civil War. Reconstructing the American nation took a long time – but eventually it was achieved to a considerable degree.

NOTES

1. Public Record Office, London (hereafter: PRO) FO 800/501/SK/46/15, 10 April 1946.
2. PRO: CAB 129/9, Cabinet Paper No. 46, 1946: 'Policy towards Germany'.
3. Ibid.
4. PRO: FO 371/55700/C 8314, 23 July 1946.
5. PRO: CAB 129/25, Cabinet Paper, 3 March 1948.
6. However, the US Embassy in Moscow did not exclude an eventual Soviet attempt at revision of this boundary. After all, it was believed that this would provide the Kremlin with 'the ultimate carrot to lead the German donkey over the hump'.
7. PRO: FO 371/103 673, 17 August 1953.
8. PRO: PREM 11/449, 6 July 1953.
9. See also Foreign Relations of the United States (FRUS) 1952–54: 1115–16.
10. See also PRO: PREM 11/449, 6 July 1953.
11. PRO: PREM 11/449, 31 May 1953.
12. The entire quote can also be found in PRO: FO 371/118254/WG 1071/G 1374, 16 December 1955.

REFERENCES

Anderson, Ch., Kaltenthaler, K. and Luthardt, W., eds (1993), *The Domestic Politics of German Unification* (Boulder, Colo.: Lynne Rienner).

Arenth, Joachim (1997), 'Die Bewährungsprobe der "special relationship": Washington und Bonn (1961–1969)', in Larres, K. and Oppelland, T., eds, ch. 6.

Bortfeldt, Heinrich (1997), 'Die Vereinigten Staaten und die deutsche Einheit', in Larres, K. and Oppelland, T., eds, ch. 10.

Balfour, M. (1992), *Germany: The Tides of Power* (London: Routledge).

Baring, A., with Görtemaker, M. (1982), *Machtwechsel: Die Ära Brandt-Scheel* (Stuttgart: Deutsche Verlags-Anstalt).

Bark, D.L. and Gress, D.R. (1989), *A History of West Germany, vol. 2: Democracy and its Discontents 1963–1988* (Oxford: Blackwell).

Bender, P. (2nd edn, 1989), *Neue Ostpolitik: Vom Mauerbau bis zum Moskauer Vertrag* (Munich: Deutscher Taschenbuch Verlag).
Bloed, A., ed. (1994), *The Challenges of Change: the Helsinki Summit of the CSCE and its Aftermath* (Dordrecht: M. Nijhoff Norwell).
Bölling, K. (1982), *Die letzten 30 Tage des Kanzlers Helmut Schmidt: ein Tagebuch* (Hamburg: Spiegel-Buch).
Borowsky, P. (4th edn, 1983), *Deutschland 1970–76* (Hannover: Fackelträger-Verlag).
Boyle, P.G., ed. (1990), *The Churchill–Eisenhower Correspondence, 1953–55* (Chapel Hill: University of North Carolina Press).
Brandt, W. (1989), *Erinnerungen* (Frankfurt/Main: Propyläen) [English abridged version: *My Life in Politics*, London: Hamish Hamilton, 1992].
Catudal, H.M. (1980), *Kennedy and the Berlin Wall Crisis: A Case Study in U.S. Decision Making* (Berlin: Berlin-Verlag).
Clemens, C. (1989), *Reluctant Realists: the Christian Democrats and West German Ostpolitik* (Durham, NC: Duke University Press).
Clemens, C. (1992), *CDU Deutschlandpolitik and Reunification, 1985–1989* (Washington DC: German Historical Institute, Occasional Paper No. 5).
Craig, G.A. (1994), 'Did Ostpolitik Work? The Path to German Reunification' (review essay), *Foreign Affairs*, vol. 73, No. 1, pp. 162–7.
Dittgen, H. (1991), *Deutsch–amerikanische Sicherheits beziehungen in der Ära Helmut Schmidt: Vorgeschichte und Folgen des NATO-Doppelbeschlusses* (Munich: W. Fink).
Dittgen, H. (1997), 'Die Ära der Ost-West-Verhandlungen und der Wirtschafts- und Währungskrisen (1969–1981)', in Larres, K. and Oppelland, T., eds, ch. 7.
Eden, A. [Lord Avon] (1960), *Full Circle* (London: Cassell).
Ehmke, H. (1994), *Mittendrin: Von der Großen Koalition zur Deutschen Einheit* (Berlin: Rowohlt).
Foschepoth, J., ed. (2nd edn, 1990), *Adenauer und die Deutsche Frage* (Göttingen: Vandenhoeck & Ruprecht).
Garthoff, R.L. (rev. edn, 1994), *Détente and Confrontation: American–Soviet Relations from Nixon to Reagan* (Washington, DC: Brookings).
Garton Ash, T. (1993), *In Europe's Name: Germany and the Divided Continent* (London: Jonathan Cape).
Genscher, D. (1995), *Erinnerungen* (Berlin: Siedler).
Glaeßner, G.J. (1992), 'German Unification and the West', in Glaeßner, G.J. and Wallace, I., eds, pp. 207–26.
Glaeßner, G.J. and Wallace, I., eds, *The German Revolution of 1989: Causes and Consequences* (Oxford: Berg).
Glees, A. (1985), 'Churchill's Last Gambit: What the "Secret Documents" Reveal about the Prime Minister's Adventurous Initiative in 1953 on the Reunification ("and Neutralisation"?) of Germany . . . and why Dr. Adenauer prevailed', *Encounter*, vol. 64 (April), pp. 27 ff.
Gorbachev, M. (1995), *Erinnerungen* (Berlin: Siedler).
Gransow, V. and Jarausch, K.H., eds (1991), *Die deutsche Vereinigung: Dokumente zu Bürgerbewegung, Annäherung und Beitritt* (Cologne: Verlag Wissenschaft und Politik).
Griffith, W.E. (1978), *The Ostpolitik of the Federal Republic of Germany* (Cambridge, Mass.: MIT Press).

Gromyko, A. (1989), *Memories* (London: Hutchinson).

Gutjahr, L. (1994), *German Foreign and Defence Policy after Unification* (London: Pinter).

Heraclides, A. (1993), *Security and Co-operation in Europe: the Human Dimension, 1972–1992* (London: Frank Cass).

Herbst, L., Bührer, W. and Sowade, H., eds (1990), *Vom Marshallplan zur EWG: Die Eingliederung der Bundesrepublik Deutschland in die westliche Welt* (Munich: Oldenbourg).

Jäger, W. (1987), 'Die Innenpolitik der sozial–liberalen Koalition 1974–1982', in Bracher, K.D., Jäger, W. and Link, W., *Republik im Wandel 1974–1982: Die Ära Schmidt*, Geschichte der Bundesrepublik Deutschland, vol. 5/2 (Stuttgart: Deutsche Verlags-Anstalt), pp. 9 ff.

James, H. and Stone, M., eds (1992), *When the Wall Came Down: Reactions to German Unification* (New York: Routledge).

Janning, J. (1996), 'A German Europe – a European Germany? On the debate over Germany's foreign policy', in *International Affairs*, vol. 72, no. 1, pp. 33–41.

Keithly, D.M. (1986), *Breakthrough in the Ostpolitik: the 1971 Quadripartite Agreement* (Boulder, Colo.: Westview Press).

Kennan, G. (1996), *At a Century's Ending. Reflections, 1982–1995* (New York: W.W. Norton).

Kessel, M. (1989), *Westeuropa und die deutsche Teilung: Englische und französische Deutschlandpolitik auf den Außenministerkonferenzen von 1945 bis 1947* (Munich: Oldenbourg).

Kissinger, H. (1994), *Diplomacy* (London: Simon & Schuster).

Koch, P. (2nd edn, 1992), *Willy Brandt: Eine politische Biographie* (Bergisch Gladbach: Bastei-Lübbe).

Köhler, H. (1994), *Adenauer: Eine politische Biographie* (Frankfurt/M.: Propyläen).

Lafontaine, O. (1990), *Deutsche Wahrheiten: Die nationale und die soziale Frage* (Hamburg: Hoffmann & Campe).

Larres, K. (1995), *Politik der Illusionen: Churchill, Eisenhower und die deutsche Frage 1945–1955* (Göttingen: Vandenhoeck & Ruprecht).

Larres, K. (1995b), 'A Widow's Revenge: Willy Brandt's Ostpolitik, Neo-Conservatism and the German General Election of 1994', *German Politics*, vol. 4, no. 1 (1995), pp. 42–63.

Larres, K. (1996), 'Germany and the West: The "Rapallo Factor" in German Foreign Policy from the 1950s to the 1990s', in Larres, K. and Panayi, P., eds, pp. 278–326.

Larres, K. and Panayi, P., eds (1996), *The Federal Republic of Germany since 1949: Politics, Society and Economy before and after Unification* (London: Longman).

Larres, K. (1997), 'Eisenhower, Dulles und Adenauer: Bündnis des Vertrauens oder Allianz des Mißtrauens? (1953–1961)' in Larres, K. and Oppelland, T., eds, ch. 5.

Larres, K. and Oppelland, T., eds (1997), *Deutschland und die USA im 20. Jahrhundert* (Darmstadt: Wissenschaftliche Buchgesellschaft).

Lehmbruch, G. (1993), 'The Process of Regime Change in East Germany', in Anderson, Ch. et al., pp. 17–36.

Lösche, P. and Walter, F. (1992), *Die SPD: Klassenpartei-Volkspartei-Quotenpartei. Zur Entwicklung der Sozialdemokratie von Weimar bis zur deutschen Vereinigung* (Darmstadt: Wissenschaftliche Buchgesellschaft).

Ludlow, P. (1991), 'The German–German negotiations and the "Two-Plus-Four" talks', in W. Heisenberg, ed., *German Unification in European Perspective* (London: Brassey's), pp. 15–27.

Lutz, D.S., ed. (1992), *Das Undenkbare denken. Festschrift für Egon Bahr zum 70. Geburtstag* (Baden-Baden: Nomos).

Mayer, Frank A. (1996), *Adenauer and Kennedy. A Study in German–American Relations, 1961–63* (New York: St. Martin's).

McCauley, M. (1992), 'Gorbachev, the GDR and Germany', in Glaeßner, G.J. and Wallace, I., eds, pp. 163–83.

Merkl, P.H. (1993), *German Unification in the European Context* (University Park, Pa.: Pennsylvania State University Press).

Neckermann, P. (1991), *The Unification of Germany, or the Anatomy of a Peaceful Revolution* (New York: Columbia University Press).

Nelson, K.L. (1995), *The Making of Détente: Soviet–American Relations in the Shadow of Vietnam* (Baltimore: Johns Hopkins University Press).

Schwartz, T.A. (1991), *America's Germany: John McCloy and the Federal Republic of Germany* (Cambridge, Mass.: Harvard University Press).

Siekmeier, M. and Larres, K. (1996), 'Domestic Political Developments II: The Years 1969–1990', in Larres, K. and Panayi, P., eds, pp. 100–36.

Smith, J.E. (1990), *Lucius D. Clay: An American Life* (New York: H. Holt).

Steininger, R. (1988), *Die Ruhrfrage 1945/46 und die Entstehung des Landes Nordrhein-Westfalen* (Düsseldorf: Droste).

Steininger, R. (1989), 'Germany after 1945: Divided and Integrated or United and Neutral?', in *German History*, vol. 7, no. 1, pp. 5–18.

Steininger, R. (1990), *The German Question: The Stalin Note of 1952 and the Problem of Reunification* (New York: Columbia University Press).

Steininger, R. (rev. edn, 1996), *Deutsche Geschichte seit 1945: Darstellung und Dokumente*, four vols (Frankfurt/Main: Fischer).

Szabo, Stephen F. (1992), *The Diplomacy of German Unification* (New York: St. Martin's).

Treverton, G.F. (1992), *America, Germany and the Future of Europe* (Princeton, NJ: Princeton University Press).

Turner, H.A. Jr. (1992), *Germany from Partition to Reunification* (New Haven, Conn.: Yale University Press).

Verheyen D. and Soe, C., eds (1993), *The Germans and their Neighbours* (Boulder, Colo.: Westview Press).

Weber, H. (1988), *Die DDR 1945–1986*, Grundriß der Geschichte, vol. 20 (Munich: Oldenbourg).

Whetten, L.L. (1971), *Germany's Ostpolitik: Relations between the Federal Republic and the Warsaw Pact Countries* (London: Oxford University Press).

Yergin, D. (1977), *Shattered Peace: The Origins of the Cold War and the National Security State* (Boston, Mass.: Houghton Mifflin).

Zelikow, Ph. and Rice C. (1995), *Germany United and Europe Transformed. A Study in Statecraft*, Cambridge, Mass.: Harvard University Press.

2 Germany in 1989: the Development of a Revolution

Klaus Larres

Initially the East German people and civil rights movements like New Forum and Democracy Now were the driving forces behind the events which led to the breaching of the Berlin Wall on 9 November 1989, the collapse of the GDR and its merger with West Germany on 3 October 1990. Even when the West German government took over as the main initiator of constitutional changes after the election of a free and democratic government in the GDR in March 1990, it was the people of East Germany who ensured that unification was entered into earlier rather than later. The wave of civil disobedience which shook the GDR between mid-1989 and late summer 1990 was certainly not merely a 'protest movement of the intelligentsia' (Reich, 1992a: 11; Reich, 1992b: 316, 319–20; Horn, 1993: 60). Rather, the protests can be characterised as widespread spontaneous uprisings of the GDR people with an evolutionary origin (Opp, 1993: 13–14, 21–5). The continuation of the mass demonstrations as well as the flood of people who were still fleeing the GDR for West Germany by the spring of 1990 put pressure on the government in Bonn and the four allied powers (USA, Soviet Union, Britain, France) to offer monetary and social union as early as 2 July 1990. Pressure by the East German people was also the main reason why the domestic process and the two-plus-four negotiations between the two German states and the four World War II allies for political unification were completed much more speedily than initially thought feasible.[1]

While the first German revolution for over a century[2] was brought to a successful end in October 1990, most of the major revolutionary events occurred in 1989. The mass demonstrations on the streets of East German cities, the flight of thousands of people to the west via Hungary and other eastern European countries, and, most importantly, the opening of the Berlin Wall and the downfall of the Honecker government all happened in 1989. In particular, the last two events helped to ensure that an irreversible process developed. After the opening of the Wall there was no way back to the *status quo ante*. It would however be wrong to claim that the continuation of the revolutionary developments in 1990 took a predetermined course towards eventual unification after the breaching of the Wall. In early 1990 there was, for example, still serious talk in many quarters within the GDR, the FRG and abroad of a democratic 'third way' for East Germany – of maintaining the GDR as an independent and alternative state to the FRG (Zelikow and Rice, 1995: 102 ff.; Padgett, 1996: 244–5; Thatcher, 1993: 792–6, 813–14). However, the successes of 1989 gave the vast majority of the East German people the motivation and stamina to continue with their own agenda: the attainment of the fruits of western capitalism and democratic freedoms which seemed to be best achieved by unification with West Germany. The first serious calls for unification could be heard on the streets of Leipzig as early as 19 November 1989. Thus, 1989 was of overall importance for the successful eruption and continuation of the revolutionary process.

This chapter will therefore concentrate mainly on the evolution of the German revolution in 1989 and the preceding years and not so much on the continuation of the process towards unification in 1990. It will analyse why it was that the year 1989 (and not any other year) saw the open outbreak of revolutionary unrest which had been lying dormant for some time. It will come to the conclusion that both internal and, initially above all, external reasons played a decisive role in turning 1989 into a truly dramatic year but that most credit for this development belongs to the East German people themselves.

WAS THERE A REVOLUTION IN GERMANY?

On the whole, it seems to be quite justified to view the events of 1989–90 as a revolutionary process. However, more than half a decade since unification this remains controversial in the literature as well as among most of the former demonstrators and civil rights groups (Thaysen, 1992: 72–3). Many attempts have been made to define precisely what kind of uprising took place on the streets of Leipzig, Dresden, East Berlin and elsewhere. However, whether the East German revolution is classified as a conservative, a compensatory or abrogated (Glaeßner, 1992: 4), an interrupted, a learning (Horn, 1993: 62, 66), a negotiated (Thaysen, 1992: 87), a peaceful (Grosser, 1992: 22) or a bourgeois and very German revolution which only took place at weekends and after working hours (Fulbrook, 1995: 250) does not seem to be of vital importance for deciding whether or not the uprising of 1989–90 qualifies to be regarded as a 'proper' revolution. Although the events of 1989–90 can at least partially be characterised as an 'importing and replacing rather than an overturning process', they also led to a 'real collapse' (Thaysen, 1992: 86).

Despite all 'revolutionary deficiencies' and the initial survival of quite a few of the old communist networks, on the whole it seems to have been a radical enough breakdown of an entire state to make way for fundamental changes. 'If a revolution is defined as the overthrow of a ruling group and the transformation of the political system by a protest movement backed by the people, what had happened might be called a revolution indeed' (Grosser, 1992: 22; Glaeßner, 1992: 4). Despite Hannah Arendt's definition of violence as an inherent factor of both war and revolution, the absence of violence does not disqualify the use of the term revolution to describe what happened in the GDR (Arendt, 1973; Glaeßner, 1992: 3–4; Opp, 1993: 25–6). Still, although a fundamental political and social transformation took place, it was also certainly an 'adopted revolution' which lacked a certain 'originality and independence' (Horn, 1992: 66–8). The East German revolution borrowed much inspiration and stimulation from the preceding developments in Poland, Hungary and, of course, from Gorbachev's Soviet Union. Despite all internal difficulties and dissatisfaction, it is doubtful whether there ever would have been a revolution in the GDR without the external stimuli.

Moreover, the mostly peaceful European revolutions of 1989–90 reflected the highpoint of a development which had begun as early as the mid-1970s. It had been the 1975 Helsinki agreements of the Conference on Security and Cooperation in Europe (CSCE) which for the first time had given eastern European political dissent an internationally recognised moral and legal basis (Heraclides, 1993: 172–5). Entirely contrary to the initial expectations in east and west, the Helsinki agreements demonstrated in the long run 'the explosiveness of the idea of human and civil rights and of the right of self-determination as formulated in basket III of the CSCE' (Thaysen, 1992: 79; Fulbrook, 1995: 87 ff., 115–25). The Final Act of the Helsinki Conference, to which the East Berlin government was a signatory, and also perhaps US President Jimmy Carter's subsequent human rights 'crusade', encouraged dissidents in the Soviet satellite countries including the GDR as well as in the USSR itself to assume gradually an ever more open political role. The Helsinki accords provided a 'rallying point' (Heraclides, 1993: 27–40, 173–4) whose explosive potential would only be realised a decade and a half later.

THE UNDERLYING CAUSES OF DISCONTENT IN THE GDR

In the GDR the Helsinki spirit led to the founding of various loosely organised groups demanding the reform of the existing system. Particularly since the early 1980s issues such as the pollution of the environment, human rights and the military policy of the Warsaw Pact were increasingly addressed by these opposition forces. Often the reform groups met in the form of discussion circles under the umbrella of the Protestant church (Thaysen, 1992: 79). As some of them represented the rough equivalent to the West German peace movement, the SED, the ruling East German communist party, itself had clandestinely encouraged the formation of several of these groups protesting against President Reagan's SDI initiative and NATO's double-track missile deployment decision. The East German security service (Stasi) proved however unable to keep the East German peace movement fully under control (Grosser, 1992: 12 ff.). Mostly young people as well as established intellectuals participated in the movement; blue collar workers and the proverbial 'man in the street' could hardly be found here (Horn, 1993: 60). In general these reform groups were in favour of a 'third way' between capitalist West Germany and too rigid, dictatorial and claustrophic East Germany. Their aim was the development of an improved socialist East German state which would observe democratic principles and human rights while being less exploitive and more humane than the West German state model. To these reformers German unification was not an issue at all (Horn, 1992: 64). By August 1989 the Stasi estimated the existence of several hundred active groups with a very unequal number of members. However, total membership was regarded as too few (merely an estimated 2500 in a population of 16 million) to cause any serious trouble (Grosser, 1992: 13; Mitter and Wolle, 1990: 46–8: Glaeßner, 1992: 13). Still, particularly in the 1980s, the Stasi had begun to prepare football stadia and other mass arenas to act as huge internment camps if need be. Moreover, in the late 1980s more and more groups left the 'church's shadow' and came out in the open and soon experienced persecution similar to the 'Initiative for Peace and Human Rights' which had been founded without any connection to the church as early as 1985–6 (Horn, 1992: 57; Fulbrook, 1995: 220 ff.).

Willy Brandt's *Ostpolitik* which had led to the 1972 Basic Treaty between the two German states and which largely recognised the GDR as an independent state probably contributed to a gradual rise in discontent among the East German people. By means of family reunions an increasing number of GDR citizens were now able to travel to West Berlin and the Federal Republic and see with their own eyes the difference in living standards and general freedom of expression between east and west. After the building of the Wall on 13 August 1961 had stabilised Cold War tension between the two superpowers, the strategy 'change through *rapprochement*', as developed by Brandt's adviser Egon Bahr in the mid-1960s, was partially successful in the 1970s and 1980s. It was a policy of westernising the GDR by cooperating closely with the regime, of supporting the country economically and avoiding all gestures and policies which might be seen by East Berlin as provocative (as this could in turn have detrimental consequences for the East German population and the continuation of the German–German *détente*) (Geiss, 1996: 152–6; McNeill, 1996: 262–5; Larres, 1996: 301–19). Until late 1989, *Ostpolitik* was pursued by all major West German parties, the Social Democrats, the Conservatives and the Liberals (Clemens, 1989). However, the lessening of political tension between Bonn and East Berlin which developed in the wake of *Ostpolitik* 'fostered the impression that a stable, almost normal situation had been attained' (Grosser, 1992: 5; Asmus, 1990: 63), thereby deluding both the western public as well as western governments (both conservative and socialist ones) about the GDR's apparent internal stability. This very widespread picture of the GDR was shattered only with the breaching of the Wall in November 1989.

Throughout the 1980s most commentators in the West entirely overlooked the precarious state of the GDR economy. However, the dire economic situation contributed decisively to the rise and eventual explosion of discontent in East Germany. In the 1970s the GDR economy did not manage to keep up with international production trends. It proved unable to turn from extensive to intensive growth thus becoming increasingly less competitive and losing out against the capitalist economies. Moreover, the GDR economy was not able to motivate its workers, engineers and managers sufficiently to develop new products and innovative production processes. Therefore, it proved impossible to increase labour and capital productivity. The GDR regime was confronted with a serious dilemma: 'Without higher labour productivity one could not increase real wages. Without product and process innovation, competitiveness in international trade had to decline' (Grosser, 1992: 11–12).

The Honecker government's short-term solution for overcoming this vicious circle consisted of subsidising basic consumer goods, housing, foodstuffs and wages as well as exports to the West at an ever increasing rate and ignoring the dangerous long-term consequences of this policy. Moreover, nothing was done to counter the increasingly dangerous level of environmental pollution in the GDR. In certain industrial areas and in cities such as Leipzig this was a much overlooked problem; discontent here was particularly widespread (Lehmbruch, 1993: 20). While high spending on external and internal security continued, investment in capital stock and the infrastructure was utterly neglected and consequently deteriorated rapidly in the 1980s. Gradually the economy stopped growing and from 1985 the budget deficit and accompanying hidden inflation became a seriously worrying factor because the Politbüro had decided to increase wages slowly and maintain the low prices for most basic commodities to fend off public dissatisfaction. Furthermore, the East German economy was much over-centralised and too bureaucratic, and its flexibility was severely impaired by the state's rigid economic planning in five-year cycles (Lehmbruch, 1993: 20).

By 1987 most economic experts within (but not necessarily outside) the GDR realised that the economy was in crisis. While the people were used to product shortages, particularly of quality goods, in the late 1980s these were noticed much more as wages had continued to rise and people now had more disposable income but there were not sufficient products available for purchase (Grosser, 1992: 11–12). Moreover, from 1987, since East German leader Erich Honecker's much celebrated state visit to Chancellor Kohl in Bonn, the number of East Germans who received permission to visit West Germany rose sharply (McAdams, 1993: 167; Grosser, 1992: 5). The GDR's severe economic crisis contributed to the increasing realisation among the East German people of how well the other German state was doing. For years this impression had been created by West German television programmes which most GDR citizens could receive but now an ever-increasing number of people were able to obtain first-hand impressions themselves. While compared with other eastern European economies the GDR was still doing fine, in comparison with the Federal Republic's economic performance and accompanying benefits for the individual consumer, East Germany was losing ground at an ever more rapid pace (Lehmbruch, 1993: 20–1; Roberts, 1991: 374–5; Anderson et al., 1993: 3–4).

Politically the Honecker regime also seemed to be increasingly out of step with the changes in the communist world since Gorbachev's rise to power in 1985. While rapid economic and social modernisation accompanied by real gains in human rights and personal freedoms was attempted in the USSR and some other Warsaw Pact countries like Poland and Hungary, the East Berlin regime stalled all of Gorbachev's attempts to export *perestroika* and *glasnost* into the GDR. Honecker's thinking had been particularly influenced by the Polish crisis of 1980 when only the imposition of martial law prevented the trade union Solidarity from gaining power. This would undoubtedly have led to the disintegration of the socialist system in Poland. The Politbüro in East Berlin was convinced that the introduction of 'premature' reforms and the legalisation of the various reform movements would only result in destabilising the GDR's 'real socialism'. However, in practical terms, martial law did not help to re-establish the communist party's leading role and authority; on the contrary it undermined the legitimacy of communism in Poland as elsewhere in the communist world even further and did not stop Lech Walesa's Solidarity from gaining power in 1989. Despite Gorbachev's new policies, the GDR's increasing economic problems and the formation of ever more outspoken reform groups in East Germany, to Honecker the continuation of his political course seemed to be well justified and the only way of guaranteeing the stability of the system (Grosser, 1992: 6). A member of Honecker's Politbüro asked reporters rhetorically: if 'your neighbour renewed the wallpaper in his flat, would you feel obliged to do the same?' (quoted in Zelikow and Rice, 1995: 37).

Within the Soviet Union Gorbachev and other reform-minded members of the Politbüro however had realised that the reform of, above all, the increasingly outdated economic system of the USSR and its satellite states was long overdue. The insight that there had to be a new drive for economic efficiency and economic growth and also towards a less confrontational new foreign policy (as outlined by Gorbachev in a speech to the British parliament in December 1984) helped Gorbachev to be elected secretary general of the CPSU in March 1985 (Gorbachev, 1995: 248, 253–62). In 1986 Gorbachev began to speak of 'radical reforms' not limited to the economy. Soon he mentioned the necessity of the 'democratisation' of the political system and the terms *perestroika* and *glasnost* became associated with the total economic and political restructuring of the Soviet system (Grosser, 1992: 6–7).

During the same year Gorbachev and his advisers came to the conclusion that the satellite countries were no longer economically and politically viable; they had become serious liabilities and also proved to be an ever increasing burden on Moscow's finances. Moreover, the reform group around Gorbachev soon realised that the West no longer constituted a direct security threat to the USSR. The various summits and disarmament agreements entered into with US President Reagan since the Reykjavik conference in 1986 had decisively contributed to this insight (Oberdorfer, 1992: 155 ff.). Consequently, a Soviet military presence in a politically autocratic and economically backward eastern Europe did not help to enhance Soviet security and even proved counter-productive as far as Moscow's new 'liberal' international prestige was concerned. And Gorbachev was always careful to boost this image with new initiatives like, for example, allowing Nobel Peace winner Andrei Sacharov to return to Moscow from his exile in Gorki (Bögeholz, 1995: 617).

In a speech in November 1987 Gorbachev declared that 'national and social differences' in the socialist world were 'good and useful' (Zelikow and Rice, 1995: 16). Four months later, in February 1988, Gorbachev told a plenum of the Central Committee that every country was free to 'choose freely its social and political system' (McCauley, 1992: 164). The period of time which was most important for the intellectual development of Gorbachev's new policy seems to have been the months from late 1987 to mid-1988 when in the course of a party conference of the communist party he speeded up the course of domestic reform (*perestroika*). His speech to the General Assembly of the United Nations in December 1988 can be regarded with hindsight as 'the culmination of a reevaluation of Soviet foreign policy and formulation of a new policy for Europe' (Zelikow and Rice, 1995: 16–17, 36). In his UN speech he announced the Soviet Union's unilateral withdrawal of 50 000 soldiers from eastern Europe. At the same time he repeated his earlier proclamations about every socialist country's right to find its own national political path without interference from Moscow. Every country could go its own way (this became soon known as the Sinatra Doctrine). And Gorbachev meant what he said. The Brezhnev Doctrine had been renounced for good (Kaiser, 1991: 182–3; Valdez, 1993). The Kremlin had finally decided that it would not again invade a satellite country to maintain a dictatorial system. It reflected the logic of this strategy that in the course of the Malta summit conference with US President Bush in December 1989, Gorbachev spoke of his belief that the changes in eastern Europe 'should be welcomed since they [were] related to the desire of the people to give their societies a democratic, human face and to open up to the outside world' (McCauley, 1992: 164). In Malta, Bush and Gorbachev announced the end of the Cold War.

It had certainly not been Gorbachev's intention to undermine the socialist system as such; on the contrary his reforms which attempted to increase consent and reduce the application of force within the communist world were the means of saving this system. He had probably hoped that 'little Gorbachevs would spring up everywhere' and that the socialist system within each eastern European country could be stabilised from within 'by increasing economic efficiency and by gaining more support from the people'. He must have envisaged that Soviet-style *perestroika* and *glasnost* would also be adopted in the Warsaw Pact countries, thus preserving the leading role of the communist party and the socialist ownership of the most important means of production (Zelikow and Rice, 1995: 5–6; McCauley, 1992: 165–7).

Neither had Gorbachev any intention of disturbing the *status quo* of the complicated German question. When Chancellor Kohl visited Moscow in October 1988 he was told that the Soviet Union genuinely wished to improve its relations with West Germany which, since the beginning of Kohl's chancellorship in late 1982, had been characterised by mutual distrust and mud-slinging. In 1988, however, Gorbachev saw no need to discuss German unification. Neither did Kohl: this belonged 'in the realm of fantasy' he told reporters (Zelikow and Rice, 1995: 62). There did not seem to be any need to put it on the international agenda. Gorbachev believed that the German problem would be solved by history in the long run (Kaiser, 1991: 183; Adomeit, 1994: 197–203). A year earlier, in July 1987, he had told visiting West German president Richard von Weizsäcker that German unification might come about in a hundred, maybe even in fifty years. As late as December 1989 Gorbachev announced to the CPSU's Central Committee that he would 'see to it that no harm comes to the GDR' (Garton Ash, 1993: 356, 349). The Soviet president certainly intended to keep Germany divided and maintain communism's leading role in the GDR as well as in the other eastern European states.

However, by early 1989 Gorbachev became increasingly worried that his strategy of saving the Soviet Union's empire by reforming it was becoming seriously undermined by the aged and unrepentant hard-line leaders in Bucharest, Sofia and above all in East Berlin. They clearly hoped that Gorbachev himself would be unseated in the Kremlin in order to return to the good old days of Brezhnev's corrupt rule. Honecker resented and repudiated all Soviet attempts to convince him of the necessity to embark upon immediate economic and political reforms. The East German leader therefore did not hesitate to have the letter by Soviet citizen Nina Andrejewa, which heavily criticised Gorbachev's reform course and first appeared in a Russian paper, translated and published in the SED daily *Neues Deutschland* (Bögeholz, 1995: 639). In November 1988 Honecker also forbade the distribution of the Soviet magazine *Sputnik* in the GDR as this publication strongly supported Gorbachev's policy, and also banned five Soviet films from being shown in the GDR (Bögeholz, 1995: 647). These were unprecedented, almost hostile measures: so far only the distribution of western media products had been forbidden in the GDR. During his visits to Moscow in September 1988 and in late June 1989 Honecker continued to insist that Gorbachev's reforms were only applicable to the USSR but not to the allegedly much more stable, modern and consumer friendly GDR (Bögeholz, 1995: 645, 655).

All these events further contributed to the rise of discontent and frustration among the East German people. As a result, for the first time since 1977 vicious hour-long street battles had occurred in East Berlin between young people and the East German police and Stasi in June 1987. The youths had assembled near the Brandenburg Gate to listen to the music of rock bands playing in the western part of the city near the Berlin Wall and had voiced their frustration with shouts for the dismantling of the Wall, the introduction of freedom and democracy and repeated calls for 'Gorbachev, Gorbachev' (Bögeholz, 1995: 623–5). The first illegal demonstrations which would find a mass following in the summer of 1989 took place in August and September 1987 (Bögeholz, 1995: 627–9). Only a few months later, in November 1987, the Stasi ransacked the flats of members of the various reform groups in several East German cities. This was followed by the arrest of several people, the confiscation of photocopiers and illegal publications as well as the closing down of the Environment Library and the Zion Church in East Berlin (Bögeholz, 1995: 631–3).

Finally, in January 1988, the Honecker regime managed to discredit itself totally in the eyes of the East German people. In the course of a demonstration in East Berlin commemorating the sixty-ninth anniversary of the murder of the socialist heroes Rosa Luxemburg and Karl Liebknecht, the Stasi used brute force to arrest some of the demonstrators and remove a poster with the Rosa Luxemburg slogan 'freedom is always the freedom of the people who think differently'. In the wake of this event the whole GDR was shaken by a wave of arrests and expulsions to West Germany of members of the various reform groups. This in turn led to huge solidarity rallies, church services and other public activities in support of the arrested and expelled. Confronted with this outcry, the regime had no choice but to release many of the arrested and allow some of the expelled to return (Bögeholz, 1995: 637; on the GDR's 'exit' policy see Hirschman, 1993: 183–5). Then, a year later, in January 1989, Honecker buried the very few remaining hopes that the GDR might embark upon some kind of reform policy after all. He announced that the Wall would continue dividing east and west as long as the conditions for its creation had not changed and expressed his belief that it might well still be in existence in a hundred years (Bögeholz, 1995: 651). Moreover, the extensive preparations for the fortieth anniversary of the founding of the GDR in October 1949 and the regime's accompanying proclamations regarding the alleged achievements of socialism in East Germany were viewed as cynical lies by many. This made people even more aware of the huge discrepancies between the official claims and real life (Opp, 1993: 20). By early 1989 and in stark contrast to the progressive changes in the Soviet Union, it appeared to the majority of the East German population that the GDR increasingly resembled a huge prison camp and was totally isolated from the hopeful developments in the USSR and some other eastern European countries.

THE BEGINNING OF THE END: THE GDR BETWEEN MAY AND NOVEMBER 1989

The increasingly widespread and largely spontaneous opposition to the Honecker regime manifested itself by means of huge demonstrations, the establishment of protest groups, the writing and distribution of letters and petitions, and not least by emigration (Opp, 1993: 13). Internal weaknesses like the lack of long overdue economic and political reforms had certainly led to an ever increasing level of discontent within the GDR (Horn, 1992). However, external factors in the form of *perestroika*, *glasnost* and the lure of West German capitalism were probably even more important.

While it is helpful to differentiate between two very different 'protest syndromes' which can be characterised as the search for political participation and the search for economic opportunities (see Lehmbruch, 1993: 21 ff.), often people's motivation was fluid and changed from day to day. Most of the disenchanted may well have been in both camps at the same time. Protesters who concentrated on political participation were often members of such groups as New Forum, Democracy Now, Democratic Awakening and others. They emphasised the importance of human rights, environmental protection, new electoral laws and the maintenance of the socialist character of the GDR. Other demonstrators, the performance and opportunity oriented people, were particularly interested in western consumer goods, a well-functioning economy and generally in obtaining opportunities to do well economically (Lehmbruch, 1993, 21–4). There is, however, no disputing the fact that it was above all the 'Gorbachev factor' which gave ordinary GDR citizens the courage to protest against the system they had tolerated for forty years (Thaysen, 1992: 72).

A case in point were the March 1989 elections to the Congress of People's Deputies in the USSR. Although the outcome of the polling was still heavily weighted in favour of the CPSU, in many constituencies voters could choose among several candidates for the first time ever (Grosser, 1992: 13). This was precisely the practical reform towards a better socialist world the people in the GDR wished to see as well. The year 1989 would prove that Gorbachev was right when he reputedly told Honecker in early October that 'history punishes those who fall behind'.[3] While it is disputable whether a sudden turn towards a reform course in 1989 would have guaranteed the further existence of the GDR for any length of time, the regime's inability to grasp what was happening in the country, its stubborn insistence on an outdated political course and not least the momentous blunders the politicians in East Berlin committed certainly hastened its demise.

On 2 May 1989 the Hungarian government, which had embarked on a carefully chosen course of 'preemptive reform from above' for some time (Garton Ash, 1993: 344), accepted the appearance of the first hole in the iron curtain by dismantling its frontier fences with Austria. This was the 'beginning of the end of the GDR . . . although this fact was by no means self-evident at the time' (McAdams, 1993: 193). Initially the government in Budapest had not withdrawn its heavily armed border guards. Nevertheless, an increasing number of GDR citizens used the holiday season to assemble near the Hungarian–Austrian border to be present should an opportunity arise to flee to the west via Hungary (Grosser, 1992: 9; Bögeholz, 1995: 653). Two days later, events unfolded in an entirely different part of the world which would have an indirect impact on the developments in the GDR. On 4 May the first demonstrations in Tiananmen Square in Beijing took place and the doomed battle for democracy in China began.

In the GDR itself the election campaign for the local elections on 7 May was used by many people to criticise the regime for the system's economic and political shortcomings to a hitherto unthinkable extent. Moreover, encouraged by the new electoral laws in the USSR, the demonstrators demanded to have a choice among several candidates in the GDR's 227 constituencies. However, when election day arrived it became clear that not only this demand had been rejected but the elections themselves were manipulated as usual. According to the official result as announced by Egon Krenz, the chairman of the election commission, there was a turnout of 98.75 per cent and 98.85 per cent of those had supported the list of the National Front headed by the communist SED. Although this was down from the usual 99.8 per cent of support for the regime, there could hardly be any doubt that this result did not reflect reality (Schabowski, 1991: 172–7). Despite the presence of Stasi observers in all constituencies, several civil rights groups had managed to monitor the polling and denounced the result as a total forgery. Unprecedented protests, discussions and demonstrations against the manipulation of the elections took place but the SED did not concede any of the demanded reform measures (Opp, 1993: 19–20). Instead in early June the regime's stubborn insistence on its orthodox political course was once again emphasised. The East German parliament, the Volkskammer, supported China's ruthless and bloody crushing of the anti-government demonstrators in Tiananmen Square. This view was confirmed by Politbüro member Günter Schabowski when he visited China at the end of June as well as a short time later by Egon Krenz's journey to China (Pond, 1993: 111–12).

While the GDR showed solidarity with a regime which had not hesitated to kill its own citizens, thus giving a clear warning signal to the East German demonstrators, in Poland the first free elections were held in the same month and secured an overwhelming victory for Solidarity. In August eastern Europe's first non-communist prime minister, Tadeusz Mazowiecki, was thus able to take over power in Warsaw. Moscow did not intervene but tolerated Solidarity's dominance of the new Polish government (it insisted however that the interior and defence portfolios would remain in the hands of communist ministers). At this point at the latest, the East Germans realised that the Soviet Union was not prepared to intervene militarily to prop up the old regimes in eastern Europe. Moreover, during his state visit to West Germany in mid-June 1989 Gorbachev declared once again that it was 'the right of all peoples and states to determine freely their destiny' and that every state was entitled 'to choose freely its own political and social system as well as unqualified adherence to the norms and principles of international law, especially respect for the right of peoples to self-determination'. This represented a clear rejection of the GDR's political course. After all, Gorbachev had hinted at the possibility of free elections in East Germany. He had also spoken of the end of the post-war era and mentioned that the Wall could be dismantled if the circumstances which had created it were to disappear. He seemed to imply that the Wall was superfluous as the East–West conflict which had dominated the post-war era was over (Kaiser, 1990: 183; Bögeholz, 1995: 664–6).

In early July 1989, during a meeting of the leaders of the Warsaw Pact countries in Bucharest, Gorbachev was faced with strong criticism for not intervening against the reformist regimes in Poland and Hungary. However, Gorbachev did not give in; instead he repeated his repeal of the Brezhnev Doctrine and he even may have begun secretly to organise the overthrow of Honecker, Husak, Ceauşescu and Zhivkov – the four eastern European leaders who were not prepared to adopt a more reform-oriented course (Gedmin, 1992; McCauley, 1992: 170–6). Gorbachev may well have believed that if the orthodox leaders in East Berlin, Prague, Bucharest and Sofia remained in charge 'they would not only be a threat to him, trying to form a coalition with his orthodox opponents within the Soviet Union, but they would go on ruining their countries until a revolution destroyed not only them but socialism as well' (Grosser, 1992: 8). Honecker had to leave the meeting in Bucharest early as he suffered a physical breakdown and was to undergo a cancer operation in the subsequent weeks. Thus, the ageing Honecker was out of action for almost three months – at a time when the situation in the GDR became increasingly critical. Only on 25 September was he able to resume his duties after having successfully weathered a 'gall bladder operation' as was officially announced.

In early August 1989 the Monday demonstrations commenced in Leipzig. They were convened every Monday after the regular evening service in the Nikolai Church which itself went back to the 'Swords into Ploughshares' movement of 1982 (Fulbrook, 1995: 249–51). In late August 1989 a new Social Democratic Party (SPD) was founded; soon the civil rights organisations New Forum and Democracy Now were officially established. Despite evidence to the contrary a considerable number of people continued to hope that public pressure and large demonstrations could convince the regime to adopt a more reform-oriented course. Yet, an ever increasing number of citizens had given up. They had resigned themselves to the fact that the only possibility to change their life was to leave the GDR as soon as possible. Most of them were young, skilled workers and professionals who the regime could hardly afford to lose. 'Particularly among young East Germans the courage of desperation grew rapidly' (Thaysen, 1992: 79).

More and more people travelled to Hungary allegedly to spend their summer holidays there.[4] However, most of them either camped near the border or – particularly from 15 July – were occupying the West German embassy in Budapest to demand exit to the west. Soon hundreds of GDR citizens also occupied the West German embassies in Prague and Warsaw. After all, on 19 August more than 600 GDR citizens had been allowed to cross the Austro-Hungarian border in the course of a pan-European 'picnic'. Hungary was obviously not prepared to force the ever increasing number of people assembling at the border to Austria back to East Germany. Although legally, due to the 1969 trade agreement with East Berlin, the Hungarian government was obliged to return the refugees to the GDR, the majority of the new Hungarian government decided to open the iron curtain. Prime Minister Nemeth and Foreign Minister Horn paid a secret visit to Bonn on 25 August to inform Chancellor Kohl of their decision. They may well have received the promise of West German financial and economic support in return; this is however rejected by the participants of the meeting (Zelikow and Rice, 1995: 66–7). Honecker's deputy Günter Mittag was told about the Hungarian government's decision on 31 August in the course of a meeting in East Berlin. The GDR leadership protested strongly but was only given the chance to visit the camps outside the Austro-Hungarian border. However, the GDR delegation was not able to persuade its citizens to return; instead Honecker's emissaries were thrown out of the camps.

On 10 September the Hungarian government renounced unilaterally the travel agreement with the GDR and announced that from midnight on 11 September GDR citizens could leave Hungary and travel to any country they wished (the border with Czechoslovakia was opened in early October). Within three days more than 15 000 people arrived in the Federal Republic and many more were to follow – more than 340 000 GDR citizens resettled permanently in the FRG by the end of the year (Bergsdorf, 1992: 90). This was the beginning of the end of the East German state. As this exodus and the emigrees' emotional arrival in the Federal Republic could be watched by the deeply moved East German population on West German television it encouraged the reform movement at home and it split the SED *nomenklatura* who at this stage was clearly in a state of panic. Within the SED the battle for Honecker's succession had begun though nobody dared to take sides too early. Above all, the Politbüro was running out of ideas on how to cope with the situation. Within the GDR the Stasi and the police attempted to contain the multiplying discussion circles and the spontaneous demonstrations with ever increasing force and brutality. But to no avail. More and more people had the courage to defy the once all-powerful state and joined in the demonstrations which were now taking place all over the country. 'The very fact that more and more citizens now dared to participate in activities which might land them in prison for years showed that the regime was no longer feared enough to be stable' (Grosser, 1992: 14).

While a considerable number of citizens were clamouring for reforms within the GDR, the stream of people who wished to escape continued unabated. In the late 1980s the CSSR was the only country where GDR citizens could travel without a visa. By 30 September 7000 GDR citizens were occupying the West German embassy in Prague, which was not able to cope with this number. Prior to the GDR's fortieth anniversary celebrations held between 6 and 8 October the Honecker regime wished to avoid any embarrassment. Therefore, West German Foreign Minister Genscher was able to negotiate a solution to the situation. The GDR allowed its citizens in the embassy to leave for West Germany. But the Honecker regime insisted on the face-saving device that the trains of the East German Reichsbahn had to cross GDR territory to enable his government to give the emigrants documents which set them free from GDR citizenship. However, soon the embassy in Prague was again filled with more than 7000 people. Again the GDR regime agreed to the solution of letting these people go west on trains which had to cross GDR territory. This time, this cumbersome procedure proved to be a debacle. Hundreds of people tried to jump onto the trains and join the emigrants when the trains passed through East German cities. On 4 October 3000 people assembled at the main railway station in Dresden looking for the opportunity to leave East Germany. Fierce battles with the police ensued. The GDR had not seen such an outburst of public discontent and violent street battles since the uprising in 1953 (Larres, 1994). Police brutality reached a peak on 6, 7 and 8 October, when in the presence of leaders from east and west the anniversary celebrations began and the regime wanted to demonstrate the GDR's stability and well-being to the world (Bögeholz, 1993: 661–3; Bortfeldt, 1993: 48 ff.)

On 7 October Gorbachev intervened. During the anniversary celebrations in East Berlin he was distinctly cool towards Honecker indicating that the latter's political days were numbered. Moreover, in the course of a meeting with the entire East German Politbüro, Gorbachev urged those present to adopt his reform course. During a public speech he repeated this and warned Honecker that without reforms his regime would be overtaken by history. Unintentionally, the speech led to widespread demonstrations and calls for reforms in East Germany throughout October. Within the SED, opportunism gradually won the day. After Gorbachev's warning a majority of the SED Politbüro was in favour of conceding certain reforms to the demonstrators to stabilise the situation. Honecker and his orthodox friends were losing their influence within the Politbüro. This was reflected in the events in Leipzig on 9 October 1989 which can rightly be called a 'turning point' and 'crucial breakthrough' (Grosser, 1992: 15; Garton Ash, 1993: 345).

Although this is still unclear, Honecker had probably given the order to dissolve the expected Monday demonstration in Leipzig on 9 October 1989 with the help of overwhelming police force. He wished to demonstrate the might of the state and end the protests and widespread civil disobedience in the country once and for all. The old man in East Berlin had decided to resort to a 'Chinese solution' of the problem. However, Honecker's decision was ignored. Local SED leaders and the respected conductor of the Leipzig Gewandhaus orchestra, Kurt Masur, appealed for non-violence on both sides. This was the beginning of the dialogue between the various reform groups and a reformist wing within the SED represented by Hans Modrow, an SED outsider who had been reprimanded in 1989 for showing too much enthusiasm for a reform-oriented course à la Gorbachev (Zelikow and Rice, 1995: 37).

70 000 people participated in the demonstration on 9 October. It was one of the biggest the GDR had ever seen and the forces of the state did not interfere. It is unclear whether, as claimed by Günter Schabowski and Egon Krenz, the majority of the Politbüro was already opposed to the use of force (Schabowski, 1990: 191; Krenz, 1992: 365 ff.). Krenz claimed later that he instructed the police and army not to use violence. It is much more likely that in East Berlin and in most regions the SED was, at this point, still not ready for entering into a constructive dialogue with the forces of reform (Thaysen, 1992: 75). It appears that there were no 'unanimous views inside the SED Politbüro about the meaningfulness of using force and thus also on how far the loyalty of the security forces could be stretched' (Horn, 1993: 58; Fulbrook, 1995: 252–7). Hannelore Horn argues that there certainly was not a peaceful revolution 'deliberately stage-managed' by the Stasi as sometimes claimed (Broder, 1993: 24; Reich, 1992b: 320). She claims however that some 'parts of the armed forces . . . intellectually defected to the opposition and that Politbüro members responded accordingly'. The ruling class wished to ensure 'the continued existence of the GDR with a reformed socialist-style system' to safeguard its privileges. Therefore, 'the question of loyal compliance with orders could not be clearly answered' on 9 October, 'thus making a withdrawal an opportune option for the political decision-makers and experts on the spot' (Horn, 1993: 59; also Asmus, 1990: 64).

This somewhat 'conspiratorial' and 'common sense' interpretation seems to go too far. Local and regional SED functionaries as well as the rather chaotic circumstances and the breakdown of communications within the SED hierarchy appear to deserve most of the credit for the absence of violence on 9 October. However, with 'Krenz's somewhat belated ratificaton of this policy of – at least implicitly – conceding the right to demonstrate, a major watershed had been passed' (Fulbrook, 1995: 257). From now on demonstrations and rallies demanding free elections and the freedom to travel spread like wildfire all over the country; the people no longer feared the SED's use of force against them. The legal demonstration on 4 November in East Berlin attracted over 500 000 people. Soon, the Politbüro attempted to regain control by declaring its interest in adopting some of Gorbachev's reforms. The will to rule had not yet disappeared. The SED intended to save itself from annihilation by sacrificing its old discredited leaders and putting itself at the head of the reform movement in the GDR.

On 18 October 1989 a *coup d'état* took place whose precise circumstances are still surrounded by mystery (see Zelikow and Rice, 1995: 82–6). Honecker had to resign all his posts on the grounds of ill health and was replaced by Egon Krenz. Other orthodox comrades like security chief Erich Mielke and Günter Mittag shared his fate. Krenz, however, was an unfortunate selection: he did not symbolise a new beginning. Krenz had been Honecker's successor designate for some time and was generally regarded as a weak and opportunistic politician in the orthodox mould of Honecker. Krenz purged the Politbüro of the 'old guard' on the eve of the huge demonstration on 4 November and elevated reformer Hans Modrow to the Politbüro. He blamed Honecker for all mistakes and even promised free elections. Hardly anyone believed Krenz. People were convinced that it was only a matter of time before the SED would return to its old course if given the opportunity. With hindsight it becomes clear that Krenz's political concessions, as far as new travel laws and other measures were concerned, constituted merely the SED's desperate attempt to cling to power (Fulbrook, 1995: 257 ff.). Not many people were fooled. The demonstrations and the exodus of people leaving the country continued unabated. Indeed, even if the GDR leaders were serious about changing their country's political course and underlying philosophy, they faced a serious, almost irresolvable, dilemma: 'What right to exist would a capitalist GDR have alongside a capitalist Federal Republic? In other words, what justification would there be for two German states once ideology no longer separated them?' (Otto Reinhold, one of the GDR's leading social scientists and ideologues, as quoted in Zelikow and Rice, 1995: 38; Gransow and Jarausch, 1991: 57).

Following the demonstration in Leipzig on 9 October, the most decisive event occurred exactly a month later: on 9 November the Berlin Wall was breached. In the long run this event would seal the fate of the GDR as an independent state. Although Egon Krenz later claimed credit for having given the order to open the border with West Berlin to pacify the demonstrating people, in fact the frontier gates between the two German states were opened as the result of a severe misunderstanding. On the evening of 9 November, SED Politbüro member Günter Schabowski announced the new travel laws to international news reporters. He explained that the SED's Central Committee had decided that all GDR citizens could get immediate permission for private travel abroad without the need of 'special prerequisites'. In the hectic and chaotic atmosphere surrounding this announcement Schabowski had not paid attention to the small print of the Central Committee's decision. The SED had almost certainly not intended to let GDR citizens go abroad without keeping a check on the travellers by issuing exit visas. Moreover, the SED Politbüro members did not plan to open the border to West Berlin; the city was after all the responsibility of the four powers. They had instead intended to open the GDR border with West Germany. Finally, the new travel law was supposed to come into effect on 10 November which would have given the government a few hours to allow for organising the necessary border and visa arrangements. However, the GDR people watching Schabowski's vague announcement on television interpreted it as the possibility to cross the border without delay. The problem was compounded when Schabowski answered an American reporter's question in English confirming that the Wall was open (Zelikow and Rice, 1995: 98–101; Pond, 1993: 131–4).

During the night of 9 November thousands of East German citizens went to the checkpoints and insisted on crossing into West Germany. As the border guards had not received any instructions at all, they had no choice, after some hesitation, but to let the mass of waiting people cross. Only a few hours later hundreds of thousands of East Germans were in West Berlin to see and experience this longstanding symbol of western freedom, culture and capitalism for themselves. Most of them returned to the GDR after a few days. But from now on almost 2000 people daily left the GDR for good (Anderson et al., 1993: 6; Zelikow and Rice, 1995: 98–101). The opening of the Berlin Wall by mistake meant that the Krenz government had 'abdicated responsibility for the most important decision in its history to the people in the street' (Zelikow and Rice, 1995: 101). The SED would never recover from this seizure of power by the East German people. It was a mortal blow. The East German people had taken over and there was nothing the SED could do to reverse this development. This constituted the highpoint of the revolution begun by the East German people in May 1989. All attempts by the Krenz regime to regain the initiative were doomed to failure.

THE POLITICIANS TAKE OVER

Almost everyone, east and west, was surprised by the opening of the Berlin Wall and the totally unexpected rapid disintegration of the GDR. However, from now on West German politicians would increasingly take charge of the developments to ensure, as was said, that the events would not get out of control. It took the Kohl government in Bonn almost three weeks to recover from its surprise regarding the fall of the Berlin Wall. Then the West German government successfully attempted to steer the East German revolution towards a more orderly and constitutional path which ultimately led to unification. This was primarily the achievement of the chancellor himself as well as that of American President Bush and their respective foreign ministers Genscher and Baker. On 28 November 1989, when Kohl announced his ten-point plan for a 'confederation' of the two German states and spoke about the need for German 'self-determination', he wrested the initiative and the international limelight away from the East German people and from his own more cautious foreign minister and forced a course which was increasingly oriented towards addressing the national question (Bortfeldt, 1993: 75 ff.; Teltschik, 1991: 42 ff.; Gransow and Jarausch, 1991: 101–4; Genscher, 1995: 669 ff.).

Although at first Kohl had not believed in the imminent possibility of unification, once he realised (between mid-December 1989 and January 1990) that this might indeed be an option, he did not hesitate to pursue this course. American support was however vital in overcoming the strong opposition to his policy from Moscow, London and Paris as well as several other EC countries once it became clear in late 1989 that unification might well be on the horizon (Merkl, 1993: 303 ff.; Pond, 1993: 153 ff.). There was one aspect which made Kohl's task easier: the lack of a concrete well-coordinated strategy in these capitals. They all seemed to 'have an attitude without a policy' (Zelikow and Rice, 1995: 138). Britain, represented by its strong-willed but often idiosyncratic and somewhat unrealistic Prime Minister Thatcher, simply did not have the political clout any more to force an anti-unification policy onto Washington. The more practical French President Mitterrand was persuaded to give up his initial opposition to unification for the promise that a united Germany would continue West Germany's policy of further integration into the European Community and of making progress towards a single market and monetary union (Merkl, 1993: 315–25; Bortfeldt, 1993: 106–13).

Gorbachev and the Soviet Union presented a much more difficult problem. Despite all attempts by Kohl (including various offers of financial and economic help on a huge scale) and Bush to dispel Soviet fears of a united Germany, in the last resort Gorbachev's eventual agreement to unification seems to have been less the outcome of a conscious decision in the Kremlin and more the result of Moscow allowing itself to drift along without being able to arrive at a coherent long-term strategy on how to tackle the looming German question. Particularly, during the bilateral Malta summit with President Bush in early December 1989, Gorbachev seems to have missed the chance to enlighten Bush about Moscow's strong opposition to unification and persuade the president to force Kohl onto a more moderate course (for example, a mere confederation of the two German states and the continuation of a separate East German government as repeatedly propagated by new East German Prime Minister Modrow in November and December 1989). Thus, the Americans received the impression that Gorbachev was uneasy but not too concerned and in the last resort 'malleable on the German question', and that the Soviet Union 'did not seem to know where it was going' (Zelikow and Rice, 1995: 130; Bortfeldt, 1993: 113–17). Only in late January 1990 did Gorbachev and GDR leader Modrow design a joint strategy of how to face the pressure for unification from the West German government and the East German people, but by then it was too late. Indeed, Gorbachev admitted to East German radio journalists just before the arrival of Modrow in Moscow on 30 January that 'no one ever cast doubt in principle on the unification of the Germans' (Pond, 1993: 171; Gransow and Jarausch, 1991: 122; Bögeholz, 1995: 687; Zelikow and Rice, 1995: 160–5; Merkl, 1993: 130). Former chancellor Willy Brandt concluded that 'now the matter is clear', only the formal modalities still needed to be worked out (Bortfeldt, 1993: 119–20).

Since the breaching of the Wall and the announcement of Kohl's ten-point plan, the East German people who had started and driven the revolution with their mass demonstrations and flights to the West had gradually lost influence. Still, until the introduction of economic unity on 2 July 1990, and political unity on 3 October 1990, the East German people continued to speed up developments by the mere threat of emigrating from the GDR to West Germany *en masse* and, consequently, of leaving an almost empty country behind and causing numerous financial and social problems in the Federal Republic. The continuation of the mass demonstrations and the convening of round table talks between all major GDR opposition forces and the new reformist Modrow government from 7 December ensured that the revolution did not lose its momentum. The round table would meet regularly several times a week until its replacement by a democratically elected government in March 1990. Modrow himself, however, would only participate from late January 1990 in the round table talks when the worsening situation in the GDR and Bonn's refusal to pour any more financial help into the bankrupt and discredited East Germany left him no other option (Bortfeldt, 1993: 118–19, 96 ff.).

There were other developments as well. The arrests of former top officials including Honecker and Mielke for corruption and abuse of power began on 3 December. The East German Volkskammer had already voted to revoke the right of the SED's leading political role as enshrined in the East German constitution on 1 December. Krenz resigned as head of state and secretary general of the SED on 6 December. Modrow, who had become head of government on 13 November, was now together with new party chairman Gregor Gysi the sole leader in charge of the reformed and renamed SED/PDS (since 18 December). In early January 1990 widespread corruption and nepotism within the top echelons of the SED was revealed. Moreover, throughout December and January several attacks on East German and Soviet military installations occurred without, however, creating much damage. But these activities ran the risk of provoking Soviet soldiers and East German security forces into becoming involved in the events in East Germany and perhaps turning the largely peaceful revolution into a violent one. In mid-January, protesters seized public buildings and stormed the Stasi headquarters in East Berlin to prevent the Stasi and government officials from destroying records of their activities during the East German dictatorship (Bögeholz, 1995: 677 ff.). Events threatened to get out of hand; chaos appeared to be looming just round the corner.

At the same time it became increasingly obvious that the economic and financial situation of the GDR was so desperate and the mood of the people so set on unification that the survival of the GDR was an ever more open question. However, the civil rights movement in the GDR, the very people who had started the revolution, played only a marginal role in the further developments. The activists had sidelined themselves by continuing to believe in the possibility of the further existence of the GDR and a 'third way' between Honecker's discredited old-style 'real socialism' and West Germany's capitalism (Pond, 1993: 134–6). This standpoint was shared by the Modrow government and, for a considerable period of time until summer 1990, it was also the position of the West German social democratic party (SPD) and their chancellor candidate Oskar Lafontaine (Padgett, 1996: 244–5). With this view the various reform groups as well as the entire round table and the West German SPD weakened and isolated itself from the East German people and made it much easier for West German Chancellor Kohl to symbolise the people's longing for unity.

It was however largely due to the continuation of the revolutionary drive of the East German people that the first free elections in the GDR took place in March 1990 rather than in May 1990 as had originally been planned by the round table. The first democratic elections in the GDR on 18 March 1990 and the overwhelming victory by the centre-right 'Alliance for Germany' which was strongly supported by Kohl's West German CDU party can be regarded as the formal end of the East German dictatorship. While unification would take another seven months – not least because of the international complexities which were tackled by the so-called Two-plus-Four Talks convened between early May and early September 1990 (Szabo, 1992) – the revolution of the East German people had already been successful by March 1990. From now on politicians and lawyers increasingly took over to work out the complex legal questions of economic, social and political merger between the two German states as well as the involvement of a united Germany in international frameworks like NATO and the EC established during the previous four decades. The western powers as well as the Kohl government had insisted on united Germany's membership of these organisations and the Soviet Union eventually had given its agreement.

The results of the GDR elections of March 1990 as well as the local elections in May and the all-German elections in December 1990 (the first since 1933) excluded most of the civil rights activists from further active political participation. Most groups and parties (with the exception of Bündnis 90/Die Grünen) had not been able to win election to the first all-German parliament. Although this left a residue of bitterness and frustration among the people who had forced down an entire dictatorship, they largely had only themselves to blame. By stopping short of endorsing unification, by attempting to preserve a socialist GDR, although a better and genuinely democratic one, they had isolated themselves from the wider East German population and in fact shown that they did not properly understand the forces they had unleashed. Revolutions tend to swallow their own children – luckily the actual East German revolution of 1989 as well as its aftermath remained largely bloodless.

CONCLUSION

External stimuli like above all Gorbachev's reform policy, the events in Hungary and Poland (and much later the activities of the West German and American administrations) were of the utmost importance in bringing about the eruption and successful conclusion of the East German revolution. However, the courage, stamina and motivation of the East German people to take on the government of a heavily fortified police state was the decisive element which ensured that general dissatisfaction, suppression and discontent would explode into a widespread but peaceful revolution – something which had never happened before in modern German history.

NOTES

1. Discontent in the GDR had always been running high. From 1949 until the building of the Wall in August 1961 almost three million people fled East Germany. Between 1962 and 1988 more than 170 000 managed to escape while 360 000 received permission to leave (Grosser, 1992: 10). The following number of people left the GDR between May 1989 and February 1991: May–Oct. 1989: 45 700; Oct.–Dec. 1989: 233 674; Jan.–June 1990: 238 384; July 1990–Feb. 1991: 110 000 (Neckermann, 1991: 101).
2. The only 'proper' revolution in modern German history was the unsuccessful revolution of 1848–9. The so-called 'November revolution' of 1918 was hardly a revolution at all as not the German people but the victorious World War I powers insisted on the abolition of the monarchy and the introduction of a republican form of government in Germany (the Weimar Republic). Whether the unsuccessful uprising in the GDR in June 1953 can be regarded as a revolution is an open question (see for the latter Larres, 1994; Fulbrook, 1995: 177–87).

3. According to Egon Krenz, Gorbachev spoke in fact less menacing words. He said: 'Our experiences and the experiences of Poland and Hungary have convinced us: if a party does not respond to life, it is condemned' (quoted in Zelikow and Rice, 1995: 84).
4. GDR citizens needed a visa to travel to Hungary. Such a visa was relatively easy to obtain as many East Germans habitually spent their summer holidays in that country. However, it was necessary to apply for a visa many months in advance. Therefore, only people who had made previous arrangements – usually with the firm intention to go on holiday – were able to benefit from the increasingly liberal attitude of the Hungarian government. Spontaneous visits to Hungary were not possible. In summer 1989 the CSSR was the only country East Germans could travel to without the need for a visa.

REFERENCES

Adomeit, H. (1994), '"Midwife of History" or "Sorcerer's Apprentice?" Gorbachev, German Unification and the Collapse of Empire', *Post-Soviet Affairs*, vol. 10, no. 3, pp. 197–230.

Anderson, C., Kaltenthaler, K. and Luthardt, W., eds (1993), *The Domestic Politics of German Unification* (Boulder, Colo.: Lynne Rienner).

Arendt, H. (1973), *On Revolution* (Harmondsworth: Penguin).

Asmus, R.D. (1990), 'A United Germany', *Foreign Affairs*, vol. 62, no. 2, pp. 63–76.

Bergsdorf, W. (1992), 'West Germany's Political System under Stress: Decision-Making Processes in Bonn 1990', in Grosser, D., ed., pp. 88–106.

Bögeholz, H. (1995), *Die Deutschen nach dem Krieg. Eine Chronik. Befreit, geteilt, vereint: Deutschland 1945 bis 1995* (Reinbek bei Hamburg: Rowohlt).

Bortfeldt, H. (1993), *Washington-Bonn-Berlin. Die USA und die deutsche Einheit* (Bonn: Bouvier Verlag).

Broder, H.M. (3rd edn, 1993), *Erbarmen mit den Deutschen* (Hamburg: Hoffmann & Campe).

Clemens, C. (1989), *Reluctant Realists: the Christian Democrats and West German Ostpolitik* (Durham, NC: Duke University Press).

Fulbrook, M. (1995), *Anatomy of a Dictatorship: Inside the GDR, 1949–1989* (Oxford: Oxford University Press).

Garton Ash, T. (1993), *In Europe's Name: Germany and the Divided Continent* (London: Jonathan Cape).

Gedmin, J. (1992), *The Hidden Hand: Gorbachev and the Collapse of East Germany* (Washington, DC: AEI Press).

Geiss, I. (1996), 'The Federal Republic of Germany in International Politics Before and After Unification', in Larres, K. and Panayi, P., eds, pp. 137–65.

Genscher, H.D. (1995), *Erinnerungen* (Berlin: Siedler).

Glaeßner, G.J. (1992), 'Political Structures in Transition', in Glaeßner, G.J. and Wallace, I., eds, pp. 3–22.

Glaeßner, G.J. and Wallace, I. (1992), *The German Revolution of 1989: Causes and Consequences* (Oxford: Berg).

Gorbachev, M. (1995), *Erinnerungen* (Berlin: Siedler).

Gransow, V. and Jarausch, K.H. (1991), *Die deutsche Vereinigung: Dokumente zur Bürgerbewegung, Annäherung und Beitritt* (Cologne: Wissenschaft und Politik) [English edition: *Uniting Germany: Documents and Debates, 1944–1993* (Providence, RI: Berghahn Books, 1994)].

Grosser, D. (1992), 'The Dynamics of German Reunification', in Grosser, ed., pp. 1–32.

Grosser, D., ed. (1992), *German Unification: The Unexpected Challenge* (Oxford: Berg).

Heraclides, A. (1993), *Security and Co-operation in Europe: The Human Dimension, 1972–1992* (London: Frank Cass).

Hirschman, A.O. (1993), 'Exit, Voice, and the Fate of the German Democratic Republic: An Essay in Conceptual History', *World Politics*, vol. 45, January, pp. 183–5.

Horn, H. (1992), 'Collapse from Internal Weakness – the GDR from October 1989 to March 1990', in Grosser, D., ed., pp. 55–71.

Horn, H. (1993), 'The Revolution in the GDR in 1989: Prototype or Special Case?', *Aussenpolitik*, vol. 44, no. 1/93, pp. 56–66.

Kaiser, K. (1991), 'Germany's Unification', *Foreign Affairs*, vol. 70, no. 1, pp. 179–205.

Krenz, E. (1992), *Wenn Mauern fallen* (Vienna: Paul Neff Verlag).

Larres, K. (1996), 'Germany and the West: The "Rapallo Factor" in German Foreign Policy from the 1950s to the 1990s', in Larres, K. and Panayi, P., eds, pp. 278–326.

Larres, K. and Panayi, P., eds (1996), *The Federal Republic of Germany since 1949: Politics, Society and Economy before and after Unification* (London: Longman).

Larres, K. (1994), 'Preserving Law and Order: Britain, the United States and the East German Uprising of 1953', *Twentieth Century British History*, vol. 5, no. 3, pp. 320–50.

Lehmbruch, G. (1993), 'The Process of Regime Change in East Germany', in Anderson, C. et al., eds, pp. 17–36.

McAdams, A.J. (1993), *Germany Divided: From the Wall to Reunification* (Princeton, NJ: Princeton University Press).

McCauley, M. (1992), 'Gorbachev, the GDR and Germany', in Glaeßner, G.J. and Wallace, I., eds, pp. 163–83.

McNeill, T. (1996), 'The Soviet Union's Policy Towards West Germany, 1945–90,' in Larres K. and Panayi, P., eds, pp. 254–77.

Merkl, P.H. (1993), *German Unification in the European Context* (University Park, Pa.: Pennsylvania State University Press).

Mitter, A. and Wolle, S., eds (1990), *'Ich liebe Euch doch alle!' Befehle und Lageberichte der MfS Jan.–Nov. 1989* (Berlin: BasisDruck).

Neckermann, P. (1991), *The Unification of Germany or The Anatomy of a Peaceful Revolution* (New York: Columbia University Press).

Oberdorfer, D. (1992), *The Turn: How the Cold War Came to an End. The United States and the Soviet Union, 1983–1990* (London: Jonathan Cape).

Opp, K.D. (1993), 'Spontaneous Revolutions: The Case of East Germany in 1989', in Kurz, H.D., ed., *United Germany and the New Europe* (London: Edward Elgar), pp. 11–30.

Padgett, S. (1996), 'The SPD: The Decline of the Social Democratic Volkspartei', in Larres, K. and Panayi, P., eds, pp. 230–53.

Pond, E. (1993), *Beyond the Wall: Germany's Road to Unification* (Washington, DC: Brookings).

Reich, J. (1992a), *Abschied von den Lebenslügen* (Berlin: Rowohlt).

Reich, J. (1992b), 'Intelligentsia and Class Power in Eastern Europe Before and After 1989', *Aussenpolitik*, vol. 43, no. 4/92, pp. 315–23.

Roberts, G.K. (1991), 'Emigrants in their own Country: German Reunification and its Political Consequences', *Parliamentary Affairs*, vol. 44, no. 3, pp. 373–88.

Schabowski, G. (1991), *Der Absturz* (Berlin: Rowohlt).

Szabo, S.F. (1992), *The Diplomacy of German Unification* (New York: St. Martin's Press).

Teltschik, H. (1991), *329 Tage. Innenansichten der Einigung* (Berlin: Siedler).

Thatcher, M. (1993), *The Downing Street Years* (London: HarperCollins) [paperback edition].

Thaysen, U. (1992), 'The GDR on its Way to Democracy', in Grosser, D., ed., pp. 72–87.

Valdez, J. (1993), *Internationalism and the Ideology of Soviet Influence in Eastern Europe* (Cambridge: Cambridge University Press).

Zelikow, P. and Rice, C. (1995), *Germany Unified and Europe Transformed: A Study in Statecraft* (Cambridge, Mass.: Harvard University Press).

Part II
The Domestic Consequences of German Unification

3 The German Economy since 1989/90: Problems and Prospects

Christopher Flockton

THE GERMAN ECONOMY, 1989/90 TO 1996: AN OVERVIEW

Throughout 1994 and 1995 there was growing optimism that the end of the deepest post-war recession in western Germany was well and truly over, and that the east was showing signs of an accelerating and broadening pattern of growth. Still by early 1996 much of the gloom over the fading international competitiveness of western Germany (the *Standortfrage*) and its ability to absorb the moribund eastern economy without a financial crisis, had not been dispelled. Moreover, the human anxiety and output losses associated with economic collapse of the old command economy upon unification will leave their mark for many years.

Politically and psychologically the eastern population still remains 'other' than the people in the western part of the country: the economic burden of a hasty unification, accompanied by in part foreseeable policy errors will remain for a decade in the form of very high state indebtedness, a high tax burden and continuing structural unemployment in the east. This burden of heavy state debt will naturally constrain the chances of domestic growth, at a time when a higher rate than the all-German trend of 2.5 per cent per annum is needed to rejuvenate the east. It is no surprise therefore that deregulation and privatisation are once again high on the policy agenda for western Germany in an attempt to escape these constraints and find a renewed growth dynamic in the freer play of market forces. The fear over *Standort Deutschland*, over Germany's weakening competitiveness, is clearly a related driving force in this more market-oriented liberal agenda. The loss of 600 000 industrial jobs in 1993 and a further half-million in 1994 and 1995, coupled with impressive though gradually weakening wage restraint since 1992, demonstrate however that the social market mechanisms, so disapproved of by Anglo-Saxon market liberals, are far from inflexibly rigid.

The economic evolution since 1 July 1990, has of course been that of a dual economy, of boom in the west and slump in the east. The German expression 'straw fire' well describes the purely temporary boost to the west which unification engendered: an inflationary overheating followed by deep recession from the second half of 1992. The responsibility for the depth of this ensuing recession, which made the task of absorbing the eastern economy all the more problematic, has been laid somewhat unfairly at the door of the Bundesbank. By raising interest rates to an all-time high (in real terms) in late 1992, so as to bring the inflationary wage claims and debt-financed overheating of the economy to an end, the Bundesbank exacerbated recessionary trends which already existed among Germany's European partners. Such is the central role of Germany in the European economy that its trading partners could not remain unscathed by the strains of unification. It is thought that in the first eighteen months following unification, partner countries received a boost through extra exports to Germany of 1 per cent of GDP, but then had to endure from late 1992 a high interest rate policy, imposed through the exchange rate mechanism (ERM) parities.

Looking back over the first half-decade to economic and monetary unification in mid-1990, the catastrophic fall in activity in the east and the fundamental restructuring there, it is a truism to say that the difficulties and costs of transforming the closed, centrally planned economy were very seriously underestimated. It will not take three to four years for the east to catch up, as was optimistically claimed in 1990, but fifteen or twenty years. As will be seen, there were warning voices which feared deep structural unemployment and the so-called 'Mezzogiorno effect' in the east, but these were brushed aside for a mixture of motives. These ranged from the urgent political imperative to stem the haemorrhage of key personnel and purchasing power from a collapsing planned economy, to the self-confidence of an ascendant Federal Republic, which believed that market forces would liberate eastern German industriousness and talent, just as it had done in 1948/49 in the west.

The state treaty on economic, monetary and social union, which entered into force on 1 July 1990, incorporated a largely closed, centrally planned and highly monopolised economy into an advanced and free-trading market economy overnight. The treaty specified the adoption of West Germany's economic constitution (the economic, social and labour market legislation and competition laws), the adoption of a monetary and banking system regulated by the Bundesbank and the substitution of the Deutsche Mark (DM) for the Ostmark (OM) at given exchange rates. It specified the organised break-up of state monopolies (the *Kombinate*) by the Treuhandanstalt (state holding trust or trustee institution, established in March 1990) with a mandate which gave first priority to privatisation. Overnight, therefore, the eastern economy had to discover free market pricing in DM and abolish the old administered pricing system. It also had to be reorganised into competing productive units to command the mass of western legislation and meet the full force of international competition, particularly that from EC partners.

The unification treaty, which ushered in formal unification on 3 October 1990 added further legislative requirements: it set out the constitution of the Treuhandanstalt holding trust (THA), and specified the restitution of compulsorily acquired land and buildings back to their original owners. This last requirement has continued to pose a substantial obstacle to new investment in the east since the treaty favours the rights of expropriated previous owners, over those of new investors. It excludes from compensation those expropriated under the Soviet land reforms of 1945–49, which poses a further point of legal contention upon which the Constitutional Court ruled finally in February 1995 (*Financial Times*, 14/2/1995, p. 2). Clearly, the two treaties specified the forms of transitional assistance in support of eastern Germany and these are treated in the following section (Sinn, 1992; Stares, 1992).

Much attention has been paid to the terms of monetary union, and it is clear that the terms for the currency exchange, adopting the Deutsche Mark (DM), have been one of several crucial factors in the eastern collapse. At the outset, there were clear warnings by economists of the consequences for output and employment of an ill-prepared and hasty currency exchange. Not only would an over-valued exchange rate expose cruelly the poor competitiveness of the eastern economy, but the tendency in any unified labour market ('social union') towards wage harmonisation would impose western labour costs on an economy with only a fraction of its labour productivity. The resulting slump and long-term structural unemployment would therefore resemble that of the 'Mezzogiorno' of southern Italy. A minority of economists favoured the 'shock therapy' of instant unification, as a way of sweeping aside the old command structures, but most feared the slump in activity which might transpire in such an internationally uncompetitive economy. Both the scientific advisory council to the economics ministry and the council of economic advisers favoured gradual integration with perhaps a staged move to monetary union with the help of a system of parallel currencies until a sustainable exchange rate was established. Lutz Hoffmann, president of the German institute of economic research, published a prescient article which foresaw unemployment of three million in the east if the productivity gap were not closed (Schäfer, 1993).

Of course, the Bundesbank itself was not a party to the Bonn government decision on 6 February 1990 to offer economic and monetary union to the east. As is well known, the central bank favoured a less favourable exchange rate of DM1 : 2OM, and eventually Bundesbank president Karl-Otto Pöhl resigned at the *lèse-majesté* displayed by Bonn towards the central bank. A monetary union has three principal imperatives: it must ensure the competitiveness of the trading sectors of the partner economy, it must ensure fairness of treatment between debtors and creditors (it has fundamental distributional consequences), and it must avoid creation of excess monetary liquidity which would threaten inflation. Often, it seemed, it was this latter concern which was uppermost in western discussions. As a final and important consideration, the exchange rate should not be so unfavourable that incomes in the east would be so low that mass migration to the west would take place. Thus, for instance, the Bundesbank's proposal of 1 : 2 would have meant that eastern average wages, then at one-third of those of the west, would have become one-sixth. Greater economic competitiveness would have been bought at the price of a huge wage gap, to be overcome only by inflation or migration. The final terms contained in the state treaty of translation of all current payments (including wages) at 1 : 1, of all savings at parity (up to a ceiling of DM2000, DM4000, DM6000 for children, adults and pensioners, with 1 : 2 for savings in excess) favoured wage-earners and savers for political reasons. The translation of enterprise debt at 1 : 2 imposed debts of DM115 billion on the state enterprises, now attracting high real West German interest rates. In aggregate, the exchange rate was DM1 : 1.81OM (Hasse, 1993; Kreile, 1992).

Clearly this imposed an almost impossible competitive challenge for the East German trading sectors, although at the time it appeared challenging, though possible. Since eastern labour productivity was assumed to be 40–50 per cent of that of the west, and wage levels only 37 per cent (with western social insurance contributions) then there was a favourable relation between relative wages and productivity. Further, there was scope for producer price falls of 30 per cent given the shift from eastern production-related taxes. However, this equation held only if the productivity calculation was correct, and if no wage inflation ensued. Neither assumption proved sustainable, with highly damaging results. The introduction of the DM did in fact lead to the creation of some excess liquidity, but overall the Bundesbank and banking system managed the currency exchange excellently, with little directly attributable rise in inflation.

There were then fundamental errors in economics, although unification was clearly driven by political imperatives. In terms of economic analysis, aside from the fateful decisions concerning the currency exchange, there were evident errors in budgetary and exchange rate policy. Unification represented a 'demand shock' for western consumer goods and investment goods: to prevent inflationary overheating of the economy a real appreciation of the DM would have been the appropriate response (Schäfer, 1993). However, this was ruled out politically, since the exchange rate mechanism had entered stage 1 of European monetary union (EMU). Likewise, the failure to raise taxes in the west, once the full budgetary consequences of the eastern collapse had become apparent, also fuelled inflationary excess demand. Public deficits, financed by borrowing, were matched for the first time since 1951 by current account deficits. Consequently the Bundesbank took its responsibilities by engineering a sharp rise in interest rates in late 1992, tipping the economy into recession.

Table 3.1 illustrates the course of the dual economic evolution from the second half of 1990, of boom and slump in the two halves of Germany. Western Germany, which had enjoyed high GDP growth rates at the end of the 1980s (partly due to the '1992' effect) experienced a sustained inflationary boom of 4.5 per cent for each year over the period to mid-1992 with growth of 2 per cent and 1 per cent respectively in the second half of 1990 and first half of 1991. This could clearly be observed by the surge of demand for western goods emanating from eastern Germany. Inflation peaked at 4.5 per cent in the west in late 1992. The scale of the shock to the eastern production sectors, and the loss of domestic and eastern European export markets brought a collapse of output in all sectors with a trough in production reached in mid-1992 and then again in January 1993. Even by July 1993 manufacturing output stood at only 69 per cent of the pre-unification level (*MRDB*, 7/1993). The labour force shrank from 10 million to 7.3 million and true unemployment was heavily disguised by the 'second labour market' measures of short-time working pay (when often there was 'zero work') and of early retirement, retraining and job creation schemes. Thus, for instance, even with a 15 per cent unemployment rate in mid-1994, if we add the 1.13 million (including early retirements) involved in special labour market schemes, this then would imply a

Table 3.1 Macroeconomic Evolution in the FRG, 1990–94

	West Germany					*East Germany*					*FRG*				
	1990	*1991*	*1992*	*1993*	*1994*	*1990*	*1991*	*1992*	*1993*	*1994*	*1990*	*1991*	*1992*	*1993*	*1994*
GNP % change (GDP E. Germany)	4.5	4.9	1.2	–2.3	1.6	–14	–28	10	7	9	–	3.7	2.2	–1.1	2.8
Gainfully employed, persons 1000 (E German estimated)	28 479	29 190	29 452	28 994	28 600	8 855	7 179	6 170	5 900	–	–	–	–	–	–
Unemployed, 1000 persons	1 883	1 689	1 808	2 270	2 556	240	913	1 170	1 149	1 142	2 123	2 602	2 978	3 419	3 698
Rate of unemployment %	6.4	5.7	5.9	7.3	7.9	–	10.4	14.8	15.8	16.1	–	–	7.7	8.8	9.6
Consumer price % change	2.7	3.5	4	4.2	3.0	–	8.3	11.2	8.8	3.0	–	–	4.6	3.9	2.6
Government borrowing (territorial authorities) DM bn											–46.3	–121.8	–110	–133	–143
Current account balance DM bn											75.7	–32.3	–34.4	–33.3	–

true unemployment rate closer to 25 per cent in the former GDR. The drastic shrinkage in the productive sectors is apparent from the bald statistics: 2 million industrial jobs have been lost and more than one-half of agricultural employment. Of course, the scale of growth, albeit from a low level, is also apparent from Figure 3.1 in the more recent period. Growth of 7.1 per cent in the east in 1993 was followed by 9 per cent in 1994, far outstripping the accelerating recovery in the west but it has since slowed markedly. Furthermore, orders in the east, rising by an annual 25 per cent for manufacturing and 33 per cent for construction in the last quarter of 1993, show that growth in the east is accelerating and broadening out. However, it remains the case that transfers from the west account for one-half of final demand in the east, and so the upturn is critically dependent on state transfers.

The causes of this economic collapse are now fairly well known, but they do deserve repetition, particularly since undue weight tends to be given to the currency exchange itself:

(a) concerning the exchange of DM for Ostmark, it is not the aggregate exchange rate of DM1 : 1.81OM which is so critical for export competitiveness but that of 1 : 1 for wages and prices. Even in 1989, it had been calculated that a rate of broadly 1 : 4 would be required for goods trade, since it took 1 OM of domestic resources to produce exports worth 23 pfennigs in the west. This effective fourfold overvaluation of the currency therefore rendered much of the manufacturing economy wholly uneconomic, but wage inflation subsequently dealt a fatal blow.

(b) the calculations of the relative productivity of the east compared with the old Länder were shown to be erroneous. Rather than the assumed productivity level of 40–50 per cent of that of the west, it was in fact closer to 30 per cent. Swathes of heavy industry were obsolescent and grossly polluting, while labour-intensive industries simply had neither the products nor the low wage levels needed to survive world competition. In agriculture the gigantic state and cooperative farms managed a productivity level of a mere 50 per cent of that of West Germany's small-farm sector.

(c) the collapse of Comecon markets upon the wholesale change in January 1991 to pricing at world price levels in dollars by the eastern bloc implied the loss of markets for swathes of heavy and light engineering. These had supplied products suited only for the eastern bloc markets under 'specialisation agreements'. Since Comecon markets accounted for 75 per cent of East Germany's exports, their almost total dissolution has dealt a mortal blow.

(d) the subsequent wage inflation, arising from wage harmonisation agreements negotiated by western German trade unions completed this almost total loss of competitiveness. Originally the achievement of western tariff wage levels by the end of 1994 was provided for, but after strikes and lock-outs in early 1993, the wage-negotiating partners agreed to extend the terminal date to July 1996. However, this offers scant alleviation, since eastern unit wage costs were 70 per cent above those of western Germany, taking the low labour productivity into account. The 'Mezzogiorno' effect was definitely realised – it is only as a result of massive state transfers that the accompanying poverty was avoided.

(e) As discussed earlier, the unresolved question of property titles has seriously hampered privatisations and new investment projects. There were 1.2 million claims for 2.5 million properties, of which 10 000 concerned titles.

The public finance consequences of this collapse have led to enormous strains in fiscal and monetary policy, which have fed through at the European level to disruption of the ERM currency parities and bands. The following section is devoted to the instruments of policy for the economic transformation in the east, and it is apparent that under every heading, expenditure was far in excess of that planned. In aggregate then, the costs of labour market support, of liquidity credits for Treuhand firms, of pensions and social security, and regional assistance and infrastructure programmes are in excess of three times that foreseen in the unification treaty of 1990. In 1993, gross public transfers from the west amounted to DM180 billion, to which one might add expenditures by the federal post and railways, bringing gross public spending to DM235 billion in one year alone. Transfers of DM150 billion or 5 per cent of GDP will be required for many years. The public finance consequences are of course most apparent in the accumulation of state debt, which in 1994 totalled 58 per cent of GDP and exceeded the Maastricht Treaty guideline of 60 per cent in 1995 as the debts of the Treuhandanstalt and Kreditabwicklungsfonds (state credit agency) had to be included in government debt (*MRDB*, 10/1994). The wholly insufficient tax rises introduced to meet this fiscal indiscipline have been dictated primarily by the electoral timetable. After a single exceptional income tax surcharge in 1991/2 of 7.5 per cent of an individual's tax liability, the 'no tax rises' promise of the Kohl government in the December 1990 election was shown to be very misleading. For the general election of October 1994, the electorate were at least forewarned that a second 7.5 per cent impost was to take place in January

1995. Clearly, had the federal government faced the deficit problem early by tax-raising, this would have cooled the inflationary boom and pre-empted the interest rate actions of the Bundesbank.

Given this course of events, it is therefore of little surprise that in order to sustain heavy subsidisation of the east, including the large core of heavy industry which remains in state hands, an almost exactly opposite policy is being pursued in the west to pay for the east. The tripartite solidarity pact of September 1993 sought to buy trade union support for wage moderation in the east, while public spending in the west was cut and redirected eastwards. Reminiscent so closely of the first Kohl government of 1982, the policy agenda concentrates once again on budget consolidation and privatisation, seeking a growth dynamic through deregulation when the economy is in recession.

THE POLICY REGIME IN EASTERN GERMANY AND ITS IMPACT (1990–95)

Economic Restructuring Policy and its Agents

With the confidence born of the boom years of the late 1980s behind it and drawing on its own experience of the 'economic miracle' in the years following the currency reform of 1948, the federal government placed great faith in the economic forces to be unleashed by the rapid transformation to market structures after 1 July 1990. Self-confidence in industrial organisation, the skills and technical knowledge of easterners, and an unforgotten market behaviour among the easterners (stretching back further than the last communist expropriation wave of 1972 to the pre-war period) would all assist in a rapid market transformation such that a catch-up period of only three to five years was required. The federal government also appeared to believe that unification would largely pay for itself, particularly once the growth process with its buoyant tax revenue were to ease initial government borrowing. Borrowings could in any case be met with the help of asset sales by the Treuhandanstalt (established by the reform communist Modrow government in early March 1990). To hold all state productive assets (valued then at DM1000 billion) the state treaty clauses provided for financial transfers from the west of DM22 billion in 1990 and DM35 billion in 1991. Hence the December election commitment of the ruling Bonn coalition parties that no tax rises would be needed to meet the costs of absorbing the east (Hüther and Petersen, 1993).

Clearly the policy was founded on the 'shock therapy' strategy, which may or may not have been economically the most efficient, but politically this was imperative, given the requirement to shore up the collapsing economy in the east and consequently remove the layers of Socialist Unity Party (SED) placemen found at every senior level. To underwrite financially a structure managed by reform communists promised little for Bonn. So the state treaty on economic, monetary and social union of July 1990 instituted overnight the economic and social welfare constitution of the west and specified the creation of competitive industrial structures through the break-up and privatisation of the old giant industrial monopoly combines. The unification treaty specified the priorities of the Treuhand as 'privatisation, restructuring and lastly closure of wholly unprofitable enterprises'. This set the direction of a policy which was market-driven through privatisation rather than the pursuit of a state intervention policy, actively restructuring and redirecting enterprises while in state hands.

In addition to the Treuhand policy, we can typify the strategy as involving start-up costs for social insurance and local administration, heavy direct infrastructural investment (exerting a Keynesian public works stimulus) and transitional assistance for the labour market. It also involved the use of regional aid to ease the profound transformation which was the inevitable result of the shift to market relations and world competition and prices. Broadly, the policy subsidised new capital investment rather than, for example, labour subsidies, since it was plain that economic renewal would be carried by new investment projects responding to world conditions, rather than the subsidising of technologies and modes of working inherited from the highly distorted command economy (*MRDB*, 3/1991). There were then six public sector funds which supported this adjustment:

— the Treuhandanstalt offered liquidity credits to keep inherited state industries afloat until they were privatised or closed. On a lesser scale it offered direct capital investment injections. Originally budgets of DM7 billion and DM10 billion were planned for 1990 and 1991, but it was rapidly apparent that much larger support was needed to avoid collapse, and so DM38 billion has been spent per year on average to the end of 1994 when the THA was wound down;
— the German unity fund (DM115 billion) was established as the main vehicle for 'pump-priming', spending programmes in the east to establish the social insurance and pension funds (whose cost increased sevenfold to DM40 billion) and for infrastructure and renovation projects by local authorities;

— the federal labour office met short-time working and retraining costs. The guarantee of short-time working pay to sustain the bulk of the labour force affected by such a profound transformation in productive structures had to be extended to 18 months, that is, to the end of 1991. In fact, of course, the 'second labour market' covering all those on retraining, job creation, or early retirement programmes and covering 1.28 million persons cost DM55 billion in 1993;
— investment assistance for new capital projects in the form of very favourable depreciation allowances and regional aid. For an interim period, special investment grants of 14 per cent were payable and, in addition, regional assistance worth 35 per cent of the project cost (subject to the number of jobs created) ensured that investors in the east had to pay less than one-half of the investment cost in the first year;
— in March 1991, when the deep slump in activity had become politically unmanageable, an additional programme was announced, the *Gemeinschaftswerk Aufschwung Ost* (the common effort for achieving an upswing in the east) to improve investment incentives, expand job creation schemes and to finance renovation by local authorities. The programme represented a further DM24 billion of funding over two years. Lastly, and having the effect of raising the relative incentive level in the east, regional aid to West Berlin and the old border zone (*Zonenrandgebiet*) was to be phased out by 1994;
— the federal railway as well as the federal post and telecommunication each instituted thoroughgoing infrastructure replacement programmes of DM1 billion each.

The fact that the strategy of the Treuhandanstalt (THA) became ever more synonymous, in the public mind, with rapid disposal of assets by privatisation meant that it also acquired the reputation of being ideologically blind to all except the market, selling off public assets at minimal prices and of insufficient audit, which allowed criminal dealings and asset-stripping to proliferate. As we shall see, behind this gross public caricature lay an important policy debate. Even under the transitional CDU-led de Maizière government in the east, the Treuhand state holding company was given the priority of privatisation first in the law of 17 June 1990. Detlev Rohwedder, the Treuhand president after unification, until his assassination by Red Army Faction (RAF) terrorists in February 1991, stressed the triad of 'rapid privatisation, decisive restructuring and cautious liquidation'. He himself valued the assets at DM600 billions, and expected disposal to last until the year

2000. In contrast, Birgit Breuel, his free market successor, insisted that the move of productive capacity into the private sector, subject to market criteria, would be the most efficient form of restructuring, offering long-term prospects of survival. She therefore set an end date for disposals of December 1994, and the tempo of privatisation reached three industrial firms per day in 1991/2, falling to two per day from the end of 1992, as the recession in the west began to bite.

The transformation process embraced by the THA comprised firstly the break-up of the 126 giant industrial combines into joint stock companies, at first 8000 firms and finally 12 000 firms. Non-core activities such as holiday homes and crèches and other welfare support were separated out and on 1 July 1990 all enterprises had to draw up an asset valuation and prepare a corporate plan. Only once this was approved, and the firm thereby considered capable of restructuring (*sanierungsfähig*) could investment credits be given. Until that point, only liquidity credits to cover running costs were offered. In the early months, important errors were made, given the disorganisation, lack of reliable management information and shortage of trained staff. Many of the illegal transactions date from this chaotic period. At the same time, however, key closure decisions concerning flagships of the East German state, such as the Interflug airline, Pentakon Cameras and the Trabant and Wartburg car plants led to social unrest against a background of collapsing industrial output. After Rohwedder's assassination, it did appear that a shift in policy direction had taken place in March 1991, with the agreement on 'principles for cooperation between the federation, Länder and Treuhandanstalt for recovery in the east'. Under these principles, the THA was enjoined to consult closely with the new Länder on the unemployment impacts of its closure decisions. Effectively this implied a moratorium on large plant closures without Land agreement and so supposedly this reflected a shift towards restructuring at the expense of rapid privatisation.

Regardless, the Treuhand, under its president Birgit Breuel, pushed harder for a rapid completion of disposals by the end of 1994. As could be expected, the easiest to privatise were firms supplying branches with good market prospects, namely construction and building materials and those serving naturally protected regional markets such as printing and food processing. Very difficult to privatise were branches suffering world competition from low-wage countries. The textiles, leather, clothing, optics and electronics branches all experienced factory liquidations or their return to the original owners.

Because of the expected repercussions of large closures, in the heavy

Table 3.2 Treuhand performance, November 1994

Of 12 370	firms
7 853	were fully privatised
3 713	were closed
536	were transferred to municipalities or majority private shareholding
268	remainded

Employment and investment guarantees:
DM206.5 billion investments and 1 487 280 jobs

Second Half 1990 – 1994:	
Income	DM41.7 bn
Expenditure	DM171.1 bn

industry sectors liquidations have been few. The steel, chemicals, shipbuilding and railway rolling stock branches all were oriented heavily to Comecon markets and are heavily polluting and technically obsolescent, producing at negative value-added under world prices. These form the so-called 'industrial core' and represent a very heavy subsidy charge for the THA. Those which have been sold have attracted a buyer only after huge public capital injections, or with other financial sweeteners (such as capital injections of DM3 billion in Jenoptik, Jena, of DM2 billion for the Baltic Shipyards, and the assumption by THA of most of the financial risk in the new oil refinery project at Leuna in conjunction with Elf-Acquitaine).

Finally, THA President Breuel has constantly reaffirmed her desire to create a raft of small and medium-sized enterprises, comparable to the West German '*Mittelstand*', so as to create a seed-bed for innovation and new entrepreneurial talent. To this end, management buy-outs (MBOs) were fostered, and accounted for 20 per cent of all privatisations. Table 3.2 gives the Treuhand's balance sheet at DM268 billion for 1994.

The fact that the DM1000 billion of assets (Modrow estimate) or DM600 billion (Rohwedder estimate) shrank to a net deficit of DM270 billion in 1994 reflected primarily the huge current losses borne by the state enterprises which clearly left few funds remaining for investment. Public attention has focused of course on the extremely low sale prices for the East German assets, seemingly given away to wealthy 'Wessies' (West Germans): total sales revenues may in the end amount to only DM50 billion. We will return to the strategic question of rapid privatisation, but let it be said that sales were typically by tender method

(MBOs and fixed price sales were restricted to the smaller enterprises). In reaching a negotiated price, the THA proceeded from the book value of the asset, given in the opening balance. Substantial remaining costs, such as inherited debt, environmental clean-up, redundancy provisions and job and investment guarantees were all included in the final price, explaining why in so many cases the ultimate price was minimal (*DIW-Wochenbericht*, 1992a).

A further common criticism of the Treuhand is that it pursued so little effective restructuring itself, waiting instead for a purchaser. It is asserted that the THA starved its enterprises of investment funds, preferring rapid privatisation to restructuring over the medium-term and therefore preventing firms from developing new products. It is the case that investment credits were accorded only after the corporate plan had been approved and meanwhile only support for running costs was given. However, an astonishing 80 per cent of its firms were considered 'capable of restructuring'. Investment levels were lower – only one-half of those of privatised firms in eastern Germany – but this doubtless reflected the fact that investment funds were very constrained when current losses were so high. In 1992, for example, investment and capital injections amounted to only DM2.8 billion while liquidity credits consisted of DM8 billion. However, a further sign that the Treuhand preferred private decision-makers to take investment decisions is evidenced by the six 'management limited partnerships' which it established to take some responsibility for restructuring. Each partnership is a mini-conglomerate grouping up to a dozen THA firms whose privatisation has proven difficult. The partnership must restructure its component firms in preparation for sale, with bonuses paid according to privatisation successes.

The Pattern of Economic Adjustment in the East

The pattern of adjustment which has emerged in the east is therefore the combined result of the policy decisions discussed above, of the relative national and international competitiveness of branches and, finally, of foreign direct investment (FDI) flows into eastern Germany. The collapse in activity which suffered a 'double dip' slump in mid-1992 and January 1993 was by the end of 1994 clearly in a sustained upturn, and the deindustrialisation process had broadly come to an end (*MRDB*, 10/1994). However, the slump and transformation have been without parallel. Eastern manufacturing output now serves only 12 per cent of total eastern effective demand (after having made up 70 per cent of net material product in 1989) and the output of the non-state service sector is 50 per cent higher than that of manufacturing (*DIW-Wochenbericht*, 1993a). Within this overall evolution, the picture by branch is very mixed, with rapid improvements in technology and product mix existing alongside obsolescent heavy industry still in the hands of the THA's successor organisations. Plainly, sheltered branches and those supplying the large infrastructure projects have prospered, while those facing world competition with obsolescent technology or a high-cost work force, faced a radical slimming cure. Successes are found in:

— *construction* which represents 15 per cent of regional output and where house building has taken over from infrastructure building as the main stimulus. Tax allowances, the resolution of ownership claims and the removal of inherited debt liabilities from housing corporations have all fostered the construction boom;
— *the car industry* is emerging from the low point of the slump in mid-1992, particularly in new plants opened by Opel and Volkswagen. Productivity equals the west, but the 'lean production methods' imply that the number employed are in the very low thousands;
— *the electrical and electronics* industry now produces only 40 per cent of the mid-1990 output level, with fewer than 25 per cent of the employees (*Wirtschaft und Statistik*, 6/1994). It does however serve the telecommunication and electricity supply monopolies, and Deutsche Telekom intends to maximise local sourcing by 1997. The electricity supply monopolies of West Germany which successfully extended their territory eastwards, are committed to a DM40 billion renewal programme. Siemens has commenced building on its DM2.4 billion microchip plant in Dresden, secured with DM700 million of regional assistance.

The problem cases remain the chemical, steel and engineering industries – the so-called 'industrial core'. The chemical triangle of Leuna-Buna-Bitterfeld/Wolfen in Saxony-Anhalt however experienced a halving of turnover in the years 1991 to 1993 and employment now stands at less than 25 per cent of the 1990 figure with a loss of more than 51 000 jobs. Dependent on basic chemicals and photosynthetics the market has collapsed with the loss of exports to Comecon and the shrinkage in fertiliser demand. As noted previously, Elf-Acquitaine agreed only to commit itself to a new refinery at Leuna if it reduced its shareholding from the initial 70 per cent to under 50 per cent and by shifting the burden of risk onto the THA. Finally in engineering, which was once the most significant branch in East Germany, most of the capacity remained in THA hands. Rationalisation was slow and output and employment at the end of 1993 stood only at 32–35 per cent of the second half of the 1990 figure (*MRDB*, 12/1993).

As implied above, the Kartellamt (Monopolies Commission) has been willing to contemplate the extension of quasi-monopoly conditions to the east in electricity supply and in potash mining, so as to secure an effective and controlled rationalisation of excess obsolescent capacity. In the case of electricity generation and supply, the dispute over the *Stromvertrag* (electricity contract) between the large western utilities and the eastern German municipal local supplies in March 1994 ensured that the big three western utilities (Bayernwerk, Preussenelektra and RWE) acquired the East German VEAG national monopoly distributor for DM10 billion and committed themselves to a further DM40 billion of investments in electricity supply. The western utilities have achieved vertical integration since Laubag, the largest brown coal producer, was acquired in early 1994 by an RWE subsidiary in which Bayernwerk and Preussenelektra have holdings. Likewise, in the case of potash, Kali and Salz (BASF) assumed control of the East German monopoly (Mitteldeutsche Kali AG) so as to rationalise excess capacity in Germany. The fact that the eastern German workers at Bischofferode went on hunger strike to protect their jobs led the THA to retain a substantial minority share.

Can the service industry take up the slack and generate sufficient employment in compensation? The sector has seen fundamental change but it remains the case that the demand for services is heavily dependent on the transfers from the west and on the evolution of real incomes. It does require a much broader industrial base. In the period since mid-1990, the net growth has been of 125 000 jobs (since the shake-out from state-owned retail distribution and transport undertakings has been substantial). There has certainly been a rapid rise among the self-employed, from 50 000 in 1989 to 300 000 in late 1993. However productivity remains at 40–45 per cent (according to activity) of the western German level, while rapid wage harmonisation ensures that unit labour costs remain far in excess of the western level. There can therefore be no substitute for an expansion in manufacturing employment.

It is beyond doubt that the prime impact on the sectoral adjustment process has been the privatisation and subsidisation (liquidity credits) policy of the Treuhand. Private investment in the east has totalled only DM26 billion, DM45 billion and DM52 billion in the years 1991 to 1993 respectively. In 1993 total investment reached DM135 billion. Foreign direct investment itself (including investment from western

Germany) has been at disappointing levels, with few 'green field' investments. It was only in 1994 that investment per head in eastern Germany substantially outpaced western Germany, and for that reason alone, one can postulate that the catch-up in productivity levels per head may take 15 years. Clearly the unresolved property restitution question continues to exact its harmful effect, but the existence of far cheaper labour in central Europe, within 70 miles of Berlin, is exacting a pull on plant location. Audi for example has switched a DM1 billion motor components project to Hungary from eastern Germany: wage rates there are one-sixth of those of the old Länder.

THE DEBATE OVER RESTRUCTURING POLICY AND LABOUR SUBSIDIES

During the first half-decade after unification the policy debate in Germany focused on the prominence given to privatisation by the Treuhand, in preference to an active industrial policy, which would seek to restructure firms while they remain in state hands. There was also the question of introducing various types of labour subsidy to avoid a free fall in employment levels. This debate is clearly reducible to that between market liberals and interventionists, but one must bear in mind that while government and Treuhand have been accused of laissez-faire liberalism, the actual degree of subsidisation presently practised is without historical parallel in Germany. Was the Treuhand at fault in pursuing a rapid privatisation and did it wilfully break-up viable units for this purpose?

Points commonly made by those broadly sympathetic to market economics are for example that the speed of privatisation necessarily led to a dramatic loss in the value of assets. The pressure for rapid disposal must depress prices in a negotiation, especially when THA sales would absorb the equivalent of three years of normal federal German investment. Further, in the prevailing market conditions of high real interest rates and low profit forecasts, the selling price was bound to weaken (Sinn, 1992; Kurz, 1993). The very lack of democratic supervision (the Bundestag set up a supervisory committee at a very late date) and the confidentiality of the sales contracts necessarily meant that viable alternative strategies were not considered, or only after the event. For example, in the case of Heckert machine tools of Chemnitz, the company's R&D division and its distribution network were sold off to a western group: it was only by the intervention of the Land Saxony and the labour union IG Metall, that the consequent closure of a dismembered Heckert AG was avoided. Saxony also stepped in, in conjunction with IG Metall, to prevent the closure of the Freital stainless steel works by finding a risk investor. More generally, Saxony has sought to pursue an active industrial policy (in contrast Thüringen has done so only on a minor scale). In the case of Saxony, its Atlas Project has given medium-term support in the form of loan guarantees to fourteen key regional employers in THA hands, with the express purpose of offering a longer-term frame for restructuring before privatisation. The success of the approach, however, remains in doubt.

Three broad alternative approaches to that of the THA have been proposed, varying from the market liberal to the expressly interventionist. Examples of the market liberal approach are those of Sinn (1992) and the DIW, the German institute for the economy (*DIW-Wochenbericht*, 1992a). Sinn proposed that minority shareholdings be attracted from 'sleeping' partners in the private sector as a first stage: as restructuring proceeds and the asset value rises, so the investor must acquire further shareholdings at a higher share price. The DIW proposal focused on an 'as-if' privatisation, which would attract investment capital as a guide to the strategic direction for the enterprise. To ensure its immediate short-term viability, inherited debt should be written off, and wage subsidies allowed but further public investment would be contingent upon attracting private investment and no further liquidity credits would be permitted.

In contrast, the expressly interventionist approach, which foresees medium- and longer-term subsidisation to maintain the integrity of the enterprise and its workforce, was postulated by then SPD leader Björn Engholm in his party's 'national recovery plan for the east' (3 August 1991) and by others (Meyer, 1991; Arbeitsgruppe, 1992). Common to such proposals is the desire to mobilise the panoply of state assistance (regional aid, R&D aid, export guarantees) to promote the reorientation to new markets, without the enterprise haemorrhaging through losses. The latter critics favour the establishment of 'technology centres' in large THA enterprises, drawing on the federal technology ministry's budget. The SPD on the other hand favours the assigning of product specialisations to plants and developing these by a combined use of investment subsidies, export guarantees and public purchasing contracts.

The federal government spoke of maintaining 'industrial cores' in the east, and these clearly comprised the heavy industrial groups left unsaleable in the THA portfolio. The proposal to sustain such cases as major regional employers derived from the chancellor's working group 'structural changes in the east' which reported in spring 1992. In September 1992, the proposal was formally made by Chancellor Kohl and separately by Finance Minister Waigel as a bargaining counter in the early stage of negotiations on a solidarity pact to contain and redirect state expenditure to the east, while buying union wage restraint. In October 1993, Mr Waigel tabled a draft law to take control of the 100 enterprises the Treuhand could not sell, and institute over the period 1995–2000 a slow restructuring, costing DM45 billion. Given the vagueness surrounding the 'industrial core' concept (Breuel et al., 1993; *DIW-Wochenbericht*, 1993a) there can be little doubt of the political motivation behind the policy and also little doubt of the extreme cost of long-term subsidisation.

The labour market debate also pitted market liberals against those in favour of a managed labour market. 'Social union' as an intrinsic part of the economic union has clearly extended the western employment legislation, social insurance and collective bargaining systems to the east. This created a single labour market (albeit one grouping two structurally very different economies with an extreme difference in productivity levels) and there is of course the danger of wage harmonisation such that, taking account of productivity, unit wage costs in the east will far outstrip those of the west.

This has clearly been the case since unification and accounts for much of the largely structural unemployment in the east. Of course it is held that social justice requires that wages be equalised with the west, otherwise large-scale migration will occur. Such social justice merely created mass unemployment. However, in these circumstances, market liberals such as the government's deregulation commission (Reports I and II, 1990–91) and Donges (1991) and Hartel (1991) stress the need to strike at the inherent rigidities in Germany's wage bargaining system and promote flexibility so that wage levels in the east will reflect more closely the marginal product of labour there. There are those who believe that these textbook recommendations hardly take existing labour market structures into consideration: rather, schemes of labour subsidisation are needed to reduce the costs of labour to the employer so that it corresponds to the productivity of the workforce in order to sustain labour demand and employment.

In a celebrated study Akerlof et al. (1991), using GDR planning data for industrial combines, showed that only 8.2 per cent of manufacturing jobs in Treuhand enterprises could survive at October 1990 DM wage levels in the east. Were wages to be subsidised at 75 per cent, then 77 per cent of jobs could survive. Akerlof therefore proposed a subsidy set in direct relation to the east–west wage gap which would be fixed in volume and over time. As jobs expanded in number, or as wage inflation proceeded, so the degree of subsidy would fall. There are clearly fears associated with such systems: fears of long-term subsidisation, of labour unions seeking to recuperate the subsidy in their wage claims, and of the wage levels fuelling price inflation. They obviously damage wage flexibility.

This wholly insufficient wage flexibility was also at the core of the debate on *ABS-Gesellschaften*, the so-called 'employment-enterprises', which the Treuhand strove to keep at arms' length. Such quasi-firms can be utilised under the 1986 *Arbeitsförderungsgesetz* (AFG) for job creation or the retraining of those unemployed or potentially unemployed. They can be used as a transitional mechanism by labour-shedding firms for the active retraining of employees facing redundancy. In eastern Germany such employment enterprises came to predominate as a vehicle for special labour market measures under the AFG law financed by the federal labour office. In 1993, there were 10 000 job creation and retraining programmes in the east. Socially, these instruments were clearly an important palliative, but economically they were open to two very serious criticisms. These schemes were legally allowed to operate only in non-profitmaking fields, in socially useful tasks such as environmental improvement or social care, but there were widespread complaints, especially by small firms, that they tendered for work outside these fields and so represented heavily subsidised competition to the struggling, newly established small firm sector. Secondly, the retrainees received 100 per cent of the (rising) tariff wage for two and sometimes three years. Here again was a mechanism for wage inflation which prevented the adjustment of wage rates to reflect the scale of unemployment. It merely strengthened the 'Mezzogiorno' effect. In 1993, paragraph 249h of the AFG Law was therefore modified in two ways. The object of the task had to be of 'community value' and beneficiaries of support could henceforth only receive four days' pay weekly at the unemployment pay rate. In mid-1994, 75 500 retrainees benefited in the east, of whom 50 000 were in Treuhand enterprises.

THE INTENSIFIED QUEST FOR COMPETITIVENESS IN POST-UNIFICATION WESTERN GERMANY

The scale of the financial transfers to the east, and the dependence of a sustained economic renewal there on western growth made painfully evident the need to achieve greater dynamism in western Germany's economy. The market liberal agenda of the first Kohl government in 1982–3 returned in the forms of a budgetary consolidation programme and solidarity pact and in a renewed deregulation drive which encompasses the partial privatisation of utilities. The consolidation programme combined near-term tax increases (e.g. solidarity surcharge of 7.5 per cent of income tax due) once again with the setting of medium-term targets to bring the deficits and escalating debt under control. The federal deficit of 4.5 per cent of GDP (or over 7 per cent if one includes the 'shadow budgets' of other federal bodies) has been targeted for reduction to 3 per cent in 1996/7 and the debt/GDP ratio, presently at 60 per cent, and therefore equal to the Maastricht ceiling, is planned to be reduced to the pre-unification level of 45 per cent at a point well into the future. This renewed stress on budget consolidation clearly seeks to redress some of the main policy errors of unification (no tax increases, haemorrhage of Treuhand losses, escalating wage rate-related social benefits in the east): however, looking to the future it also points to stagnant or slowly growing disposable incomes, and high tax levels, including high corporate tax. Where then will be the stimulus for growth, in exports or through supply-side efficiency gains?

After the 'straw fire' or evanescent boom induced by unification the question resurfaced of whether Germany would remain on the slow growth trajectory which prevailed from the first oil crisis of 1973/4 to 1987. The depth of the recession in 1992/3 intensified this soul-searching as to the competitiveness of Germany as an industrial location, the so-called *Standortfrage*. That western Germany has the highest production costs in the world (though matched by high productivity) is well known, and the report published in September 1993 (*Zukunftssicherung des Standorts Deutschland*) by the free market economics minister Günther Rexrodt highlighted the scale of the competitiveness problem and proposed 147 measures for deregulation. The report cited what are now quite well-known statistics: that the ageing of the population means that 33 per cent of Germans will be aged over 60 years in 2030, compared with 20 per cent now; that the German manufacturing worker works only 82 per cent of the hours of his Japanese equivalent; and that Germany, apart from having the shortest working week, has the shortest machine running times. Moreover, the level of corporate taxation, the restrictiveness of environmental legislation, the constraining effect of the centralised wage bargaining system on wage rate differentials as well as the shop closing hours (relatively successfully tackled in mid-1996) were all listed, among many other cases. Clearly then, the reforms proposed were for greater privatisation, reduction in red tape constraining businesses, a reduction in corporation tax rates and a shift in government spending towards the promotion of investment, innovation and employment. Among a range of other policy changes announced, the *Standortsicherungsgesetz* (law to ensure the competitiveness of Germany as an industrial location) of 1993 included provisions for a reduction in corporation tax, and the promotion of part-time working in the civil service.

This debate in West Germany surfaced at least twice in the 1980s, following phases of currency appreciation which hit exports, but was then followed by periods of record export surpluses. Two studies (*DIW-Wochenbericht*, 1992b, 1993b) stress that the problem is not structural but engendered by a DM appreciation. They point out that, in the period to 1991, high productivity, falling unit labour costs and record export surpluses, were only matched by those of Japan. Only twice in 25 years did West German unit wage costs rise faster than in competing countries and West Germany has maintained world export share (if this includes shipments to East Germany). Can one say then that the present difficulties are just a mixture of the merely cyclical, of the temporary DM appreciation by 5 per cent after unification, and of tariff wage rises of over 6 per cent in 1991 and 1992? Have the rise in the yen, and wage moderation in Germany since 1993 now resolved the matter?

The fact that export demand in late 1993 and 1994 served largely to pull western Germany out of recession does point to the Federal Republic's ability to regain competitiveness. Real incomes of employees have been stagnant or falling in response to the 2.6 million (8.6 per cent) unemployed in the west in June 1994 (*MRDB*, 5/1994). This trend continued in 1995. In fact, German industry has engaged in unprecedented cost-cutting and restructuring since the onset of recession in 1992, in order to reduce production costs by the 20–30 per cent which it was commonly said was required to hold off south-east Asian competition. Unit wage costs have been falling since 1992 and a gradual re-establishment of the profit rate occurred. However, the loss of many hundreds of thousands of jobs could be observed at the same time.

The enormous scale of job cuts, and the acquiescence of the workforce in real income losses and increased flexible working hours all point to certain strengths in the centralised bargaining system, which is so maligned among Anglo-Saxon market liberals. The point is that sector-wide bargaining fosters real wage moderation, since unions are seen to be responsible for employment outcomes. Union representation on the supervisory boards of larger companies does also lead to greater responsibility. In 1994 effective wage increases were brought down to 1.5 per cent or half the inflation rate. In addition, unions have agreed a range of concessions on working time reductions (without compensation) or, for example, the recruitment of the long-term unemployed at rates 10 per cent lower than the tariff wage. The four-day working week (without compensation) at Volkswagen, enabled the company to spread working time among the labour force without job losses.

Reform in Germany is typically incremental, painstaking and legalistic, acknowledging employee rights within an (admittedly strained) social market consensus. This is evidenced in the slowness of privatisation and in other loosening of regulatory constraints. The decisions of the federal government to privatise utilities such as the post and telecommunications, the Lufthansa airline and railways date back to mid-1992. Of course the opening of competition in telecommunications, air transport and electricity supply is to a significant degree a result of single market directives emanating from Brussels. One does suspect, however, that the federal government, hamstrung by constitutional provisions in this area and by the SPD majority in the Bundesrat, is driven primarily by the prospect of financial gains from asset sales rather than ideological fervour. Recent decisions comprise:

— the establishment in December 1993 of the Deutsche Bahn AG, which unites the western and eastern railway companies. It is divided into three subsidiaries covering network, passenger and freight, granting much greater managerial freedom, and opening the possibility of private railway operating concessions as well as private capital injections;
— the Lufthansa AG is being privatised in three steps, reducing federal participation from 51.4 to 38 per cent by the end of 1995 and subsequently to zero;
— the break-up of the Bundespost into three joint stock companies of Telekom, Postdienst and Postbank in 1993, followed by the decision to commence privatisation of Deutsche Telekom in 1996. It will retain its telephone monopoly according to a timetable set by Brussels, ending in 1998 or in the year 2000.

In each of these privatisation projects, the question of the civil servant status (i.e. job tenure for life) of employees, other employment rights, and their pension entitlements proved major obstacles and, in the end, a substantial continuing burden. Only in the case of Lufthansa have employees lost their job tenure, and the inherited pension costs (leaving out of account the huge cost to the finance ministry) have burdened Telekom with DM40 billion in pension entitlements and Lufthansa with DM4 billion. There is also no clear break with the past in the regulatory conditions for the Telekom voice monopoly. So much in its operating environment remains to be resolved but it clearly can block entry to the market by the many substantial potential entrants. In the huge growth sector of multimedia services (including pay TV) the Telekom presides over the densest fibre-optic net in the world and may yet retain monopoly rights to the year 2000.

There is plentiful evidence of the powerful constraints on regulatory change in a federation which operates in a legalistic and consensual way. One may cite in support the imperceptible attack on subsidies (which amount to a relatively low 1.2 per cent of GDP for federal subsidies, but up to 6 per cent of GDP in the widest definition), the lack of relaxation in shop pricing freedom (*Rabattgesetz*) and the limited changes to working time regulations and shop opening hours. All are evidence of the slow and deliberate nature of changes in regulation. However, there is no doubt that competitiveness in the exposed manufacturing sector is gradually regained: the question is whether Germany can produce domestic sources of demand growth in the coming years, or whether it is largely dependent on world export demand. Will its powerful export industry further locate abroad in low cost locations, squeezed as it is by intense competition from south-east Asia in the higher technology products, and from central and eastern Europe in ordinary commodities? There is considerable evidence of increased flexibility in working patterns and of a surgical restructuring in western German manufacturing. The question remains however whether Germany can sustain a sufficiently large and high value-added manufacturing sector in the face of relentless world competition.

REFERENCES

Akerlof, G.A., Rose, A.K., Yellen, J.L. and Hessenius, H. (1991), 'East Germany in from the Cold. The Economic Aftermath of Currency Union', paper presented to the Conference of the Brookings Panel on Economic Activity, Washington, D.C. (4–5 April), p. 12.

Arbeitsgruppe Alternative Wirtschaftspolitik (1992), *Memorandum '92 – Gegen den ökonomischen Niedergang – Industriepolitik in Ostdeutschland* (Cologne: Pappyrossa Verlag).

Breuel, B. et al. (1993), 'Erhaltung industrieller Kerne in Ostdeutschland?', *Wirtschaftsdienst*, no. 2, pp. 59–70.

DIW-Wochenbericht (1992a), 'Zur Politik der Treuhandanstalt – eine Zwischenbilanz', no. 7, pp. 62–8.

DIW-Wochenbericht (1992b), 'Industrieller Mittelstand in Ostdeutschland', no. 11, pp. 103–9.

DIW-Wochenbericht (1993a), 'Stand der Privatisierung, Achter Bericht', no. 13, pp. 131–58.

DIW-Wochenbericht (1993b), 'BRD: Strukturkrise oder konjunktureller Einbruch?', no. 26–27, pp. 360–8.

Donges, J.B. (1991), 'Arbeitsmarkt und Lohnpolitik in Ostdeutschland', *Wirtschaftsdienst* (1991), no. 6, pp. 283–91.

Financial Times (14/2/1995), 'German Court Rejects Property Claims', p. 2.

Ghaussy, A.C. and Schäfer, W., eds (1993), *The Economics of German Unification* (London: Routledge).

Härtel, H.H.(1991), 'Lohnpolitik im vereinten Deutschland', *Wirtschaftsdienst* (1991), no. 1, pp. 7–10.

Hasse, R. (1993), 'German–German Monetary Union: Main Options, Costs and Repercussions', in Ghanie-Ghaussy, A. and Schäfer, W., eds, pp. 26–59.

Hüther, M. and Petersen, H.G. (1993), 'Taxes and Transfers: Financing German Unification', in Ghanie-Ghaussy, A. and Schäfer, W., eds, pp. 73–91.

Kreile, M. (1992), 'The Political Economy of the New Germany', in Stares, P., ed., pp. 55–92.

Kurz, H.D., ed. (1993), *United Germany and the new Europe* (Aldershot: Edward Elgar).

Kurz, H.D. (1993), 'Distributive Aspects of German Unification', in Kurz, ed., pp. 134–62.

Meyer, W. (1991), 'Welchen Beitrag können Beschäftigungsgesellschaften leisten? Anforderungen aus gewerkschaftlicher Sicht', *Wirtschaftsdienst* (1991), no. 8, pp. 385–8.

MRDB – Monthly Report of the German Bundesbank (various issues).

Schäfer, W. (1993), 'The Unification of Germany, the DM and European Monetary Union', in Kurz, H.D., ed., pp. 217–30.

Sinn, G. and Sinn, H.W. (1992), *Jumpstart – the Economic Unification of Germany* (Boston, Mass.: MIT Press).

Stares, P., ed. (1992), *The New Germany and the New Europe* (Washington, DC: Brookings).

Wirtschaft und Statistik (various issues).

4 The German Party System since Unification

William M. Chandler

THE PARTY SYSTEMS IN GERMANY BEFORE UNIFICATION

The post-1945 division of Germany created two radically different regimes, each with it own distinctive party system. In West Germany (FRG), the first Bundestag (federal parliament) election in 1949 produced a fragmented multiparty array but also established the Christian Democrats (CDU) and Social Democrats (SPD) as pre-eminent contenders for power. By 1953, in part due to the national application of the five per cent minimum for the proportional allocation of parliamentary seats, the post-war party system took on its essential character, thereafter evolving gradually without traumatic disruptions (Smith, 1986: 88–124).

The West German version of party-government blends a Westminster-like competition between two major parties with a continental multiparty tradition of coalition-building. Elections are strongly oriented towards a choice between two chancellor-candidates, yet alternation in power between the major parties has been a function of the crucial pivot role played by the small but influential Free Democratic Party (FDP), which has tended to form alliances with both Christian Democrats and Social Democrats. As a Grand Coalition alliance of the two *Volksparteien* proved viable, the party system also took on a triangular character, with a strong convergent dynamic of power-sharing. The 1983 Bundestag entry of the Greens challenged but did not destroy the workings of this model (Pappi, 1984; Dalton, 1992: 52–76).

In the German Democratic Republic (GDR), an entirely different and artificially created party system emerged under Soviet tutelage. The forced merger of the eastern SPD with the communist KPD produced a communist-controlled Socialist Unity Party (SED). By assuming the role of vanguard party, the SED governed the GDR for 40 years under a multiparty façade of smaller parties designed to provide legitimacy for both the SED and the regime. These were the so-called block-parties as they tended to side and vote with the SED *en bloc* (Lapp, 1988: 7–47; Glaessner, 1992: 103–7). All Volkskammer (East

German parliament) representatives were elected by means of a unity list in which each party or group was allocated a pre-set number of seats. Importantly, block-parties participated on condition of their recognition of the constitutionally ordained 'leading role' of the SED (Glaeβner, 1992: ch. 1; Merkl, 1993: ch. 3).

Almost half a century after the division of Germany, unification brought these two party systems together through an unequal merger. The sudden collapse of the regime and the peaceful democratisation in the GDR prior to unification created unique circumstances for a total restructuring of the party political landscape. It can be summarised as follows:

1. Dissolution of the GDR's party system.
2. Sprouting of indigenous protest movements.
3. Extension and importation of the organisation as well as the financial means and expertise from western parties.

By 1989 the transformation of the party political structures in the GDR was immediately visible in the rise of opposition groups and mounting protests. With Honecker's ouster in October 1989 and the dramatic opening of the Berlin Wall one month later, there followed a brief but crucial phase in which the SED/PDS leadership (first led by Egon Krenz and then by Gregor Gysi) attempted to salvage the regime by means of a damage control approach. However, concessions only served to fuel public pressure for democracy. In the Volkskammer election of March 1990 East Germans voiced an unmistakable preference for rapid unification by electing the Christian Democratic umbrella organisation 'Alliance for Germany'. With this mandate, the new de Maizière government, the first and last democratically chosen in the history of the GDR, initiated negotiations with Bonn, leading to the complete absorption of the former GDR into the Federal Republic, an event without historical precedent.

Although 'instant' fusion could be seen as a vote of confidence in western parliamentary democracy and the social market economy, it also imposed immense challenges affecting all aspects of German politics. Political parties were confronted with the task of absorbing some 16 million citizens into the institutions and practices of parliamentary democracy.

FRAMEWORK FOR ANALYSIS

Because party systems are multifaceted, the following analysis distinguishes among three forms of change in the context of unification: intra-party organisational integration, inter-party patterns of competition, and coalition relations as far as both the governing parties and the parties in opposition are concerned. Table 4.1 presents these distinctions.

Table 4.1 A framework for analysing party change

Intra-party organisational adaptation	Integration, founding, mergers, membership change
Inter-party relations	Electoral bases, patterns of competition
Coalition politics	Governing/ Opposition roles

ORGANISATIONAL ADAPTATION OF THE PARTY SYSTEM IN THE GDR

The end of the SED's hegemony led directly to the development of competitive politics and imposed on all parties new challenges of integration. The introduction of pluralism by the citizen protest groups created a multiplicity of weak proto-parties, which lacked developed infrastructures or active memberships. Most of these formations proved ephemeral and were, for the most part, absorbed within the established parties which were organisationally much stronger (Richter, 1994: 101–10; Niedermeyer and Stöss, 1994: 11–17). Imminent free elections in the GDR required all parties to begin with building organisations suitable for electoral competition.

For the established parties (CDU, SPD, FDP and Greens), integration occurred within two stages. Following the founding of new parties and the reform of the existing block-parties, the first stage involved the fusion of the eastern parties and groups with each other and the formation of alliances. During the second stage western and eastern organisations merged. The integration process carried over into the post-unity period and more than half a decade after unification it has still not been entirely completed.

The CDU, SPD and FDP quickly formed working alliances with

Table 4.2 Patterns of party merger

Phase	*CDU*	*FDP*	*SPD*	*Greens*
Emergent opposition	DA, DSU	DFP, east FDP	SDP, Oct 1989	Dissident groups, east Grüne
Block party adaptation	Reform in Ost-CDU	Reform in LDPD	none	none
Consolidation, alliances pre-VK election	Alliance for Germany	Liberal regrouping in BFD	SDP renamed SPD	Alliance of three groups: Bündnis 90
Fusion of eastern and western wings	East–west merger, Oct 1990	Fusion, Oct 1990	Fusion December 1989	1993 east–west merger

their eastern counterparts, leading to 'friendly takeovers'. This shaped the kind of parties that would prevail through the elections of 1990 and the immediate post-unity era (Eisenmann and Hirscher, 1992: 8). The overall effect of the mergers was to simplify the configuration of parties into certain patterns of organisation and competition in the new Länder, which to a considerable extent mirrored the system of the old Federal Republic.

For the Christian Democrats, the early integration phase comprised three steps:

1. an internal renewal of the eastern CDU (Ost-CDU), starting with the ouster of its chairman Gerald Götting and the election of Lothar de Maizière,
2. the founding of new opposition groups, especially the Democratic Awakening (DA) and the German Social Union (DSU), both of which were naturally apprehensive about dealing with the Ost-CDU (the DSU was created under the sponsorship of the Bavarian CSU, the CDU's sister party, which sought to establish links with the east),
3. as free elections approached, finding a viable partner in the east became a priority, culminating in the building of the 'Alliance for Germany' in February 1990 to contest the forthcoming Volkskammer election (Richter, 1993: 119–21; Clemens, 1993: 200–23).

For the western CDU, integration meant an awkward partnership with a former block-party. The CDU in Bonn had long avoided contact with the Ost-CDU, which was regarded as nothing more than a 'transmission belt' for the SED. However, the Ost-CDU, unlike the newly formed opposition forces, promised substantial property holdings and had a large membership (although many quit during the collapse of the GDR). Once this former block-party became the principal partner for the CDU in Bonn, rebuilding meant a western input of money, resources and personnel. Organisational integration was complemented by the importation of political leaders and top civil servants to staff key ministries in the new Länder (König, 1993: 386–96). Increasing western involvement in the process of party-building naturally paved the way to ultimate fusion, but this did not resolve persisting tensions between older 'Blockis' and the newer 'Renewalists', which since unification has cast a shadow over the CDU's ability to mobilise new support and to recruit candidates (Schmidt, 1994: 59–60).

For the FDP, organisational change was shaped by a similarly awkward fusion with a block-party, the LDPD (the Liberal Democratic Party of Germany). Existing contacts between the two increased sharply after October 1989. By early 1990 the renamed LDP had undergone significant programmatic transformation, but its chairman Manfred Gerlach, a leading figure in the old regime, remained in office and also became the last head of state in the final days of the GDR. For the newly founded eastern FDP and the German Forum party (DFP), distrust of the LDP made cooperation difficult (Roberts, 1993: 154–8), yet political survival made merger inevitable. The early Volkskammer election, first planned for May then scheduled for March 1990, forced all these liberal formations to regroup under the umbrella of the BFD (*Bund freier Deutscher*, Union of Free Germans). This coalition captured an unimpressive 5.3 per cent of the Volkskammer voting. Shortly thereafter another block-party, the National Democratic Party (NDPD) also fused with the BFD. Five months later, in anticipation of federal elections in December 1990, the FDP's party congress in Hanover ratified the merger of the party's eastern and western wings.

Merger provided an extraordinary boost for this small pivot party. Instant inclusion of the LDP also gave the FDP substantial property holdings, and total membership more than doubled. The FDP temporarily became the only party with more members in the new Länder than in the old. However, many of its nominal 200 000 members dwindled away after 1990. According to one reliable estimate, from some 136 000 eastern members only about 58 000 remained by 1992 (Soe, 1992). By

1995 federal party membership was estimated at only 80 000 (50 000 west, 30 000 east). Grass-roots weakness has remained a persisting flaw, confirmed after 1993 by the FDP's dismal electoral performance in both the old and new Länder. However, from late 1994 a gradual rise in the electoral fortunes of the FDP could be observed (see below).

For the Social Democrats, more than for any other party, a preoccupation with internal cohesion pre-dates unification. Its own success in achieving the 1959 Bad Godesberg goal of a broad, inter-class *Volkspartei* led to social diversification of both party membership and electorate. This had a profound impact on internal party relations. The inflow of new members accentuated divisions between a rising new middle class espousing post-materialist priorities and the party's traditionally materialist milieu of skilled workers and trade union members. Such internal dissension prevented the SPD from effectively capitalizing on the frequent unpopularity of CDU/CSU-led governments. Furthermore, in the 1980s, the SPD became the primary victim of the advances made by the Green party. The gradual erosion of its electoral base, especially after it lost power in 1982, exposed a crisis of identity and prompted endless debate about electoral strategy and organisational renewal (Silvia, 1993: 171–9).

Compounding these internal problems, unification imposed new challenges of integration. However, the SPD was spared the block-party collaborationist legacy, and the newly created eastern SDP seemed at first a promising partner, but its organisation was feeble, lacking in resources and personnel. Thus, as elections approached the SPD found itself at a disadvantage to the CDU. More fundamentally, the task of recruiting activists was thwarted by the SPD's own ambivalence to unification, which rendered the party largely irrelevant to most eastern voters during the crucial phase of party-building. The consequences were found in the meagre support the party received both in the Volkskammer (21.9 per cent) and in the Bundestag (23.6 per cent in the new Länder) elections of 1990. Although the east–west merger was accomplished by December 1989, persisting organisational weaknesses in the new Länder continued to plague the SPD's electoral efforts (Tiemann, 1993: 415–21; Silvia, 1993: 180).

Unification presented a difficult adaptation for the Greens. Of all the parties represented in the Bundestag, only the Greens failed to merge prior to unity. Two separate organisations competed regionally through the 1990 elections: Bündnis 90 (Alliance of '90) in the east and the Green Party in the west. East–west merger was delayed due to both a basic imbalance in membership and inherent policy differences. By

1993 an uneasy integration of the eastern and western wings was accomplished under the name Bündnis 90/die Grünen, but easterners have remained fearful of being swallowed up by the much larger western party (Poguntke and Schmitt-Beck, 1993: 191– 213; Frankland and Schoonmaker, 1993: 215–34). The concern to preserve an eastern identity in an unbalanced relationship was accentuated by defeats in several eastern Landtag elections in 1994. Federally, Green membership in 1995 has been estimated at 40 000 but with only 2000 in the east. While activists total 10 000, just 150 are located in the east (Hoffmann, 1995: 5).

For the Party of Democratic Socialism (PDS), the SED's reformed successor party, survival rather than merger became the paramount task. With its SED legacy, the problem was primarily one of adaptation to pluralist politics, that is, a transformation from democratic centralism and a vanguard function to participation in competitive democracy. It also led to a generational change through the departure of most of the older members of the SED leadership, but there have been few new entrants. The strength of the PDS remains based on the cadres of the former SED (still some 130 000). They have provided a grass-roots organisational presence across the new Länder, something that other parties have failed to establish (Falter and Klein, 1994: 22–34). In the 1994 Bundestag election this was undoubtedly a key to the ability of the PDS to win four direct mandates in Berlin.

BASES OF PARTY COMPETITION

Partisan dealignment has altered patterns of competition in all advanced democracies. As a consequence of increasing voter mobility and the erosion of traditional loyalties, the two large German *Volksparteien* (CDU/CSU and SPD) have suffered decline in both membership and electoral support. Dealignment has, correspondingly, provided a potential for 'new politics' and populist protest (Dalton, 1992: 69–72; Schultze, 1994: 472–93). Initially, unification appeared to facilitate even greater volatility, in part because many eastern voters lack firm party loyalties and have tended to be issue-oriented.

Trends on the Right

Urbanisation, secularisation and increasing affluence have all slowly reduced the weight of rural Catholic bastions. Similarly, alterations in occupational structures have gradually expanded the electoral weight of a new middle class which is relatively detached from traditional party loyalties. Thus despite four successive Bundestag election victories between 1983 and 1994, Christian Democratic membership and support stagnated. Importantly, however, the CDU/CSU did not suffer alone. Both *Volksparteien* lost ground due to dealignment effects. The weakening of the SPD was even more severe than that of the CDU, so that by 1990 the gap of popular support between the two expanded to about 10 per cent. After the 1987 election – and especially after the Barschel affair in 1988 – but prior to the pressures of unification, the vulnerability of the CDU/CSU had become evident by the party's slump in opinion polls and in Landtag elections (Chandler, 1993: 42–3). These setbacks appeared to threaten the leadership of Chancellor Kohl. However, his political fortunes suddenly reversed when the GDR collapsed. Although unification brought immediate benefits for the CDU as eastern Germans voted massively in support of the chancellor and his 'fast track' approach, the longer term implications of unification were less clear. Victories in the unity election of December 1990 postponed but did not erase electoral anxieties for the CDU/CSU.

The new Länder offered no natural social bastion for the CDU. The more Protestant and more secular eastern electorate has tilted the party base away from its traditional core. As the 1990 elections demonstrated, it was, however, significant that the CDU and not the SPD became the primary party for eastern blue-collar workers.

In 1990 Chancellor Kohl promised that no one would be worse off as a result of unification, yet unification exposed the reality of economic collapse, job losses and dependence. This confronted Bonn with the immediate need to instigate new policies in an atmosphere of massive economic, social and emotional stress. As the major governing party, the CDU/CSU had to wrestle with the dilemma of how to retain popularity while pursuing painful policies. Its inability to provide immediate relief led to mass disillusionment. Across the new Länder (where the CDU won convincingly in 1990), CDU popularity dropped to the 20 per cent level, while SPD support rose to around 40 per cent.

At the same time, an influx of refugees made the asylum question politically destructive. In this festering atmosphere, CDU popularity eroded further. In the western bastion of Baden-Württemberg, the 1992 Landtag election resulted in significant gains by the far-right Republican Party (*Republikaner*) and forced the CDU into a grand coalition Roth, 1993: 1–20; see also Chapter 6 by P. Panayi in this book).

By early 1994, Helmut Kohl was down but not out. Benefiting from a long awaited economic recovery, he again was able to engineer a remarkable reversal of fortunes, first evidenced by a strong CDU/CSU showing in the European elections of June 1994. Economic upturn, the resolution of the asylum issue with the help of a change of the constitution, plus victory in the federal presidential election of May 1994 all contributed to a strong recovery, notably in the new Länder. Eastern voters responded quickly to improving prospects. Despite this sharp turnaround, CDU support in the 1994 Bundestag election remained considerably weaker in the east than in the west. Only among western voters was the CDU/CSU fully effective in mobilizing its core electorate. Although these elections produced only a very slim overall majority of ten seats between the government and all opposition parties (however, when not counting the PDS's 30 seats, the gap between the government and the combined number of SPD-Green MPs amounts to 40 seats), they confirmed the stabilisation of CDU/CSU support.

As the Free Democrats have lacked a loyal electoral base throughout the history of the Federal Republic, they always have had to rely on ticket-splitting on the part of other party supporters. This has perpetually put the FDP in danger of slipping below the crucial 5 per cent minimum. However, unification appeared to strengthen the liberal electoral base, and the 1990 campaign focus on Genscher and Lambsdorff produced an enormous victory, with the FDP winning their first ever direct mandate. Yet after 1990 the FDP squandered its electoral windfall because of the party's inability to transform immediate gains into a solid base and a more modern organisation. By mid-1993, polls showed a weakening of support for the FDP. Electoral defeats in a string of seven consecutive Landtag elections prior to the October Bundestag election – plus a weak 4.1 per cent in the June 1994 Euro-elections – signalled a looming crisis of existence. In the general election of October 1994 the FDP absorbed massive losses compared to 1990 but did survive, with 6.9 per cent. However, without firm roots or a stable core, the FDP's reliance on 'itinerant' voters remains an Achilles heel (Søe, 1992: 32). In the public mind, the party no longer has a distinctive role. In 1994 an estimated 63 per cent of FDP voters were strategic ticket-splitters who identify more closely with the CDU/CSU (Jung and Roth, 1994: 14).

With persisting dissension over the leadership of Klaus Kinkel, the FDP tottered on the verge of extinction. Although the February 1995 Hessian Landtag contest provided a reprieve, the FDP's crisis was intensified by devastating setbacks in North Rhine-Westphalia and Bremen in May 1995. These results meant that the FDP would be excluded from 11 of the 16 state legislatures and forced the resignation of Kinkel. To a considerable degree, the FDP has been overtaken by the Greens as the third party in the Länder. However, the new FDP leadership consisting of chairman Wolfgang Gerhard and secretary-general Ingo Westerwelle have vigorously attempted to establish the FDP as a modern capitalist party and have had some moderate success.

Trends on the Left

The collapse of communism caught the SPD off guard. The party's *Ostpolitik* of small steps to humanize authoritarianism in the GDR rested on the assumption of the *de facto* permanent division of Germany. When unification became unstoppable, adjustment was more difficult for the SPD than for the CDU/CSU (for whom unification seemed natural, even if wholly unexpected). Although by early 1990 public opinion massively supported rapid unification, chancellor-candidate Oskar Lafontaine warned against the economic problems associated with speedy unification. This tactic divided the party and left the SPD out of step with the wider public, especially in the new Länder. It also allowed the chancellor and his majority coalition to capture the emotive groundswell of support for the fast-track to unity. By the time of the crucial Volkskammer election in March 1990, the SPD had wasted its broad but tenuous base in the east. In the 1990 Bundestag election, its 33.5 per cent marked its lowest share of the vote since 1957.

However, in the several Landtag contests between 1991 and 1994, the SPD made significant gains in several Länder, pushing the CDU out of power or forcing grand coalitions. Regional recovery has meant a federalisation of power, with the SPD's rising stars increasingly to be found among its minister-presidents and opposition leaders in the Länder (see Chapter 5 by C. Jeffery in this book).

After 1990, Björn Engholm assumed the leadership and served as a moderating force, often opting for a pragmatic resolution of policy issues rather than confrontational politics. But his sudden resignation from all leadership posts in May 1993 threw the SPD into further disarray. The resolution of the leadership problem by means of an unprecedented direct election by party members of the SPD's national chairman led to the election of Rudolf Scharping, the minister-president of Rhineland Palatinate. This provided an unexpected boost to the SPD just when Kohl was particularly unpopular. The leadership change furthered the generational turnover that had been observed for some time. It also restored both internal confidence and public approval. However, the Scharping honeymoon with the electorate could not be sustained. Late in the election campaign of 1994, as Scharping's appeal faded and Kohl's image gained strength, the SPD resorted to a strategy based on a leadership team personified in the *troika* of Scharping, Lafontaine and Gerhard Schröder, the minister-president of Lower Saxony. This led to the stabilisation of support for the SPD and to limited gains (3.4 per cent) in the Bundestag election of October 1994, but this fell short of what was necessary for a new coalition on the left. At the party conference in Mannheim in November 1995 Scharping was quite unexpectedly deposed as party chairman (though he remained the SPD's parliamentary leader) and Lafontaine managed to become his successor.

With unification as the preoccupying question, the Bündnis 90/Greens became temporarily irrelevant and lost their entire western parliamentary delegation in the 1990 Bundestag election. This interruption by no means signified the end of green politics, for recovery in the old Länder became evident over the next three years. As Green popular support revived to about 10 per cent, a Bundestag re-entry became a virtual certainty. The 1994 results produced a modest but satisfying return to federal politics for a more pragmatic Green alliance. However, the demise of the eastern wing over the same period has meant that the Greens have become a party heavily dominated by its western wing.

1995 regional election victories in Hesse, North Rhine-Westphalia and Bremen attest to the expanding strength of the Greens in the old Länder where it is assuming the role of third party, displacing the FDP. Once the 'anti-party' party, the Greens have emerged as a force of considerable experience at many levels: they are hardly outsiders any longer. Considering the poor performance of the SPD opposition, Joschka Fischer, one of the Green's most prominent politicians and former environment minister in Hesse, is regarded by many as the real leader of the opposition in the Bundestag since 1994.

Due to the electoral rules exceptionally in effect for the 1990 election, the 5 per cent minimum applied separately within two districts, east and west. This permitted the PDS to gain a foothold of 17 seats in the Bundestag, providing national exposure, which was effectively exploited by the leadership of Gregor Gysi. At that time, many observers expected that, once the electoral law reverted back to a national minimum of 5 per cent, the PDS could not survive as anything more than a fringe party.

However, the unpopularity and organisational weakness of other parties in the new Länder gave the PDS a chance to consolidate its base after

1990. With a solid membership and local roots deriving from the former SED, it became a voice of discontent among eastern German voters. By 1994 the durability of the SED-successor had become fully evident. In all five eastern Landtag contests in 1994, the PDS substantially advanced, winning on average an additional 5 per cent of the popular vote. These gains attest to the diverse appeal of the PDS. It cannot be labelled the party of the working class, despite its socialist ideology, for its electorate is a social cross-section, consisting not only of the disadvantaged.

It is worth noting that in the 1994 Bundestag election, reverse ticket-splitting in key districts aided the PDS to win its direct mandates. An estimated 18 per cent of second votes cast for the SPD and 25 per cent of second votes given to the Bundnis 90/Grüne cast their first ballot for the PDS candidate in the four crucial Berlin districts. Moreover, the revival of the PDS blocked the chances of the SPD in the new Länder, a trend already found in communal elections.

Populist Extremism

Following unification, disillusionment with the established parties widened and deepened. As Germans increasingly voiced scepticism about the competence of the established parties, the potential for protest and extremism increased correspondingly. Although the far right remained insignificant in the unity elections of 1990, it resurfaced in several Land elections in conjunction with the economic slow-down and an influx of asylum-seekers. By mid-1993, national support for the Republican Party was slightly above the 5 per cent minimum, suggesting a possible 1994 entry into the Bundestag. Such an outcome would have plunged the party system into crisis and could have altered dramatically coalition alternatives, perhaps forcing a CDU/CSU-SPD grand coalition. As in the 1966–9 period, the consequent lack of any major party on the opposition benches could have then further intensified rejection of the 'cartel of élites' in Bonn. Some two-thirds of extremist support was based on diffuse discontent and frustration. When translated into populist protest (Lepszy, 1993: 2), this made for an unstable electorate, without firm social anchoring (Veen et al., 1993: 56–64; Roth, 1993: 17–19). However, when the numbers of asylum-seekers began to diminish, partly due to the implementation of new restrictive procedures, and as the economy began to recover, extremist appeals from the far right dissipated. The CDU/CSU had successfully managed to reintegrate many of the potential right-wing protest votes into its ranks.

COALITIONAL POLITICS SINCE UNIFICATION

Unification has provoked no reversal in the dominant role of the federal parties. Coalition formation has remained anchored in the triangular model in which two Volksparteien and one smaller pivot party, define the three coalitional options (Smith, 1992: 79–83; Pappi, 1984; Chandler and Siaroff, 1992). However, signs of new coalitional options, especially red-green alliances within the Länder, may suggest the demise of the triangular model.

In Bonn, relations within the CDU/CSU majority party can be summarised by the CDU's relations with its two smaller partners, CSU and FDP.

The relationship between CDU and CSU in the post-unity period has undergone subtle but significant changes. From the perspective of the CSU, two crucial developments reshaped its role. The 1988 death of its charismatic leader Franz Josef Strauss obliged the CSU to renew its leadership. Theo Waigel was chosen as party chairman, while in Munich Max Streibl became minister-president. However, by late 1993, scandals (notably the so-called Amigo affair) were undermining the CSU's traditional grip on Bavarian voters. When Streibl was replaced by Edmund Stoiber, the CSU was able to overcome its internal crises. The more vigorous leadership tandem of Waigel and Stoiber put the CSU in a strong position for the electoral battles of 1994.

Unification also confronted the CSU with the reality of becoming a smaller regional force in a larger Germany. While the CDU expanded eastward through merger, the CSU's effort at building a CSU-like DSU in the new Länder faltered. Yet by 1994 the CSU, in the context of economic recovery in the country at large, went on to impressive victories in the European, Landtag and Bundestag elections. The post-Strauss and post-unity phase for the CDU-CSU relationship has become one of relative harmony, evident in the cooperative partnership between Kohl and Waigel but enforced by the CSU's realisation that it has much less bargaining power in post-unification Germany than the party had in the days of Franz-Josef Strauss.

The FDP's coalitional significance is found in its pivot role rather than in its popular base. Although the 1990 election results denied the FDP its arithmetic balancer role, it emerged as the primary partner for the CDU, ahead of the CSU, largely because the FDP was able to expand eastward while the CSU, confined to Bavaria, lost leverage in national politics. CDU-FDP relations were tested in the presidential election of May 1994. With government popularity crumbling away in the wake of recession, speculation mounted about a possible renewal of a social-liberal coalition after the 1994 general election. The FDP candidacy of Hildegard Hamm-Brücher, a well-respected former foreign office minister, posed the question of the party's intentions as far as coalition-building was concerned. However, Kinkel remained opposed to any deal with the SPD, which could have provided the FDP with a victory but would have split the coalition. Kinkel's support for the CDU's candidate, former supreme court justice Roman Herzog, on the decisive third ballot gave a psychological boost to Kohl as the hot phase of the election campaign of 1994 unfolded.

For the opposition, significant SPD gains in the Länder have given the party a controlling majority in the Bundesrat and a *de facto* power-sharing with the Kohl government in Bonn. However, this also has posed the internally very controversial question regarding the extent to which the SPD should cooperate with the government and what alliances it should pursue. Within the left, the main inter-party relations have become those between the SPD and Bündnis 90/Greens (although the PDS's consolidation of its electoral support has complicated the relations among the opposition parties in the new Länder). As the SPD has emerged as the dominant party in many Länder and as the Greens have advanced in most of the western Länder, red-green majorities have become much more prevalent than in the past. Even though debate over alliance strategy continues within all parties in the post-unity period, there are three factors which account for the increasing viability of the red-green option.

First, and most obviously, as the FDP has lost its representation in most Länder, the party has almost vanished as a coalition partner for either Volkspartei.

Second, although factional struggles have plagued the Greens throughout their existence, the exit of hardline fundamentalists has cleared the air and has given an advantage to the pragmatic wing of the party. The increasingly mature and professional Greens have developed into a party interested in sharing power. This internal transformation has effectively altered their political style and made them more acceptable to the SPD, signifying a normalisation of relations. In the February 1995 Hessian Landtag victory, Green professionalism produced popular gains, which translated for the first time into a major portfolio (Justice). Three months later in North Rhine-Westphalia and Bremen as well as in Schleswig-Holstein, while the SPD slipped, the Greens emerged as clear winners and have become partners in government, though partners the SPD finds it difficult to deal with.

Third, the presence of the PDS on the left has made the Greens look less radical and therefore more acceptable to moderates in other parties.

In the new Länder, SPD efforts to build up both organisation and support have been made difficult by a revitalised PDS. With the left-wing electorate split between these two, the CDU has been able to stabilise its support in most of eastern Germany with the exception of Brandenburg and former East Berlin. The presence of the PDS has posed a strategic dilemma for the SPD: should exclusion or accommodation define future relations with the reformed communists? The Magdeburger Modell, that is, an SPD-Green minority government tolerated by the PDS (as developed in Saxony-Anhalt in June 1994) created divisions within the SPD and became a political target for the CDU/CSU's attacks on the SPD during and after the many elections in 1994.

Changing coalitional patterns in the Länder (as seen in Table 4.3) reflect some of the post-unity complexities of German party politics. Beyond the increasing viability of red-green alliances and the partial demise of the FDP, indications of change at the Land level have been seen in the transitory 'traffic-light' coalitions (*Ampelkoalitionen*) in Bremen and Brandenburg, in the revival of grand coalition politics in Berlin (1990), Baden-Württemberg (1992), Mecklenburg-West Pomerania and Thuringia (both 1994), and in the SPD-Green minority government in Saxony-Anhalt (Sturm, 1993).

Transition without Transformation

Historically, German party politics have been subject to periodic trauma through war, regime collapse and dictatorship. Unification, although positive in character, constitutes the most recent system shock. How well has the post-war party system survived the strains of unification? To what extent has the party system been reshaped? Several general patterns appear evident.

Even when acknowledging the indisputable reality of the dealignment phenomenon, what is striking in the recent German experience is the remarkable endurance of the party system as a whole. Although unification has brought disruptions and has provoked uncertainty to 'politics as usual' in the Federal Republic, the accession of the new Länder has involved a process of incorporation that, on balance, has enhanced the legitimacy of the German state, while simultaneously normalising its international status. Thus, despite the turmoil of unification, the party system has been contained within its institutional boundaries.

Table 4.3 Coalition patterns: stability/change in the Länder

Land (Bundesrat seats)	*Unity phase, 1990–94*	*Post-1994*
Bremen (3)	1991 Traffic light (SPD-FDP-Green)	1995 Grand Coalition (SPD-CDU)
Hamburg (3)	1993 SPD accord with STATT Party	1994 SPD
Schleswig-Holstein (4)	1988 SPD; 1992 SPD-Green	1996 SPD-Green reconfirmed
Lower Saxony (6)	1990 SPD-Green	1994 SPD
North Rhine-Westphalia (6)	1990 SPD	1995 SPD-Green
Hesse (5)	1991 SPD-Green	1995 SPD-Green reconfirmed
Rhine-Palatinate (4)	1991 SPD-FDP	1995 SPD-FDP reconfirmed
Baden-Württemberg (6)	1988 CDU; 1992 CDU-SPD Grand Coalition	1996 CDU-FDP
Bavaria (6)	1990 CSU	1994 CSU reconfirmed
Saarland (3)	1990 SPD	1994 SPD
Berlin (4)	1990 Grand Coalition (CDU-SPD)	1995 CDU-SPD continued
Mecklenburg-West Pomerania (4)	1990 CDU-FDP	1994 Grand Coalition (CDU-SPD)
Saxony-Anhalt (4)	1990 CDU-FDP	1994 SPD-Green minority (Magdeburger Modell)
Brandenburg (4)	1990 SPD-FDP-B90 (Traffic light)	1994 SPD
Thuringia (4)	1990 CDU-FDP	1994 Grand Coalition (CDU-SPD)
Saxony (4)	1990 CDU	1994 CDU reconfirmed

Sources: Sturm 1993, 123; Smith 1996, 68–9

The implantation of western party organisation and competition occurred without fundamental alteration in the character of the existing national party system, although some signs of change are more visible within the Länder.

Despite the collapse of the GDR, including the fundamental restructuring of its parties in the last days of this regime, since 1990 the changes in the electoral bases of support have remained remarkably incremental and modest in scope. Recent Bundestag elections have shown no great popular reversals. If anything, they have tended to demonstrate a consolidating effect, even allowing for a notable tendency towards non-voting (Feist, 1994).

In contrast to 1990, the 1994 Bundestag elections suggest that, whereas the two Volksparteien, CDU/CSU and SPD, have halted their downward slide, the more significant changes apply to the smaller parties. The Free Democrats have lost almost half of their 1990 vote and despite a recent modest recovery are still an endangered species. The Greens have recovered from a devastating defeat and appear positioned to displace the FDP as Germany's third force. The PDS has demonstrated surprising regional strength. Its emergence as a viable opposition force marks an exception to the general case for endurance, but it should also be remembered that this party is a residue of the past rather than an expression of some new dynamic force.

A certain regionalisation of party electorates is evident across the Länder. Comparisons of east–west voting patterns in the first five to six years of unity suggest little evidence of convergence. Here party competition appears to have crystallised into two broad patterns. In the old (western) Länder, the Greens have expanded their base of support, while the FDP electorate to crumble. In the new Länder, a distinctive three-party configuration has developed. Here both Bündnis 90/Greens and FDP have faded away, leaving the PDS as the only viable third party, but one that is unable to play the pivot role. Finally, even if it is not yet possible to decipher any emergent fundamental restructuring of the national party system and its electoral support, more extensive change could be in store if the social and economic problems of unified Germany remain unresolved. Ultimately, the endurance of the post-war governing model depends on a consolidation of existing party loyalties. Should dealignment persist and extend, the foundations of the established governing model would gradually erode. As the increasing complexity of coalitional options within the Länder attests, a loss of social anchoring and consequent fragmentation could presage the emergence of some new party balance.

REFERENCES

Chandler, W. (1993), 'The Christian Democrats: Responses to Unification', in Padgett. S., ed., pp. 129–46.

Chandler, W. and Siaroff, A. (1992), 'Party Government in Advanced Democracies', in Bakvis, H., ed., *Canadian Political Parties* (Toronto: Dundurn Press).

Clemens, C. (1993), 'Disquiet on the Eastern Front: The Christian Democratic Union in Germany's New Länder', *German Politics*, vol. 2, no. 2, pp. 200–23.

Dalton, R.J. (1992), 'Two German Electorates?', in Smith, G. et al., eds, pp. 52–76.

Eisenmann, P. and Hirscher, G., eds (1992), *Die Entwicklung der Volksparteien im vereinten Deutschland* (Bonn: Bonn Aktuell).

Falter, J. and Klein, M. (1994), 'Die Wähler der PDS bei der Bundestagswahl 1994', *Aus Politik und Zeitgeschichte*, B51/52, pp. 22–34.

Feist, U. (1994), *Die Macht der Nichtwähler* (Munich: Knaur).

Frankland, E.G. and Schoonmaker, D. (1993), *Between Protest and Power: the Green Party in Germany* (Boulder, Colo.: Westview Press).

Glaeßner, G.J. (1992), *Der Schwierige Weg zur Demokratie. Vom Ende der DDR zur Deutschen Einheit* (Opladen: Westdeutscher Verlag).

Hoffmann, G., 'Was wollen sie . . .', *Die Zeit*, 24 March 1995, p. 5.

Jung, M. and Roth, D. (1994), 'Kohls knappster Sieg', *Aus Politik und Zeitgeschichte*, B51/52, pp. 3–15.

König, K. (1993), 'Bureaucratic Integration by Elite Transfer: the Case of the Former GDR', *Governance*, vol. 6, no. 3, pp. 386–96.

Lapp, P.J. (1988), *Die Blockparteien im System der DDR* (Melle: Ernst Knoth).

Lepszy. N. (1993), 'Die Republikaner', in Hirscher, G., ed., *Repräsentative Demokratie und Politische Partizipation* (Munich: Hanns Seidel Stiftung), pp. 99–114.

Merkl, P. (1993), *German Unification in the European Context* (University Park, Pa.: Pennsylvania State University Press).

Niedermeyer, O. and Stöss, R., eds (1994), *Parteien und Wähler im Umbruch* (Opladen: Westdeutscher Verlag).

Padgett, S., ed. (1993), *Parties and Party Systems in the New Germany* (Aldershot: Dartmouth).

Padgett, S. (1993), 'The New German Electorate', in Padgett, ed., pp. 25–46.

Pappi, F.U. (1984), 'The West German Party System' in Bartolini, S. and Mair, P., eds, *Party Politics in Contemporary Western Europe* (London: Frank Cass), pp. 7–26.

Poguntke, T. and Schmitt-Beck, R., 'Still the Same with a New Name? Bündnis 90/die Grünen after the Fusion', *German Politics*, vol. 3, no. 1, pp. 91–113.

Richter, M. (1993), 'Exiting the GDR: Political Movements and Parties between Democratization and Westernization', in Hancock, D. and Welsh, H., eds, *German Unification: Process and Outcomes* (Boulder, Col.: Westview), pp. 93–138.

Roberts, G. (1993), 'The Free Democratic Party and the New Germany', in Padgett, S., ed., pp. 147–69.

Roth, D. (1993) '*Volksparteien* in Crisis? The Electoral Success of the Extreme Right in Context', *German Politics*, vol. 2, no. 1, pp. 1–20.

Søe, Ch. (1992), 'Germany's United Liberals: the Making and Testing of their Electoral Triumph', (unpublished) paper given at the annual conference of the German Studies Association of the USA in Minneapolis.

Schmidt, U. (1994), 'Transformation einer Volkspartei – die CDU im Prozess der deutschen Vereinigung', in Niedermeyer, O. and Stöss, R., eds, pp. 37–74.

Schultze, R.O. (1994), 'Aus Anlass des Superwahljahres: Nachdenken über

Konzepte und Ergebnisse der Wahlsoziologie', *Zeitschrift für Parlamentsfragen*, no. 3, pp. 472–93.
Silvia, S.J. (1993), 'Loosely Coupled Anarchy: the Fragmentation of the Left', in Padgett, S., ed., pp. 171–89.
Smith, G. (1996), 'The Party System at the Crossroads', in Smith, G., Paterson, W.E., Padgett, S., eds, *Developments in German Politics* 2 (London: Macmillan), pp. 55–75.
Smith, G. (1993), 'Dimensions of Change in the German Party System', in Padgett, S., ed., pp. 87–101.
Smith, G., Paterson, W.E., Merkl, P.H. and Padgett, S., eds (2nd edn, 1992), *Developments in German Politics* (London: Macmillan).
Smith, G. (3rd edn, 1986), *Democracy in Western Germany, Parties and Politics in the Federal Republic* (New York: Holmes & Meier).
Sturm, R. (1993), 'The Territorial Dimension of the New Party System', in Padgett, S., ed., pp. 103–25.
Tiemann, H. (1993), 'Die SPD in den neuen Bundesländern – Organisation und Mitglieder', *Zeitschrift für Parlamentsfragen*, vol. 24, no. 3, pp. 415–21.
Veen, H.J., Lepszy, N. and Mnich, P. (1993), *The Republikaner Party in Germany* (Westport, Conn.: Praeger).

5 German Federalism in the 1990s: On the Road to a 'Divided Polity'?

Charlie Jeffery

One of the central debates about contemporary Germany concerns the extent to which the established political structures and policy processes of the pre-unification Federal Republic can absorb the shock of incorporating the new Länder of the former GDR. Some, most recently Douglas Webber (1995), have identified a high capacity for adaptation in the structures and traditions of the 'old' Federal Republic and for accommodating the former GDR without undue disruption. Others, though, have argued that the incorporation of the former GDR will, over time, produce 'far-reaching' (Lehmbruch, 1990) or even 'fundamental' (Veen, 1993) change. The latter has been the case particularly in assessments of the impact of unification on the federal system in Germany. A number of the most prominent commentators on German federalism – Heidrun Abromeit (1992), Arthur Benz (1991), Jens Hesse and Wolfgang Renzsch (1990), Hartmut Klatt (1993), Fritz Scharpf (1990, 1994) and Roland Sturm (1991) among them – all predicted in the aftermath of unification that, on balance, the integration of the five new German Länder into the federal system would modify the relationships between Länder and central institutions in favour of the centre, in particular the federal government. Common to these assessments was the view that unless the federal system underwent far-reaching reform, the divergences of interest between eastern and western Länder thrown up by the problems of transformation in the east would predispose the eastern Länder to accept a high degree of federal intervention in their affairs. This would result in a net process of political centralisation and imply a 'permanent loss of substance' (Sturm and Jeffery, 1993) for a federal system designed to deconcentrate and disperse power between federal and Länder institutions.

This prospect of centralisation and 'loss of substance' was enhanced by a second challenge to the balance between the federal state and the Länder identified by these authors at the time of unification: the debates and negotiations on the future of European integration launched at the end of the 1980s which were to lead to the Maastricht treaty on European union. Since the 1950s, the European integration process had typically tended to tip the internal balance between federation and Länder in favour of the former, and now stood to compound the tendency to centralisation which unification was seen to have encouraged. As a result, Germany, according to Scharpf (1994: 55), was moving 'a big step closer' to becoming, in effect, a unitary state.

These are the issues which this contribution seeks to review more than half a decade on from unification. The chapter seeks to assess whether the situation observable in 1996/7 confirms, modifies or rejects the pessimistic prognoses made in the aftermath of unification in the early 1990s. Its first section identifies the inheritance of federal state–Länder relations bequeathed by the 'old' Federal Republic. Section two then sets out the dual challenge posed for the inherited procedures and balance of the federal system by unification and deepening European integration back in 1990–1 before examining the options which were discussed at the time for meeting those challenges. The third section discusses the way these challenges were (in the case of Europe) or were not (in the case of unification) met. The final section then seeks to exemplify the practical policy implications of these developments by focusing on the highly divergent roles eastern and western Länder have come to play in regional economic policy, traditionally a litmus test of the wider policy role performed by the Länder. This will lead to a conclusion which, building on Roland Sturm's image of a polity divided between old west and new east (Sturm, 1993a: 110), broadly reaffirms the pessimistic tide of opinion about the future of the federal system expressed in the immediate aftermath of unification.

THE INHERITANCE FROM THE 'OLD' FEDERAL REPUBLIC

The Structures of Cooperative Federalism

Any assessment of the impact of unification on the German federal system requires a brief review of the character and evolution of the pre-unification federal system, in particular of the way that the interrelationships of federation and Länder had been shaped prior to 1990. These interrelationships were highly distinctive. Neither the federal nor the Länder levels possessed a great range of exclusive fields of competence in which they were responsible both for the formulation and the implementation of legislation. Exclusive powers were held by the federation in foreign affairs and defence, citizenship and migration, currency, customs and trade, rail and air transport, post and telecommunications, some aspects of policing and internal security, and a number of other more minor areas. The exclusive powers of the Länder were restricted to aspects of educational, cultural and media policy, and policing. Other policy areas – the vast majority – were subject to some form of shared competence. In most cases the federal level had the power of legislation and the Länder (or more precisely the governments of the Länder) the corresponding power – in terms of financial and technical resources and personnel – to implement that legislation. Moreover, the federal level lacked extensive supervisory powers over the implementation process. Article 83 of the Basic Law awarded the Länder a high level of discretion in implementing federal law 'as matters of their own concern' and in the light of the particular circumstances which exist in each Land. This pattern of federal legislation combined with discretion in Länder implementation was one which became ever more pervasive after the establishment of the Federal Republic in 1949. Its pervasiveness was the result of a gradual but persistent process of constitutional and procedural adaptation which was justified by the requirement in Articles 72 and 106 of the Basic Law that 'living conditions' should be broadly 'uniform' across the Federal Republic, in other words that general national standards of legislation should normally apply across the Federal Republic as a whole.

The division between federal legislation and Länder implementation created a relationship of interdependence between the federal government and the Länder governments. Because the Länder governments possessed the lion's share of implementive responsibility, resources and expertise, their input and know-how was required by the federation in order for it to formulate effective legislation. As a result, they were increasingly drawn into the co-formulation of federal legislation alongside the main initiator of legislation, the federal government. This co-formulation role was facilitated and strengthened by the position of the Bundesrat, the legislative body of the Länder governments on the federal level, which acts as Germany's second parliamentary chamber alongside the directly elected Bundestag. The Bundesrat's legislative power is based on the absolute veto it possesses over all federal legislation deemed to affect the interests, duties or administrative procedures of the Länder (alongside a lesser, suspensive veto over all other federal legislation). Buttressed by supportive decisions of the federal constitutional court (Blair, 1991: 70–2), the Bundesrat was able to secure a broad definition of the scope of its absolute veto power to cover, by the 1980s, some sixty per cent of all federal laws. The scope of the absolute veto strengthened the imperative on the federal government to bind the Länder into the process of co-formulating federal legislation, and thus cemented the relationship of interdependence inherent in the division of legislative and implementive powers between federation and Länder.

An important variant on this pattern of interdependence was introduced by a series of constitutional reforms enacted in 1969. These redesignated former Länder responsibilities in the fields of university construction, regional economic development, agricultural structures and coastal preservation as the so-called 'joint tasks' of federation and Länder. These reforms were justified by a modified version of the principle of maintaining a uniformity of living conditions across the federation: the inability of the Länder otherwise to fund high expenditure policy fields which were important, according to a new Article 91a of the Basic Law, in the 'improvement of living conditions' of 'society as a whole'. Policy responsibility in these fields was subsequently exercised jointly by the federal government and the Länder governments, setting the seal on the emergence of what became known as 'cooperative' federalism in Germany: a relationship of interdependence in the making of nationally applicable legislative standards, which was conducted through an ongoing process of coordination between the two levels of government.

A crucial point to note at this stage is that for cooperative federalism to work effectively from a Länder perspective, the Länder had to be able to generate a strong collective voice in order to make their implementive expertise, their Bundesrat veto and their 'joint task' role count in framing national legislative standards. Cooperative federalism therefore required a high degree of solidarity among the Länder. An important mechanism for maintaining this solidarity was the Federal Republic's system of financial equalisation. Rudimentary financial equalisation mechanisms had existed since the foundation of the Federal Republic in 1949, but only reached their fully fledged form in reforms passed in 1969 to accompany the entrenchment of cooperative federalism through the 'joint tasks'. These established a highly complex equalisation system which redistributed resources according to fixed formulas both vertically (between federation and Länder) and horizontally (between more and less affluent Länder) and were designed to ensure that each Land had more or less the same level of income per head of population. This process of resource redistribution was supposed to guarantee that each of the Länder had both sufficient and similar levels of resources for the fulfilment of their various constitutional responsibilities and could not, as a result, be 'divided and ruled' by the additional financial incentives a hypothetically devious federation might offer to any Länder suffering temporary or structural financial weakness.

The Weakening of Cooperative Federalism in the 1980s

The 1969 financial equalisation reforms were designed to fine-tune the relatively minor disparities in resource base which existed in a then economically relatively homogeneous Länder community. This was a task they performed effectively enough in the 1970s. However, the long-term effects of the recessions of the 1970s and early 1980s had produced, by the mid-1980s, far wider economic disparities than the financial equalisation had been designed to bridge. These disparities reflected the growing economic divergence between a predominantly northern 'rust-belt' of Länder facing structural economic decline, particularly in heavy industry, and a group of predominantly southern 'blue chip' Länder which had proven successful in exploiting new technologies to ensure continuingly high levels of economic growth. Widening inter-Länder disparities placed tremendous pressure on the financial equalisation system. This, as noted above, was geared towards the equalisation of income per capita in each Land. It therefore provided (at the growing expense of the economically stronger Länder) compensation to the economically weaker for the declining income levels caused by economic decline. It however took no account of the higher expenditures per capita – on social security and structural adaptation policies – which economic decline generates. As a result, the economically weaker Länder increasingly felt that the financial equalisation system was no longer adequate for their needs and sought to extract higher contributions from the economically stronger Länder. The latter, understandably, were not keen to be penalised for their economic success and equally sought to limit their contributions to the equalisation mechanism.

The result was a partial breakdown of inter-Länder solidarity which led to a number of complaints about the (depending on the perspective) supposedly inadequate or over-generous redistributive effects of financial equalisation being brought by representatives of both groups of Länder before the federal constitutional court (Mackenstein and Jeffery, forthcoming). More importantly, the growing divergence of economic and financial interests threatened to create a lasting strategic divide in Länder priorities. The financially weaker Länder displayed an increasing propensity to look to the federation for financial assistance, for example in the 1988 Structural Aid Law and the discussions, led by Lower Saxony, which preceded it (Exler, 1993: 25–6). Some of the more affluent Länder – notably Baden-Württemberg, Bavaria and North Rhine-Westphalia – on the other hand sought in part to turn away from their obligations to their weaker counterparts – and more broadly from cooperative federalism – by devoting their greater resource base to supporting autonomous Länder policies, most notably in the field of regional economic policy (Götz, 1992; Jürgens and Krumbein, 1991).

The growing divergences of interest and strategy which became evident in the 1980s threatened to knock the established mechanisms of cooperative federalism out of equilibrium, opening up for the federation the opportunity to drive a wedge between the two groups of Länder and thus to impose its priorities on a fractious Länder community. The full effect of declining inter-Länder solidarity had not, however, become clear by the time unification emerged to dominate the political agenda in Germany. It did, though, point to a growing prospect of the Länder losing their ability to act collectively as a counterbalance to the federation. This prospect of a shift in the balance between federal state and the Länder in favour of the federation was significantly enhanced following the incorporation of the five new Länder of eastern Germany into the federal system in 1990.

THE CHALLENGES OF UNIFICATION AND EUROPEAN INTEGRATION I: THE PROBLEMS

The East–West Divide

The central problem faced by the new Länder after unification has been the economic near-collapse in the east which followed German economic and monetary union in July 1990 and the slow pace of economic reconstruction ever since (see Chapter 3 by C. Flockton in this book). The economic problems of transformation have inevitably posed, in their wake, immense financial problems for the new Länder. The low level of economic activity in the east means that the new Länder raise far fewer tax revenues per head of population than their western counterparts. At the same time, though, they face far higher expenditure burdens per capita. These reflect in part the costs of social dislocation and economic reconstruction – including massive outlays on improvements to the communications and environmental infrastructure

– thrown up by the transformation process. More broadly, though, they have also reflected the immense burden, imposed by the treaty of unification, of assuming the '*acquis fédéral*' accumulated by the western Länder over the forty years since the Federal Republic was founded in 1949 (Jeffery, 1995: 257).

The combination of low income and extraordinarily high expenditure created a tremendous potential for distributional conflict between east and west, far greater than that carried out over financial equalisation between economically stronger and weaker Länder in the west in the 1980s. In addition, the difficulties of the transformation process in a more general sense created policy priorities in the east vastly different from (and therefore difficult to coordinate with) those which had been developed in the west. The implications of such a deep east–west divide for a cooperative federal system in which the role of the Länder was primarily based on the generation of a collective voice *vis-à-vis* the federation were clear. Some kind of far-reaching reform was clearly necessary if the expanded and far more diverse Länder community of the 1990s was to retain an 'efficient' (Sturm and Jeffery, 1993: 174) role in German government in the future. As Fritz Scharpf (1994: 58) drily noted: 'German federalism can only win or lose in the coming years, but it cannot remain as it was before'.

Accommodating the New Länder: Options for Reform

A clear window of opportunity to seek reform was given by the terms of unification in 1990. Firstly, any immediate pressure on the financial equalisation system was avoided under the terms of the treaty on economic and monetary union of July 1990. This made provision for the establishment of a German Unity Fund, co-financed by federation and western Länder, which was intended as a substitute for the financial equalisation in the new Länder until the end of 1994, by when a more enduring solution to the equalisation problem was to be found. This solution on financial equalisation was supplemented by a provision in the October 1990 treaty of unification. It allowed for wider discussion of constitutional changes which were deemed necessary to shore up the federal system after unification. Together these provisions gave the Länder a breathing space to consider the options for reshaping and revitalising the federal system for the post-unification context.

The options for reform which were considered can be divided into three main groups – legislative competences, financial equalisation, and territorial reform. Significantly, they revealed two competing and to a large extent contradictory (Jeffery, 1995: 258–60) directions for reform, the one implying a revamping of the inherited structures and practices of cooperative federalism, the other a move away from cooperative federalism. The first group of reform proposals – by no means representing a consensus view across the Länder community (Jeffery, 1995: 261–2) – suggested a partial move away from the ethos of cooperative federalism and foresaw a change in the division of competences between federation and Länder. The prime concern here was to restore to the Länder more exclusive competences in part by returning the fields covered since 1969 by 'joint task' arrangements to Länder jurisdiction, and more generally by rejigging the distribution of legislative competences in the Basic Law in favour of the Länder. The aim was evidently for the Länder not to have all their eggs in the now rather dubious basket of cooperative federalism, but rather to break some of the ties of interdependence with the federation and move more generally towards the more autonomous policy role some had begun to develop in the later 1980s.

The reform discussion centred secondly on the possibility of reform to the financial equalisation process. A simple incorporation of the new Länder into the existing system would, quite simply, have ruined most of the western Länder, but would still not have addressed fully the extraordinary expenditure needs faced in the east (Peffekoven, 1990: 348). The only conceivable outcome would have been the financial dependence of both east and west on the federation. Some kind of rethink was therefore necessary which could take into account the expenditure side of the equation, while leaving all of the Länder in east and west in the position to carry out their constitutional responsibilities and maintain an effective balance between Bonn and the Länder. A wide variety of ideas were discussed (see Jeffery, 1995: 264–5) which focused in essence on two alternative approaches: the first supported the mooted move away from cooperative federalism proposing to grant the Länder the necessary fiscal autonomy to support a more autonomous legislative role; the second sought to shore up cooperative federalism by ploughing sufficient additional resources into the new Länder (either through the equalisation mechanism or through separate, targeted grants) to secure a viable basis for maintaining inter-Länder solidarity across the east–west divide.

Many of the suggestions on financial equalisation – of both variants – were accompanied by proposals for a territorial reform of Länder boundaries. Territorial reform had long been a topic for debate in the 'old' Federal Republic before 1990 (Sachverständigenkommission, 1973), where Länder boundaries had been set largely according to the military and diplomatic considerations of the post-war occupation zones rather than any 'technocratic' (Benz, 1993: 38–9) administrative or economic criteria. The debate flared up again after unification when the short-lived (and equally 'untechnocratic') Länder in the former Soviet zone of occupation, abolished in 1952, were revived as part of the unification process. The aim of the proponents of reform (for an overview of the debate, see *Presse- und Informationsamt der Bundesregierung*, 1993, vol. 7, section 1.2.2.2) was to create out of the haphazard, post-unification map of sixteen Länder of widely varying size, population and economic potential a new map of seven or eight Länder of broadly equivalent size, population and (in the case of the east, long-term) economic potential. A smaller number of larger Länder would, it was argued, have been administratively and economically more efficient and would have removed some of the controversies of financial redistribution. Such Länder would also – depending on the preferred viewpoint – have been easier to coordinate with one another *vis-à-vis* the federation and could therefore help to shore up cooperative federalism, or would have provided a more effective basis for a more autonomous Länder policy role and a move away from cooperative federalism.

The contours of the reform debate certainly suggested a widespread conviction in the Länder that, as Scharpf suggested, some form of decisive action needed to be taken to secure the future role of the Länder in the federal system. Importantly, though, it was also evident that no clear agreement existed as to how reform should be approached, with two broad alternative strategies emerging, the one committed to revitalising the inheritance of cooperative federalism in the new 1990s context, the other looking to a more autonomous Länder role distanced from the traditional pattern of interdependence with the federation. This divergence in responses to the challenge of unification had important implications for the outcome of the reform debate, and is discussed further below. First, though, attention is given to the simultaneous challenge posed at the start of the 1990s by the European integration process.

European Integration and German Federalism

The problem here was in some respects even more fundamental than that posed by unification. Rather than undermining the solidarity of the Länder in their dealings with the federation, the mechanics of the European integration process tended to tilt the broader, overall balance of relationships between federation and Länder to the detriment of the Länder. The central problem was that European policy was defined as a foreign policy responsibility and thus fell under the exclusive competence of the federation. This had two main implications. Firstly, the federal government possessed the sole right to transfer the sovereign powers of the Federal Republic to European institutions, including those powers hitherto exercised or co-exercised by the Länder. Such transfers of sovereignty, over which the Länder had no constitutionally guaranteed right of control, could therefore undercut the rights of the Länder in their remaining exclusive fields of legislative responsibility. Importantly, transfers could also undermine the implemention-based input of the Länder into any federal-level powers transferred to the European level where the Länder had previously played an interdependent role alongside the federation. Although the Länder are still responsible domestically for implementing the lion's share of legislation enacted at the European level, they generally have less discretion in doing so than in the implementation of federal laws, particularly where European regulations, with direct binding effect in the member states, are concerned (Bulmer and Paterson, 1987: 190). Adding insult to these injuries to Länder legislative and implementive competences, the federal government was then able, on the basis of its powers in foreign relations, and through its seat on the Council of Ministers, to help shape legislation in Brussels in areas of responsibility previously exercised by the Länder. Such transfers of sovereign powers often had the effect – normally *de facto* and rarely *de jure* – of amending the distribution of competences in the Basic Law to the detriment of the Länder and to the (indirect) benefit of the federal government.

The problems raised by this indirect shift of responsibilities from Länder to federation had been experienced, with uneven intensity, since the establishment of the European Coal and Steel Community in 1951. They became, however, especially severe from the mid-1980s, when the Single European Act produced the biggest integrative 'jump' since the Rome Treaties and also laid the groundwork for the further 'jump' which was ultimately set out at the Maastricht European Council at the end of 1991. Although the Länder had, over time, managed to accumulate a number of procedures which enabled them to be consulted and to comment on European level initiatives (Bulmer and Paterson, 1987: 191–5), they lacked full, constitutional rights of input into the European policy process either within the Federal Republic or in Brussels. The acceleration of integration in the 1980s created a new imperative to secure such rights. Initial progress was made in the discussions between the federal state and the Länder which accompanied the ratification of the Single European Act (Hrbek, 1991: 92–8). More importantly, though, the Single European Act raised a collective awareness among the Länder of the potential dangers posed to their position by a 'deepening' EC. The result was the preparation of a coherent, collective Länder strategy for meeting the challenges of European integration which could be – and, in negotiations surrounding the Maastricht treaty, was – mobilised to secure a fuller Länder role in the European integration process.

The strategy of the Länder was characterised by the employment of three different approaches (Jeffery, 1994: 7–25). The first sought to exert greater control over the federal government's European policy, more or less by subjecting this policy to the internal procedures of cooperative federalism. Here, the Länder were concerned on one level to restrict the federal government's right to transfer sovereign powers both where their exclusive powers of legislation and their cooperative powers of implementation were concerned. They were also concerned to establish a fuller role in the wider, day-to-day process of European policy-making within the Federal Republic. Secondly, they were concerned to enter into direct relations with European institutions in policy fields which fell domestically under their exclusive legislative competence. And thirdly, and as a rather more long-term aim, they hoped to generate and shape a wider subnational voice in the EC which could be brought to bear on European policy-making and lend a broader base of support across the EC for their European policy aims.

THE CHALLENGES OF UNIFICATION AND EUROPEAN INTEGRATION II: THE OUTCOMES

Unity and Success in the European Arena

Quite remarkably, the Länder made substantial progress on achieving all of these aims in the domestic and international negotiations and debates which surrounded the formulation and ratification of the Maastricht treaty. Two factors facilitated these achievements. First, compliance with the terms of the Maastricht treaty on EU citizenship and economic and monetary union required amendments to the Basic Law. Such amendments are subject to the support of two-thirds of the Bundesrat and gave the Länder, through the Bundesrat, a veto power over the ratification of the treaty. The federal government, as a prime mover behind Maastricht, was unwilling to countenance any threat of German non-ratification, and was therefore under pressure to make substantial concessions to the Länder. Secondly, and in order to make this veto power credible and operative, the Länder succeeded in maintaining a tightly united front throughout the Maastricht debates. This reflected the unifying force of the common, external threat posed by the deepening integration process and, as a result, the carefully coordinated preparation of European strategy which followed the Single European Act. The united front was, moreover, in no sense weakened by the incorporation of the new Länder, although this probably had more to do with the inexperience of the new Länder in European affairs and their preoccupation with, for them, far more pressing domestic problems than any deep-seated unity of European interest with their western counterparts.

As a result, Länder unity endured, and was mobilised to secure concessions in the treaty itself and a number of domestic constitutional changes. The latter were enshrined mainly in a new Article 23 of the Basic Law, whose effect was to break the exclusive power of the federation in European policy and to extend cooperative federalism arrangements to the domestic process of European policy-making. The Länder won, through the offices of the Bundesrat, a veto over all future transfers of sovereignty to the EU, thereby ensuring for themselves input into the disposal of both their exclusive powers and their implementive role in the federal legislative process. They also won full rights of information and consultation in day-to-day German European policy-making to the extent that where their legislative powers or their 'authorities and administrative procedures' are concerned, their word is normally 'decisive'. Again, this solution covers both their own exclusive legislative powers and their work in implementing federal legislation, and would seem to offer effective protection against what had previously been for them the detrimental and inaccessible mechanics of the European policy process.

Additional protection was given by the clauses inserted under Länder pressure into the Maastricht treaty. Most importantly and concretely, the Länder (working in coordination with the Belgian regions) were able to secure a right for representatives of the Länder to sit for the Federal Republic on the Council of Ministers in policy areas (mainly in education and culture) where the Länder hold responsibility domestically. Länder pressure was also decisive in securing the establishment of the Committee of the Regions in the treaty, and in shaping the final wording of the subsidiarity clause in Article 3b. Though neither was entirely what the Länder had envisaged (see Jeffery, 1994: 10–11), both offer direct or indirect opportunities for subnational input into the European integration process and can be seen in part at least as initial fruits of extensive efforts made by the Länder in the run-up to Maastricht to generate a wider subnational lobby in European affairs (cf. Jeffery, 1994: 9–10, 20–5).

By any standards, the negotiating efforts of the Länder in and around Maastricht were extremely successful and have done much to meet the challenge posed by European integration to the wider balance between the federal state and the Länder. The Länder have certainly created a favourable framework for asserting their interests in EU-related matters. The key to this success was undoubtedly the united front they were able to bring to bear on the Maastricht process. A note of caution has, however, to be entered at this point. It is not entirely clear that the Länder will be able to maintain their sense of unity over European policy in the coming years in the practice of using the new powers gained in and around Maastricht. This is a point the discussion returns to later. It is prefigured, though, in an examination of the less than satisfactory outcomes of the reform debate sparked by the domestic challenge of unification. Here, as the following discussion makes clear, the Länder were unable to maintain a unity of purpose, and as a result failed to confront effectively the problems raised by the east–west divide created by unification.

Division and Non-reform in the Domestic Arena

Put baldly, no significant progress was made in reshaping the federal system in the light of the challenges posed by unification. This scenario of non-reform applied equally to the ideas mooted for adjusting the distribution of legislative competences, for overhauling the financial equalisation system and for redrawing the territorial boundaries of the Länder. Territorial reform, after an initial flurry of debate in the Länder, soon emerged as a non-starter. Despite the vociferous advocacy of Hamburg, supported to greater or lesser extents by Schleswig-Holstein, Baden-Württemberg and North Rhine-Westphalia (*Presse- und Informationsamt der Bundesregierung*, 1993: vol. 7, sections 1.2.2.1 and 1.2.2.2) the reform impetus stumbled on three hurdles (Benz, 1993: 50–2; *Presse- und Informationsamt der Bundesregierung*, 1993: vol. 7, 4522). Firstly, reform would have been a protracted, expensive and, in the short term, administratively disruptive process. A consensus emerged, particularly in regard to the eastern Länder struggling anyway with the problems of administrative reconstruction, that territorial reform would be an unnecessary distraction. Secondly, there was considerable popular opposition in the east to any change in the boundaries of the Länder reconstituted in 1990. The reconstitution of the territorial units abolished by the GDR regime in 1952 was a heavily symbolic feature of the transition to democracy. Any move to redraw their boundaries (beyond the merger of Berlin and Brandenburg proposed in the treaty of unification but rejected by the two states' parliaments in early 1996) would have been an uncomfortable echo of what happened in 1952. And thirdly, there were also considerable popular attachments to existing Länder boundaries in the west, but, probably more importantly, extremely strong attachments to those boundaries among the politicians and civil servants of some of the Länder – Bremen, Saarland and Rhineland-Palatinate – whose positions were likely to be affected by any reform.

Equally, but for reasons indicative of the wider problems of the post-unification federal system, no far-reaching changes came to be instituted in the fields of financial equalisation and legislative competences. Rather, differences in priority and strategy among the various Länder cancelled each other out in reform discussions and produced 'fudges' which left the bases of the existing system untouched. Regarding financial equalisation, any considerations of the urgency of reform were submerged under narrow and short-term calculations of immediate financial self-interest. Especially instructive were the detailed proposals for reform put forward by a number of the western Länder – Hesse, Baden-Württemberg, Bavaria, Saarland and Bremen – during 1992. These, with the honourable exception of Bremen (but only just), managed to burden the home Land less than all the other competing proposals. In similar, self-interested vein, clear indications emerged towards the end of 1992 that the eastern Länder were preparing to cut a deal with the federal finance minister Theo Waigel which would be highly disadvantageous to the 'old' Länder (Jeffery, 1995: 265–6).

In the end though, the Länder ultimately managed to unite on – and eventually implement against federal opposition – probably the only course of action which could have produced consensus among them: a vast transfer of additional funds at the expense of the federation to prop up the existing system of financial equalisation. This 'solution' to the financial equalisation problem was of course trumpeted as a vital success for the Länder and for the federal system (Jeffery, 1995: 268). A more sober assessment would suggest otherwise. The equalisation system remains income-oriented, and takes no account of the differential expenditure needs faced in different parts of the Länder community, but in particular in the east. A continuation of income-based form of equalisation, given the experiences of the 1980s in the west, presages future conflict between stronger and weaker Länder around the east–west divide (especially in light of the difficulties in papering over the differences of perspective which emerged between the Länder during the 1992 reform debate).

A similar outcome of non-reform emerged in the debate over the distribution of legislative competences. The proposals to restore legislative competences to the Länder and move away from cooperative federal arrangements were championed by Hesse and Baden-Württemberg – the two Länder with the highest *per capita* incomes in the Federal Republic and, therefore, with the soundest financial basis to pursue a vision of enhanced legislative autonomy. Support for their proposals was conspicuously lukewarm among other western Länder, and was wholly absent in the east. The priority of the new Länder was, above all else, to haul up living standards towards the western level, not to extend, or even necessarily to preserve autonomy. This latter point was clearly illustrated by Gottfried Müller, President of the Thuringian Land Parliament, in May 1992:

> The enormous legislative catching-up process which the parliaments of the new Länder are having to undertake leaves us groaning too much under the weight of existing Länder competences to regret their diminution in favour of the federation. (Gemeinsame Verfassungskommission, 5. Sitzung, 7 May 1992: 9)

The net result of these conflicting viewpoints was a wholesale failure by the Länder to make use of the opportunity presented to them in the treaty of unification to reshape the constitutional bases of the federal system. Differences of perspective again largely cancelled each other out, leaving the inheritance from the 'old' Federal Republic broadly intact (Jeffery, 1995: 260–3). The Länder therefore remain bound into a distribution of competences in which the effectiveness of their input remains dependent on maintaining a high degree of inter-Länder solidarity *vis-à-vis* the federation.

What has emerged, in other words, is a no more than marginally modified version of the *status quo ante* of 1989. As was argued earlier, this *status quo* was increasingly inadequate to the task of maintaining an effective balance between federation and Länder before 1990. If that is the case, it is hardly likely to provide for such a balance in the far more difficult circumstances of the 1990s. The German federal system is thus highly vulnerable to the dangers which had become apparent at the end of the 1980s: a punctured solidarity, clashes of financial interest and, as a result, the opportunity for a divide-and-rule strategy of the federal government.

These dangers have been manifested in a number of ways since 1990. Firstly, the new Länder have demonstrated a readiness to meet separately from their western counterparts to formulate common positions on a range of policy areas where the transformation has placed particular burdens on them: for example school and university education, social policy, trade with eastern Europe and, in particular, budgetary matters (Sturm, 1993b: 122–4; 1994). The prominence of the latter budgetary issue has been, of course, a reflection of an economic and financial weakness, which has predisposed them, secondly, to accept high levels of federal intervention in their policy programmes in return for financial support. This was a pattern established in the period directly after unification, when agreement was reached for the federation to play a limited, transitional role in financing new Länder policy responsibilities in economic reconstruction (the 'joint task' for recovery in the east) and even in the core areas on exclusive Länder competence, education and culture. As Hartmut Klatt (1993: 10–12) warned at the time, the danger clearly existed, given the long-term economic weakness of the new Länder, that such support would become institutionalised and leave a persistent divergence in the quality of the relations between the federal state and the Länder in east and west. This seems to have become the case in key policy areas like higher education (Neuweiler, 1994: 11) and health-care provision. Concerning the latter, for example, Regine Hildebrandt (1994: 25) has noted that 'Land-level efforts alone will not be sufficient to meet fully the catch-up demand for hospital provision' in the east, with the result that the new Länder have negotiated a ten-year programme for co-financing hospital investment with the extensive support of federation and the health insurance funds. Extended and extensive support of this kind would seem to give substance to Klatt's warning. The scenario which exists is one, to follow Roland Sturm's (1993: 110) description, of 'policy-making for a divided polity', a scenario which runs counter to the ethos and procedures of the flawed inheritance with which the Länder, despite the reform debates of the early 1990s, are still lumbered.

THE DIVIDED POLITY: REGIONAL ECONOMIC POLICY IN THE NEW FEDERAL REPUBLIC

This scenario can be illustrated especially clearly in the field of regional economic policy. This is a field of policy which, for obvious reasons, is of central importance to the Länder. It is also a field which has tended to exemplify wider changes in the pattern of the relations between Bonn and the Länder in policy-making since 1949. In the early years of the Federal Republic, regional economic policy was considered to be one of the exclusive fields of competence of the Länder. By the 1960s, however, changing policy problems and priorities – notably the decline of key, often regionally concentrated industrial sectors of national importance and the then enthusiasm for 'Keynesian' forms of economic interventionism – had led to greater central government involvement in regional economic management. These changes were institutionalised in 1969 in a series of constitutional changes which, with a 'joint task' of the federation and the Länder for regional economic development, established a fully fledged cooperative federalism in regional economic policy. It also instituted a period of joint planning, implementation and financing of regional economic initiatives.

The 1980s saw, though, a renewed period of change which in part dismantled the cooperative structures of 1969. This renewed change had three main sources. The first reflected a growing disillusionment with the instruments of Keynesian economic management in Germany (as elsewhere) and saw the partial withdrawal of the federal government from its commitment to co-financing joint initiatives with the Länder in regional economic policy. The process of withdrawal was confirmed secondly by the deepening of European integration in the 1980s, in particular by the commitment to create a single, barrier-free European market by 1993. Under the rules of EC structural policies and of the Single Market programme, the instruments on which previous joint central-regional policies had been based – above all the subsidisation of declining industrial sectors – were progressively outlawed. The third force for change reflected the divergences of economic performance and interest which had emerged among the Länder in the 1980s. Disillusioned by some of the rigidities inherent in the 'joint task' arrangements, some of the more affluent Länder sought to place a new emphasis on a more autonomous and often innovative role in regional economic policy (Allen, 1989). While their less prosperous counterparts also sought to develop a similar, more autonomous policy role, their financial position gave them less leeway and left them to a large extent still reliant on the now downgraded 'joint task' structures (Scharpf, 1988: 250).

Before unification, therefore, a situation of growing differentiation in regional economic policy processes across the Länder had emerged which reflected a changing international economic environment and the strains placed on cooperative federalism by an increasingly divergent Länder community. The scale of regional economic policy differentiation has, however, been markedly widened since unification. In three key respects, a more or less separate set of policy structures has been established in the new Länder and starkly distinguishes east from west. The first concerned the role of the Treuhandanstalt, the federal agency set up to execute the restructuring, privatisation or liquidation of former GDR state enterprises, a series of functions obviously of crucial importance for the regional economy. Despite this crucial importance, the new Länder made relatively little impact on the work of the Treuhand (or of its successor institutions, now that the main task of the Treuhand, industrial privatisation, has been completed: the Treuhandanstalt was wound up in late 1994).

There exist a number of reasons for this. Most fundamentally, the Länder were excluded from a full role in the Treuhandanstalt simply because it and its remit were set up before they were established themselves in 1990 (although they did subsequently receive places on the Treuhand board). With notable exceptions (such as the Saxon Atlas-Project to save 'regionally significant firms' with good medium-term profitability prospects (Anderson, 1995)), the Länder failed to push for a full role (Seibel, 1994: 10–13). On the one hand, their bargaining hand was weakened because of the vast sums the federal government was pouring into industrial subsidies, which, of course, they did not want to (and indeed could not conceivably) take over. On the other, they were reluctant to shoulder co-responsibility for the unpopular decisions the Treuhand made concerning restructuring and, in particular, liquidation. The net result has been, and remains, a degree of federal involvement in the management of the regional economy vastly out of step with the much more limited federal role in the west.

An equivalent situation exists, secondly, with regard to the 'joint task' of the federation and the Länder in regional economic development. As noted above, the scope of the 'joint task' in the west was narrowed in the 1980s, and has been cut back further since unification. These latest cut-backs have, however, been used to free resources for the east, where the 'joint task' has been revamped and represents a major tool of economic regeneration and industrial subsidy (Anderson,

1995). Taken together with *ad hoc* federation-new-Länder initiatives like the 'joint task' for recovery in the east (a two-year DM 24 billion programme of investment in infrastructure, housing and urban development begun in 1991) an extraordinary east–west policy divide has emerged: on the one hand, the western Länder have opted – or, increasingly, have been forced – to develop the autonomous form of regional economic policy initiative noted above; and on the other, the eastern Länder are bound tightly into a policy process between Bonn and the Länder funded largely by the federation.

The same pattern can be identified, thirdly, with regard to the EU Structural Fund, whose primary function is to support regional economic development. The western Länder have never achieved Objective One status for structural funding, have never received large amounts from the European purse, and have seen those amounts reduced since unification. The new Länder on the other hand have blanket and well-funded Objective One status and are as a result tightly bound into a structural funding process involving close coordination with the federal government (through the structures of the 'joint task' in regional economic development) and the European Commission (Benz, 1996; Anderson, 1995).

CONCLUSIONS

This scenario of divided policy-making in regional economic policy, with the new Länder bound tightly to the federal government and the old Länder left largely to go their own way, may be something of an extreme case, bound up as it is with the overriding imperative of economic reconstruction. But, taken with the other examples briefly mentioned earlier, it does seem indicative of a wider schism between east and west and of a tendency of the eastern Länder to accept the support and intervention of the federal government in their affairs.

The reason for stressing this is not to castigate the eastern Länder for their lack of solidarity; they have in part been forced to resort to the federal government by the unwillingness of the western Länder to make sacrifices on their behalf. The point rather is to stress the inadequacies of the present unreformed structure of German federalism in maintaining the kind of balance between the federal state and the Länder which existed, albeit under increasing strain, before 1990. As Scharpf implied in the aftermath of unification, the worst-case scenario for the federal system would be for its structures to remain as they were before. This does not mean, as Scharpf also implied, that one should talk of a 'unitary state'. Nevertheless, the stark divisions which exist between east and west, and which suggest the emergence of a form of 'divided polity', do seem to imply an upward movement in the balance of power between Bonn and the Länder in favour of the federation which will not easily be reversed.

With this in mind, it is worth making a final comment on the new European policy powers won by the Länder in and around Maastricht. As was stressed earlier, these powers provide an impressive framework for Länder input into European policy-making which, on paper, have eliminated the disadvantages which have traditionally accrued to the Länder because of the peculiar, nation-state-focused mechanics of the European integration process.

The thrust of the above discussion suggests, however, that the Länder may not be able to use those powers to their full extent. As in the cooperative federalism of domestic politics, they will only be fully effective if the Länder can generate a solid, collective voice. It is a moot point whether they can attain such a voice. In the European arena as in the domestic arena, there are clear differences of interest between Länder in east and west. The driving interest of the western Länder has been to stop the drift of competences to Brussels and to have a greater say in how European policy is made. Given their present economic and financial situation, the driving European interest of the eastern Länder is to secure high levels of structural funding. It is not clear that these differences of interest are easily reconcilable. This may have something to do with the rather muted voice of the Länder regarding the Maastricht review, the intergovernmental conference which met in 1996–7 to evaluate the Maastricht Treaty. This compared poorly with the clear and vocal strategy they developed for Maastricht in 1991.

These comments lend weight to a pessimistic conclusion. The east–west divide bequeathed by the unification process in 1990 has not only undermined the sense of unity necessary for the assertion of collective Länder interests in an unreformed domestic federal structure. It also threatens to create weighty obstacles for the Länder in their pursuit of a fuller European policy role. Germany is, it seems, at the expense of the Länder, firmly on the road to a divided polity.

REFERENCES

Abromeit, H. (1992), *Der verkappte Einheitsstaat* (Opladen: Leske & Budrich).

Allen, C. (1989), 'Corporatism and Regional Economic Policies in the Federal Republic of Germany: The "Meso" Politics of Industrial Adjustment', *Publius: Journal of Federalism*, vol. 19, pp. 147–64.

Anderson, J. (1995), 'Regional Policy and Politics in a United Germany: The Institutional Foundations of Continuity', *Journal of Regional and Federal Studies*, vol. 5.

Benz, A. (1991), 'Perspektiven des Föderalismus in Deutschland', *Die öffentliche Verwaltung*, no. 14, pp. 586–98.

Benz, A. (1993), 'Redrawing the Map? The Question of Territorial Reform in the Federal Republic', in Jeffery, C. and Sturm, R., eds, pp. 38–57.

Benz, A. (1997), 'Rediscovering Regional Economic Policy: New Opportunities for the Länder in the 1990s', in C. Jeffery, ed. [forthcoming].

Blair, P. (1991), 'Federalism, Legalism and Political Reality: The Record of the Federal Constitutional Court', in Jeffery, C. and Savigear, P., eds, pp. 63–83.

Bulmer, S. and Paterson, W. (1987), *The Federal Republic of Germany and the European Community* (London: Allen & Unwin).

Exler, U. (1993), 'Financing German Federalism: Problems of Financial Equalisation in the Unification Process', in Jeffery, C. and Sturm, R., eds, pp. 22–37.

Gemeinsame Verfassungskommission, ed. (1992), *Sitzungsprotokolle* (Bonn: unpublished official papers).

Götz, K. (1992), *Intergovernmental Relations and State Discretion: The Case of Science and Technology Policy in Germany* (Baden-Baden: Nomos).

Hesse, J-J. and Renzsch, W. (1990), 'Zehn Thesen zur Entwicklung und Lage des deutschen Föderalismus', *Staatswissenschaften und Staatspraxis*, no. 4, pp. 562–78.

Hildebrandt, R. (1994), 'Die Einrichtungen des Gesundheits- und Sozialwesens in der DDR und in den neuen Bundesländern', *Aus Politik und Zeitgeschichte*, no. B3/94, pp. 15–25.

Hrbek, R. (1991), 'German Federalism and the Challenge of European Integration', in Jeffery, C. and Savigear, P., eds, pp. 84–102.

Jeffery, C. and Savigear, P., eds (1991), *German Federalism Today* (Leicester: Leicester University Press).

Jeffery, C. and Sturm, R., eds (1993), *Federalism, Unification and European Integration* (London: Frank Cass).

Jeffery, C. (1994), 'The Länder Strike Back: Structures and Procedures of European Integration Policy-Making in the German Federal System', *University of Leicester Discussion Papers in Federal Studies*, no. FS94/4.

Jeffery, C. (1995), 'The Non-Reform of the German Federal System after Unification', *West European Politics*, vol. 18, no. 2, pp. 252–72.

Jeffery, C. (1997), *German Federalism in the 1990s: The Challenges of Unification* (London: Leicester University Press), [forthcoming].

Jürgens, U., Krumbein, W. (1991), *Industriepolitische Strategien. Bundesländer im Vergleich* (Berlin: Edition Sigma).

Klatt, H. (1993), 'German Unification and the Federal System', in Jeffery, C. and Sturm, R., eds, pp. 1–21.

Lehmbruch, G. (1990), 'Die improvisierte Vereinigung: Die dritte deutsche Republik', *Leviathan*, vol. 18, no. 4, pp. 462–86.

Mackenstein, H. and Jeffery, C. (1997), 'Financing German Federalism: Financial Equalisation in the 1990s', in Jeffery, C., ed. [forthcoming]

Neuweiler, G. (1994), Das gesamtdeutsche Haus für Forschung und Lehre', *Aus Politik und Zeitgeschichte*, no. B25/94, pp. 3–11.

Peffekoven, R. (1990), 'Finanzausgleich im vereinten Deutschland', *Wirtschaftsdienst*, no. 8, pp. 346–52.

Presse- und Informationsamt der Bundesregierung, ed. (1993), *Deutschland 1990*, 99 volumes (Bonn: Presse- und Informationsamt der Bundesregierung).

Sachverständigenkommission für die Neugliederung des Bundesgebiets, ed. (1973), *Vorschläge für die Neugliederung des Bundesgebiets gemäß Artikel 29 des Grundgesetzes* (Bonn: Bundesministerium des Inneren).

Scharpf, F. (1988), 'The Joint-Decision Trap: Lessons from German Federalism for European Integration', *Public Administration*, vol. 66, pp. 239–78.

Scharpf, F. (1990), 'Föderalismus an der Wegscheide: eine Replik', *Staatswissenschaften und Staatspraxis*, no. 4, pp. 579–87.

Scharpf, F. (1994), *Optionen des Föderalismus in Deutschland* (Frankfurt: Campus).

Seibel, W. (1994), 'Das zentralistische Erbe: Die institutionelle Entwicklung der Treuhandanstalt und die Nachhaltigkeit ihrer Auswirkungen auf die bundesstaatlichen Verfassungsstrukturen', *Aus Politik und Zeitgeschichte*, no. B43-44/94, pp. 3–13.

Sturm, R. (1991), 'Die Zukunft des deutschen Föderalismus', in Liebert, U. and Merkel, W., eds, *Die Politik zur deutschen Einheit* (Opladen: Leske & Budrich), pp. 161–82.

Sturm, R. (1993a), 'Government at the Centre', in Smith, G., Paterson, W., Merkl, P., Padgett, S., eds, *Developments in German Politics* (London: Macmillan), pp. 103–18.

Sturm, R. (1993b), 'The Industrial Policies of the Länder and European Integration', in Jeffery, C. and Sturm, R., eds, pp. 102–18.

Sturm, R. (1994), 'The Constitution under Pressure? Emerging Asymmetrical Federalism in Germany', unpublished paper presented to the XVIth IPSA World Congress, Berlin, August 1994.

Sturm, R. and Jeffery, C. (1993), 'German Unity, European Integration and the Future of the Federal System: Revival or Permanent Loss of Substance?', in Sturm, R. and Jeffery, C., eds, pp. 164–76.

Veen, H-J. (1993), 'The First All-German Elections', in Padgett, S., ed., *Parties and Party Systems in the New Germany* (Aldershot: Dartmouth), pp. 47–86.

Webber, D. (1995), 'The Second Coming of the Bonn Republic', *University of Birmingham Institute for German Studies Discussion Papers*, no. 95/1.

6 Racial Exclusionism in the New Germany[1]

Panikos Panayi

As artificial ethnic entities, nation-states tend to exclude the groups and individuals who do not conform to their rules of citizenship. The methods of exclusion vary from one state to another and depend upon the national traditions existing within an individual nation-state and the system of government. Obviously, a dictatorship like the one which existed in Germany between 1933 and 1945 will behave in a much more extreme way than any contemporary European liberal democracy. The methods of exclusion in the former were ruthless and brutal, while those employed by the latter are of course far more 'genteel'. Nevertheless, while the methods of discrimination or persecution clearly differ from one country to another and from one system of government to another, all nation-states are ultimately in the same business: the inclusion of those who meet the necessary ethnic criteria for citizenship and the exclusion of those who do not.

In post-war European liberal democracies the methods of exclusion have been basically consistent throughout the continent and have involved both governments and populace with the assistance of an omnipresent, and perhaps omnipotent, media which popularises views sometimes also held in academic circles.

It is useful to distinguish between official and unofficial forms of anti-foreigner prejudice in modern liberal democracies. Beginning with the former, these are basically three in number. They can be described as structural components of the liberal-democratic nation-state. The first of these elements consists of immigration controls, whose existence means that individuals not born within a country are not offered the economic, social and political benefits to which the native population is entitled. The second structural component consists of nationality laws, which, again, are designed to exclude foreigners from the benefits enjoyed by natives. The final element in the structural racism of the nation-state consists of the forces of law and order in the form of the police and judiciary which implement the measures outlined above.

Popular racism in liberal democracies also manifests itself in a variety of unofficial ways. The most potent of these includes the development of pressure groups and extreme parties. In post-war Europe these have not been able to seize power but, instead, have forced the ruling parties, terrified of losing votes, to adopt some of their policies, albeit in an assimilated form. Racial violence might be seen as the most potent manifestation of unofficial hostility varying, in liberal democracies, from attacks upon individuals to nationwide riots.

The official and unofficial manifestations of racism are not constant and are determined by short-term factors which can be narrowed down to three in post-war Europe. First, political changes, especially in the nature or system of government; second, economic downturns; and, third, large influxes of immigrants who inevitably receive attention in the racialised discourse which controls politics in the nation-state.

GERMAN ATTITUDES TOWARDS IMMIGRANTS IN HISTORICAL PERSPECTIVE

Since unification in 1990, Germany has experienced all of the above short-term changes, and this has inevitably meant that the position of immigrants has deteriorated. Nevertheless, in the case of Germany, historical traditions are important. Any study of race in contemporary Germany cannot ignore the historical situation of minorities within the country, not only during the Nazi period, but also in the late nineteenth and early twentieth century and continuing after the Second World War.

Various factors have been constant. First, the importation of foreign labour, which began at the end of the nineteenth century, by which time Germany had changed from being a net exporter to a net importer of population (Bade, 1983). In all subsequent periods of economic growth in German history, labour has been imported from a variety of countries (Dohse, 1981). During the Nazi period the newcomers originated in eastern Europe and involved as many as twelve million people in the exploitative labour system established during the Second World War (Homze, 1967). In the early post-war years the labour shortage was met by Germans from eastern Europe. They consisted of refugees who had fled the Russian advance at the end of the war as well as ethnic Germans affected by boundary changes. Together they represented approximately 20 per cent of the population of the Federal Republic in 1960 (Bethlehem, 1982; Lehmann, 1990).

When this source of labour was no longer available, especially after the construction of the Berlin Wall in 1961, the Federal Republic had to turn to new areas of Europe. Beginning with Italy in 1955, the German government concluded agreements with southern European countries which, by the late 1960s, included Spain, Greece, Turkey, Portugal and Yugoslavia. This process was halted during the economic recession caused by the oil crisis of 1973–5 (Bade, 1992b), but by 1989 the foreign population of Germany had reached 4.9 million (Bade, 1992a: 1983).

By this time, however, this figure also included an uninvited component in the country – asylum seekers. Due to the comparatively liberal German asylum laws their numbers had begun to grow dramatically by the end of the 1980s. As a result of the decay of eastern European communism and the loosening of its shackles, vast numbers of ethnic Germans from eastern Europe began to enter the country (Bade, 1992: 198, 199; Kemper, 1993).

The non-German population developed many of the characteristics of immigrants in a liberal democracy. They resided predominantly in urban geographical concentrations, usually in the more deprived areas of cities, including West Berlin, Cologne, Frankfurt and Stuttgart (Blotevogel et al., 1993: 89–96). The overwhelming majority of migrant workers were employed in unskilled and low-skilled jobs, involving heavy, dirty and dangerous work, especially in iron and other metallurgical production, as well as in the construction industry (Castles et al., 1987: 127–38, 159–89).

All non-German groupings who made their way to the Federal Republic have attempted to re-create their original ethnic environment in their new country of residence. Religion has played an important role in this process so that by 1987 a city such as Duisburg had thirty mosques. In addition, cultural organisations have been created at both a local and national level among most groups. Similarly, countless newspapers were founded for the newcomers in post-war West Germany. With the increase in religious refugees, political activity has become important, a good example being the Kurds (Nielsen, 1992: 29–33; Schlaffke and von Voss, 1992: 98–9, 159–64).

Some integration has also taken place. This has partly occurred through education of second generation immigrants in German schools, although the children of immigrants have a lower success rate at school than the children of Germans (Faist, 1993). Integration is more clearly indicated in the incidence of marriages between Germans and non-Germans, which in 1990 made up 9.6 per cent of all such unions in the country (Schumacher, 1992: 144).

Just as constant as the presence of migrant and refugee communities in the Federal Republic of Germany has been the hostility towards them. The remainder of this article will focus upon three indicators of racial exclusionism: unofficial racial violence; the existence of extreme right pressure groups; and the use of official immigration control and nationality legislation by the German state.

Racial violence, endemic in the nation-state, began to develop in Germany during the 1920s with the rise of violent anti-semitism, connected especially with the Nazis. After 1933 the extermination of European Jewry became the central goal of the National-socialist state (Dawidowicz, 1987). In the liberal-democratic Federal Republic the manifestations of racial violence have been far milder, reaching a peak in 1959–60 with a wave of anti-semitic daubing of Jewish targets (Dudek and Jaschke, 1984: 266–7). Attacks upon foreigners began to develop during the 1980s, connected with both football supporters and extreme right groupings (Husbands, 1991). By the end of the 1980s violence against foreigners was also not uncommon in East Germany (Ammer, 1988).

Since the end of the Second World War overtly racist political parties have always been present and obtained votes, often on a significant level, in the Federal Republic. In the late 1940s and early 1950s the two major groupings consisted of the Socialist Reichs Party and the German Reichs Party, the former of which obtained 11 per cent of the vote in the Lower Saxony Landtag election in 1951 only to be banned in 1952. The German Reichs Party had less support and in 1964 reconstituted itself into the National Democratic Party (NPD), the major right-wing force during the 1960s. The NPD's success reached a highpoint in 1969 when it secured 4.3 per cent of the vote in the general election with a peak membership of 28 000. The 1970s 'were a dismal period for the far right in Germany', a situation which continued into much of the 1980s (Childs, 1991). However, apart from the major groupings mentioned above, one should also consider the countless smaller organisations which have always existed (Hirsch, 1989: 314–39).

Until the 1980s the main manifestations of official hostility to immigrants consisted of labour importation and nationality laws. The significance of the former basically lies in the fact that German governments simply viewed migrant workers as a commodity which could be imported during times of economic growth, as in the 1950s and most of the 1960s, and expelled in a time of economic recession, such as happened to a limited extent in 1966. Although this policy was not re-adopted during the recession of the mid-1970s, labour recruitment stopped (Bendix, 1990: 10–87).

Nationality laws, meanwhile, have operated on the basis of *jus sanguinis* rather than *jus solis*, meaning that, unlike the classic liberal democracies of Britain and the USA, nationality is determined, literally, by blood, or the ability to prove German origin, rather than place of birth. This situation has remained constant since the formation of the German Empire at the end of the nineteenth century. It originates in the lack of a German state before this time, which meant that birth within territorial boundaries was less important than ability to prove German origin. Nevertheless, because of the constant presence of *Auslandsdeutsche* throughout German history, *jus sanguinis* has remained the constant principle. Two basic pieces of legislation have upheld this situation. First, the Nationality Law of 1913 and, second, the federal constitution, especially article 116 which recognises a German citizen as a person or his/her descendants who held German nationality according to the German borders of 1937 or refugees or deportees with German ethnicity (Wilpert, 1991; Brubaker, 1992; Hoffman, 1993; Aziz, 1992).

The main consequence of the above is that aliens and their descendants are deprived of basic civil rights such as voting in elections while those of German ethnicity, who, in some cases, trace their German origins back to the twelfth century, can enjoy these priviliges if they move to Germany. Because of the complications involved in obtaining German nationality, it has been difficult for non-Germans to improve their position (Hoffman, 1993: 88–91, 139–40; Aziz, 1992; Steger and Wagner, 1993: 67)

One aspect of the Federal Republic which would suggest a more open and tolerant attitude towards aliens consisted of the old Article 16 of the federal constitution. Section 2, sentence 2, declared that 'Political refugees enjoy the right to asylum' (Steger and Wagner, 1993: 59; Münch, 1993: 13–37). During the explosion of potent racism which occurred after unification, the article was viewed by the press and conservative political opinion as one of the causes of the upsurge because of the ever-increasing number of asylum seekers who were entering Germany.

However, the causes of the growing attention which focused upon race in the new Germany are far more complicated than this and attention should be drawn to a complexity of factors which considers historical traditions, socio-economic conditions, and political causation. Historical traditions can simply be viewed as an underlying factor, but, to use the currently popular historical jargon, one must question whether the 'memory' of Nazism can ever be eradicated from German national consciousness. Moreover, racial exclusionism has guided the history of Germany in the same way as it has done in all other nation-states. It has always been a core ideology.

THE UNIFICATION CRISIS

What was needed for the demons of the Nazi past to make another appearance was a short-term crisis which worked against the background of the milder forms of racism characteristic of the German nation-state. The crisis took the form of unification, which had both socio-economic and political effects. Beginning with the former, unification had serious consequences upon economic production and employment, especially in the east, which, before the collapse of the eastern bloc, claimed to have eradicated all unemployment. Therefore, between 1990 and 1993 the unemployment rate in the new Länder increased from zero to 17 per cent in January 1994. In addition, there also existed 'hidden unemployment' in the form of people engaged in job creation programmes financed by the government. The western German economy also went into recession. While the change was not as dramatic as in the east, an increase in unemployment from 6.2 per cent in 1990 to 8.8 per cent in January 1994 took place. Moreover, the bill to restructure the eastern half of Germany, which included cuts in public spending had negative effects (Flockton, 1993; OECD, 1993; *Süddeutsche Zeitung*, 9 February 1994).

The second socio-economic factor which led to the upsurge of hatred consisted of the mass migrations into Germany since the end of the Cold War, a process which, as mentioned above, actually began to develop in the increasingly tolerant last years of many east European regimes. Between 1983 and 1992, 1 397 640 asylum seekers entered the country, together with 1 556 060 ethnic Germans (Press and Information Office of the FRG, 1993: 77). Furthermore, in 1992 Germany received 79 per cent of all applications for asylum in EC countries (*Guardian*, 1 June 1993). These totals have to be contextualised by considering the history of population movements into the Federal Republic since 1945. Although Germans never perceived their country as one of mass immigration, this was in fact the case as West Germany accepted, as we have seen, a combination of eastern German refugees, ethnic Germans, foreign workers and refugees who were fundamental to the reindustrialisation of the West German economy (Bade, 1983: 59–81). As a consequence one third of the population of the

Federal Republic in 1989 was the result of immigration while in the period 1945–80 the Federal Republic admitted 17 million newcomers compared with just 11 million admitted in the USA (Hoffman, 1993: 28-9).

Despite this important tradition of immigration into the Federal Republic, links can clearly be drawn between the rise of racism and the recent influx of newcomers into Germany. In general, however, the rise in racism and increased immigration need not necessarily be connected, unless the latter occurs on a large scale during a time of crisis. This would differentiate the early 1990s newcomers from those who entered the country during much of the period from the late 1940s until the early 1970s. The latter were needed for the reindustrialisation of Germany, and therefore fitted into the classic post-war European pattern of the importation of foreign workers during times of economic growth and a reduction of foreign labour during times of economic recession (Castles, et al., 1987). The perceived problem for the German government as well as for the press and the public in the first half of the 1990s was that they all felt powerless to halt the influx, as it had been possible to do in 1966 and 1973 as far as foreign workers were concerned. Consequently, obsessive attention focused upon the assumed abuse of Germany's asylum laws by so-called 'economic immigrants', although, in reality, it is very difficult to distinguish between an economic and a political refugee. Therefore, asylum seekers became scapegoats for the economic recession in Germany. The link between public and media attention to this issue and the outbreaks of racial violence is striking. Newspapers and periodicals carrying accounts of racial violence often also printed details about the abuse of the asylum laws.[2]

However, there are also more political reasons for the growth of potent racism and again one can discern several causes. The most important is simply the enormous significance of unification and the end of the Cold War. The latter had a global impact in releasing pre-1945 nationalist tensions. In the German case, simply the act of unification has given a boost both to virulent nationalism and potent xenophobia. Returning to historical traditions, the situation in Germany in the late twentieth century resembles the period of time which followed the original unification in 1871 when the euphoria over this event also led to a rise in popular anti-semitism (Dawidowicz, 1987: 62–75).

The most potent manifestation of the rise of racism following unification came in the form of racist violence. This violence has basically taken two forms. Firstly, small-scale attacks which include homicides, arsons, bombings, assaults, and property damage. They have affected the entire country. Secondly, large-scale riots, which have been small in number and have only affected eastern Germany.

The year of unification, 1990, actually represented a quiet twelve months as far as racial violence was concerned, with a fall in the number of attacks carried out by right-wing extremists compared with the previous year (Bundesministerium des Innern [BMI], 1990: 124). However, a dramatic increase occurred in 1991 with a rise, compared with the previous year, from 270 to 1483 in the number of right-wing offences – attacks both against people or their property – which resulted in three deaths (BMI, 1992: 75). Most of the incidents took place between August and October. Before the late summer incidents had occurred in a series of locations including Bad Krotzingen-Schlatt in Baden-Württemberg; Eisenhüttenstadt near the Polish border; East Berlin; Pirna near Dresden; Grossenhain in Saxony; and Gelsenkirchen in the west of the country (BMI, 1992: 79–80; *Searchlight*, May 1991; ibid., July 1991: 15–16; ibid., October 1991: 15).

The most serious incident occurred in Hoyerswerda in Saxony, which had developed during the 1960s and 1970s into 'an industrial barracks' of 70 000 people dependent for its economic existence upon a nearby electric power plant and brown coal mines. Following unification the unemployment rate rose, remaining at 7 per cent and rising by the autumn of 1991. Social facilities were extremely limited. A few hundred foreign workers lived in the town together with 230 asylum seekers. After an increase in hostility towards these two groups during the summer, a full-scale riot broke out between 17 and 22 September involving hundreds of local residents, together with skinheads who had made their way to the town from other locations in eastern Germany (Hockenos, 1993: 23–5; *Searchlight*, November 1991: 10; *Spiegel*, 30 September 1991: 48–51; *Die Zeit*, 26 September 1991; *Stern*, 2 October 1991: 24).

Even as the events in Hoyerswerda unfolded, further isolated attacks took place all over Germany. Between 18 and 23 September the most significant incident occurred in Saarlouis where a Molotov cocktail thrown into a refugee hostel burnt to death a Ghanaian and severely injured two Nigerians (Jürgs and Duve, 1992: 109–12). Attacks continued on a nationwide scale, unabated and uncontrolled, reaching a crescendo in the week following the day of the anniversary of German unification. It is difficult to offer a full explanation for the events in Germany in the first two weeks of October 1991 when frequent attacks on foreigners were taking place. Morning radio news broadcasts often began by listing the attacks which had occurred the previous evening. The violence did not subside until mid-October. The 490 attacks in that month fell to less than 200 in November and under 100 in December (BMI, 1992: 75).

The high number of attacks carried out by extremists in Germany during 1991 increased even further during the following year, from the total of 1483 for that year to a new height of 2584 in 1992, an increase of 74 per cent. Just as notable was the rise in the number of racist murders from three in 1991 to 17 in the following year. However, only one month, September, surpassed the number of attacks which had occurred in the previous October, with 536 in the former and 488 in the latter.

The pattern for the course of 1992 was similar to that of 1991, with a relatively small number of attacks until the autumn, although at a higher level, followed by an explosion. In the case of 1992 this occurred one month earlier, sparked off by a similar event to the one in Hoyerswerda, which, on this occasion, took place in Rostock at the end of August (BMI, 1993: 69–71).

The city of Rostock faced an economic crisis following unification as about fifty per cent of the working population had lost their jobs. Discontent began to focus on an asylum home in the city throughout the summer and violence exploded against it, involving thousands of local residents and travelling neo-Nazis, between 22 and 27 August (Funke, 1993: 106–7, 111–12; *Süddeutsche Zeitung*, 24–31 August 1992; *Ostsee Zeitung*, 24–31 August 1992).

The events in Rostock gave rise to racial violence throughout Germany. On the weekend beginning Friday 28 August as many as 50 incidents may have taken place, a significant percentage of them involving neo-Nazi youths attacking refugee hostels in the former GDR (*Searchlight*, October 1992: 21). Such events continued throughout September 1992 when, as in the previous October, immigrants and refugees were attacked, with the state apparently powerless to halt the violence or arrest the perpetrators. The disorder declined somewhat in October, although the number of attacks still stood as high as 364 in that month and 344 in November (BMI, 1993: 69). On 23 November one of the most notorious incidents took place in the town of Mölln in Schleswig-Holstein when three Turks were murdered in a firebomb attack (*Hamburger Abendblatt*, 24 November 1992; *Die Zeit*, 27 November 1992).

The year 1992 represented the high point in racial violence in post-war Germany. The following years resulted in a decline in the number of attacks against asylum seekers and foreign workers and their families. In addition, no riots occurred comparable with Hoyerswerda or Rostock. Nevertheless, the number of attacks which took place during 1993–4 still exceeded the total for 1991, although, significantly, they represented a fall of over fifteen per cent compared to 1992.

The major incident of 1993 occurred on 29 May when a firebomb attack on a Turkish house in Solingen resulted in the death of three children and two women. The significance of this incident lies not just in the tragic loss of life but also in the revulsion against it, manifesting itself most spectacularly in violence and civil disobedience by Turks (*The Times*, 31 May 1993; *The European*, 3–6 June 1993).[3] However, even as the above events took place, a further spate of attacks against the foreign population of Germany occurred. June represented the highpoint of racist violence in 1993, with 256 attacks occurring in that month.

The major incidents of 1994 occurred in March and May. The first involved an arson attack on a synagogue in Lübeck on 25 March, just before the start of the Passover. This was the first time such an event had happened since the Nazi era (*Frankfurter Rundschau*, 26 March 1994; *Searchlight*, May 1994: 18; *The European*, 1–7 April 1994). A few weeks later, on 12 May, foreigners were attacked in the streets of Magdeburg by 60 neo-Nazi youths (*Searchlight*, June 1994: 18).

As indicated in the table below, a geographical analysis of the racial attacks which occurred in 1991 and 1992 indicates that most of the violence, simply in terms of numbers, has taken place in western, as opposed to eastern Germany. Nevertheless, a breakdown of attacks per 100 000 of the population in individual federal states has demonstrated that those with the highest proportions consisted of the new areas of Mecklenburg-Vorpommern and Brandenburg, with a figure of over nine attacks per 100 000, followed, however, by Schleswig-Holstein, Saarland, Sachsen-Anhalt and North Rhine Westphalia, the last of which actually counted the highest total number of attacks. Perhaps most significantly, the states with the seven lowest totals all lay in western Germany (BMI, 1992: 76; BMI, 1993: 72–3).

Just as significant as the above statistics is the fact that there have been variations in the nature of the violence between east and west. While both the new and the old federal states have experienced small-scale attacks, riots in the form of Hoyerswerda and Rostock have only occurred in the east. The explanation for this would lie in the fact that western Germany, with a greater experience of large-scale immigration, has reached a more mature phase of race relations, in which anti-

Table 6.1 Racial attacks in Germany in 1991–92

	1991			*1992*		
	East	*West*	*Nationwide*	*East*	*West*	*Nationwide*
Homicides	1	2	3	7	10	17
Arson and bombings	123	260	383	222	500	722
Assault	198	251	449	307	418	725
Property damage	171	477	648	329	791	1120
Total	493	990	1483	865	1719	2584

Sources: BMI, 1992: 76; Press and Information Office of the Federal Government, 1993: 39.

immigrant riots are unacceptable, a situation which also exists in Britain, whereas the new Länder have yet to reach this stage (Panayi, 1993: 17).

THE EXTREME RIGHT IN UNITED GERMANY

Analyses of the perpetrators of racist crimes in Germany carried out by the federal office for the protection of the constitution in Germany (*Amt für Verfassungsschutz*, AVS) reveal that the overwhelming majority are youths. In 1991, 69 per cent of suspected perpetrators were under 20 years of age, including 22 per cent between 16 and 17, while less than 3 per cent were over 30. The figures for 1992 are similar. These statistics are not surprising and demonstrate that youth expresses racism in the basic form of violence (BMI, 1992: 84; BMI, 1993: 82). In addition, young people also form an important component of support for neo-Nazi groupings in the new Germany. Such groupings have always been present since the end of the Second World War, but increased their support in the early 1990s.

Neo-Nazi bodies usually consist of groups with a small number of members who are not afraid of participating in criminal activity as defined by the AVS, especially of a violent nature (Husbands, 1991: 89–90). In the Federal Republic during the 1980s the total of these bodies fluctuated just above 20 while their total number of members fell from 1800 in 1980 to 1150 in 1984 to reach 1800 again by the end of the decade (Husbands, 1991: 91; Hennig, 1993: 103). The major organisation was the Free Workers Party (*Freiheitliche Deutsche Arbeiterpartei*, FAP), established in 1979, with over 450 members by 1988 and responsible for 34 per cent of all right-wing acts of violence in 1987. However, the party received just under 0.1 per cent of the vote in the 1989 European election. Other organisations have emerged but soon disappeared, as a result of being banned by the federal government (Paul, 1989; Husbands, 1991).

By the time of the fall of the Berlin Wall neo-Nazism had also made an appearance in the GDR, especially revolving around a skinhead youth subculture which had developed in the early 1980s. At the time of unification there may have been as many as 1500 people in organised groups, with West German neo-Nazi groupings also active in East Germany. These activities were known to the authorities in the GDR, who, in 1988 and 1989, carried out over 60 prosecutions against youths involved in extreme right-wing offences (Farin and Seidel-Pielen, 1992: 74; Bergmann, 1994: 266; Ködderitzch and Müller, 1990).

In contrast to the extreme right as a whole and to the increase of incidences of racial violence, the numbers of neo-Nazi groups and their membership did not grow significantly after unification. In 1990 there were 27 organisations with 1400 members which increased to 30 and 2200 in 1991 and stood at 33 and 1400 members in 1992. However, during the same period, the number of extreme right-wing groups (including the German People's Union [*Deutsche Volksunion*, DVU], and the National Democratic Party [NPD] but excluding the Republican Party [*Republikaner*]) grew from 69 to 82 with their membership increasing from 33 600 to 43 100 (BMI, 1993: 66).

The major neo-Nazi groupings included the FAP, with a membership of only 220 in 1992. It received just 0.37 per cent of the vote in a local election in Berlin in May 1992 (BMI, 1993: 135; *Stern*, 24 February 1994: 105). New groupings also came into existence, including the German Alternative established in Bremen in May 1989; it received much support in eastern Germany (Farin and Seidel-Pielen, 1992: 88–9). On 1 February 1990 six young men founded the National Alternative in East Berlin. It reached a membership of 500 by June (Lynen von Berg, 1994: 117). The National Offensive, meanwhile, was founded in Augsburg in July 1990.

The federal government decided to take action against neo-Nazi groupings when it banned several of them at the end of 1992, including the National Offensive, the National Front and the German Alternative, with moves considered against the FAP in the autumn of 1993. Nevertheless, these groups continued to function, and some of their members reconstituted themselves into new organisations. In addition, there have always existed several thousand unorganised skinheads. At the end of 1994 the federal government outlawed the Viking Youth (*Wiking Jugend*), a right-wing youth organisation (Institute of Jewish Affairs, 1994: 37; *Spiegel*, 1 February 1993: 71–3; ibid., 8 August 1993: 93–8; *Searchlight*, December 1994: 15; Skrypietz, 1994).

Just as important as the neo-Nazi groupings which have remained on the fringe, and have made an impact essentially through the violent actions of their members against foreigners, are the more mainstream organisations which attracted attention due to the support they gained during local and regional elections after 1989. The major parties consisted of the old-established NPD, which reached its highpoint during the late 1960s, the DVU founded as early as 1971, but only making an electoral impact after unification and, above all, the Republican Party. It was established in 1983 by Franz Schönhuber who had served in the *Waffen SS* and who left the CSU in 1983 because of its, as he saw it, too conciliatory attitude towards the GDR (Weissbrod, 1994: 227; Childs, 1991: 79).

As these groups and parties would be banned if their ideology was overtly neo-Nazi they have presented themselves as centre-right organisations. Still, they have been much more openly nationalistic than any of the mainstream parties. They all support the collective over the individual, the collective consisting of a homogeneous nation, people or state. They have been overtly racist and have called for more extreme measures to deal with the 'threats' posed by foreigners within Germany, including deportation and a further tightening of the right of asylum, guaranteed under the federal constitution. They have blamed immigrants for unemployment and for social problems and fear that German national identity will be destroyed by foreign cultures. All three groups have also advocated a move away from the feeling of guilt they believe Germany has suffered due to its Nazi past, asserting that the country should take pride in its history. Furthermore, they are hostile to the European Union and want to see Germany return to its 1937 borders (Weissbrod, 1994: 227; Saalfeld, 1993; Gessenharter, 1991).

In the early 1990s the above nationalistic mix appealed to many groups in the country, especially within particular geographical locations. The Republican Party climbed to a membership total of 25 000 while the DVU reached 11 500 and the NPD totalled over 6100 (Jaschke, 1993: 118; BMI, 1993: 36). More spectacular was the electoral support obtained by the DVU and, more importantly, the Republican Party. In fact, the former grouping only really made a major breakthrough in the regional elections in Bremen in October 1991 and in Schleswig-Holstein in April 1992, on both occasions obtaining over six per cent of the vote. The NPD, meanwhile, only obtained such a vote in the local election in Frankfurt in 1989 (Feist, 1992; Falter, 1994: 21).

It was the electoral successes of the Republican Party which really grabbed the headlines. After obtaining 3 per cent of the vote in the Bavarian regional election of 1986, it faded into the background until 1989 when it was catapulted into the limelight again by gaining 7.1 per cent in the election to the European Parliament and 7.5 per cent in the regional election in Berlin. In the former, the highest support was obtained in Bavaria (14.6 per cent) and the lowest in North Rhine-Westphalia (4.1 per cent). The Republican Party fell back to just 2.1 per cent in the federal election of 1990. However, the party subsequently achieved its most spectacular success in the early years of the new Germany, rocketing to 10.9 per cent of the vote in the regional election in Baden-Württemberg in 1992 and gaining just around five per cent on several other occasions. The party has managed to perform significantly better in the old Federal Republic than in the areas which have been added to it since unification, where voters, if they do not support the established centre parties, tend to choose the reformed communist party, the PDS (Falter, 1994: 21; Childs, 1991: 80; *Die Zeit*, 12 March 1993; Lynen von Berg, 1994: 119–22; *Die Woche*, 17 March 1994; Krisch, 1993; *Stern*, 24 February 1994: 103).

Several political scientists and journalists have analysed the electoral support of the extreme right, focusing especially upon the results in Baden-Württemberg and Schleswig-Holstein. In terms of gender, two-thirds of both DVU and Republican Party voters were men. Both parties also had a disproportionate percentage of voters among the younger age groups. Socially, the parties of the right were successful in attracting members of the working classes and lower middle classes, as well as the unemployed: all felt that their economic position was threatened (Jaschke, 1993: 123–36; Feist, 1992; Falter, 1994; Roth, 1993; Wüst, 1993: 28–9; Minkenberg, 1992: 72–76).

Nevertheless, in the federal election of October 1994, the extreme right did not make the breakthrough which had seemed to be imminent in 1991 and 1992 but which appeared increasingly less likely since 1993. While the DVU did not contest the election, the Republican Party gained just 1.9 per cent of the vote, falling below the 2.1 total it achieved in 1990 and thereby polling considerably less than the 4.3 per cent gained by the NPD in 1969 (*Die Zeit*, 21 October 1994; *Searchlight*, January 1995: 13; Childs, 1991: 73; Falter, 1994: 21).

Several explanations can be offered for this poor showing. First, the Republican Party suffered internal divisions which came to a head two weeks before the election when the party's executive voted 'to dump' Schönhuber as its leader (*Searchlight*, November 1994: 21). Second, the strength of support for the extreme right mirrored the incidence of racial attacks, both of which reached a peak in 1991–2. This would suggest that the highpoint of post unification xenophobia, fuelled by economic difficulty, was reached in these two years, after which it declined. A third explanation is that the election results were typical protest votes characteristic of a contemporary liberal democracy in the middle of a parliament, with voters moving back to the mainstream for the 'real thing'. However, at least part of the answer seems to lie in Germany's liberal asylum laws which were tightened in 1992–93. This resulted in the ruling coalition's ability to woo some of the protest votes away from the extreme right and back to Chancellor Kohl's centre-right coalition government.

CONCLUSION

An enormous influx of refugees and ethnic Germans into Germany took place immediately after unification, so that in 1992, 438 191 asylum seekers and 230 565 ethnic Germans entered the country. This represented an increase from the previous year's figures of, respectively, 256 132 and 221 995 (Wüst, 1993: 30). These statistics became a media obsession which often dominated the evening news broadcasts. Similarly, newspapers and magazines also focused heavily upon this issue. Chancellor Kohl's governing coalition also contributed to the general hysteria by speaking about the 'uncontrolled flood' of refugees and of the 'boat being full' (*Searchlight*, December 1992).

Throughout the early 1990s and, in fact, over a longer period of time, the CDU-CSU government had wanted to change Article 16 of the constitution, but this task proved difficult because a two-thirds majority is needed in the Bundestag to amend the Federal Republic's Basic Law. Without the support of the opposition SPD, which at first proved reluctant to toe the government's line, no change could take place. However, during the second half of 1992 the main opposition party eventually accepted the necessity of change, so that by the end of the year Chancellor Kohl and the SPD had reached an agreement to amend Article 16 of the constitution. It came into effect in July 1993 (Steger and Wagner, 1993: 61–2).

The changes meant that asylum seekers could not enter Germany if they came from a country in which they did not face persecution, either originally or on their way to Germany. Under the new legislation deportation was also made much easier (Steger and Wagner, 1993: 61–3; Wüst, 1993: 31; Kuechler, 1994: 51–2). The new measures seem to have been effective because a significant decrease occurred in the number of asylum seekers in the second half of 1993. Nevertheless, these figures may be illusory because illegal immigration takes place on a massive scale so that many refugees may simply have gone 'underground' (*Stern*, 7 October 1993: 51–8; *Focus*, 4 October 1993: 52–4, 10 January 1994: 27). It may well be the case that the federal government is powerless to halt the mass immigration from post-Cold War eastern Europe and beyond and that in this respect Germany has now become the new America (Berschin, 1995).

The German government's reaction to the ever-increasing number of attacks on foreigners living in Germany consisted of intensifying its racial exclusionism. In contrast to the change in the asylum laws, little progress has been made towards a radical change in nationality legislation, despite the fact that the issue has been on the public agenda for some time (*Focus*, 14 June 1993: 28–30; *Stern*, 7 June 1993: 18). After all, part of the compromise between government and opposition regarding Article 16 consisted of the agreement to simplify the process of naturalisation for foreigners who wish to obtain German citizenship (Kuechler, 1994: 52–3).

In the early 1990s Germany's behaviour towards newcomers paralleled that of liberal democracies throughout the twentieth century. An economic crisis combined with a large influx of unwanted newcomers, and, in this instance, a resurgence of nationalism, led to an increase of moves towards racial exclusionism. Another example of a country where such a situation occurred was Britain in the late 1950s and early 1960s. Increased right-wing activities, racial violence and government concern led to the introduction of legislation in 1962. In the British case this process has been continuing ever since with a constant tightening of controls on immigrants and refugees (Layton-Henry, 1992).

It remains to be seen whether this will happen in united Germany. This is one possible scenario. However, the determining factors will probably be the need of the German economy for cheap labour and the strengthening of the discriminatory economic and political forces which drive people out of eastern Europe. Certainly, the racial crisis of the early 1990s has passed because the factors which caused it in the form of the combination of an economic crisis and the national hysteria resulting from unification have faded away. However, these were potent manifestations of the racial exclusionism which underlies the existence of the modern nation-state, and there is little doubt that the everyday exclusionism will continue, as it has done in almost all nation-states throughout the twentieth century.

NOTES

1. I am grateful to the following for financing the research for this chapter: the Alexander von Humboldt Foundation, the Nuffield Foundation, and the Department of Historical and International Studies at De Montfort University.
2. See for instance *Spiegel*, 9 September 1991, lead story, 30 September 1991, pp. 30–8; *Frankfurter Rundschau*, 23 September, 7 October 1991; *Welt am Sonntag*, 6, 13 October 1991; *Rheinischer Merkur*, 2, 9, 16 August 1993; *Stern*, 15 August 1991, p. 107.
3. These developments were far more dramatic and spectacular than the rather timid 'candlelight' processions against racism in which Germans participated. These demonstrations had occurred sporadically since the end of 1991. See for instance *The European*, 12–18 November, 1993 and 10–13 December, 1993.

REFERENCES

Ammer, T. (1988), 'Prozesse gegen Skinheads in der DDR', *Deutschland Archiv*, vol. 21, no. 8, pp. 804–7.

Aziz, N. (1992), 'Zur Lage der Nicht-Deutschen in Deutschland', *Aus Politik und Zeitgeschicte*, no. B9/92, pp. 37–44.

Bade, K.J. (1983), *Vom Auswanderungsland zum Einwanderungsland? Deutschland 1880–1980* (Berlin: Colloquium Verlag).

Bade, K.J. (2nd edn, 1992a), *Ausländer, Aussiedler, Asyl in der Bundesrepublik Deutschland* (Hanover: Niedersächsische Landeszentrale für politische Bildung).

Bade, K.J. (1992b), 'Einheimische Ausländer: "Gastarbeiter" – Dauergäste – Einwanderer', in Bade, K.J., ed., *Deutsche im Ausland, Fremde in Deutschland* (Munich: Beck).

Bendix, J. (1990), *Incorporating Foreign Workers: A Comparison of German and American Policy* (New York: Peter Lang).

Bergmann, W. (1994), 'Anti-Semitism and Xenophobia in the East German Länder', *German Politics*, vol. 3, no. 2, pp. 265–76.

Berschin, H. (1995), 'Migrationsland Deutschland', *Die Politische Meinung*, vol. 40, no. 302, pp. 11–14.

Bethlehem, S. (1982), *Heimatvertreibung, DDR-Flucht, Gastarbeiterzuwanderung: Wanderungsströme und Wanderungspolitik in der Bundesrepublik* (Stuttgart: Klett-Cotta).

Blotevogel, H.H., Müller-ter Jung, U. and Wood, G. (1993), 'From Itinerant Worker to Immigrant? The Geography of Guestworkers in Germany', in R. King, ed., pp. 83–100.

Brubaker, R. (1992), *Citizenship and Nationhood in France and Germany* (Cambridge, Mass.: Harvard University Press).

Bundesministerium des Innern (BMI), ed. (1991), *Verfassungsschutzbericht, 1990* (Bonn: Bundesministerium des Innern).

Bundesministerium des Innern (BMI), ed. (1992), *Verfassungsschutzbericht, 1991* (Bonn: Bundesministerium des Innern).

Bundesministerium des Innern (BMI), ed. (1993), *Verfassungsschutzbericht, 1992* (Bonn: Bundesministerium des Innern).

Castles, S., with Booth, H. and Wallace, T. (2nd impression, 1987), *Here for Good: Western Europe's New Ethnic Minorities* (London: Pluto).

Cheles, L., Ferguson R. and Vaughan M., eds (1991), *Neo-Fascism in Europe* (London: Longman).

Childs, D. (1991), 'The Far Right in Germany since 1945', in L. Cheles et al., pp. 62–75.

Dawidowicz, L.S. (1987), *The War Against the Jews, 1933–45* (Harmondsworth: Pelican)

Dohse, K. (1981), *Ausländische Arbeiter und bürgerlicher Staat: Genese und Funktion von staatlicher Ausländerpolitik: Vom Kaiserreich bis zur Bundesrepublik Deutschland* (Königstein: Anton Hain).

Dudek, P. and Jaschke, H.G. (1984), *Entstehung und Entwicklung des Rechtsextremismus in der Bundesrepublik*, vol. 1 (Opladen: Westdeutscher Verlag).

Faist, T. (1993), 'From School to Work: Public Policy and Underclass Formation among Young Turks in Germany during the 1980s', *International Migration Review*, vol. 27, no. 2, pp. 306–31.

Falter, J.W. (1994), *Wer Wählt Rechts? Die Wähler und Anhänger rechtsextremistischer Parteien im vereinigten Deutschland* (Munich: Beck).

Farin, K. and Seidel-Pielen, E. (1992), *Rechtsruck: Rassismus im neuen Deutschland* (Berlin: Rotbuch).

Feist, U. (1992), 'Rechtsruck in Baden-Württemberg und Schleswig-Holstein', in Starzacher, K., Schacht, K., Friedrich, B. and Lief, T., eds, *Protestwähler und Wahlverweigerer: Krise der Demokratie* (Cologne: Bund-Verlag).

Flockton, C.H. (1993), 'The Federal German Economy in the Early 1990s', *German Politics*, vol. 2, no. 2, pp. 311–27.

Gessenharter, W. (1991), 'Die Parteiprogramme der Rechtsparteien', *Sozialwissenschaftliche Information*, vol. 20, no. 1, pp. 227–33.

Hennig, E. (1993), 'Rechtsextremismus: Kontinuität und Brüche zwischen Weimar, Bonn und Berlin (1932/33, 1945, 1949 und 1990)', in Sicking, M. and Lohe, A., eds, *Die Bedrohung der Demokratie von Rechts: Wiederkehr der Vergangenheit?* (Cologne: Bund Verlag).

Hirsch, K. (1989), *Rechts von der Union: Personen, Organisationen, Parteien seit 1945* (Munich: Knesbech & Schuler).

Hockenos, P. (1993), *Free to Hate: The Rise of the Right in Post-Communist Eastern Europe* (London: Routledge).

Hoffman, L. (1993), *Die Unvollendete Republik: Zwischen Einwanderungsland und Deutschem Nationalstaat* (Cologne: PapyRossa Verlag).

Homze, E. (1967), *Foreign Labour in Nazi Germany* (Princeton: Princeton University Press).

Husbands, C.T. (1991), 'Militant Neo-Nazism in the Federal Republic of Germany in the 1980s', in L. Cheles et al., pp. 86–113.

Funke, H. (1993), *Brandstifter: Deutschland zwischen Demokratie und völkischem Nationalismus* (Göttingen: Lamuv).

Institute of Jewish Affairs, ed. (1994), *Antisemitism World Report 1994* (London: Institute of Jewish Affairs).

Jaschkc, H.G. (1993), *Die 'Republikaner': Profile einer Rechtsaußen-Partei* (Bonn: Dietz).

Jürgs, M. and Dave, F., eds (1992), *Stoppt die Gewalt! Stimmen gegen Ausländerhass* (Hamburg: Luchterhand).

Kemper, F.J. (1993), 'New Trends in Mass Migration in Germany', in R. King, ed., pp. 257–74.

King, R., ed. (1993), *Mass Migrations in Europe: The Legacy and the Future* (London: Belhaven Press).

Ködderitzch, P. and Müller, L.A. (1990), *Rechtsextremismus in der DDR* (Göttingen: Lamuv).

Krisch, H. (1993), 'From SED to PDS: The Struggle to Revive a Left Party' in R.J. Dalton, ed., *The New Germany Votes: Unification and the Creation of the New German Party System* (Oxford: Berg).

Kuechler, M. (1994), 'Germans and "Others": Racism, Xenophobia or "Legitimate Conservatism"?', *German Politics*, vol. 3, no. 1, pp. 47–74.

Layton-Henry, Z. (1992), *The Politics of Immigration* (Oxford: Blackwell).

Lehmann, A. (1990), *Im Fremden ungewollt Zuhaus: Flüchtlinge und Vetriebene in Westdeutschland 1945–1990* (Munich: Beck).

Lynen von Berg, H. (1994), 'Rechtsextremismus in Ostdeutschland seit der Wende', in Kowalsky, W. and Schroeder, W., eds, *Rechtsextremismus: Einführung und Forschungsbilanz* (Opladen: Westdeutscher Verlag).

Minkenberg, M. (1992), 'The New Right in Germany: The Transformation of Conservatism and the Extreme Right', *European Journal of Political Research*, vol. 22, no. 1, pp. 55–81.

Münch, U. (2nd edn, 1993), *Asylpolitik in der Bundesrepublik Deutschland: Entwicklung und Alternativen* (Opladen: Leske & Budrich).

Nielsen, J. (1992), *Muslims in Western Europe* (Edinburgh: Edinburgh University Press).

OECD, ed. (1993), *Economic Surveys, 1992–1993: Germany* (Paris: OECD).

Panayi, P. (1993), 'Anti-immigrant Riots in Nineteenth and Twentieth Century Britain', in Panayi, P., ed., *Racial Violence in Britain, 1840–1950* (Leicester: Leicester University Press).

Paul, G. (1989), 'Der Schatten Hitlers verblaßt: Die Normalisierung des Rechtsextremismus in den achtziger Jahren', in Paul, G., ed., *Hitlers Schatten verblaßt: Die Normalisierung des Rechtextremismus* (Bonn: Dietz).

Press and Information Office of the Federal Government, Foreign Affairs Division, ed. (1993), *Hostility Towards Foreigners in Germany: New Facts, Analyses, Arguments* (Bonn: Foreign Office/Auswärtiges Amt).

Roth, D. (1993), '*Volksparteien* in Crisis? The Electoral Success of the

Extreme Right in Context', *German Politics*, vol. 2, no. 1, pp. 1–20.
Saalfeld, T. (1993), 'The Politics of National Populism: Ideology and Politics of the German Republican Party', *German Politics*, vol. 2, no. 2, pp. 177–99.
Schlaffke, W. and Voss, R. von, eds (1992), *Vom Gastarbeiter zum Mitarbeiter: Ursachen, Folgen und Konsequenzen der Ausländer-beschäftigung in Deutschland* (Cologne: Infomedia).
Schumacher, H. (1992), *Einwanderungsland BRD: Warum die deutsche Wirtschaft weiter Ausländer braucht* (Düsseldorf: Zebulon Verlag).
Skrypietz, I. (1994), 'Militant Right-Wing Extremism in Germany', *German Politics*, vol. 3, no. 1, pp. 133–40.
Steger, M. and Wagner, P.F. (1993), 'Political Asylum, Immigration and Citizenship in the Federal Republic of Germany', *New Political Science*, vol. 24–25, pp. 59–73.
Weissbrod, L. (1994), 'Nationalism in Reunified Germany', *German Politics*, vol. 3, no. 2, pp. 222–32.
Wilpert, C. (1991), 'Migration and Ethnicity in a Non-Immigrant Country: Foreigners in a United Germany', *New Community*, vol. 18, no. 1, pp. 49–62.
Wüst, A.M. (1993), 'Right-Wing Extremism in Germany', *Migration World*, vol. 21, nos. 2–3, pp. 27–31.

Part III
The External Consequences of German Unification

7 The German Model and European Integration

Eric Owen Smith

Even though there are far-reaching political implications involved in any free trade area, customs union, common market and/or currency union, this chapter is confined to the economic, fiscal, monetary, social and anti-trust policy aspects of the German model and European integration. The basic argument will be that a number of features of the German economy have already been adopted, or would lend themselves to adoption, at the European level.

What, then, is the German model? The social market economy (SME) can be defined in general terms. Freedom, efficiency and equity all receive equal weight (Wiseman, 1989). The SME was the product of opposition to both fascist and communist economic systems, as well as to the *laissez-faire* school epitomised by von Hayek (Nicholls, 1994: 102–3, 146; Owen Smith, 1994: 16–20). As Helm (1995) points out, to Anglo-American economists the Germans do all the wrong things: they protect their companies from hostile take-overs; they cosset their employees with generous social security provisions; they have allowed employees to have a say in business since long before the social chapter was enacted in the Maastricht treaty; they face heavy taxation; monopolies dominate important sectors of the economy; and the role of local and national government is extensive. An independent central bank is also a product of German history, that is to say a product of two humiliating inflations. International financial markets hold this bank – the Bundesbank – in such high esteem that the exchange rate of the Deutsche Mark (DM) has been continually revalued. The highly regulated dual system of vocational training is jointly provided by the state and employers. In short, by Reagan-Thatcher standards, the German economy should be a major disaster area. Yet the industrial wasteland of East Germany has been incorporated into the Federal Republic as a result of German economic, monetary and social union (GEMSU). After some needless prevarication, during which theoretical Anglo-Saxon neoclassical competitive models were considered for the former East Germany, fiscal transfers from western to eastern Germany have financed fundamental infrastructure reforms in the former GDR (Owen Smith,

1996a). But European integration represents a far greater degree of heterogeneity than that exemplified by GEMSU.

Secondly, therefore, what is the nature of the heterogeneity which bedevils European integration? Dyker (1992: 1) gives an excellent perspective of European problems in this respect. Europe is unique among the high income regions of the world. It is extraordinarily heterogeneous, boasting some fifty major nationalities (not all enjoying separate statehood), and nearly as many languages. Economic development has therefore proceeded in the face of a whole range of cultural and linguistic barriers. Yet in spite of the comparative poverty of Europe in raw materials, its economies typically trade a relatively high proportion of its GNP. The contrast between all this and the richly endowed USA is impressive. Several other factors must be added. The USA is a single currency area and possesses a common working language. In area, even the united Germany is smaller than California, Montana or Texas; for that matter it is smaller than Spain and France, and not much bigger than Italy or Poland (Sinn and Sinn, 1992: 22).

It follows that a useful third and final introductory item would be to summarise the relevant elements of the German model. Germany is the EU's dominant member. This is attributable to her general economic prowess. Many developments within the EU have reflected, or will take account of, German practices and experiences:

— If monetary union is realised, the European central bank will probably enjoy the degree of autonomy accorded to the Deutsche Bundesbank. Outside of the economies of the Benelux countries, probably Austria, and possibly France, this appears to be a constraint on deepening.
— In the less likely event of full fiscal harmonisation being achieved, and/or a significant amount of tax revenue accruing to Brussels, the German model of fiscal equalisation would become a constitutional feature. On the expenditure side, the question of subsidies – especially in the agricultural sector – would pose significant problems for the Germans themselves. This appears to be a constraint on widening.
— If a full European economic and monetary union (EMU) is ever achieved, the lessons learned from German unification may be heeded by policy makers. The problems resulting from uniting dissimilar economies by introducing common exchange rates, particularly against the US dollar and Japanese yen, is one such lesson. Assuming such a currency union, the exchange rates of the currencies to be absorbed

against the Euro, as the currency will be called, may be a potential cause of price instability.

— The EU social chapter contains provisions which resemble the German social insurance and industrial democracy provisions.
— EU anti-trust legislation corresponds closely to the German model.

In the following each of these features will be considered in turn.

MONETARY POLICY

The European monetary institute, the forerunner of the European Central Bank (ECB), is situated in Frankfurt am Main – a city which is also the seat of the Deutsche Bundesbank. It is not surprising that this is the only major European institution to be located in Germany. The ECB will certainly be a clone of the Bundesbank (BBk). Above all, it will enjoy the degree of independence from political influence enjoyed by both the Bundesbank and its predecessor (Bank deutscher Länder – BdL). It is important to understand the historical reasons for this independence, the differences between the BdL and the BBk and the policy implications of central-bank independence, although these implications have been far more widely investigated than any other aspect of the German model (Marsh, 1992; Owen Smith, 1994, ch. 4).

When Germany was blockaded during the First World War, it chose to finance what was expected to be a short conflict by a significant increase in government borrowing. There was a consequent increase in the money supply. After the war the allies made extortionate reparation demands which caused a balance of payments deficit and a disastrous fall in the exchange rate. In 1919 the annual inflation rate was 70 per cent but by 1923 it was 1.9 billion per cent (Owen Smith, 1994: 4). This hyperinflation stands in contrast to the suppressed inflation after the Second World War, although government debt was again created with the help of a servile central bank. During the latter inflation there were white markets in which the allies allowed the Nazi price and wage freeze to continue, grey markets in which money substitutes were used and black markets which accounted for 10 per cent of trade but 80 per cent of monetary circulation (ibid.: 6). It was the consequent need to induce dishoarding and give a further stimulus to industrial production that caused the draconian allied currency reform which saw the launch of the BdL and the introduction of the Deutsche Mark.

The BdL coordinated the policies of the central banks in each of the

Länder (federal states). It predated the election of the first post-war federal government by eighteen months and was thus already exercising the large degree of policy independence bequeathed by the western allies when an elected government came to power. Both the BdL and the BBk – which was established in 1957 – have almost invariably succeeded in winning any policy conflict with federal politicians (ibid.: 185–93). Moreover, the BBk is more centralised than its predecessor. It is owned by the federal government. Its eight-strong directorate – notwithstanding their subsequent independence – are federal appointees. Länder representation on its governing council was reduced to nine as a result of GEMSU and its attendant threat of an unwieldy council. Together with the directorate, therefore, the policy making council now consists of 17 members. In order to achieve its sole goal of price stability, it uses its contemporaneous interest-rate instruments and currently targets the monetary aggregate M3 (ibid.: 143–78). Because the DM is a major trading, investment and reserve currency, the fortnightly deliberations of its council are an internationally important event.

A number of issues would have to be resolved before the ECB could be modelled on the BBk. First, even if all fifteen EU members were in a position to move simultaneously to the third and final stage of EMU, would all fifteen central-bank presidents or governors be accorded a council seat? If so, BBk experience with GEMSU indicates that very few additional places would be available for other representatives. Secondly, what type of securities would be acceptable collaterals for discounting by the ECB? Because of its restrictive approach to dealing in public-sector debt, the BBk has evolved its own 'flexible' securities for this purpose. Thirdly, would politicians retain the right to negotiate exchange-rate treaties? If so, central bankers would be perturbed by the possibilities of imported inflation.

FISCAL POLICY

Because GEMSU incorporated East Germany into an existing economic, monetary and social union, tax rates were already established – albeit that some transitional arrangements were made. Such a degree of tax harmonisation was not, of course, made possible by the Single Market Act. VAT rates still differ widely within the EU, as do excise duties. Citizens of member states living near Luxembourg, for example, make considerable savings by purchasing motor-vehicle fuel and tobacco products in the Grand Duchy – in some cases merely by crossing a road or bridge!

There is an even greater problem. It was shown in the last section that the establishment of a centralised ECB is at an advanced stage of preparation. By way of complete contrast, the EU's fiscal powers are relatively negligible. Basically, the ceiling on 'own resources' until 1999 is 1.27 per cent of the EU's GNP, a reduced share of VAT but a contribution related to each member state's GNP (BMF, 1994: 174). In 1992 the budget totalled ECU61.1 billion – about the same size as the combined general-government and the Treuhand privatisation agency's budgetary deficits in Germany, and not a great deal larger than the solidarity surcharge enhanced federal unshared tax yield in that year (ibid.: 110–11; MRDB, 1/94: 75* and 4/95: 55*; OECD, 1994: 153). Even more significantly, it was trivial compared to the magnitude of flows from western to eastern Germany (Ifo, 1994: 5). By 1997 (in real terms) the EU's budget will total ECU74.5 billion, 28.4 per cent (gross) of which will be contributed by Germany (von Laun, 1994: 55). This 22 per cent budgetary expansion is, however, dwarfed by the costs of GEMSU – an exercise analogous to including Sweden and Greece (to say nothing of the central European aspirant members) in EMU.

On the expenditure side, the common agricultural policy (CAP) still accounts for a half of the total EU budget, with Germany faring better than the UK. At an early stage in the emergence of the social market economy, German farming interests were soon able to evade market forces, and accommodating the French farmers as European integration progressed meant that agriculture would remain protected and subsidised (Nicholls, 1994: 345). In fact, despite its comparative disadvantage, Germany became a major food exporter (Flockton, 1992: 58). Reform of such a fiscal arrangement is supposedly to be undertaken by 1999, although in the spring of 1995 Bavarian farmers demonstrated against the loss of southern EU markets as a result of the revaluation of the DM being unaccompanied by the CAP's MCAs. Indeed, food prices throughout the EU were set at German levels, by far the highest in Europe. Pegging farm prices to the DM, which was introduced on German insistence in 1984, was brought to an end only after it had cost EU taxpayers ECU 35 billion. *The Economist* (8 July 1995) predicted that food stocks in the EU will rise again unless prices are further reduced. Given the electoral and lobbying power of German farmers that seems unlikely. The two policy options for European integration therefore appear to be either delaying any further EU enlargement, or not permitting new members into the CAP until after a long transitional period. This latter option effectively means according virtual associate membership to successful applicants from central Europe.

The quantitative and qualitative magnitudes of both revenue raising and expenditure are thus respectively too insignificant or misdirected to provide any countervailing power to the envisaged degree of centralisation in monetary policy. Price stability will therefore be the only policy goal, even if employment creation by public-sector spending is considered a viable alternative policy scenario. Any clone of the BBk will normally view public-sector expenditure as suboptimal.

On the other hand, the German model has a potentially useful device for fiscal equalisation – although the donor Länder within the Federal Republic were critical of the system even before GEMSU. In view of what was said in the previous paragraph, the German model demonstrates the fairly obvious proposition that each level of government must be allocated a revenue flow which corresponds to its implicit expenditure commitments (= vertical equalisation). It also indicates the need for fiscal transfers from more affluent to less affluent areas, especially in the event of an economic, monetary and social union (= horizontal equalisation). By referring to Table 7.1, it is possible first to consider German vertical equalisation.

There are several points worthy of note. Above all, the federal share of VAT has fallen over the years, not least as a result of 'compensating' the western Länder for the full inclusion of the new Länder in the system as from 1 January 1995. (Between 1990 and 1994 these obligations were met out of the German unity fund, to which the federal government was by far the largest contributor.) Hence the federal government's share of VAT fell from 65 per cent in 1986–92, to 63 per cent in 1993–4, and to 56 per cent in 1995. The shortfall was in turn partially met by increasing the independently levied federal duty on hydrocarbon oils, the revenue which almost doubled between 1989 and 1994 (*MRDB*, 4/95: 55). An income tax solidarity surcharge was reintroduced as from 1 January 1995, again amounting to 7.5 per cent. It should also be noted that the tax revenue of local authorities – regarded by the federal president as the 'schools of democracy' in June 1995 – is insufficient to cover expenditure needs. They admittedly retain 86 per cent of their trade-tax yield which, while significant, is not shown in Table 7.1 because its fundamental reform is under active consideration (Owen Smith, 1994: 100–1, 107–8; FAZ, 29 April 1995). Interestingly enough, the larger local authorities are pressing for a constitutionally guaranteed share of VAT revenue in return for the complete abolition of the trade tax. When the payroll element of this

Table 7.1 Vertical fiscal equalisation (percentage shares in principal tax revenues)

Government level	*Federal*	*Länder*	*Local*	*Total*
Income tax	42.5	42.5	15	100
Corporate tax	50	50	–	100
Value-added tax	56	44	–	100
Excise duties[1]	100	–	–	100
Inheritance/wealth tax	–	100	–	100
Property tax	–	–	100	100

[1] Excluding beer, which is a Länder tax.
Sources: *Grundgesetz* Article 106, as amended in 1995, 1956 and 1969; *MRDB* 4/95: 55*; OECD 1993: 122

tax was abolished in 1979, the local authorities received an additional percentage point share in the income tax yield. But the trade tax not only undermines industrial competitiveness. The virtual cap on further increases means that alternative sources of revenue have to be found. Above all, fee income from services such as sewage disposal totalled DM34 billion in 1994, having grown by almost 50 per cent in the period 1989–93 (*Die Zeit*, 15/94).

Now consider horizontal equalisation. Articles 106(3) and 107(2) of the Basic Law respectively require the federal and Länder governments to promote uniform living standards throughout the republic, achieving this by means of fiscal equalisation between financially strong and financially weak Länder. It is difficult to think of a more instructive model for any genuine deepening (= EMU) or widening (= admission of former communist economies) of the EU. There are three fundamental lessons. First, GEMSU was also a costly exercise in this respect. Second, Bremen and Saarland – the two weakest Länder in western Germany – have remained eligible for additional assistance between 1995 and 1998. Third, both the federal and the richer Länder governments were significant contributors. Table 7.2 illustrates all three features.

Basically, the 'fiscal power' of any Land is its tax revenue raising powers. If this indicator exceeds the Land's 'equalisation indicator', the Land becomes a net contributor and vice versa. The first round of equalisation process then results in each Land being brought up to a minimum share of 95 per cent of the average tax revenue raised by the Länder. Hence, the first three columns of data in Table 7.2 illustrate this process. Next, the second round of federal grants-in-aid would

Table 7.2 GEMSU and horizontal fiscal equalisation (as from 1995)

Land	*Unadjusted fiscal power*[1,2] *(per cent of average)*	*Horizontal transfer [+= recipient] [−= contributor] (DM million)*	*Adjusted fiscal power (per cent of average)*	*Federal grants-in-aid minus German unity annuity (DM million)*	*Readjusted fiscal power (per cent of average)*	*Average adjustment (per cent of average)*
North-Rhine Westphalia	107.2	–3 892	102.3	–2 176	99.5	95.4
Bavaria	106.8	–2 359	102.3	–1 439	99.5	94.0
Baden-Württemberg	113.2	–4 320	103.3	–1 250	100.7	96.7
Lower Saxony	96.8	397	98.0	858	100.6	93.8
Hesse	116.8	–3 345	104.0	–732	101.2	97.2
Rhineland Palatinate	95.9	267	97.4	727	101.6	94.3
Schleswig-Holstein	98.4	71	99.0	353	102.0	94.3
Saarland	88.7	301	95.0	2 017	103.7	93.4
Hamburg	106.7	–440	102.3	–235	99.9	129.7
Bremen	82.8	538	96.2	2 117	104.1	128.1
Saxony	81.4	2 818	95.0	6 318	125.4	105.0
Saxony-Anhalt	81.7	1 667	95.0	3 975	126.8	105.9
Thuringia	81.6	1 517	95.0	3 657	127.3	106.0
Brandenburg	82.1	1 452	95.0	3 598	127.0	106.1
Mecklenburg-W. Pomerania	81.0	1 167	95.0	2 716	127.5	106.8
Berlin	74.7	4 161	95.0	4 830	118.6	140.1
Old Länder	106.0	–12 782[3]	101.5	241	100.4	96.5
New Länder	79.9	+12 782[3]	95.0	25 086	124.6	112.4
Total	100.0	–	100.0	25 327	100.6	100.0

[1] Shared and separately levied taxes of Länder, plus half of imputed local tax revenue, [2]Includes DM19.5 billion VAT transfer from Federal and old Länder governments to the new Länder; [3]net transfer from old Länder to new Länder.

Sources: BMF (1993) and 1994: 153–4: Ifo (1994): 9–11; OECD (1993): 123; Owen Smith (1994): 68–71

normally bring every Land up to a minimum revenue level of 100 per cent of average revenue. But the remaining three columns of data illustrate the exceptional measures associated with the integration of the new Länder, all of which, including the amalgamated two halves of Berlin, lie below the bold line in Table 7.2. It will be seen that the federal cost of this exercise alone was DM25.327 billion. This statistic consists of the second round of federal grants, plus a number of special grants designed to reduce the administrative and financial burdens of transition between 1995 and 2004 (BMF, 1993: 42). In addition, the new Länder will receive infrastructure renewal grants, also for the period 1995–2004. Finally, the old Länder's annuity payments to the German Unity Fund have been deducted. As can be seen from the penultimate column, this all results in a rough equalisation of the old Länder relativities (recall that Bremen and Saarland receive supplementary assistance). On the other hand, the new Länder are on average almost 25 per cent better off. Alternatively, (final column) the relationship between the degree of equalisation in this widest sense results in a 10 percentage-point difference between the non-city states in western and eastern Germany. The problems of the city states were to be partially resolved with the merging of Brandenburg and Berlin, however this failed in early 1996 (note that these two Länder in any case have only one seat on the BBk's Council; Hamburg and Bremen similarly share representation with their surrounding Länder).

Summarising, it can be said that integrating the new Länder into the fiscal equalisation system will cost the federal government DM41.9 billion annually over the next ten years. This consists of DM16.6 billion in forgone VAT revenue, plus DM18.7 billion in grants-in-aid and DM6.6 billion infrastructure assistance. Grants-in-aid to the old Länder will cost the federal government an additional DM6.9 billion, although these will decline after 1998. The old Länder will in addition contribute a gross DM15.7 billion to the costs of integration: DM2.9 billion in forgone VAT revenue, plus horizontal equalisation payments of DM12.8 billion. Hence, over the next few years the total equalisation flow to eastern Germany from the federal and old Länder governments amounts to DM57.6 annually (Ifo, 1994: 5). The German unity annuities increase this sum to DM67.2 billion (ibid.). Total transfers are even higher, of course. In net terms – that is eliminating double counting, deducting the federal government's tax yield in eastern Germany and deducting privatisation revenue from the losses of the privatisation agency – transfers between 1991 and 1994 totalled DM626 billion (Deutsche Bank Research, 1994: 21). As well as the continuing costs of the now defunct privatisation agency, there is a social insurance transfer which in 1993, for example, cost DM42 billion (Ifo, 1994: 5). This latter cost, given the advanced social policy embodied in the SME, was inevitably high. But before analysing this aspect of the German model, some of the reasons for the high costs of GEMSU can be specified. They represent grave shortcomings in the introduction of an economic, monetary and social union.

GEMSU (GERMAN ECONOMIC, MONETARY AND SOCIAL UNION)

GEMSU turned conventional economic thinking on its head. The orthodox approach to a union between two such vastly dissimilar economies would have been one of gradual assimilation and convergence. GEMSU was, in other words, a 'big bang approach': a step-by-step approach would have been normally expected. For this reason, exchange-rate determination is arguably the most important lesson from this leap into full union. Put at its simplest, the GDR had in effect employed long-run average shadow export pricing of Ostmark (OM)3.73:DM1 (Akerlof et al., 1991: 17–18). Even short-run average cost pricing meant, in DM terms, an average loss of 84 per cent on each item exported to non-socialist economies (ibid.). The politics of GEMSU meant flows were converted at OM1:DM1, and stocks generally at OM2:DM1. This clearly resulted in most eastern German products being price uncompetitive, especially given that they were now officially priced in the world's hardest currency and the former GDR's export markets were in the reserve-impoverished Comecon. In addition, eastern German products were also uncompetitive on qualitative grounds – a characteristic that reflected the technological backwardness of the industrial base. This was in contrast to the viable industrial base which existed when the social market economy emerged in West Germany. Had it been possible to retain two segmented labour markets at the time of GEMSU, the average lower productivity level in eastern Germany would have been reflected by lower money wage rates converted at 1:1. But segmentation was by definition ruled out. Either there would be a high degree of migration and commuting to higher paid jobs in western Germany, or money wage rate equalisation, initially through subsidisation, would have to occur (Owen Smith, 1994: 317).

Eastern German industrial production consequently plummeted to a third of its former level within a year of GEMSU, a fall even more catastrophic than the five-year Great Depression of 1928–33 (Sinn and Sinn, 1992: 29–30). Commuting and migration to western Germany, training schemes, early retirement and short-time working did not prevent a headline unemployment rate of 17 per cent (ibid.; Owen Smith, 1994: 259). Actual unemployment probably peaked at three times the official figure (Steinherr, 1994: 27). Total exports fell by 60 per cent during 1989–91, and three-quarters of this decrease was due to the decline in Comecon trade (ibid.). One-third of the fall in industrial production was due to the decline in exports, and the other two-thirds by the shift within eastern Germany to foreign products (ibid.). Such a series of repercussions begs the following central question. Could a more rapid and thorough recovery be anticipated in eastern Germany than in the relatively more gradualist Poland, Hungary and the then Czechoslovakia – three aspirant members of the EU? Yet as early as 1990 the estimated catching-up period for eastern Germany lay between 15 and 30 years, assuming a net investment of at least DM1.0 trillion (Lipschitz and McDonald, 1990: 77; OECD, 1990: 51; Owen Smith, 1994: 22–4). Nonetheless, eastern Germany could rely on the SME into which she had been incorporated, a treaty which in addition carried automatic membership of the EU (Kurz, 1993: 193).

Major blunders were also made in the fields of monetary and fiscal policies, both of which had implications for the German model. Within the paradigm of this model, as already shown above, the monetary policy reactions were predictable, whereas the fiscal policy mistakes were avoidable. The latter errors emanated from the promises made by members of the federal coalition parties prior to the first all-German election in December 1990. It was contended that GEMSU would make no one in western Germany poorer, but would improve everyone's economic lot in the eastern part of the newly united economy. The mounting debt required to finance transfers to eastern Germany, which was in turn initially financed by borrowing, ultimately led to rising short-term interest rates and taxation. Two income tax surcharges of 7.5 per cent, a 1 percentage point increase in the top rate of VAT to 15 per cent and increases in the excise duty on hydrocarbon oils were necessary. Raising taxes to reduce the public deficit was justifiable – if arguably suboptimal – under the circumstances. Widening the income tax base by abolishing numerous tax exemptions was one alternative. Even so, the overall tax rate, at about 43.6 per cent, was not seriously out of line with the average for 13 OECD countries (although the USA, Japan and the UK were significantly below the average of 43.1 per cent in 1993 [OECD, 1994: 96]). On the grounds of inflation, however, the hike in short-term interest rates by the BBk is more difficult to justify. Analogies may be drawn with the first two crude oil price shocks (Owen Smith, 1994: 158–60). At their peak, current real short-term rates in 1974, 1981 and 1992 were respectively –0.9, 0.2 and 3.2 per cent (Owen Smith, 1996a). There could surely not have been such a vast difference in the implied expected rates of inflation.

Analysis of the wider exchange-rate implications of the BBk's interest-rate policies is rendered more difficult by the apparent stubborn refusal of other ERM members to agree to a realignment. For example, the Canute-like attitude of the British government, culminating in two hikes in short-term interest rates on Black Wednesday, withdrawal from the ERM and retraction of the second interest-rate rise, was a stylised example of British exchange-rate policy – as was the decision to enter the mechanism at DM2.95 : £1. Along with the fact that, following Black Wednesday, there was an immediate and dramatic fall in the DM:£ rate, the episode was an extremely costly lesson in how not to approach currency union. Among the resource costs were avoidable bankruptcies and an increase in unemployment. Nonetheless, EU states retained high interest rates just as their economies were facing a major slow-down in growth (Chauffour et al., 1992: 251). In discussing Steinherr (1994: 1), de Cecco compares the manner in which GEMSU was implemented with the decision in the USA to rapidly increase public expenditure in the 1960s, without a commensurate increase in taxation. He traces the destruction of the Bretton Woods international monetary regime to this policy scenario. Whereas Hobsbawm (1994: 241–2) agrees with this view, he correctly adds that the French availed themselves of the option of converting US dollars into gold, thereby drastically reducing the initially large gold reserves at Fort Knox. Had policymakers at the BBk also chosen to use their significant reserves to purchase gold, they would have profited considerably and the US-dominated international monetary and trading systems would have collapsed even earlier (ibid.: 275–6; Smyser, 1993: 221). Further policy inferences for European integration can thus be drawn from this process, not least the presence of a dominant member. This is precisely the position that Germany is assiduously trying to avoid – with varying degrees of support within the EU. Nonetheless, the handling of GEMSU was inept. Because the necessarily huge rise in public expenditure could not be monetised through a compliant central bank, the rise in interest rates induced a massive inflow of capital. Since international investors were guaranteed instruments denominated in a high interest, low inflation and revaluing currency, they were enticed to invest in Germany.

De Cecco (in Steinherr, 1994) plausibly sees the ERM as being the 'first international victim' of this policy. Domestically, the boom in western Germany ended and unemployment rose. Significantly, capital controls had been an important element in the success of the EMS during the 1980s (Higgins, 1993: 33). It follows that there are clear policy implications for the system's reform (ibid.: 37). The three options are: (1) reduce capital mobility; (2) accept a single monetary policy; (3) allow exchange rates to adjust freely. In other words, GEMSU and unsound macro-economic policies undoubtedly contributed to strains within the ERM, but fundamental reform may be required as a precursor to EMU.

There were further differences between the emergence of the SME and GEMSU (Owen Smith, 1993 and 1996a). Briefly put, they can be summarised as follows. Markets still functioned, albeit imperfectly, after the Second World War. Federal subsidies and tax relief induced investment during the 1950s. Following GEMSU, the German government procrastinated over the property-rights question and also failed to offer significant subsidies for investment in real capital (Thornton, discussant in Steinherr, 1994: 6). Hölscher (1994) usefully postulates three stylised facts for the development of the SME. They are the 1948 currency reform, the 1950 EPU credits and the 1953 London treaty. On the whole, West Germany gained extremely beneficial relief from internal and external debts, along with invaluable balance of payments assistance. Yet one of the most impressive accomplishments during the GEMSU process was western German thoroughness in drawing up various accounts setting out the degree of eastern German indebtedness. This was a major contributory factor to their becoming collectively known as '*Besserwessie*' in eastern Germany – a corruption of the German term for 'know-all' (*Besserwisser*). Moreover, some western German commentators insisted on market principles for eastern Germany that had been ignored in western Germany for decades (Owen Smith, 1996a; Smyser, 1993: 167). A good half of the savers' conversion loss was probably siphoned off by the BBk. Moreover, the privatisation process transferred whole enterprises to western German ownership without according an opportunity for share ownership to easterners, and the restitution process transferred a large part of housing wealth to western Germany (Kurz, 1993: 135; Sinn and Sinn, 1992: 74, 117; Smyser, 1993: 178). The Deutsche Bank accepted DM12 billion in eastern deposits, but made loans of only DM6.8 billion (Smyser, 1993: 157). Hence, if the eastern Germans believed that the adoption of the DM would make them wealthier in the short term, they were cruelly disabused (Flockton, 1992: 60). GEMSU was implemented in a manner which made eastern Germans 'victims' (de Cecco, discussing Steinherr, 1994: 2).

SOCIAL POLICY

Initially the introduction of the single market in 1993 was seen by the EC as generating the need for the protection of fundamental social rights because of the threat of cross-border mergers and the attendant process of concentration (Owen Smith, 1994: 310). Although this was the genesis of the social chapter, it is necessary to recall that such developments date from the Rome treaty itself. This notion of countervailing power is also a built-in feature of the SME. In any case, the firm is not the black box assumed in neoclassical economic theory; social efficiency is as important as economic efficiency (FitzRoy and Kraft, 1987: 496; 1993: 366, 374–5; Owen Smith, 1996a). Indeed, there is some evidence that, contrary to the predictions of property rights theorists, employee participation in managerial decision-making may improve efficiency (Gurdon and Rai, 1990). Similarly, Kersley and Martin (1995) demonstrate that productivity growth is increased by improving conditions of work and communications. Finally, trends at the micro-level of the firm, and of production, which exert a potentially major impact on trends at the macro-level have only recently, and only partially, become an integral part of the paradigm of political economy (Regini, 1995: 7).

Article 118 of the Rome treaty requires the EC to promote cooperation between member states 'in the social field'. In the present context it is instructive to note that social security, the right of association and collective bargaining between employers and employees are all among the several policy areas specified. Similarly, Annex 1 to the Maastricht treaty requires the Community (Article 2[1]) to support and complement the activities of member states in, for example, informing and consulting employees. Article 2(3) mentions such items as 'the social protection of employees', 'codetermination' and, in effect, the need to determine common conditions of employment within the EU. Annex 1 is more popularly known as the 'social chapter' – from which the UK government 'opted out'. During the first half of the 1980s, however, the European Court of Justice (ECJ) forced the Major government to introduce amendments to its equal pay and sex discrimination legislation. Moreover, in 1994 the House of Lords ruled that, by EU standards, the UK's effective exclusion of part-time employees from employment protection legislation was illegal.

Admittedly, the EU standards for part-time employees had been arrived at as a result of a series of German nationals appealing to the ECJ between 1987 and 1992. Nonetheless, it can be generally shown that the German model scores highly on all of these social policy features. Two basic aspects of social policy in the SME can be cited in support of this assertion. There is first a high degree of social protection and, second, there are constitutionally protected collective bargaining rights, along with statutory provision for a highly developed system of industrial democracy (Owen Smith, 1994: chs 5 and 6; 1996b). Social protection encompasses social insurance, social security and social welfare. Industrial democracy is defined here as employee participation in managerial decision-making. Since this is partly accomplished by means of codetermination, consultation and the right to information, collective bargaining between works councils and individual employers takes place at the level of the firm. As such it supplements collective bargaining at district level by the relevant trade union and employers' association. Hence, both dimensions of employee participation are in evidence: specific participative machinery exists alongside more unblurred conflicts of interest (Bean, 1994: 161–2).

Such generalisations are not, however, meant to imply that the various social policy features of this model are the subject of perfect economic and social consensus. There are several outstanding examples of conflict in what has nevertheless been a remarkably consensual society in the post-war period. First, some of the economy's largest employers and their associations resorted to litigation over the property rights implications of the 1976 Codetermination Act. Significantly, the case was heard by the Federal Constitutional Court, and its verdict went against the employers (Berghahn and Karsten, 1987: 124–6). Second, in 1984, during the lengthy strike in support of the 35-hour week, the employers and the Federal Labour Office took legal action in order to prevent employees indirectly affected by strike action in another district from drawing short-time benefits (ibid.: 98–9; Owen Smith et al., 1989: 205–6). The issue here was whether the neutrality of the Office during an industrial dispute was impaired. It duly reached the Constitutional court in 1995. Whereas the court thought the contested provisions acceptable at that juncture, it also envisaged their statutory revision at some future date (*Süddeutsche Zeitung*, 5 July 1995). Third, in 1993 the largest employers' association (Gesamtmetall) repudiated the agreement to bring about a step-by-step equalisation of money wage rates between eastern and western Germany, followed by its unprecedented announcement that the wage agreement in western Germany was to be terminated (Bastian, 1995; Sadowski et al., 1994: 533). These events confirmed the view that trade unions were on the defensive (Silvia and Markovits, 1995a and 1995b). Even so, some aspects of the UK's Trade Union Reform and Employment Rights Act (*sic!*) of 1993 would probably have been unconstitutional in Germany. Finally, over the last two decades, the costs of social insurance, assistance and welfare have all become critical policy issues (Owen Smith, 1996b). Since social insurance costs are principally met by equal contributions from employers and employees, unemployment among the indigenous labour force – particularly in construction – has increased as a result of their counterparts from member states with less developed systems not having to meet these high non-wage costs when in Germany. This problem of social dumping is exacerbated by the lower wages paid to EU citizens working in Germany. This latter reason lies behind the German government's desire to see a single market for labour whereby local rates of pay would have to be paid by all employers. The EU supports this initiative (TU Information Bulletin, 1/95).

ANTI-TRUST POLICIES

By 1949 it was obvious that the British and Americans – particularly the latter – were determined to use German industrial power as a means of strengthening the West in general against communism (Nicholls, 1994: 340). The dilemma facing the French was recognising German sovereignty while keeping German industry from threatening the French economy (ibid.). As early as the negotiations over the Schuman plan, the French attempted to reconcile allied anti-cartel policies with their anxieties about 'German remilitarisation' (Berghahn, 1986: 134–54). First the allies, and later sections of the CDU and industry, insisted that the German legislators should concentrate on cartels (ibid.: 100; Owen Smith, 1994: 436–7). Hence, any enterprise may acquire and maintain a market-dominating position as long as the Federal Cartel Office cannot demonstrate that this position is being, or would be, exploited. A notion of 'workable competition' is thus part of the SME. Moreover, the courts and the federal Minister of Economics can overturn the office's rulings. All such intervention is, however, of negligible significance when compared to the total merger scene (Owen Smith, ibid. 438–43). The Minister may also permit cartels in the public interest (ibid.: 437).

Jean Monnet saw the ECSC treaty as the 'first European anti-trust law' (Berghahn, 1986: 145). It had, in effect, emerged to accommodate the new German model in this field. Articles 60, 61, 65 and 66 prohibited cartels in principle, but permitted them where productivity and distribution would be improved; similarly concentration short of monopoly was also permitted (ibid.: 144–5). Moreover, Articles 85 and 86 of the Rome treaty, on which current European anti-trust legislation is based, contained very similar provisions – with a specific clause requiring that any abuse of a dominant position should be the subject of an EC investigation (Morgan, 1995: 7; Owen and Dynes, 1992: 155). Finally, two issues gained prominence following the single market treaty. The first was prompted by the increase in cross-border mergers and acquisitions (M&As), while the second was government subsidies to industry (state aids) (Woolcock et al., 1991: ch. 2). The West German views on both issues were absolutely crucial. They argued for a retention of some national control over mergers, and for a separate and politically independent competition authority. As a result the 1990 merger-control regulation issued in 1990 was closer to the German model than any other (ibid.: 20). Likewise, within the framework of the SME, 'industrial policy' has negative connotations. It is normally associated with the subsidisation of declining industries but also has wider implications. Although all member states – including Germany – have used such policies, they are considered by many German observers to be more important in frustrating competition than industrial concentration (Owen Smith 1994: 416–17). By implication, therefore, the enforcement of Article 92, which in such cases gives powers of veto to the EU, received enthusiastic German support. After all, although spending had decreased slightly, the aggregate level of EU state aids during the period 1988–90 averaged ECU89 billion – excluding aid given to eastern Germany (Morgan, 1995: 10). Such a sum again illustrates how the size of the EU's budget places it in a disadvantaged fiscal policy position. Moreover, until the 1980s there had been a reluctance on the part of the EC to challenge these aids. During the 1990s, Germany's state aids averaged 2.5 per cent of the economy's GDP, but the EU average fell from 3 to 2.2 per cent (EC, 1989, 1990 and 1992). Enforcement took the form of requiring the repayment of illegal aid – witness British Aerospace's refund of a £44.4 million 'sweetener', plus interest, to the UK's government. In terms of the German model, however, the level of aid to the former GDR, and the application of competition rules there, are portentous issues facing the EC.

A final area is the continued divergence between the British and

German models in the retention of national ownership of key industries and services, especially as the position in other member states is closer to the German model (Woolcock et al., 1991: 23). There is no German policy designed explicitly to prevent foreign ownership, but the system favours a long-term commitment to a company's development. Interlocking directorates, proxy voting and voting restrictions at general meetings ([and AGMs), as well as accounting procedures, form the basis of the system (Owen Smith, 1994: 338, 355, 455–6). Whereas the universal banks play a crucial role in this system, there is a range of other features which demarcate the German and Anglo-Saxon systems, not least the clear delineation of responsibilities between the non-executive and executive boards of directors (ibid.: ch. 7). Nonetheless, the role of banks as such has been widely researched, usually under quite evocative titles (see for example Pfeiffer, 1993). The flotation of Daimler-Benz on the New York stock exchange and, even more so, the privatisation of Deutsche Telekom, may be signs of an emergent 'shareholder value' culture, but a crucial inference is that the principal/agent problem for small shareholders is no better resolved in Germany than in Britain. In the latter case large institutional shareholders almost always support the [single] board's recommendations, a situation analogous to the collective use of proxy votes in the German system. An equally important inference is that the British system explicitly encourages the inflow of foreign capital, an inflow facilitated by persistent current account deficits. In the present context, the acquisition of Rover by BMW, and of Morgan Grenfell, Standard Chartered and Kleinwort Benson respectively by the Deutsche Bank, Westdeutsche Landesbank and Dresdner Bank reflect the differences between the two systems. Ironically enough, it is the capital-market expertise of these merchant banks which was highly sought after by their German purchasers (Owen Smith, 1994: 342, 379–80, 456). Capital inflows into Britain have not been confined to German, or even intra-EU, acquisitions, of course. But this seems to emphasise even more clearly the differences between, on the one hand, the German-type capital markets and, on the other hand, Anglo-Saxon models in which the potential threat of hostile takeover is a central dynamic (Cutler et al., 1989: 117). The German model thus creates wealth; the Anglo-Saxon system manipulates it. For instance, privatisation flotations brought very welcome grist to the City of London's mill.

CONCLUSION

Apart from the strong political motivation underlying the German economic, monetary and social union in mid-1990, there were obvious historical, cultural and geographical features which favoured integration. Historically, Article 116 of the West German constitution accorded German nationality to all those living within the area of the former 'Third Reich'. In many respects, these factors bind Germany as much to central and eastern Europe as to the western part of the continent. Such unifying factors are almost completely absent within the EU. Indeed, the point made at the outset about heterogeneity can be usefully supplemented at this juncture. Tichy (1993) lucidly considers the optimal conditions for European integration. Quite apart from the contrasting logical extensions to the political, historical, cultural and geographical arguments just made about Germany, there are many critical policy differences. The simultaneous existence of the EU, EFTA and Comecon bore testament to these differences. True, Scandinavian countries and Austria also have a tradition of SMEs which, as in the German case, has not reduced growth and efficiency (ibid.: 164). But Norway and, even more so, Switzerland, are able to serve their economic interests best by remaining outside of the EU. In this way, they avoid the potential fiscal transfer costs which membership would incur. Moreover, trade intensities (normalised export ratios [ibid.: 169, 177]) reveal a closely integrated Scandinavian bloc with Britain and Ireland loosely attached. Portugal, Spain, France, Belgium and the Netherlands are linked consecutively but not commonly. There are central and southern triangles comprising Germany, Switzerland and Austria on the one hand, with Italy, Greece and the former Yugoslavia on the other hand. These two triangles are bridged via France to Italy, and Austria to the former Yugoslavia and Greece. The Yugoslavian crisis isolated Greece in this respect. A similar degree of potential isolation could not conceivably affect the Iberian peninsular. Yet one must never overlook the relative openness of the EU (imports plus exports as a percentage of GDP – Higgins, 1993: 29). Even the very lowest statistic (Italy with 36 per cent, compared to Belgium's 136 per cent) was still ahead of the USA's 22 per cent and Japan's 18 per cent. In 1990, the ratio of Germany's exports to GDP was 32 per cent, compared to 11 per cent for Japan and 10 per cent for the USA (Stein, 1994: 367). Nonetheless, European trade intensities, the degree of intra-trade, along with price and production structures, all suggest a variety of 'optimal' customs unions (Tichy, 1993).

Of greater significance in terms of the Maastricht treaty is the even more pronounced degree of heterogeneity as far as the criteria for 'optimal' currency unions are concerned. Perhaps above all else, the above study has demonstrated that the formidable strengths of the Bundesbank and the DM are *the* features of the German model which will most affect EMU. The titles of contributions to the policy debate in this area are as evocative as those which address the German financial system (Goos, 1994; Hafer and Kutan, 1994; Smeets, 1990). The facts that these strengths had their origins in a draconian Allied currency reform and an undervalued international exchange rate are nearly always overlooked. The contrast with GEMSU could not be greater. Nonetheless, the emergent strong economic and political position of the DM implies that any optimal currency union with which Germany is associated would have to be based on strict price stability. Tichy (1993, 172) estimates that this union could comprise Germany herself, along with the Netherlands, Austria, probably Belgium and Switzerland. Presumably the exclusion of Luxembourg is an oversight. But the inclusion of Switzerland is at once incongruous and unrealistic: its international 'neutrality' and cumbersome political decision-making process, as well as the costless benefits endowed by being an outsider with access to EU markets, all indicate that the country will retain its present position. In addition, Switzerland has important holdings within the EU. France, on the other hand, has incurred high opportunity costs, not least in terms of unemployment, in maintaining a *fort franc* stance. Short of dramatic policy changes, she may qualify for this currency union. Meanwhile, in spite of a great deal of trepidation within Germany, the Maastricht criteria were virtually met in 1995–6 (BBk Report, 1995: 99). True, the budget deficit reached 3.5 per cent of GDP in 1995, mainly due to the incorporation of some shadow budget items arising from GEMSU. For much the same reason, gross government debt jumped from 50 to 58 per cent of GDP. But inflation and long-term interest rates were well within the relevant criteria. It is in any case inconceivable that the country would be left out of EMU for any relatively minor transgression. On the contrary: the efforts to meet the criteria notwithstanding the costs of GEMSU may prove too onerous and consequently EMU will be postponed.

Moderate wage claims, increased productivity and under-utilised production capacity all contributed to 'the fight against inflation' in 1994 (BBk Report, 1994: 103). Since this is central bankers' code for falling real wages accompanied by rising unemployment, it brings the implications of the present plans for EMU into sharp relief. But the causal flow should surely be from the real economy to nominal variables. The bottom line is that without the addition of the German model's fiscal and social policies, politically stable and viable progress with European integration and EMU will not be feasible.

REFERENCES

Akerlof, G.A., Rose, A.K., Yellen, J.L. and Hessenius, H. (1991), 'East Germany in from the Cold: The Economic Aftermath of Currency Union', *Brookings Papers on Economic Activity*, no. 1, pp. 1–105.

Bastian, J. (1995), 'Brothers in Arms or at Arms? IG Metall in 1994: Confronting Recession and Unification', *German Politics*, vol. 4, no.1, pp. 87–100.

Bean, R. (2nd rev. edn, 1994), *Comparative Industrial Relations* (London: Routledge).

Berghahn, V.R. (1986), *The Americanisation of West German Industry 1945–1973* (Leamington Spa: Berg).

Berghahn, V.R. and Karsten, D. (1987), *Industrial Relations in West Germany* (Oxford: Berg).

Chauffour, J.P., Harasty, H. and Le Dem, J. (1992), 'German Reunification and European Monetary Policy', in Barrell, R. and Whitley, J., eds, *Macroeconomic Policy Coordination in Europe: The ERM and Monetary Union* (London: Sage).

Cutler, T., Haslam, C., Williams, J. and Williams, K. (1989), *1992 – The Struggle for Europe* (New York: Berg).

Deutsche Bank Research (1994), 'East Germany: Progress and Problems', *Bulletin* (17 October), pp. 19–25.

Die Zeit (various issues), (Hamburg).

EC – European Commission (1989, 1990, 1992), *First, Second and Third Survey on State Aids in the European Community* (Luxembourg: Commission of the European Communities).

Dyker, D.A., ed. (1992), *The National Economies of Europe* (London: Longman).

Frankfurter Allgemeine Zeitung – [FAZ] (various issues), (Frankfurt).

FitzRoy, F. and Kraft, K. (1987), 'Efficiency and Internal Organization: Works Councils in West German Firms', *Economica*, vol. 54, no. 4, pp. 493–504.

FitzRoy, F. and Kraft K. (1993), 'Economic Effects of Codetermination', *Scandinavian Journal of Economics*, vol. 95, no. 3, pp. 365–75.

Flockton, C. (1992), 'The Federal Republic of Germany', in Dyker, D.A., ed., pp. 32–68.

Goos, B. (1994), 'German Monetary Policy and the Role of the Bundesbank in the ERM', *Economic and Financial Review*, vol. 1, no. 1 (spring), pp. 3–12.

Gurdon, M.A. and Rai, A. (1990), 'Codetermination and Enterprise Performance: Empirical Evidence from West Germany', *Journal of Economics and Business*, vol. 42, no. 4, pp. 289– 302.

Hafer, R.W. and Kutan, A.M. (1994), 'A Long-Run View of German Dominance and the Degree of Policy Convergence in the EMS', *Economic Inquiry*, vol. 32, no. 4 (October), pp. 684–95.

Helm, D. (1995), 'Anatomy of a Giant', *Times Higher Education Supplement* (27 January).

Higgins, B. (1993), 'Was the ERM Crisis Inevitable?', *Economic Review* (Federal Reserve Bank of Kansas City), vol. 78, no. 4 (fourth quarter), pp. 27–40.

Hobsbawm, E. (1994), *Age of Extremes: the Short Twentieth Century, 1914–1991* (London: Michael Joseph).

Hölscher, J (1994), *Entwicklungsmodell Westdeutschland: Aspekte der Akkumulation in der Geldwirtschaft* (Berlin: Duncker & Humblot).

Ifo – Institut für Wirtschaftsforschung (1994), 'Die Neuordnung des bundesstaatlichen Finanzausgleichs im Spannungsfeld zwischen Wachstums- und Verteilungszielen', *Ifo-Schnelldienst*, 3/94, pp. 3–11.

Kersley, B. and Martin, C. (1995), 'Should the UK Adopt the Social Chapter?', *Research Paper* (Department of Economics, Queen Mary and Westfield College, University of London).

Kurz, H.D., ed. (1993), *United Germany and the New Europe* (Aldershot: Edward Elgar).

Laun, K. von (1994), 'Europäische Union: Die Finanzlast für die Bundesrepublik', *Orientierungen zur Wirtschafts- und Gesellschaftspolitik*, vol. 59, no. 1, pp. 55–61.

Lipschitz, L. and McDonald, D., eds (1990), German Unification: Economic Issues, *Occasional Papers*, no. 75 (Washington, DC: International Monetary Fund).

Marsh, D. (1992), *The Bundesbank: the Bank that Rules Europe* (London: Heinemann).

Morgan, E.J. (1995), 'EU Competition Policy and the Single Market', *Economics and Business Education*, vol. 3, no. 1, pp. 7–11.

MRDB – Monthly Report of the Deutsche Bundesbank (various issues).

Nicholls, A.J. (1994), *Freedom with Responsibility: The Social Market Economy in Germany 1918–1963* (Oxford: Oxford University Press).

OECD – Organisation for Economic Co-operation and Development (1990) (1993) (1994), *Economic Surveys* (Germany).

Owen, R. and Dynes, M. (1992), *The Times Guide to the Single European Market* (London: Times Books).

Owen Smith, E. (2nd edn, 1993), *The German Economy in Western Europe* (London: Europa Publications).

Owen Smith, E. (1994), *The German Economy* (London: Routledge).

Owen Smith, E. (1996a), 'Incentives for Growth and Development', in Frowen, S.F. and Hölscher, J., eds, *The German Currency Union of 1990 – A Critical Assessment* (London: Macmillan).

Owen Smith, E. (1996b), 'Determinants of German Socio-Economic Policies' in Shackleton, J.R. and Lange, T., eds, *Germany – An Economy in Transition* (Oxford: Berghahn Books).

Owen Smith, E., Frick, B. and Griffiths, T. (1989), *Third Party Involvement in Industrial Disputes: A Comparative Study of West Germany ad Britain* (Aldershot: Avebury Press).

Pfeiffer, H. (1993), *Die Macht der Banken* (Frankfurt: Campus).

Regini, M. (1995), *Uncertain Boundaries: The Social and Political Construction of European Economies* (Cambridge: Cambridge University Press).

Sadowski, D., Schneider, M. and Wagner, K. (1994), 'The Impact of European Integration and German Unification on Industrial Relations in Germany', *British Journal of Industrial Relations*, vol. 32, no. 4, pp. 523–37.

Silvia, S.J. and Markovits, A.S. (1995a), 'The New World of German Trade Unions: Still Essential Pillars of "Modell Deutschland"?', *Business and the Contemporary World*, vol. 8, no. 1, pp. 52–66.

Silvia, S.J. and Markovits, A.S. (1995b), 'The Reform of the German Trade Union Federation', *German Politics*, vol. 4, no. 1, pp. 64–85.

Sinn, G. and Sinn, H.-W. (1992), *Jumpstart: the Economic Unification of Germany* (Boston, Mass.: MIT Press).

Smeets, H.D. (1990), 'Does Germany Dominate the EMS?', *Journal of Common Market Studies*, vol. 29, no. 1, pp. 37–52.

Smyser, W.R. (2nd edn, 1993), *The German Economy: Colossus at the Crossroads* (Harlow: Longman).

Stein, J.L. (1994), 'Fundamental Determinants of Real Exchange Rates and Capital Flows and their Importance for Europe', *Economic Notes*, vol. 23, no. 3, pp. 367–87.

Steinherr, A. (1994), 'Lessons from German Unification', *CIDEI Working Paper*, no. 33 (December).

Süddeutsche Zeitung [SZ], (various issues), (Munich).

Tichy, G. (1993), 'European Integration and the Heterogeneity of Europe', in Kurz, H.D., ed., pp. 163–180.

Wiseman, J. (1989), 'Social Policy and the Social Market', in Peacock, A. and Willgerodt, H., eds, *German Neo-Liberals and the Social Market Economy: Origins and Evolution* (London: Macmillan), pp. 160–78.

Woolcock, S., Hodges, M. and Schreiber, K. (1991), *Britain, Germany and 1992: the Limits of Deregulation* (London: Royal Institute of International Affairs/Pinter Publishers).

8 Believing in the Miracle Cure: The Economic Transition Process in Germany and East-Central Europe*

Till Geiger

The policy recommendations of western economists looking at eastern Europe after the velvet revolutions of 1989 predicted a fairytale ending to a story as yet untold: '[A former state socialist country] was poor, then it chose capitalism, then as a result it became rich' (adopted from McCloskey, 1990: 26). Faced with an uncertain future, this prophecy proved compellingly seductive. It intuitively appealed to policy-makers confronted with the aftermath of the collapse of state socialism for a variety of reasons. At first sight, it offered a simplistic historical interpretation. In particular, its rhetorical message reflected an unquestioned belief in the crisis of one system (Schabowski, 1992: 8). However, the imaginary plot alluded to an existing solution without examining the appropriateness of the proposed policy recommendations (Keegan, 1993: 1–2).

Since the heady days of the velvet revolutions, economic transition has not stuck to the script. Indeed, the chequered history of economic reform since 1989 has exposed the extent to which the predictions of western economists raised false hopes. In the popular imagination, the end of the Cold War liberated Europe from the political, economic and social structures of the previous four decades. However, this perceived radical discontinuity presented particular problems for policy-makers. The stability of the Cold War order created a false sense of predictable interstate relations between the two blocs and among European nations. With *perestroika* and ultimately the fall of the Berlin Wall, this stability gave way to a period of uncertainty which is still continuing. Western European policy-makers faced these new challenges ill-prepared. Taken by surprise, they clung to existing institutional arrangements or bowed to the inevitable turn of events. Faced with uncertainty, policy-makers attempted to rely on some assumed 'certainties' implying their ability to manage economic transition.

In the days of the Cold War, the tensions between the two military blocs had been partially articulated through a stylised competition between the 'two' economic systems. This aspect of the conflict reflected the ideological nature of political and economic thought on both sides of the iron curtain. The revolutions of 1989 allowed for a reunification of language and political discourse in eastern and western Europe (Dahrendorf, 1990: 11–12). The new unified language reinforced the perception of a complete catharsis of the political discourse as well as of the political, economic and social structures. However, the end of the ideological confrontation only started the much-needed re-evaluation of the discursive interpretations of these institutional arrangements which emerged during the Cold War. In the immediate aftermath, the perceived radical break with the past obscured reality. Indeed, the velvet revolutions did not undermine many of the myths and 'instant histories' about the Cold War. These discursive structures of the Cold War influenced, if not shaped, the transformation from state socialism to pluralist democracies and market economies in eastern Europe. At first, the presumed destruction of the political, economic and social structures fostered unrealistic expectations among policy-makers. For example, many of the policy solutions adopted suggest the widespread belief among politicians that one economic system could just be replaced with another like equipping a car with a new engine. Indeed, this assumption reflects the degree to which institutional structures are internalised. Therefore, the complexity of rearticulating and reinventing the political, economic and social structures has been underestimated. Developments since 1989 have shown that institution-building is a far more cumbersome process than policy-makers and observers had asserted and imagined. Among the folk tales of the Cold War period, five myths about economic development, in particular, seem relevant to a discussion of economic transition of Germany and eastern and central Europe:

— *National reconstruction myths*: In 1945 Europe lay in ruins. The state reconstructed the economy and as a result Europe experienced an unprecedented boom.

— *Competition of ideologies*: At the end of the Second World War, there existed ideological differences between the United States and the Soviet Union. Soon each side felt threatened by the actions of the other. As a result both sides rearmed and engaged in economic competition.

— *European dream*: In the immediate post-war period, the German problem dominated the agenda. Each bloc created institutional frameworks to contain the German threat; this led to a period of relative stability.

— *Convergence hypothesis*: At the beginning of the great boom, economies conformed to either the capitalist or state socialist economic structures. Economic reforms transformed the national economies and as a result the economic systems started to converge.

— *Thatcher revolution*: In the 1970s, capitalist economies stagnated. Therefore, governments disassembled the Keynesian welfare state and privatised nationalised industries and as a result economic performance in western Europe recovered.

At various stages, these myths simultaneously articulated and influenced the politico-economic relationships in the European nation states as well as between the two economic blocs. Being interrelated, these discursive structures reflected and moulded the institutional arrangements as well as political, economic and social structures. In 1989, the conjunction of these discursive practices fostered the conviction that the adoption of capitalism would overcome the economic backwardness of the former state socialist economies. Under the influence of these discursive practices, policy-makers adopted certain policies over alternative approaches to the economic transition process.[1]

Consequently, the first section of this paper is devoted to reconstructing the historical developments underlying these patterns. The following section will analyse how the various stories influenced the actions of policy-makers in the aftermath of 1989. The last section examines the economic consequences of some of these choices.

DISCURSIVE STRUCTURES OF THE COLD WAR ERA

National Reconstruction Myths

At the end of the Second World War, Europe lay in ruins. In the immediate aftermath, national governments in both east and west lacked political legitimacy to some degree. This lack arose from the long absence of governments in exile or from the imposition of a particular government by the victorious liberators. Despite national differences, the maxim 'never again' became the *leitmotiv* underlying national reconstruction policies. Governments set out to address some long-standing economic and social problems which ministers perceived as contributory causes

Table 8.1 Growth of output
(average annual percentage changes)

	GDP 1950–52 to 1967–69		
West Germany	6.2	East Germany	5.7
Austria	5.0	Czechoslovakia	5.2
Italy	5.4	Hungary	4.8
Spain	6.1	Poland	6.1
Greece	6.0	Bulgaria	6.9
Portugal	5.1	Romania	7.2
Total	5.9	Total	6.0

Source: Nita Watts, 'Eastern and Western Europe', in *European Economy: Growth and Crisis*, ed. Andrea Boltho (Oxford: Oxford University Press), 1982, 259–86.

of the world crisis of the 1930s and ultimately the Second World War. In western Europe, national governments pursued a combination of five policy objectives: social welfare, full employment, development of national agriculture, economic growth, and later military security (Milward, 1994: 21–45). Similarly, eastern European countries embarked on ambitious reconstruction programmes directed toward rapid industrialisation. On both sides of the emerging iron curtain, the state assumed a more visible role in the management of the economy. As Table 8.1 shows, national reconstruction policies resulted in rapid economic development in both eastern and western Europe in the 1950s and 1960s. On both sides, politicians attributed the economic boom to the restructuring of the economy and choice of economic system. These decisions about national reconstruction policies became part of the mythology of the new European nation states.

In the case of West Germany, the 'economic miracle' myth celebrated the currency reforms and the associated reforms creating Erhard's *soziale Marktwirtschaft* (social market economy) (Giersch et al., 1994: xi–xiii). The success of the Monnet plan paved the way for the enduring commitment of the French government to *planification* (Hall, 1986: 139–91; Sautter, 1982: 450–71). Even in the dying days of the German Democratic Republic (GDR), reformist politicians defended the achievements of state socialism. In the case of East Germany, policy-makers proudly remembered overcoming the massive problems of the reconstruction period (Schabowski, 1992: 37–9, 281–2). The reformers of the Prague Spring saw the social-democratic reconstruction policies pursued by the democratic coalition government between 1945 and 1948 as a model for future economic development (see the guarded references in Šik, 1967: 44–77).

Competition of Ideologies

During the Cold War, the ideological conflict between the superpowers led to the primacy of the security structure. In the immediate post-war period, the opposing ideological standpoints led each of the main players to misperceive the other superpower's intention which resulted in an unprecedented military build-up in peace-time. Both the Soviet Union and the United States embarked on policies directed towards containing the perceived expansionism of the other superpower. Once the formation of two opposing blocs became inevitable, both superpowers sponsored the creation of military alliances in Europe. By the mid-1950s, military competition had assumed the form of exceedingly dangerous posturing. To an overwhelming degree, the national security interests of the hegemon determined the parameters of all relationships between the two blocs. On both sides of the iron curtain, the different production structures reflected the economic system of the dominant economy. As Stalin had insisted in conversation with Milovan Djilas during the Second World War: 'whoever occupies a territory also imposes on it his own social system. Everyone imposes his own system as far as his army has power to do so. It cannot be otherwise' (Djilas, 1963: 90).

In eastern Europe, the Soviet leadership coerced most states into adopting the Stalinist model of central planning. In contrast, American policy-makers mainly relied on Marshall aid to promote the American model of capitalism (Carew, 1987). In such a climate, any attempt to steer a middle way between state socialism and capitalism soon floundered. For a time, the post-war Czechoslovak government tried to implement an alternative socialist system. In 1947, even the communist ministers supported defying the Soviet leadership and participated in the Marshall Plan. Under Soviet pressure, the cabinet was forced to reconsider and soon ended its act of defiance. Indeed, this episode paved the way for the communist *putsch* in February 1948 (Kaplan, 1981; Krátky, 1994: 9–25). From the early days of the Cold War, any attempt to bridge the two systems became impossible. Any departure from the 'right' economic system under the communist power monopoly prompted massive coercive pressure to bring the truant state back to the fold. As a consequence, by early 1948 the Cold War divided the world into two rival military and economic blocs. The clearest statement of the competition between the economic systems remains Khrushchev's 1959 boast that the Soviet economy would overtake the American economy by 1970 or 1980 at the latest. After the launch of Sputnik, many western observers feared the economic challenge of state socialism (Nye, 1990: 116; Nove, 1984: 356). Western analysts made similar claims for capitalism. The strong ideological content of such debates is reflected in the subtitle of Walt Rostow's influential study on the stages of economic growth – 'A Non-Communist Manifesto' (Rostow, 1960). In such comparisons, each side emphasised the advantages of their system in terms of stable economic growth, employment opportunities and economic security. Far from being constructive, this discourse reinforced the ideological nature of the economic structures underlying the Cold War.

The European Dream

On both sides of the iron curtain, the 'German problem' exercised national governments worried about the re-emergence of German military expansionism in the future. The wartime allies fiercely debated an array of plans to guard against such an eventuality. All these plans envisaged the division of Germany into a number of smaller states, reparations, total disarmament, the prohibition of the production of military equipment, and severe restrictions on many important industries. France and the Soviet Union counted on German reparations and deliveries from current production to assist their own reconstruction plans. In contrast, Britain and to a lesser extent the United States promoted the reconstruction of their occupation zones to limit the growing financial cost of the occupation, relief and rehabilitation effort. To assuage French concerns, American policy-makers tied German reconstruction to the provision of Marshall Plan aid for western European modernisation (Milward, 1984). By then, Stalin himself had abandoned hope for a unified, state socialist Germany and proceeded to integrate East Germany into the eastern bloc (Djilas, 1963: 119). After the Marshall Plan paved the way for a separate West German state, the French government sought a defence guarantee from Britain and the United States against a future German threat. At the same time, French ministers persisted in their quest to attain some form of international control over the heavy industry in the Ruhr. Protracted negotiations initially resulted in an institutional framework satisfying none of the contracting parties. The Schuman Plan broke the deadlock in 1949/50 by reconciling the different interests among western Europeans.

While the European Coal and Steel Community (ECSC) failed to create an integrated market, the rhetoric established an aura around the project of European integration. Arguably, the liberalisation of intra-European trade and the formation of the European Payments Union engendered western European economic integration. The tangible benefits of economic integration convinced western European policy-makers to establish the common market (Milward and Sorensen, 1993: 1–32). Since 1957, the member states of the European Economic Community (EEC) continued, albeit more slowly than intended, to translate the treaty of Rome into reality. Implementing the European dream created its own historical dynamic. In the changed circumstances of the 1980s, western European policy-makers adopted the Single European Act (SEA) to revitalise a sluggish European economy. As hoped, this bold initiative accelerated economic growth and seemed to cure the so-called Euro-sclerosis which had plagued western Europe since the early 1970s. At the same time, the single European market heightened the impetus for European monetary union (EMU) (Altvater and Mahnkopf, 1993: 72–92). Indeed, the French government saw EMU as a means to break the Bundesbank's rule over western European monetary policy (Dyson, 1994: 171–2). The relative success of the SEA initiative revived the dream of European integration as a solution to all European woes (Altvater and Mahnkopf, 1993: 11–15).

The Convergence Hypothesis

Historians have argued that the division of the world into two rival blocs was completed by the mid-1950s. After years of intense confrontation, policy-makers in east and west accepted the emerging ground rules underlying the Cold War (Loth, 1989). The threat of mutual destruction convinced policy-makers of the futility of any major military confrontation. Indeed, both sides felt that the economic burden of the arms race had become excessive (Ambrose, 1984: 541–53). Peaceful coexistence, however, did not imply an end to the ideologically motivated competition between the two hegemonic blocs. By the 1960s, the state had assumed a more prominent role within capitalist economies. Meanwhile, economic reformers in eastern Europe argued for the creation of markets within state socialist economies. However, such reforms only partially succeeded. As a consequence of these developments, some analysts argued that two economic systems were converging towards a third way between capitalism and socialism. Economic convergence would eventually remove the underlying reasons for the superpower confrontation (Wiles, 1990: 73–6). Indeed in the 1970s, *détente* created a climate of accommodation between the blocs.

The Thatcher Revolution

As a backlash against the role of the state in the west, monetarists such as Milton Friedman blamed governments for economic stagnation, rising unemployment and spiralling inflation after the massive oil price increases of 1973 and 1979. Higher unemployment was attributed to 'excessive' welfare provisions and trade union powers. All economic woes arose from expansionary fiscal and monetary policies. Unemployment benefits and state subsidies for failing nationalised industries contributed to the rigidities in the labour market and further increased unemployment. Based on their analysis, monetarists recommended the severe pruning of public expenditures, restrictive monetary policies, curbs on trade unions, and the liberalisation of the economy through privatisation of the nationalised industries and public services. In Britain after 1979, conservative politicians embraced this radical programme as a first step to regain the competitiveness of the British economy. Margaret Thatcher presented her programme rhetorically as a fight against 'socialism' blurring the distinction between the Keynesian welfare state and state socialism. After a decade of the Thatcher experiment, some economic indicators seemed to support the idea of a rejuvenation. The globalisation of the world market forced national governments to pursue similar economic policies of privatisation, deregulation and reducing welfare. However, other western European governments adopted quasi-Thatcherite policies more slowly. As the Mitterrand experiment in France in the early 1980s demonstrated, the globalisation of the world economy restricted the scope for any national expansionary programme. Moves to improve national competitiveness reflected concerns about Euro-sclerosis in the early 1980s. However, compared with Japan and the United States, western Europe seemed to fall behind and suffer increasingly from structural unemployment. Arguably, national developments persuaded politicians that Euro-sclerosis could only be addressed through deregulation at western European level. The relative success of the SEA initiative reinforced the rationale underlying national deregulation policy.

As the above summary shows, the five myths about economic development during the Cold War emerged at different times and in different contexts. To some extent, their messages varied in importance and changed over time. Individual myths overlapped and enhanced one another, but they also contradicted and excluded other assumptions. This raises the vital question: how did these myths – the national reconstruction myths, the competition of ideologies, the European dream, the convergence hypothesis, and the Thatcher revolution – influence the policy choices of policy-makers during the early stages of the economic transition process in Germany and east-central Europe?

NEW UNCERTAINTIES, OLD CERTAINTIES AND THE ECONOMIC REFORM PROCESS

In 1989, the velvet revolutions accomplished the unforeseen. With remarkable ease, the collapse of state socialism occurred through the surrender of the East European regimes first in Poland and Hungary, later in East Germany and Czechoslovakia. Even more striking is the fact that the rapid demise of state socialism remained an unforeseen contingency for policy-makers in both east and west, even on the very eve of the respective revolutions. Unprepared, policy-makers relied on the relative certainties of the Cold War structures when confronted with the uncertainties of the politico-economic aspects of the post-Cold-War world. Western analysts and statesmen, in particular, followed events from the sidelines in stunned surprise. State socialist politicians did not fare any better in dealing with the unpredicted turn of events. On both sides, policy-makers miscalculated their responses under the pressure of constantly changing developments.

The question, as to why no one accurately predicted the demise of state socialism and the centrally guided economies in eastern Europe, has exercised many social scientists since.[2] One possible explanation is that the inaccurate expectations of the policy-making community reflected recent historical developments. Paradoxically, the collapse of the convergence hypothesis reinforced assumptions about the stability of the Cold War structures in the 1980s. In addition, the ability of both economic systems to overcome repeated economic failures created the impression of the reformability of the economic structures in the east as well as in the west.

How did policy-makers interpret the unpredicted? Far from questioning the failure of past theories, political discourse immediately historicised the events within the context of the Cold War structures. Policy-makers, who had come of age in a world of ideological competition, naturally interpreted the sudden demise of state socialism as the victory of capitalism and western democracy. Taking this interpretation to an extreme, Francis Fukuyama heralded the events by claiming that modern societies had reached the 'end of history' (Fukuyama, 1992). In eastern Europe, meanwhile, politicians suggested that the new democracies had returned to Europe. Having shaken off the Russian yoke, little in their eyes separated the emerging civil societies in eastern Europe from their western neighbours (Dahrendorf, 1990: 93–100).

Beyond instant history, the Cold War's discursive structures shaped the aspirations of policy-makers, élites and the public. The long years of ideological competition contributed to the apprehension about the 'reintroduction' of capitalism among many eastern European intellectuals. In their eyes, the end of Soviet domination would not only speed the end of state socialism but also open the floodgates to the worst excesses of capitalism. In 1985 György Dalos summed up this ambivalence in the following ominous conclusion, about what would happen if a modernising Soviet leader wanted to reduce the massive expenditure of its vast Empire:

> [After] the Soviet troops have been seen off with marching music and flowers . . . the countries of the former eastern bloc will create parliamentary institutions, they will open their borders and guarantee individual rights including a sensibly regulated right to private property. Everything else – the McDonald's chain, unemployment, and peep shows – will emerge by itself. (Dalos, 1991: 185)

Faced with this nightmare senario, many on the left in eastern and western Europe expected (or hoped) that the new democracies would adopt a 'third way' – an economic system between state socialism and capitalism (Lipp, 1989: 5–7). To some extent, this support for a 'third way' reflected the admiration that many intellectuals felt for the experiment of 'socialism with a human face' in the Prague Spring of 1968. Hoping to preserve the cultural credo of the underground, these dissident intellectuals expected the implementation of Ota Šik's *humane economic democracy* to pave the way to a more egalitarian society (Dahrendorf, 1990: 53–69; Engler, 1991: 48–75). These discussions soon fizzled out due to the lack of a coherent blueprint for such an alternative economic model (Nuti and Portes, 1993: 1). Moreover, existing models were themselves flawed to varying degrees. For example, Šik's vision of a 'third way' overburdens the democratic process with detailed economic allocation decisions. To be operable, the system would have to rely heavily on state intervention. Therefore, this blueprint would lack the legitimacy of an alternative model of economic reform in eastern Europe where state institutions were thoroughly discredited

(Geiger, 1995). Adopting an alternative economic system would have clashed with the desire of many eastern Europeans for an early 'return to Europe' and ruled out their integration into a wider European Community (Sachs, 1993: 3–26).

The twin objectives of a rapid transition to democracy and early membership of the European Union almost necessitated the switch to a market economy (Przeworski, 1991: 8). Against this background, eastern European policy-makers attempted to model a post-reform economic system on western European mixed economies. To legitimise their reform programmes, policy-makers borrowed from the treasure trove of historical examples. In 1989, the Polish prime minister Tadeusz Mazowiecki sought to appoint the Polish Ludwig Erhard to spearhead the new government's radical economic reforms (Sachs, 1993: 83–7). By associating the 'Balcerowicz Plan' with Erhard's radical reforms in 1948, Mazowiecki created the impression that the future path of Polish economic development would evolve along the lines of the West German post-war miracle – the *Wirtschaftswunder*. West German politicians made a similar mental link drawing a direct parallel between post-war reconstruction in West Germany and economic unification of post-Cold War Germany. Through the currency reform and the introduction of the market economy in former East Germany, German economic, monetary and social union (GEMSU) would trigger another economic miracle at a single stroke (Heilemann and Jochimsen, 1993: 14–16). In the case of Germany, the national reconstruction myth proved politically potent despite the tarnished recent record of the West German economy. The questionable historical analogy notwithstanding, the *Wirtschaftswunder* myth became a source of inspiration for the unification process (Carlin, 1992: 335). In Poland, another western myth influenced the initial formulation of policy. The Thatcher government's sell-off of nationalised industries and public services provided the framework for the first Polish privatisation law. Perceived success in the west recommended the British model to Polish policy-makers. In their initial judgement, policy-makers ignored the totally different scale of privatising the state sector in eastern Europe (Sachs, 1993: 83–7).

These examples show that policy-makers in east and west sought refuge in the reassuring security of established political discourses. Through these rhetorical allusions, policy-makers plotted for themselves and their electorates the path to a 'better future'. Armed with reassuring economic advice from western economic advisers, policy-makers boldly faced the future under the banner of 'democracy, market, Europe'. The search for a paradigm for political and economic transition in the former state socialist countries stood in the way of understanding the institutional barriers to implementing the policy-makers' dream for a brighter future (Hirschmann, 1970: 329–43). Initially, the rhetoric deflected from the fact that once the iron curtain had been perforated, the post-Cold War era would quickly turn into a policy-maker's nightmare. Confronting this nightmare, old certainties offered solutions, albeit illusory ones to the unanticipated and as yet unknown problems of political, economic and social transition.

Evolving discursive practices quickly narrowed the potential for change by defining and limiting the political agenda. During the velvet revolutions, events also dictated, shaped and altered the options for policy-makers. A dramatic example of the rapidly changing agenda remains the East German street demonstrations. On the streets, the initial call for change, associated with 'we are *the* people', soon evolved into the demand for unification, expressed by 'we are *one* people' after the fall of the Wall (Heilemann and Jochimsen, 1993: 57; Engler, 1991: 48–75). As the fog lifted, the emerging but still shifting agenda pointed in the direction of an uncertain and indeterminate future driven by the aspirations, imagination and rhetoric of the velvet revolutions. In this context, the role of policy-makers became crucial in translating the agenda of the street into a coherent political and economic programme.

However, how far did these discursive structures not only shape the perceptions of policy-makers but also influence their actual behaviour and policy response? The velvet revolutions marked the beginning of an historically unique period of social change. This uniqueness implies that the eventual result of redefining political, economic and social relationships is *ex ante* not only uncertain but indeterminate. This difference is vital. In an established democracy, the outcome of a decision might be uncertain, yet, the process by which decisions are reached, implemented or contested is constrained by an institutional framework. However in eastern Europe, these institutions have not yet been firmly embedded within society. After all, the eastern European experiments of transition to democracy might well end in renewed authoritarian rule. In this situation, economic development could be an important element to ensure the future social cohesion of a new democracy (Przeworski, 1991: 10–40).

In an historically unique situation, certain discursive practices may not be appropriate. For example, the discursive practice of economists rests on the assumption that economic laws apply everywhere, even in different cultural settings or in exceptional circumstances. Their optimism regarding the universal applicability of economic laws represents the proverbial straw which western economic advisers are offering to policy-makers to grasp (Adams and Brock, 1993: 21–43). Initially, these economists seemed to ignore the antagonism between their universal rules and the historical uniqueness of economic transition (Hirschmann, 1970: 329–43). Tainted by the deceptive simplicity of their economic models, economists exclude political complexities from their discussion of the economic transition process (Adams and Brock, 1993: 103–17; the missionary zeal of economists is often reflected in the titles of their works, see for example Kornai, 1990; Sachs, 1993). For many economic advisers, policy-makers should take decisive action to rearticulate all economic relationships according to the blueprint of western market economies while ignoring the cost involved. Indeed, a sense of historical occasion seemed to breed its own unique bravado among policy-makers. Policy-makers trusted their own historical metaphors rather than their customary caution regarding institutional change. In this context, the imperative for decisive change crowded out the incremental nature of institutional change in times of *normal* politics (Dahrendorf, 1990: 71–108). However, such trust may lead to hasty solutions which will prove defective in the long run.

Together with existing institutional structures, historical discourses contributed to the *historical uniqueness* of the velvet revolutions. However, discursive structures are just one element among a number of independent factors 'over-determining' the course of history (Hirschmann, 1970: 329–43). In different historical circumstances, a post-communist government would in all likelihood have received different economic advice. In the immediate post-war period and in the 1960s, Keynesian economists might well have counselled a more gradual approach. Today, economists favour a big bang and a radical approach to economic reform which reflects the dominance of neoclassical and monetarist ideas in the profession. Despite overwhelming support among economists, such ideas might not have appealed to post-communist governments under different circumstances. Through the Thatcher revolution, a monetarist policy regime acquired around 1989 the kudos of knowing the recipe for economic success. The World Bank spread this message by claiming that a diminished role for of the state would engender economic development after the Cold War (World Bank, 1991: 109–47).

Therefore, discursive structures matter, because they shape perceptions, set the agenda and determine the choices of policy-makers.

RÉGULATION IN A MOMENT OF HISTORICAL UNIQUENESS

The emerging discourse of instantaneous history resumed the 'as yet untold story' of the economic reform process and its 'fairytale ending' by investing the story with new meanings: 'In a former state socialist country, the old political system collapsed. The process of economic transition freed society and reintroduced the (universal) economic incentives of a market economy, then as a result the country became rich.'

Elements of the five discursive structures outlined at the beginning of this chapter projected a homogeneity onto the events of 1989. The past did not just explain events, but neatly fitted them into established discourses. According to the script of the 'untold story', economic success depends on putting in place a catalogue of 'freedoms' (the right to own private property, to trade, to contest markets, to enforce contracts, to compete, etc.) (Dahrendorf, 1990; Kornai, 1990). In surrendering the mind (state intervention), the body (society/market economy) will follow. However, the assumption that it is best to leave economic development to the automatism of market mechanisms is one of the myths of our age (i.e. a crucial element of the Thatcher revolution) (Laclau, 1990: xi–xv). It ignores the fact that these fundamental elements are only given meaning as the articulation of economic relations in a particular social context. In the end, the 'untold story' ignores the discursive nature of the reform process itself.

This analysis has treated myths as a reflection of how communities (i.e. policy-makers, economists, citizens, the Atlantic ruling class, the *nomenklatura*) construct social identities by identifying elements of political or economic developments as defining moments. These moments in concrete discourses (particular stories, specific myths) are perpetuated through articulatory practice (Bertramsen et al., 1991: 55–7). Through discursive practice, any concrete discourse is constantly renegotiated and constructed. In this open-ended process, the meanings of moments are reinterpreted as the discursive practice changes. In the case of West Germany, economic prosperity (the result of the *Wirtschaftswunder*) became a defining moment of citizenship (Habermas, 1990: 209). To some extent, this discursive practice ignores major elements and the material basis of the West German mode of *régulation* (i.e. the articulation of economic relations and institutional structures).[3] While forgotten in discursive practice, these elements underpin modes of *régulation* potentially outlasting a concrete discourse. In a situation of unique change, concrete discourses offer meaning to developments in their own logic until new social identities have been renegotiated. While any concrete discourse can inform social action (our myths influencing governments' policy agenda), only through discursive practice can social identities be renegotiated and constructed redefining the relationship and structure of state, economy and society.

In the field of economic reform, three myths proved particularly influential: the economic competition between the two economic systems, the 'return to the market' battle-cry of the Thatcher revolution, and the *Wirtschaftswunder* myth. These concrete discourses interpreted the reform process in terms which equated the transition of establishing institutional forms with the defining moments of these three discursive structures (capitalist economic development, privatisation and deregulation, political stability of the social market economy). In an historically unique situation, the discursive practices of the revolutionary force may be influenced by established stories offering concrete articulations of their aims (e.g. to establish a civil society, human rights, economic freedom and prosperity). In a revolutionary situation, the persuasiveness of concrete discourses lies precisely in the fact of their concreteness compared with the yet undefined new social identities.

The process of transition from one mode of *régulation*/development to another requires the discursive renegotiation of economic relationships. However, the institutional economic and political structures cannot be changed within a short period of time (Bertramsen et al., 1991: 193–5). Even in circumstances of normal economic development, changes of production methods trigger a difficult and lengthy adaptation of the economic arrangements governing wage determination, forms of competition, financing of investments, nature of state, degree of openness of the economy and international trade (Boyer, 1993: 7–80; Boyer, 1992: 55–103).

The structural limits to discursive practice or decisive intervention redefining the mode of *régulation* are substantial in East Germany and east-central Europe. For example, the industrial base is outdated, the infrastructure in serious disrepair and the service sector underdeveloped. While the legitimacy of the central planning authorities and the *nomenklatura* has been eroded, the arrangements governing worker representation and/or management of state enterprises in Poland and Hungary remain virtually unaffected by the collapse of communist party rule. By 1989 institutional arrangements had already weakened the control of the state over economic relationships in both countries. The public demand for a radical break with the past was loudest in East Germany and Czechoslovakia, where state control had been the tightest (Frydman and Rapaczynski, 1994: 141–67). East Germans opted to transplant the existing arrangements of another system. Only in the Czech Republic did the unique opportunity materialise to start with a clean slate as far as economic management was concerned (Kosta, 1991: 301–25).

In this model, the state is a crucial, but not the only, determinant of the mode of *régulation*. Despite the collapse of state socialism, existing interest groups who have a vested interest in current institutional arrangements may resist change. The reform process may be historically unique, but its inner dynamics are shaped by past arrangements which survived the collapse of the old system. The ability of societies to redefine an appropriate mode of *régulation* will determine whether the transition from a state socialist economy to a market economy will be successful. By extension, this theoretical approach rejects the notion of a universal economic policy regime (or mode of *régulation*). Societies have to find an 'appropriate' mode of *régulation* which accommodates its institutional structures and changes in the economic arrangements. Only a sufficient degree of flexibility to social change will engender harmonious economic development (Altvater, 1992: 50–68).

The reform process is a subject of constant debate. Compared with the detailed economic advice offered to western governments, many policy proposals are characterised by uncharacteristic fervour (given the normal discursive practices among economists). The policy proposals are very essentialist, focusing on the major tasks of renegotiating economic institutions and arrangements. This discourse demands an 'end to state control' and a 'return to the market'. As these economists realise, decisive action to establish competitive market structures requires determined state intervention on a massive scale. Consequently, only a strong government will end the uncertainty about a return to state socialism (Sachs, 1993; Kornai, 1990). In east-central Europe, state socialism thoroughly undermined the legitimacy of government. The new governments will need time to acquire a sufficient degree of legitimacy to risk unpopularity. At the same time, the government has to strike a balance between the programme of radical reform and pursuing economic stability (full employment, low inflation, sustainable economic growth) (Dahrendorf, 1990: 71–108). For example, to avoid price reform leading to hyperinflation, the government has to negotiate with other agents to contain inflation. In economic theory, it might be sufficient to adopt a restrictive monetary policy regime limiting monetary growth and bank lending. Beyond this theoretical discourse, state intervention alone is not enough as managers and trade unionists will have to exercise wage restraint as well. Such cooperation might be difficult to achieve or maintain because in the past firms circumvented wage restrictions by borrowing from other state enterprises. As long as state enterprises cannot go bankrupt, managers would rather agree to the wage demands of their employees in response to price rises. In Poland, the expansion of informal credit between enterprises has at times undermined the government's anti-inflation policy (Calvo and Coricelli, 1992: 176–226).

Therefore, policy-makers have to renegotiate new discursively constructed arrangements and institutional structures to facilitate cooperation between all economic agents and to achieve longer-term economic stability. In this process, the government will meet opposition, if other groups feel their interests are threatened. Thus, to ensure political acceptability of the economic reform process, governments have to address social concerns and reform the welfare system. The government's discursive strategy should take account of the fact that all transition strategies require a massive leap of faith across all sectors of society. As any policy choice might have lasting implications for the emerging mode of *régulation*, policy-makers have to find a discursive strategy which will attract sufficient consent.

If economic transition is an intensely discursive process, then the debates over key elements in the reform process will be marked by the clash of differing discursive practices. For example, the debate over the conversion rate of the East German currency (*Ostmark*) shows the process of renegotiating economic relationships while failing to construct a unifying discourse around the decision. In early 1990, the European Commission outlined the conundrum faced by policy-makers:

> [a] crucial point will be the conversion rate(s) of East German marks into Deutschmarks. The choice of the rate(s) must hold the balance between the need to avoid creating excessive purchasing power, weakening the competitiveness of East German enterprises and causing unemployment as a result, and the need to take account of the German Democratic Republic population's expectations that wages and pensions will catch up with West German standards. (EC Commission, 1990: 11)

Chancellor Kohl seized the opportunity and intervened decisively. Concentrating on the historical task of unification, Kohl emphasised meeting the expectations of the East German population. Without consulting his cabinet and the Bundesbank, Kohl offered the principle of an 1:1 exchange rate for most money and small savings (Marsh, 1993:

206–17). This surprise move reflected Kohl's ambition to achieve an early settlement of the terms of unification. To justify the 1:1 conversion rate, Kohl and his ministers drew a discursive link between the 1948 currency reform and the 1990 currency conversion suggesting that the introduction of the West German currency into the GDR (D-Mark) would result in another *Wirtschaftswunder* (Schmieding, 1991: 189–211).

Given the discursive practice linking citizenship with West Germany's economic strength, any other exchange rate would have amounted to excluding East Germans from full participation in the West German state. Moreover, the chancellor's agreement to the favourable terms of GEMSU should be interpreted as a move to prevent the potential mass migration of East Germans to the west, undermining the existing institutional arrangements underpinning the West German economy (Rothschild, 1993: 259–66). The chancellor's action established a moment in unification discourse. However, this decision flew directly in the face of the advice given by the Bundesbank or professional economists. Their discursive practice focused much more on the future competitiveness of East German industry and potential implications for unemployment resulting from choosing the wrong rate. Kohl's political choice did not reflect either the black market rates for the eastern Mark (7:1 to 11:1) (Sinn and Sinn, 1993: 67) or the official rates for commercial transactions[4] or tourists (2 : 1 to 5 : 1) (Deutsche Bundesbank, 1991: 128–9) at the time. After GEMSU, purchase power comparisons have shown that the 1 : 1 exchange rate did roughly reflect the correct rate (Sinn and Sinn, 1993: 65–72). However, as the East German official rates extremely overvalued the currency in terms of international competitiveness, East German export industry could no longer compete in eastern European markets, industrial production collapsed, and unemployment rose to unexpected levels (Priewe and Hickel, 1991: 56–81). Despite this structural spanner in the works of Kohl's discursive promise of a bright future, a political U-turn to take account of the misgivings among Bundesbank officials and sceptical economists became impossible. Once the offer had been announced publicly, any adjustment to ease the consequences for the competitiveness of East German industry or reduce the financial implications for West Germany could not be contemplated. The open disagreement between the Bundesbank and the Kohl government soured and altered the relationship between the two, as would become visible again over EMU (Dyson, 1994: 348–51). In the context of domestic politics, the Kohl government appeased West Germans by promising nothing would change and

East Germans by offering economic prosperity as symbolised by the D-Mark. According to the chancellor's rhetoric, the settlement offered unification without tears as a fitting end to the years of 'unnatural' division (Offe, 1993: 282–301).

The terms of GEMSU ruled out alternative economic strategies or a more gradual transition. Kohl's discursive practice suggested that West German economic institutions and arrangements could be simply transferred. However, as the East German example shows, institutional arrangements do not transfer easily or adjust as flexibly as past experience would suggest. The collective wage-bargaining arrangements in the former West Germany were renowned for the ability of both employers and trade unionists to accommodate economic change. The conversion rate for the East German Mark had disastrous consequences for East German industry, raising their unit wage costs above West German levels. With a different conversion rate, this problem would have been avoided. To correct its mistake, the Kohl government called for wage restraint. Accepting the political inevitability of unification and the terms of GEMSU, economists started to preach similar wage restraint. In line with the government's optimistic rhetoric, economic advisers now claimed that the healthy state of West German public finances would enable the government to finance the implications of unification by increased borrowing. The extent of this self-deluding optimism is revealed by the assumption that the additional public expenditure could be met by the peace dividend.[5] West German politicians and government economic advisers constructed a new unifying discursive practice proclaiming that the *Aufschwung Ost* (Upswing East) was just around the corner provided everyone pulled together. To many East and West Germans, this discursive practice seemed designed to whip up courage while blithely ignoring the reality of unemployment and deindustrialisation (Priewe and Hickel, 1991: 195–8). This differing interpretation became obvious over the issue of wage restraint. Where in the past unions might have heeded such an appeal, trade unionists now resisted the government's attempts to shift the economic cost of unification on to the workforce. Within the trade union movement, the radical nature of economic change led to divisions over a national wage strategy rather than to solidarity among workers (Altvater and Mahnkopf, 1993: 185–214; Busch, 1994: 188–91). While demanding wage restraint, the discursive strategy of politicians to 'rebuild one nation' assumed new additional financial commitment, such as moving the seat of the federal government from Bonn to Berlin (Dornbusch and Wolf, 1992: 235–72). The government's line on unification assumed that solidarity would emerge spontaneously and ignored the growing rift between the discursive practices in East and West Germany (Offe, 1993: 282–301).

The government's discursive strategy over unification raised a few eyebrows abroad. During the negotiations of GEMSU and political unification, Kohl asserted the primacy of his domestic political mission. Later, the government would argue that given the unstable nature of Russian politics a speedy settlement had to be found in order not to miss this unique opportunity for unification (Rothschild, 1993: 259–66). This imperative, however, does not excuse the hair-raising manner in which Kohl bulldozed through the unification settlement at European and international level (Habermas, 1990: 205–06). After all, Kohl might have been expected to inform, if not consult, his friend François Mitterrand over the conversion rate before making his infamous offer (Dahrendorf, 1990: 127–8). As the chancellor normally likes to portray himself as a staunch believer in the European dream, ignoring the legitimate interests of the FRG's neighbours reinforced the apprehension of West Germany's EC partners about unification. The Cold War discursive practice of decrying the iron curtain and the division of Germany now made it hard for the western European countries to object to unification. From the start of the unification process, the other EC partners (in some cases reluctantly) accepted that East Germany represented a special case for accession to the Community.[6] As paymaster of the Community, the Kohl government could, to some extent, disregard the objections of other western European governments to unification. Despite this turn of events, the legal hairsplitting of the Kohl government over the terms of unification did little to improve the legitimacy of the settlement domestically or at European level (Offe, 1993: 282–301).

Since the formation of the European Coal and Steel Community, a defining moment in the European dream had been the construction of an institutional framework not merely as a basis for peaceful cooperation but also as a safeguard against future German expansionism. Even NATO and the common market never offered more than this rhetorical guarantee for continued cooperation on the basis of good neighbourliness. The primacy of the domestic agenda seemed to push the European dream off the West German policy agenda adding to the suspicions that a unified Germany would become a bully rather than remain the trusted partner within the EC. Believing in the stabilising nature of European integration, the EC members decided to deepen the economic union at Maastricht. By drawing the unified Germany deeper into the institutional framework, the French government believed the potential threat could be contained (Dyson, 1994: 12). To assuage its western European partners, the Kohl government signed up for the next stage in the integration process, the European monetary union (EMU). Despite the initial tensions, the discussions among EC members renegotiated the European dream to accommodate German unification in the Maastricht treaty. In the member states, the new discursive consensus among policy-makers did not necessarily meet the support of the electorate. Despite the efforts of the Mitterrand government to persuade the public, French voters came close to rejecting the Maastricht treaty. The attempt to reassure western European partners similarly backfired on Kohl as (West) German taxpayers increasingly resented the tax increases resulting from the government's largesse over the EC budget. Moreover, the Bundesbank, having lost the argument over currency conversion, openly defied the German government's commitment and actively undermined the EMU process (Eichengreen and Wyplosz, 1993: 109–13).

Another challenge to the new European élite consensus came from the declared desire of the new democracies in east-central Europe to join the EU. Early EC membership came to be seen as a 'return to Europe' by many policy-makers in east-central Europe, stabilising the achievements of political revolution and modernising their economies through participation in the European dream. The rapid modernisation of Spain after the death of Franco seemed to confirm the benefits of economic integration into the European market (Sachs, 1993: 3–26). Western policy-makers responded to this plea for admission into the fold of the EC with some scepticism about the ability of eastern European states to adhere fully to the *acquis communautaire*.

While sharing this view, leading politicians close to the Kohl government argued in a policy document on European policy that unless the EU accepted a major role, '. . . Germany might be called upon . . . to try to effect the stabilisation of eastern Europe on its own and in the traditional way' (Schäuble and Lammers, 1994: 3). This discursive practice fuelled the apprehensions in east-central Europe about Germany's future role in Europe (Dahrendorf, 1990: 114–28). Without the experience of the extensive dialogue between the EC member states, such fears reflect the unhealed scars of previous German attempts to control the region through economic imperialism in the 1930s and the Second World War. During the years of Cold War confrontation, reconciliation proved difficult since both sides lacked any shared discourse through which to confront the past constructively (Ibid., 10–13). After the revolutions of 1989, West German politicians did not treat the ceaseless demands for reassurance of its peaceful intentions with the required sensitivity. The initial refusal to guarantee Poland's western border and entertain compensation claims reeked of an emerging D-mark imperialism (Habermas, 1990: 205–6). Since then, German politicians have become the leading lobbyists for a financial aid package for east-central Europe. This reflects the growing awareness that Germany should not contemplate assisting east-central Europe without support from its EC partners. As the other member states lacked Germany's direct security interest, the EC aid effort has remained a trickle compared to the need for another Marshall Plan (Cox, 1993).

From the perspective of the new market economies, the objective of gaining access to the EU internal market acquired paramount importance. The 'trade not aid' rhetoric fell foul of the protectionist outlook of some EU member states (Inotai, 1994: 139–65). One of the major concerns is the economic impact from certain 'sensitive' imports from the new market economies in the east. In the case of full membership, members would lose the existing degree of protection from these imports and the financial support from the structural fund. To some extent, the European Commission mitigated these protectionist inclinations of member governments in the negotiations of the Association Agreements with the east-central European states (Nicolaïdis, 1993: 196–245). The Commission thus pursued a 'dual' strategy and was in favour of member states constructing a Europe of concentric circles. While continuing the process of economic integration, the association agreements failed to reduce the EU's trade barriers sufficiently despite the EU's rhetorical commitment to trade liberalisation (Busch, 1992: 323–6). The half-hearted approach of the association agreements bars the east-central European market economies from full integration into the world economy. Rather than interpreting the original provisions of the agreements restrictively, the EU countries should liberalise trade relations further. Such a strategy would be mutually beneficial improving western European competitiveness in the world economy (Inotai, 1994: 139–65; Schumacher and Möbius, 1993: 113–75).

The EU's invidious reluctance to open its markets to 'sensitive' imports from eastern Europe, calls into question the wisdom of the economic advice that openness to the global economy will speed the modernisation of domestic industry. Under pressure from the protectionist member states, the EU has been reluctant to grant immediate access to east-central European imports of agricultural products, basic materials, semi-manufactured goods and textiles (see Inotai, 1994: 146). Trade liberalisation rules out any attempt to pursue a strategic trade policy which affords domestic industry a degree of infant industry protection.

At the same time, east-central Europeans cannot in the short term earn enough foreign currency through exports to finance the modernisation of industry. Therefore, east-central Europeans rely on a rescheduling of the existing external debt, massive capital imports and foreign direct investment from the west (Houbenova-Dellisivkova, 1994: 217–32; Vincentz, 1994: 175–95). Western economic advisers justified their rhetorical adherence to openness by insisting that imports will increase internal competition and curb the monopoly power of large state enterprises before their privatisation (Sachs, 1993: 47–52; Adams and Brock, 1993: 58–9). In the end, this rhetorical strategy recognised that the government can decide to open the economy in concert with financial assistance from abroad, but the mass privatisation of state enterprises needs to be discussed more fully (a survey of the privatisation policies in the various east-central European countries can be found in Frydman et al., 1993; the merits and disadvantages of the various approaches are discussed in Bornstein, 1994: 233–58).

The debates over privatisation have focused on whether state enterprises should be sold off to the highest bidder or distributed through vouchers to the general public or to the employees of state enterprises. The crucial issue remains the establishment of a system of corporate governance which ensures competitive behaviour by the newly privatised firms (Frydman and Rapaczynski, 1994). While any settlement has to safeguard the interests of employees and the public in an equitable distribution of the national wealth, the state should maximise the potential revenue to help finance economic transition (Bolton and Roland, 1992: 275–309). In this respect, the greatest threat to social stability is the process of spontaneous privatisation whereby managers sell company assets below price and acquire them for their newly formed companies (Frydman and Rapaczynski, 1994: 141–67). The gradual progress of economic reform in east-central Europe (Poland, Czech Republic, Slovakia and Hungary) reveals that, contrary to economic advice, price and macro-economic stabilisation are by themselves insufficient to achieve the transition to a market economy (Portes, 1993). To transform the system, governments will have to attach more importance to privatisation and trade liberalisation (Welfens, 1993: 319–44). Such progress will only be possible in dialogue between all interests in society and at a European level. Maybe the time has come to consider a more gradual conversion which preserves social stability and prevents a redistribution of social wealth to the old *nomenklatura* in east-central Europe. But even gradualism needs a strategy, rather than become a third way by default.

CONCLUSION

In the new Europe, political stability depends to a large extent on securing economic prosperity in the medium term. At present, existing domestic and intra-European institutions are under great strain. The current problems require reform of existing agreements or new, possibly more flexible, institutional arrangements. Only open dialogue among all Europeans can find new solutions to recast the current European order. Among the alternatives, further and wider economic integration might offer the best route to attaining economic and political stability at the doorstep of the European Union (Buzan et al., 1990: 202–28, 253–60). The multilateral institutions created in the post-war period provide useful models for such efforts (Ruggie, 1993: 3–47). Intergovernmental cooperation (e.g. in a reformed EU) depends on assuring indivisibility of benefits (east-central European states should become full members), generalised organising principles (*acquis communautaire*), and diffuse reciprocity. This programme demands that EU members abandon their current dual strategy and adopt a more flexible approach to the integration of east-central Europe. Given the political will, the European dream should be opened to aspiring members to renegotiate and construct the European house of the future. Within the current institutional framework, east-central Europe will have to wait until its economies converge with those of the current members. To serve the wider European community, old discursive structures should themselves be rethought and replaced as a part of finding new institutional arrangements appropriate for a new Europe. In an atmosphere of good neighbourliness, Europe would be more likely to thrive if the strains and costs of economic transition could be better accommodated. This, in turn, would ensure Europe's economic and political security.

NOTES

* I would like to thank Niamh Early and Michelle Twoomey for their useful criticisms of an earlier draft of this paper. I am grateful to Hilary Owen for reading the final draft and making some invaluable suggestions. All mistakes, however, are entirely my own.

1. This analysis defines discourse as an 'open and decentred structure in which meaning is constantly renegotiated and constructed'; see Bertramsen et al.,

1991: 55–6. Stories and myths form part of concrete discourses established through articulatory (or discursive) practices and reflect how communities define their social identity. Discursive structures refer to the structural relationship between these five privileged discursive practices in a wider sense. See also the discussion in the final section of this chapter.

2. For the reasons of this failure to predict the collapse of the Soviet empire, compare Collins and Waller, 1993: 302–25; Waldrauch, 1994: 433–45.; Gaddis, 1993: 5–58; Cox, 1994: 29–44.; Ticktin, 1994: 45–58. Even the most critical analysts did not predict that the centrally planned economies faced such an immediate end; compare Winiecki, 1986: 543–61.
3. In the French *régulation* theory approach, the concept *régulation* refers to the institutional structures and arrangements governing the economy including the government, the representation of industry, and trade unions. The mode of *régulation* refers to the national articulation of the institutional accommodation of economic relationships. On this point, see the translator's note to Boyer, 1979: 99–118. For a critical survey of this approach, see Boyer, 1986.
4. The GDR's State Trade Bank (Deutsche Aussenhandelsbank) often operated with a myriad of different exchange rates depending on the transaction. For an indication of the various rates, see Marer et al., 1992: 144–5. Under state socialism, both east-central European countries and East Germany sustained their over-valued exchange rates by carefully managing their foreign trade through state trading organisations.
5. For an optimistic assessment of economic transition by a senior economic adviser to the Kohl government, see Siebert, 1991: 289–340. On the peace dividend, see Dornbusch and Wolf, 1992: 235–72. For an openly critical assessment of such suggestions, see Deutsche Bundesbank, 1992: 5–6.
6. Article 23 of the West German Basic Law provided for the accession of the former East German states to the Federal Republic. If the two German states had chosen the alternative route to unification enshrined in article 146 of the Basic Law, the procedure might have been more difficult from the perspective of the EC; see EC Commission, 1990: 9–10.

REFERENCES

Adams, W. and Brock, J.W. (1993), *Adam Smith Goes to Moscow: A Dialogue on Radical Reform* (Princeton: Princeton University Press).

Altvater, E. (2nd edn, 1992), *Die Zukunft des Marktes: Ein Essay über die Regulierung von Geld und Natur nach dem Scheitern des 'real existierden' Sozialismus* (Münster: Westfälisches Dampfboot).

Altvater, E. and Mahnkopf, B. (1993), *Gewerkschaften vor der europäischen Herausforderung: Tarifpolitik nach Mauer und Maastricht* (Münster: Westfälisches Dampfboot).

Ambrose, S.E. (1984), *Eisenhower: The President* (New York: Simon & Schuster).

Bertramsen, R.B., Thomsen, J.P.F. and Torfing, J. (1991), *State, Economy and Society* (London: Unwin Hyman).

Bolton, P. and Roland, G. (1992), 'Privatization policies in Central and Eastern Europe', *Economic Policy*, vol. 7, no. 15, pp. 275–309.

Bornstein, M. (1994), 'Privatization in Central and Eastern Europe: techniques, policy options and economic consequences', in Csaba, L., ed., pp. 233–58.

Boyer, R. (1979), 'Wage formation in historical perspective: the French experience', *Cambridge Journal of Economics*, vol. 3, no. 2, pp. 99–118.

Boyer, R. (1986), *La théorie de la* régulation*: une analyse critique* (Paris: Éditions la Découverte).

Boyer, R. (1992), 'Neue Richtungen von Managementpraktiken und Arbeitsorganisation: Allgemeine Prinzipien und nationale Entwicklungspfade', in Demirovic, A., Krebs, H.P. and Sablowski, T., eds, *Hegemonie und Staat: Kapitalistische Regulation als Projekt und Prozess*, (Münster: Westfählisches Dampfboot), pp. 55–103.

Boyer, R. (1993), 'Première Partie: Comment émerge un nouveau système productif?', in Boyer, R. and Durand, J.P., eds, *L'après-fordisme* (Paris: Syros), pp. 7–80.

Busch, K. (2nd edn, 1992), *Umbruch in Europa: Die ökonomischen, ökologischen und sozialen Perspektiven des einheitlichen Binnenmarktes* (Köln: Bund Verlag).

Busch, K. (1994), *Europäische Integration und Tarifpolitik: Lohnpolitische Konsequenzen der Wirtschafts- und Währungsunion* (Köln: Bund Verlag).

Buzan, B. et al. (1990), *The European Security Order recast: Scenarios for the Post-Cold War Era* (London: Pinter).

Calvo, G.A. and Coricelli, F. (1992), 'Stabilizing a previously centrally planned economy: Poland 1990', *Economic Policy*, vol. 7, no. 14, pp. 176–226.

Carew, A. (1987), *Labour under the Marshall Plan: The politics of productivity and the marketing of management science* (Manchester: Manchester University Press).

Carlin, W. (1992), 'Privatization in East Germany, 1990–92', *German History*, vol. 10, no. 3, pp. 335–51.

Collins, R. and Waller, D. (1993), 'Der Zusammenbruch von Staaten und die Revolutionen im sowjetischen Block: Welche Theorien machten zutreffende Voraussagen?', in Joas, H. and Kohli, M., eds, *Der Zusammenbruch der DDR* (Frankfurt: Suhrkamp), pp. 302–25.

Cox, M. (1993), 'The Lessons of the Present: Understanding the Marshall Plan historically', Paper presented at the ECPR workshop *The Political Economy of Postwar Reconstruction* in Leiden, 3–7 April.

Cox, M. (1994), 'The End of the USSR and the Collapse of Soviet Studies', in Dunleavy, P. and Stanyer, J., eds, pp. 29–44.

Csaba, L., ed. (1994), *Privatization, Liberalization and Destruction: Recreating the Market in Central and Eastern Europe* (Aldershot: Dartmouth).

Dahrendorf, R. (1990), *Reflections on the Revolution in Europe: In a letter intended to have been sent to a gentleman in Warsaw, 1990* (London: Chatto and Windus).

Dalos, G. (1991), 'Über die Verwirklichung der Träume,' in Deppe, R. et al., pp. 182–205.

Deppe, R., Dubiel, H. and Rödel, U., eds (1991), *Demokratischer Umbruch in Osteuropa* (Frankfurt/Main: Suhrkamp).

Deutsche Bundesbank (1991), *Geschäftsbericht der Deutschen Bundesbank für das Jahr 1990*, vol. 42 (Frankfurt/Main: Deutsche Bundesbank).

Deutsche Bundesbank (1992), *Geschäftsbericht der Deutschen Bundesbank für das Jahr 1991*, vol. 43 (Frankfurt/Main: Deutsche Bundesbank).
Djilas, M. (1963), *Conversations with Stalin* (Harmondsworth: Penguin).
Dornbusch, R. and Wolf, H. (1992), 'Economic Transition in Eastern Germany', *Brookings Papers on Economic Activity*, no. 1, pp. 235–72.
Dunleavy, P. and Stanyer, J., eds, *Contemporary Political Studies 1994*, vol. 1 (Belfast: Political Studies Association).
Dyson, K. (1994), *Elusive Union: The Process of Economic and Monetary Union in Europe* (London: Longman).
EC – European Communities: Commission (1990), *The European Community and German Unification*, Bulletin of the European Communities, Supplement 4/90 (Luxembourg: Office of Official Publications of the European Communities).
Eichengreen, B. and Wyplosz, C. (1993), 'The unstable EMS', *Brookings Papers on Economic Activity*, no. 1, pp. 109–13.
Engler, W. (1991), 'Stellungen, Stellungnahmen, Legenden: Ein ostdeutscher Erinnerungsversuch', in Deppe, R. et al., pp. 48–75.
Frydman, R. and Rapaczynski, A. (1994), 'Insiders and the State', in Frydman, R. and Rapaczynski, A., eds, *Privatization in Eastern Europe: Is the State Withering Away?* (Budapest: Central European University Press), pp. 141–67.
Frydman, R., Rapaczynski, A. and Earle, J.S. (1993), *The Privatization Process in Central Europe* (Budapest: Central European University Press).
Fukuyama, F. (1992), *The End of History and the Last Man* (Harmondsworth: Penguin).
Gaddis, J.L. (1993), 'International Relations Theory and the End of the Cold War', *International Security*, vol. 17, no. 3, pp. 5–58.
Geiger, T. (1995), 'Economic transition in Eastern Europe and Ota Šik's *Third Way*: What future a radical "alternative" to the reform process?,' unpublished manuscript.
Giersch, H., Paque, K.H. and Schmieding, H. (rev. edn, 1994), *The Fading Miracle: Four decades of market economy in Germany* (Cambridge: Cambridge University Press).
Habermas, J. (1990), *Die nachgeholte Revolution* (Frankfurt/Main: Suhrkamp).
Hall, P. (1986), *Governing the Economy: The Politics of State Intervention in Britain and France* (Cambridge: Polity Press).
Heilemann, U. and Jochimsen, R. (1993), *Christmas in July? The Political Economy of German Unification Reconsidered*, Brookings Occasional Papers (Washington, DC: Brookings).
Hirschman, A. (1970), 'The Search for Paradigms as a Hindrance to Understanding', *World Politics*, vol. 22, no. 3, pp. 329–43.
Houbenova-Dellisivkova, T. (1994), 'Liberalization and Transformation in Bulgaria', in Csaba, L., ed., pp. 217–32.
Inotai, A. (1994), 'Central and Eastern Europe', in Randall Henning, C., Hochreiter, E. and Clyde Hufbauer, G., eds, *Reviving the European Union* (Washington: Institute for International Economics).
Kaplan, K. (1981), *Der kurze Marsch: Kommunistische Machtübernahme in der Tschechoslowakei, 1945–1948* (Munich: Oldenbourg).
Keegan, W. (1993), *The Spectre of Capitalism: The Future of the World Economy after the Fall of Communism* (London: Vintage Books).

Kornai, J. (1990), *The Road to a Free Economy: Shifting from a Socialist System: The Example of Hungary* (New York: W.W. Norton).

Kosta, J. (1991), 'Ökonomische Aspekte des Systemwandels in der Tschechoslowakei', in Deppe, R. et al., pp.301–25.

Krátky, K. (1994), 'Czechoslovakia, the Soviet Union and the Marshall Plan', in Westad, O.A., Holtsmark, S. and Neumann, I.B., eds, *The Soviet Union in Eastern Europe, 1945–89* (London: Macmillan), pp. 9–25.

Laclau, E. (1990), *New Reflections on the Revolution of Our Time* (London: Verso).

Lipp, E.M. (1989), 'The GDR undergoes dramatic change: outlook for 1990 and beyond', unpublished manuscript.

Loth, W. (7th edn, 1989), *Die Teilung der Welt: Die Geschichte des Kalten Kriegs, 1941–1955* (Munich: Deutscher Taschenbuch Verlag).

Marer, P. et al. (1992), *Historically Planned Economies: A Guide to the Data* (Washington: World Bank).

Marsh, D. (1993), *The Bundesbank: The Bank that rules Europe* (London: Mandarin Paperbacks).

McCloskey, D.N. (1990), *If you are so smart: The narrative of economic expertise* (Chicago: University of Chicago Press), 1990.

Milward, A.S. (1984), *The Reconstruction of Western Europe, 1945–51* (London: Methuen).

Milward, A.S. (1994), *The European Rescue of the Nation-State* (London: Routledge).

Milward, A.S. and Sorensen, V. (1993), 'Interdependence or integration? A national choice,' in Milward, A.S. et al., eds, *The Frontier of National Sovereignty: History and theory, 1945–1992* (London: Routledge), pp. 1–32.

Nicolaïdis, K. (1993), 'Eastern European Trade in the Aftermath of 1989: Did International Institutions Matter?', in Keohane, R.O., Nye, J.S. and Hoffmann, S., eds, *After the Cold War: International Institutions and State Strategies in Europe, 1989–1991* (Cambridge, Mass.: Harvard University Press).

Nove, A. (1984), *An Economic History of the U.S.S.R* (Harmondsworth: Penguin).

Nuti, D.M. and Portes, R. (1993), 'Central Europe: the way forward', in Portes, R., ed., pp. 1 ff.

Nye, J.S. (1990), *Bound to Lead: The changing nature of American power* (New York: Basic Books).

Offe, C. (1993), 'Wohlstand, Nation, Republik', in Joas, H. and Kohli, M., eds, *Der Zusammenbruch der DDR* (Frankfurt/Main: Suhrkamp).

Portes, R. (1993), *Economic Transformation in Central Europe: A Progress Report* (London: Centre of Economic Policy Research).

Priewe, J. and Hickel, R. (1991), *Der Preis der Einheit: Bilanz und Perspektiven der deutschen Vereinigung* (Frankfurt/Main: Fischer Taschenbuch).

Przeworski, A. (1991), *Democracy and the market: Political and economic reforms in Eastern Europe and Latin America* (Cambridge: Cambridge University Press).

Rostow, W.W. (1960), *The Stages of Economic Growth: A Non-Communist Manifesto* (Cambridge: Cambridge University Press).

Rothschild, K.W. (1993), 'Like a *Lehrstück* by Brecht: notes on the German reunification drama', *Cambridge Journal of Economics*, vol. 17, no. 3, pp. 259–66.

Ruggie, J.G. (1993), 'Multilateralism: The Anatomy of an Institution', in Ruggie, J.G., ed., *Multilateralism Matters: The Theory and Practise of an Institutional Form* (New York: Columbia University Press), pp. 3–47.
Sachs, J. (1993), *Poland's Jump to the Market Economy* (Cambridge, Mass.: MIT Press).
Sautter, C. (1982), 'France', in Botho, A., ed., *European Economy: Growth and Crisis* (Oxford: Oxford University Press), pp. 450–71.
Schabowski, G. (1992), *Der Absturz* (Reinbek: Rowohlt Taschenbuch Verlag).
Schäuble, W. and Lamers, K. (1994), 'Reflections on European Policy', policy document published by the CDU/CSU-Fraktion des Deutschen Bundestages, Bonn, 1 September.
Schmieding, H. (1991), 'Deutschlands Weg zur Marktwirtschaft: Die westdeutsche Währungsreform von 1948 und die gesamtdeutsche Währungsunion von 1990 im Vergleich', *ORDO: Jahrbuch für die Ordnung von Wirtschaft und Gesellschaft*, vol. 42, pp. 189–211.
Schumacher, D. and Möbius, U. (1993), 'Eastern Europe and the EC – trade relations and trade policy regards to industrial products', in Heitger, B. and Waverman, L., eds, *German Unification and the International Economy* (London: Routledge), 1993, pp. 113–75.
Siebert, H. (1991), 'German unification: the economics of transition', *Economic Policy*, vol. 6, pp. 289–340.
Šik, O. (1967), *Plan and market under socialism* (White Plains, NY: International Arts and Sciences Press).
Sinn, G. and Sinn, H.W. (3rd edn, 1993), *Kaltstart: Volkswirtschaftliche Aspekte der deutschen Wiedervereinigung* (Munich: Deutscher Taschenbuch Verlag).
Ticktin, H. (1994), 'The State of Soviet Studies in the Post-War Period: A View from the Left', in Dunleavy and Stanyer, eds, pp. 45–58.
Vincentz, V. (1994), 'Internationaler Handel auf unvollkommenen Märkten: Implikationen für Osteuropa', *Konjunkturpolitik*, vol. 40, no. 2, pp. 175–95.
Waldrauch, H. (1994), 'Theoretische Erklärungsansätze der Transitionsprozesse der kommunistischen Länder Osteuropas (1988–1990)', *Österreichische Zeitschrift für Politikwissenschaft*, vol. 23, no. 4, pp. 433–45.
Welfens, P.J.J. (1993), 'Privatisierung und externe Liberalisierung: Probleme der Systemtransformation in Polen', *ORDO: Jahrbuch für die Ordnung von Wirtschaft und Gesellschaft*, vol. 44, pp. 319–44.
Wiles, P.J.D. (1990), 'The Convergence Hypothesis', in Eatwell, J., Milgate, M. and Newman, P., eds, *Problems of the Planned Economy* (London: Macmillan).
Winiecki, J. (1986), 'Soviet-type economies: considerations for the future', *Soviet Studies*, vol. 38, no. 4, pp. 543–61.
World Bank (1991), *World Development Report 1991: The Challenge of Development* (Oxford: Oxford University Press).

9 Germany's Security Policy Dilemmas: NATO, the WEU and the OSCE

Adrian Hyde-Price

More than half a decade after unification it is appropriate to assess Germany's changing role in the European security system. What has been the response of the Bundesrepublik Deutschland (BRD) to the new responsibilities placed on it by the ending of the east–west conflict and with it, of the 'short' twentieth century (Hobsbawm, 1994)? What is the wider significance for Europe of post-war Germany's foreign and security policies? Bonn's evolving security policy must be seen not only in the light of changes since 1990, but also in terms of Germany's troubled history and its unique geopolitical situation.

The concern of this chapter is thus to assess the main trends, directions and dynamics of Germany's security policy since unification in 1990, and to situate them in their historical and geopolitical context. The chapter begins by considering the implications of the 'German problem' for European security, and goes on to assess the implications of Cold War bipolarity for West German security policy. It then seeks to identify the distinctive features of German security policy since 1990, and to assess the implications of the Federal Republic's (FRG) security policy for European international relations and the changing nature of global politics in the late twentieth century. What emerges from this study is that Bonn's security policy cannot be understood in terms of clear-cut choices and distinct strategies, but rather as a series of policy dilemmas. They revolve around three international organisations (NATO, the WEU and the OSCE, formerly the CSCE) and three capitals (Washington, Paris and Moscow). These dilemmas cannot be resolved, only managed. Consequently, the task facing Bonn in the 1990s is to manage its security dilemmas in ways which contribute to the consolidation of the European integration process and a lessening of tensions and conflicts in the wider continent – in short, to lay the foundations for a Europe 'whole and free'.

GERMANY AND EUROPEAN SECURITY BEFORE 1990

German security policy is inextricably bound up with reference to three decisive factors: geography, economics and politics. This trinity provides the key to understanding Germany's role in the modern states system. Germany has long been the fulcrum of the European balance of power. At the time of the formation of the modern European states system (a long and complex process given legal expression in the 1648 treaty of Westphalia[1]), Germany – in the shape of the Holy Roman Empire – was a weak and divided land. The weakness of the Holy Roman Empire left the plethora of German principalities and statelets as the pawns in the wider struggle for mastery between Europe's great powers. It was only in 1871 that Germany emerged as a powerful and united state – a European great power in its own right.

From the start, the Bismarckian Reich – created through 'blood and iron' under Prussian hegemony – posed a challenge to the established system of European international relations. Simply put, Germany was too big, and too centrally located, to fit easily into the European states system. From this was born the 'German problem': the problem, in other words, of how to integrate – or at least contain – the prodigious economic strength and military potential of a united German state, situated at the very heart of the European continent. It was the failure to resolve this conundrum that led to the two world wars of the twentieth century.

It is important to note that the German problem derived not from some intrinsic character flaw in the German people, but rather from the geography, economics and politics of the German state. To begin with, Germany's central geographical location – its *Mittellage* (or central location) – has given it a pivotal role in European affairs. Few countries have as many neighbours as Germany. Situated at the heart of the European continent, straddling its two major waterways (the Rhine and the Danube) and standing at the crossroads between Latins and Slavs, Germany has long been destined to play a central role in Europe's international relations. On the positive side, its *Mittellage* gives Germany economic and cultural interests in both east and west. On the negative side, Germany 'was born encircled' (Calleo, 1978: 206), its *Mittellage* creating a difficult and demanding geopolitical situation in which the nightmare of a war on two fronts was an ever-present danger.

Germany's central geographical location would not have been so much of a problem for its neighbours if it were not also for Germany's size, its vibrant economy and its authoritarian political character. 'What is wrong with Germany', A.J.P. Taylor once wrote, 'is that there is too much of it' (Taylor, 1967: 21). With unification in 1871, Germany became the largest state in central and western Europe. Only Russia in the east was larger, both geographically and in terms of population. But in contrast to Russia, the German economy since the late nineteenth century has been arguably the most dynamic and productive in Europe. Industrialisation transformed the German economy into the manufacturing and financial powerhouse of Europe. Germany, in the words of John Maynard Keynes, became the central support around which the rest of the European economy grouped itself, and 'on the prosperity and enterprise of Germany the prosperity of the rest of the continent mainly depended' (quoted in Wallace, 1990: 15). It also gave the Berlin government the wherewithal to build up a formidable military machine, harnessing Prussian militarism to the productive capacity of the *Ruhrgebiet*, the country's foremost industrial region.

At the same time, Germany has been a problem for European security not just because of its structural position within the international system (i.e., its geopolitical location and economic potency), but because of its political character. Domestic political considerations are often discounted by realist or neo-realist theorists of international relations when analysing the functioning of the states system. Yet in the case of Germany, this is patently absurd. The unified Germany forged by Bismarck, upon which Hitler constructed the national socialist state, was characterised by a propensity towards authoritarianism, militarism, intolerance and economic protectionism (see the controversial book by Blackbourn and Eley, 1984). The domestic political complexion of Germany has thus long been an issue of crucial importance for European peace and stability.

THE BUNDESREPUBLIK AND COLD WAR EUROPE

With the exception of the ill-fated Weimar Republik, security policies of successive German states prior to 1945 tended towards militarism and an aggressive assertiveness. The comprehensive military and political defeat of the 'Third Reich' in May 1945 provided a historic opportunity to break with this self-destructive pattern of behaviour. Early post-war hopes of building a new democratic and peaceful Europe were thwarted by the onset of the Cold War. Yet the Cold War also gave the West Germans the opportunity to redeem themselves by integrating into western multilateral structures and acting as a bulwark for western democracy. Moreover, the bipolar division of Europe, with the division of Germany and Berlin at its heart, meant that Germans were increasingly seen not as the recent perpetrators of aggression, but as the hapless victims of Soviet perfidy.

The Cold War also changed the geopolitics of what was now a divided Germany. Germany was no longer at the heart of European affairs, pursuing its own *Sonderweg* ('special path') between east and west, and playing a pivotal role in shaping the future of the continent. Instead, Germany found itself forming the front-line in a new global struggle between east and west. The fault-line of the east–west conflict ran through the heart of Germany, and was epitomised by the division of Berlin – a division given concrete form on 13 August 1961 when the Berlin Wall was erected. The Cold War led to the division of Germany into two new states, each of which was from the very start firmly integrated into their respective alliance systems, and aligned closely with their respective superpower patron. Germany thus became the focus of the Cold War in Europe. As such it constituted what a British Foreign Office memorandum of the time referred to as the 'pawn which both sides wished to turn into a queen' (quoted in Moreton, 1987: 32).

This division of the former German Reich into two rival states, each laying claim to Germany's democratic and humanist traditions, was a brutal and ultimately unsustainable violation of the national and democratic rights of the German people. Yet at the same time, it also seemed to have 'provided a solution, inadvertently, to the problem which the countries of Europe had faced and failed to master since 1890: the place of a too-powerful Germany in a European system which could not of itself preserve the independence of its members in the face of German strength' (DePorte, 1986: 116). In both east and west, the division of Germany was thus often quietly accepted as a pragmatic solution to the problem of integrating German power in Europe. One oft-quoted example of this is the aphorism of François Mauriac, who declared that 'I love Germany so much that I rejoice at the idea that today there are two of them' (quoted in Moreton, 1987: 76).

The changed political and strategic environment in which post-war West Germany found itself necessitated a dramatically new approach by the Bonn government to its defence and security policy. From the very start, German security policy – indeed, its foreign policy in general – was characterised by a pronounced commitment to multilateralism. The Bonn government, conscious of the lingering suspicion harboured by its neighbours and former enemies, sought to pursue its own national interests through multilateral cooperation with its new western allies. Indeed, *Westbindung* became part of the very *raison d'état* of the FRG (Juricic, 1995: 111–12). West Germany subsequently became one of the firmest supporters of both the European integration process and the Atlantic Alliance. Multilateralism also provided the means for the country to regain its sovereignty in the post-war period, and has subsequently become deeply internalised in the contemporary German mind. As Jeffrey Anderson and John Goodman have argued, precisely because 'the Federal Republic was a semi-sovereign state operating within a bipolar system, the country was forced to rely almost entirely on international institutions to achieve its objectives'. Yet despite the instrumental origins of its commitment to multilateralism and institutional cooperation, the FRG has developed 'a reflexive support for institutions' which has become 'one of the principal legacies of the Cold War period':

> Over the course of forty years, West Germany's reliance on a web of international institutions to achieve its foreign policy goals, born of an instrumental choice among painfully few alternatives, became so complete as to cause these institutions to become embedded in the very definition of states interests and strategies. (Anderson and Goodman, 1993: 24, 60)

Post-war West German security policy itself was built on three key planks. First, a transatlantic alliance with Washington, and integration into NATO. The FRG joined NATO in 1955, and since then the alliance has provided the bedrock of West German security. Second, a West European alliance with Paris, and integration into the European Economic Community (EEC) and the Western European Union (WEU). The Franco-German axis was formally institutionalised in the 1963 treaty of friendship and cooperation, and Paris and Bonn have consistently coordinated their *Europapolitik* in order to further their shared commitment to European integration. Third, a policy of détente towards the Soviet Union and the Warsaw Pact countries, including East Germany – a policy which became most pronounced with the adoption of *Ostpolitik* in the late 1960s and 1970s, and which achieved institutional expression in the Conference on Cooperation and Security in Europe (CSCE) (Ash, 1993). From the late 1960s, the tensions between these three policy orientations became increasingly more obvious. The policy of close alliance with Washington and commitment to NATO was not wholly compatible with Franco-German 'tandem' in

Europe, given French aspirations to create a more autonomous West European defence identity. Similarly, tight integration into the western alliance made the pursuit of *détente* with the East more difficult. Nonetheless, these underlying tensions were largely suppressed given the overarching security imperatives of the east–west conflict.

While the Adenauer government was laying down the key planks of a new security policy, the *Bundeswehr*, purged of Prussian militarist values and imbued with the spirit of *innere Führung*, was being fully integrated into NATO's military command structures. It was also forbidden by the *Grundgesetz* (the West German federal constitution) from acting outside the area covered by the 1949 Washington treaty. These political and constitutional changes, along with the experience of the war, gave rise to a very distinctive post-war West German 'strategic culture'. Painful memories of the Nazi era and trauma of defeat and national division led many West Germans to reject militarism and advocate peaceful modes of international intercourse. Post-war West Germany emphasised deterrence rather than defence. The aim of the German security policy was to prevent rather than to fight a war. As Peter Stratman has argued,

> Since the 1950s nearly all aspects of defence, i.e., objective conditions and requirements of military operations in case of war, have been fundamentally eradicated from the security consciousness of the West German population. This eradication was an understandable political reflex in view of the fact that the Federal Republic can expect to be secure only if war is entirely prevented. Confronted with the conventional and nuclear offensive and destructive potential of the Soviet Union, it would be meaningless for this tiny, densely populated and highly-industrialised country, which might be the potential battlefield, to seek security in the capability for successful defence . . .
>
> Under these circumstances there was a gradual development of a studied amilitary, i.e., purely political, understanding of security policy. The interpretation of NATO strategy as a political means to avoid war by the threat of nuclear retaliation was portrayed positively in contrast to 'war-fighting strategies', which were declared to be out-of-date in the nuclear age . . . In the popular version of this argument, the mission of the Bundeswehr would be seen to have failed as soon as the first shot was fired. (Stratman, 1988: 97–8)

This amilitary strategic culture contrasts starkly with Germany's pre-1945 strategic culture, and reflects the far-reaching changes that have taken place in West German society and politics. The terrible legacy of Nazism and the trauma of defeat in war, coupled with the 'civilising' impact of a rising standard of living and a social market economy, led to a widespread rejection of militarist values and substantial support for neutralist and even pacifist sentiments. This amilitary strategic culture continues to exert a profound influence on contemporary German security thinking, and colours Bonn's approach to the post-Cold War security agenda in Europe and the wider international system.

POST-WAR WEST GERMANY AND THE TRANSATLANTIC 'SECURITY COMMUNITY'

The evolution of contemporary German security policy cannot be understood without reference to one further development in the post-war period – the emergence of a 'pluralist security community' embracing the North Americans and the West Europeans. Although post-war hopes for a new democratic and peaceful Europe were thwarted by the onset of the Cold War, the bipolar divide had the unintended result of stimulating new forms of cooperation and integration in western Europe. In 1949 the NATO alliance was created. In 1951, the European Coal and Steel Community (ECSC) was formed. This in turn was subsumed within the European Economic Community, established in 1957. The long-term political and economic vision underpinning these last two bodies was ambitious: it was to 'lay the foundations of a destiny henceforth shared', and to make war between its diverse peoples both politically unthinkable and economically impossible. At the heart of this integration process was the process of Franco-German rapprochement – a development which has proved of major consequence for the stability and security of Europe (for a discussion of these and related aspects see Jopp et al., 1991).

The process of formal integration and institution-building in western Europe was both facilitated by, and helped stimulate and channel, processes of informal integration. The processes of informal integration – by which is meant 'those intense patterns of interaction which develop without the intervention of deliberate governmental decisions, following the dynamics of markets, technology, communications networks and social exchange, or the influence of religious, social or political movements' (Wallace, 1990 : 54) – have acquired a pronounced importance in contemporary western Europe. The emergence of a regional micro-economic division of labour, transnational corporations, cross-border production systems, global financial markets, rapid communications and transportation systems, constant technological innovation, transnational social movements and political forces – these developments have created a new Europe characterised by complex interdependence and globalisation.

At the same time, the nature of western European societies has changed, with the development of social market economies, pluralist civil societies and democratic polities. Throughout western Europe, a broad consensus has emerged around shared values and principles, particularly as regards human rights, liberal-democracy and basic social welfare provisions. These developments, together with the emergence of a dense institutional complex and a high degree of economic and social interaction, have had a profound impact on the nature of international relations in the region. As Karl Deutsch has written, a 'pluralistic security community' has emerged embracing the North Americans and the West Europeans (Deutsch et al., 1957). Within this pluralistic security community, the threat and use of force plays no part in interstate relations. War is no longer a rational instrument of policy in relations between states in the transatlantic community (for an interesting perspective on this see Coker, 1992 : 189–98). In Hedley Bull's terms, an 'international society' has developed within the transatlantic states system, in which cooperation and 'sociability' between states has largely superseded traditional *Realpolitik* instincts (Bull, 1977).

This constitutes a dramatic and far-reaching change in the nature of contemporary West European politics – a change which has profound implications for the European security system. Prior to Cold War bipolarity, Europe's great powers were locked into a multipolar balance of power arrangement. These states jealously guarded their sovereignty, and engaged in power politics based on *Realpolitik* calculations. Within these *Realpolitik* considerations, military assets constituted the key element in the assessment of relative power relationships. It was in the context of this anarchical international system that the rise of Germany proved so destabilising to the prevailing balance of power.

However, post-war social, political, economic and institutional developments have radically changed the nature and functioning of international relations in western Europe and North America. As William Wallace has argued in the case of western Europe, '[i]nteractions between governments, economies and societies . . . have moved well beyond the traditional model of relations among nation-states' (Wallace, 1990 : 21). The very structural dynamics of the Westphalian states system have been altered, given the emergence of an 'international society' embracing the mature industrial pluralist democracies of the transatlantic community. Within this international society, relations are conducted on the basis of international law within a complex institutional ensemble. The states within this community share common normative values, associated primarily with human rights, liberal democracy and market economics (Hanson, 1993 : 28–41). Most significantly, relations between them are no longer conducted against the background of a threat to resort to force. This is the most startling and most positive change: after centuries of internecine warfare, the peoples of the transatlantic area now enjoy peaceful interstate relations. In this part of the world at least, Kant's dream of a 'pacific union' has at last become a reality.[2]

The emergence of the pluralist security community has tremendous significance for German security policy, and Germany's place in the new post-Cold War Europe. Prior to 1945, the 'German problem' – namely how to incorporate a country as large and dynamic as Germany into the established European states system – had proved an insoluble problem for European security. The power of the German nation-state had been fatally destabilising for the European balance of power. With the end of Cold War bipolarity and the unification of Germany some have feared that German power will once again destabilise Europe. However, complex interdependence, economic globalisation, institutionalised multilateral cooperation and the consolidation of stable liberal democracies have transformed the nature of sovereignty and state power in the late twentieth century. This has affected the nature of German power in four significant ways and made possible a resolution of the age-old 'German problem'.

First, the power of a united Germany will be not be concentrated in the hands of a centralised government as it was during the Wilhelmine or 'Third' Reich because substantial state functions and responsibilities have been devolved downwards to the Länder and local government level. Second, Germany is integrated into both the European Union and NATO, and this means that some power has been devolved *upwards*, particularly to the EU. Third, the rise of transnational corporations, strategic corporate alliances and cross-border mergers means that economic power no longer accrues directly to the nation-state, but is diffused *outwards*, beyond the confines of the nation-state. Finally, the political culture and social structure of contemporary Germany is fundamentally different from what it was in the first half of the century. Germany today has a democratic and liberal ethos, in which, if anything, pacifism, not militarism, is the concern of its allies. As Alfred

Grosser has commented, 'Germans today are different from those who supported Hitler. They have accepted democratic values. They have done everything possible to demonstrate their good faith' (quoted in *Newsweek*, 26 February 1990 : 10; see also Enzensberger, 1989 : 100–1).

The changing nature of German power is related to changes in the nature of power in the wider international system. The end of the Cold War, the advent of an increasingly globalised economy and the emergence of a transatlantic security community have changed the currency of power. In the new pattern of international relations in Europe, military force is of declining utility in contrast to the economic and political indices of power (Luard, 1988). The changed nature of power is reflected in the debate on European security, where a broad consensus has emerged that security is much more than a problem of weapons: it is increasingly tied up with economic, political, social and environmental issues (Buzan, 1983 : 253). This is particularly significant for the FRG, whose international power is primarily based on its economic dynamism and the overall attractiveness of its society, culture and way of life, rather than its military capabilities (Garton Ash, 1993 : 381–3).

Associated with the changed nature of power in the modern European security system is a shift in the meaning and content of 'sovereignty'. Sovereignty was the constitutive principle of the Westphalian states system, and generations of Germans have fought wars, first to achieve sovereignty, and later to defend it. But the Bundesrepublik, as a member of the European Union, has 'pooled' certain sovereign rights and prerogatives in a body which has been described as 'a union of states without a unity of governments' (Brewin, 1987 : 1). Conceptualising the European Union is a notoriously difficult task, given its *sui generis* nature: the EU is neither an unambiguously supranational organisation nor simply an intergovernmental body. Murray Forsyth has argued that the EU should be regarded as a 'federal body'.[3] A more nuanced approach has been taken by Lisbeth Aggestam, who has suggested that the EU should be seen as a form of 'cooperative federalism', given its hybrid decision-making process combining both intergovernmental and supranational dimensions (Aggestam, 1997). Whatever concepts one uses to categorise the nature of EU decision-making, few would deny that it has transformed the meaning and content of sovereignty for its members. In the German case, European integration has become such an integral part of the FRG's *raison d'état* and so deeply embedded in popular political culture, that a 'postmodern conception of sovereignty' has emerged in the country. Moreover, 'if Germany were to realize its vision of Europe, it would emerge as a consequential but *semi-sovereign* member of a supranational authority' (Anderson and Goodman, 1993 : 62).

BEYOND THE COLD WAR: GERMANY'S CHANGING SECURITY AGENDA

The post-war transformation of West European politics and international relations – with political democratisation, economic interdependence, multilateral integration and the emergence of a pluralist security community – has fundamentally and irrevocably changed the nature of German security. It has also changed the geopolitical context within which German security policy is made. Germany's traditional geopolitical dilemmas arose from its central geographical location within a European balance of power between the continent's great powers. The emergence of a pluralistic security community has made redundant such traditional balance of power considerations within the West European context. Today, the dilemmas of Germany's *Sicherheitspolitik* derive from the country's position on the eastern edge of the transatlantic security community: Germany is an integral member of this security community, but borders on the zone of incipient conflict and instability in the east. It is this new geopolitical landscape which has produced the current foreign and security policy dilemmas of the Bonn government – dilemmas which are only superficially similar to those of the Bismarckian Reich or the Germany of the interwar years.

With the end of the Cold War, the reunited Germany faces a radically different security agenda from that which faced the Bundesrepublik for nearly forty years. Until the late 1980s, West German security concerns were focused on the perceived threat posed by the concentration of Soviet and Warsaw Pact armoured forces forward-deployed in Eastern Europe. This 'Soviet threat' provided the rationale for the Bundeswehr itself, and for the FRG's alliance commitments within NATO and the WEU. The demise of the east–west conflict has thus called into question the very purpose of Germany's armed forces and the fundamental underpinnings of its foreign and security policies.

The break-up of the Soviet Union and the unfreezing of the Cold War divide has left the FRG in a historically novel and uniquely privileged international situation. Germany today has no obvious enemies, and faces no clear and specific security 'threat'. As former president Richard von Weizsäcker observed, '[f]or the first time [in history] we Germans are not a point of contention on the European agenda. Our uniting has not been inflicted on anybody: it is the result of peaceful agreement' (Joffe, 1991 : 84). In contrast to Bismarck's policy of 'blood and iron', German unification in 1990 was brought about following peaceful popular demonstrations for national self-determination in East Germany, along with democratic elections and the 'two plus four' international negotiations agreed at the open skies conference in Ottawa in February 1990. German security policy is thus being framed and conducted in a uniquely benign international environment, in which the *Bundesrepublik* is in the fortunate situation of having no enemies on or near its borders.

Nevertheless, although Germany today enjoys a relatively benign security environment, violent conflict remains endemic in the wider international system, while in Europe new security problems have arisen. The Bonn government recognises that it cannot exist as an isolated island of peaceful prosperity and liberal-democratic stability in an otherwise turbulent world. United Germany is therefore having to confront a radically different security agenda. This security agenda is new in that it is no longer dominated by one single, overriding security 'threat': rather, it is composed of a series of potential 'risks' and 'challenges'. Moreover, not only are these new security concerns increasingly diffuse, multifaceted and intangible, they are also often concerned with the non-military dimensions of security. In other words, they are neither military in nature nor amenable to military solutions: rather, they are economic, social, political or environmental in character (on this wider security agenda see Kolodziej, 1992 : 421–38).

The first of these potential security 'risks' and 'challenges' comes from the residual military arsenal of the former Soviet Union. The Russian Federation itself remains a major military superpower with substantial conventional and military assets. Even though the operational effectiveness of the Russian army has been called into question by the conduct of its campaign in Chechnia, Russia's military strength continues to cast a long and dark geopolitical shadow over the European continent. This, coupled with the continuing political instability of many post-Soviet republics and the dangers of nuclear proliferation, will be a major security concern for the Bundesrepublik until well into the twenty-first century.

Second, there are the security problems generated by the resurgence of ethno-national conflict in much of eastern Europe and the Balkans. The collapse of communism, and the socio-economic costs created in transforming authoritarian communist systems into democratic market-orientated societies, has fuelled long-suppressed historical animosities and kindled new patterns of ethnic, religious and national conflict. As the bitter fighting in the former Yugoslavia and around the fringes of the former Soviet Union demonstrates all too vividly, ethno-national conflict has emerged as one of the most pressing concerns on the post-Cold War European security agenda. Bonn's worry is not only that such intercommunal conflict could spread across the often arbitrarily delineated borders in the post-communist east, but that such conflict will encourage further waves of refugees seeking security and prosperity in Germany's social market economy.

Third, there are security concerns arising from developments in the wider international system. The FRG is a major trading nation, and cannot but be concerned about potential threats to supplies of vital raw materials, markets and maritime trade routes. Technological developments also mean that the international system is increasingly subject to global security concerns, above all the spread of ballistic missile technology coupled with the proliferation of chemical, biological and nuclear weapons. On top of this, Germany remains concerned with the problems of international terrorism (especially state-sponsored terrorism); with economically motivated immigration from North Africa, the eastern Mediterranean and Asia; and with the instability generated by the appalling levels of poverty and underdevelopment in many countries in the south. Many of these international security concerns are focused on the emerging southern 'arc of crisis', which stretches from the Balkans and the eastern Mediterranean, through the Middle East and the Persian Gulf, to the Mahgreb and the North African littoral.

Germany thus faces a radically changed security environment. Although the FRG is no longer confronted by any identifiable enemies or direct security threats, it nonetheless has to address a security agenda constituted by a series of diffuse and multifaceted security 'risks' and 'challenges'. As the newly united Germany struggled to come to terms with the new demands and responsibilities placed upon it by the end of the Cold War, it was confronted by the need to respond to the first major test of the 'new international order' – the Gulf War. This was a test which, in the eyes of many both inside Germany and without, found Bonn severely wanting (Thies, 1991 : 89–90). Constrained legally and politically from deploying Bundeswehr forces outside the NATO area, Germany was left in the secondary role of paymaster and diplomatic cheerleader for the allied coalition in the Gulf. Since then, Germany has faced growing domestic and international calls to make a more positive contribution to the maintenance of international security in an increasingly turbulent and uncertain world. At the same time,

German foreign and security policy-makers are operating within a distinctive political environment, marked by a largely amilitary strategic culture and widely held pacifist and neutralist sentiments. As Karl Kaiser has written,

> A united Germany free of the East–West confrontation on its soil and now one of the world's wealthiest democracies, must face a novel and difficult task: to reconcile its foreign policy traditions with the new responsibilities that inevitably accompany its enhanced position and require the – sometimes unpopular – use of its political, economic and military resources in partnership with others to preserve peace on an unstable globe. (Kaiser, 1991 : 205)

GERMANY AND EUROPE'S SECURITY 'ARCHITECTURE'

As Germany continues to work out its response to the new demands and responsibilities placed upon it by the end of the Cold War, it is doing so within a firmly multilateral framework. As we have already noted, the post-war Bundesrepublik has consistently pursued its foreign and security policy within multilateral frameworks. This commitment to institutionalised multilateral cooperation continues to permeate the assumptions and approaches of Germany's political class. Bonn's post-Cold War *Sicherheitspolitik* is therefore being pursued within a dense institutional framework consisting of a series of regional, European and international organisations. These include the Council of Europe, the Council of Baltic Sea Cooperation, the Schengen Group and the European Union: however, the three key organisations for German security policy are NATO, the WEU and the OSCE (formerly the CSCE).

As a new, post-Cold War security 'architecture' evolves, many of Germany's allies and partners favour a distinct hierarchy of organisations. The Americans, British and Dutch, for example, favour a privileged role for NATO; the French and Belgians, on the other hand, would like to see the Western European Union play a leading role, functioning as the defence arm of the EU; meanwhile, the Russians would like to see both NATO and the WEU subordinated to a pan-European collective security system based on the OSCE. The current Bonn coalition, however, favours a *Verflechtung* (a network) of institutions without any distinctive and overarching hierarchy between them. This approach was summed up by Helmut Kohl when he declared that in the security field, 'I am against "all or nothing"; I am in favour of "but also"' (quoted in the *Financial Times*, 31 May 1991). In policy terms, this approach has been clearly evident from Bonn's resolutely ambiguous stance on the WEU, describing it both as the 'European pillar' of NATO and as the 'defence arm' of the European Union.[4] Such a network of multiple, overlapping and interlocking institutions, it is felt, would provide Germany with the best framework for managing the dilemmas of its foreign and security policy.

Although German security policy since 1990 has sought to create a network of overlapping and interlocking institutions, post-war West German *Sicherheitspolitik* was based first and foremost upon NATO. The NATO alliance provided the indispensable bedrock of West German security, and NATO remains central to post-Cold War security policy. It is thus appropriate that we begin our discussion of contemporary German security by focusing first on Bonn's policy towards and within NATO.

NATO AND GERMAN *SICHERHEITSPOLITIK*

From its very first hours, the fledgling FRG was reliant on the transatlantic alliance for its security and territorial integrity. After becoming a member of NATO in 1955, the Bundesrepublik played an increasingly important role in the alliance, both as a base for forward-deployed NATO forces, and as a major contributor to the conventional military strength of the sixteen nation alliance. Although the Bonn government has collaborated with France in seeking to develop a European defence and security identity, and has also been keen to see the development of a more cooperative European security system based on the CSCE/OSCE, this has not yet resulted in any significant weakening of Germany's commitment to NATO. Even with the end of the Cold War, the NATO alliance remains the bedrock of German security policy.

There are four main reasons why the Bonn government remains so resolutely committed to NATO. First, the alliance provides an invaluable security guarantee against a resurgent and revanchist Russia. It also offers an insurance policy in the event of instability in the former Soviet Union generating large-scale military conflict in the east. Second, German participation in NATO's integrated military command provides a very visible demonstration of its continuing *Westintegration* and its commitment to multilateral defence cooperation (Wettig, 1991 : 15). Third, the German government enjoys a close relationship with the USA (as 'partners in leadership'), and remains convinced that a strong US military commitment to Europe is essential for the peace and security of the continent. Finally, NATO is seen as a tried and tested alliance based on democratic principles, and one which makes a vital contribution to the security and stability of the wider European continent. Although there are some Germans who favour the development of a common European defence and security policy, or an OSCE-based collective security system, most are unwilling to risk giving up an established bulwark of security until a more viable security structure has been created.

Yet while NATO remains the bedrock of German security policy, a broad consensus has developed since unification that the alliance must significantly reform its structure and functions if it is to remain relevant to the changed security environment of post-Cold War Europe. To begin with, there is broad agreement in Germany that NATO must become a more European organisation. The belief that the Europeans need to assume a greater responsibility for their own defence is widely held on both sides of the Atlantic. The German government has therefore supported the idea of a stronger 'European pillar' within the alliance, based primarily on the WEU. The problem with this, however, is that building a more cohesive 'European pillar' risks undermining America's self-styled 'leadership role' within NATO. The worry is that by strengthening the political cohesion and operational effectiveness of the WEU – which also serves as the 'defence arm' of the European Union – Washington may increasingly feel marginalised within the North Atlantic Council, and may therefore lose interest in maintaining a substantial commitment to European security. Managing the tension between the transatlantic alliance and the development of a common European security and defence policy has been a major concern of the Bonn government in recent years, and is an issue to which we will return below.

The second set of changes to NATO championed by the Germans concern the alliance's relationship with the countries of the former communist east. The Bonn government was a prime mover behind NATO's 'London declaration' of July 1990 which, amongst other important changes, offered to extend 'the hand of friendship' to its former enemies in the Warsaw Pact. Since then, the Germans have actively encouraged the development of a more complex network of bilateral diplomatic and political links between NATO on the one hand, and the new democracies of the former Soviet Union and eastern Europe on the other. For example, in October 1991, the then foreign minister Hans-Dietrich Genscher, in a joint initiative with his American counterpart,

James Baker, proposed the creation of an institutionalised forum for regular high-level consultation and discussion between the NATO sixteen, the USSR, the three Baltic states and the countries of eastern Europe (for details see Kurt Kister in *Süddeutsche Zeitung*, 4 October 1991). This US–German initiative was formally endorsed by the Rome NATO summit in November 1991, which agreed to establish a 'North Atlantic Cooperation Council' along the lines of the Baker-Genscher plan. By strengthening political dialogue across the former east–west divide, the German government hopes that greater mutual understanding and tolerance can be fostered. This is something very much in the interests of Germany, given its geographical proximity to potentially unstable countries in the former communist east (Rühe, 1993 : 135).

In the spring and summer of 1993, influential voices from within the ruling coalition could be heard arguing for the selective expansion of NATO eastwards. In particular, it was suggested that the countries of east-central Europe should be offered early membership of the alliance in order to bring greater security and stability to the region (Garton Ash, 1994 : 65–81). This caused growing anxiety in Moscow (thereby undermining Bonn's other security interest, namely the construction of an OSCE-based pan-European system of cooperative security), and was coolly received in a number of other NATO capitals. Instead of offering either firm security guarantees or the promise of early membership of the alliance to the east-central Europeans, a new initiative was launched. This was the 'partnership for peace' scheme, formally inaugurated in January 1994. The 'partnership for peace' strategy offered individual countries from the former communist east tailor-made packages of bilateral military cooperation with NATO. It was designed to prepare some of the new democracies for membership of NATO, and to consolidate the emerging patterns of functional military cooperation and security dialogue the alliance had been advocating since the end of the Cold War (for the relevant documents and commentaries see *Nato Review*, 1994). The 'partnership for peace' scheme was warmly embraced by the Germans, who have been fully involved in a series of joint military exercises with the cooperation partners from the east, as was the NATO–Russia Council established in May 1997.

The third set of changes sought by Germany within NATO have been to the organisation's military strategy and force structure. Germany played an important role in shaping NATO's far-reaching 'strategic review', a review made necessary by the withdrawal of Soviet troops from central and eastern Europe and the disbandment of the Warsaw Pact. The 'strategic review' was completed in late 1991, and subsequently NATO's 'new strategic concept' was adopted at the November 1991 Rome summit. This advocated a greater reliance on reinforcements in the event of war, and smaller, more mobile stationed forces configured in multinational corps (Weisser, 1992 : 51–68). The subsequent creation of a rapid reaction corps was welcomed by the German government, although the leading role assigned to British forces within it was the source of some contention. Of considerable importance for German domestic opinion, was the statement in the 'London declaration' of July 1990 defining nuclear weapons as 'weapons of last resort' and the call for the negotiated elimination of all ground-launched nuclear forces of the shortest range. The new strategic concept also reduced the emphasis attached to maintaining a robust ladder of nuclear escalation. This removed what had been a major bone of contention between Germany and some of its NATO allies (particularly France and the USA), and helped diffuse one of the most divisive aspects of NATO's military strategy and force posture. Today, the issue of most concern to both German public opinion and German policy-makers is not NATO's nuclear strategy, but rather the risks of nuclear proliferation arising from the disintegration of the former Soviet Union.

TOWARDS A EUROPEAN DEFENCE AND SECURITY IDENTITY?

While NATO remains the bedrock of German security policy, the Bonn government is also a firm proponent of a more pronounced 'European defence and security identity'. The precise meaning of this phrase remains institutionally ambiguous and politically contentious. Nonetheless, for the ruling coalition, it means the fostering of a more consistently multilateral approach to foreign and security policy issues by EU members, and the gradual development of an operational European military capability. Chancellor Kohl has consistently pursued this line since late 1989. He joined with French President Mitterrand to advocate an accelerated transition to political union within the European Community (in joint initiatives issued on 18 April and 6 December 1990), and called repeatedly for the development of a common European defence and security policy. This was reflected in the Maastricht treaty, which announced the formation of a 'common foreign and security policy', which may in time include defence. The treaty also recognised the WEU as 'an integral part of the development of the European Union', which may ask the WEU 'to elaborate and implement [the Union's] decisions and actions . . . which have defence implications'. A declaration on the WEU attached to the treaty also noted the member states' intention to 'build up the WEU in stages as the defense component of the Union' (Treaty on European Union, 1992; Dinan, 1994 : 472). In the course of the preparation for the 1996–7 intergovernmental conference (IGC) with the task to review the Maastricht treaty, the Bonn government has made it clear that it would like to see a further strengthening of the EU's common foreign and security policy, 'of which a common European defense policy and defense force must form an integral part' (Seiters, 1995 : 6). Germany, in tandem with France, is also the driving force behind the 'Eurocorps', a multinational force of 35 000 which became operational in 1995.

The German government recognises that these 'europeanist' initiatives have caused unease in Washington, London and other more 'pro-atlanticist' capitals. Bonn has had to work particularly hard to convince the Americans, British and Dutch that the Eurocorps is not a threat or rival to NATO. Chancellor Kohl believes that the tensions between these two seemingly contradictory approaches to European security – Atlanticist and Europeanist – can be finessed through the medium of the WEU, which he envisages as the bridge between NATO and the EU (Kohl, 1991 : 40). For this reason, the Germans have welcomed the NATO decision of January 1994 to create 'combined joint task forces' (CJTF). These will be command and control structures within NATO's integrated military command structure which will be 'separable but not separate'. It is planned that these CJTF could then be placed under a WEU operational command in order to allow the WEU to conduct humanitarian and peacekeeping operations (the so-called 'Petersberg tasks' defined by the June 1992 WEU Petersberg declaration).

The German government thus hopes that by formulating ambiguous statements on the role of the WEU, and encouraging the formation of the CJTFs (a development which is proving very difficult to realise in practice) it can overcome the tensions between its commitment to NATO and its desire to see a more coherent and effective European defence and security entity. But this position will prove increasingly hard to sustain in the medium to long term. As the Americans have pointed out, the decisive issue is where security decisions are taken: in the Atlantic Alliance (which would leave the United States as *primus inter pares*), or in the EU/WEU (which would exclude the USA, along with non-EU NATO members like Norway and Turkey) (*Neue Zürcher Zeitung*, 5 May 1991). At some stage in its development, therefore, a robust security and defence dimension within the EU would inevitably undermine the current centrality of NATO to German security.

For some in Germany, this would be a very welcome development. Although the dominant school of thought within the German security community has been Atlanticist, there has been a significant minority of German 'Gaullists' who have advocated an unambiguously 'europeanist' approach. These Europeanists can be found on both sides of the political spectrum, from anti-Americans in the SPD to leading politicians in the CDU. They would like to see NATO replaced by an autonomously European security organisation, analogous to the failed European Defence Community (EDC) of the early 1950s.

Although there is undoubtedly broad support for a robust common European foreign and security policy (including defence) in Germany, such overtly Europeanist perspectives remain marginal to the security debate. The central aim of the current Bonn government is to manage the dilemmas of its security policy, which aspires to be both Atlanticist and Europeanist at the same time. While NATO remains the only tried and tested collective defence alliance, and the role of the WEU continues to be shrouded in a studied ambiguity, these dilemmas will be easy to manage. But if transatlantic relations were to deteriorate seriously, or if European integration were to result in an effective common foreign and security policy including defence, then the dilemmas at the heart of German security will become virtually impossible to conceal. At that point, the Bundesrepublik will be forced to confront some tough decisions concerning the very foundations of its security policy.

THE OSCE AND A COOPERATIVE SECURITY SYSTEM?

The Organisation for Security and Cooperation in Europe began life in 1975 as the CSCE (Conference on Security and Cooperation in Europe). Since its formation in Helsinki at a time of blossoming *détente* in Europe, the Bundesrepublik has been one of the staunchest supporters of the CSCE process. From Bonn's perspective, the CSCE provided an ideal pan-European framework for regulating the east–west conflict, and provided a welcome multilateral forum for pursuing its *Ostpolitik*.

With the end of the Cold War, the CSCE acquired a new lease of life. In Germany there was a widespread feeling that, freed of the debilitating effects of the east–west conflict, the CSCE would finally be able to fulfil its promise as the institutional setting for new forms of pan-European cooperation and interaction (Bernt Conrad in *Die Welt*, 28 March 1992). Hans-Dietrich Genscher, the long-serving foreign minister at this time, was a determined advocate of the CSCE, and strongly believed that the CSCE could provide an invaluable framework for integrating the former communist states into a new, more cooperative security structure. He also saw the CSCE as 'a framework for stability for the dynamic, dramatic and sometimes revolutionary developments in Eastern Europe and the Soviet Union' (quoted in *Atlantic Council Policy Paper*, 31 October 1990). Thus, following the end of the Cold War, Genscher played an important role in outlining ideas for the 'institutionalisation' of the CSCE. This was achieved at the Paris summit of CSCE heads of state and government in November 1990. As well as providing the CSCE with a number of permanent institutional structures, the grandly named 'Paris charter for a new Europe' also codified a series of principles for the conduct of interstate relations and human rights.

The Paris charter reflected the mood of tremendous optimism which swept Europe in the wake of the collapse of communism. However, as ethno-nationalist conflicts erupted in the Balkans and around the fringes of the former Soviet Union, this mood of optimism gave way to a deepening sense of *Angst* and foreboding. This was reflected at the CSCE summit in Helsinki in the summer of 1992, which issued a more sober-sounding document called 'the challenges of change'. Since then, the CSCE has focused primarily on early warning, preventive diplomacy and crisis management. The established place of the CSCE in Europe's post-Cold War security architecture was acknowledged in December 1994 at the Budapest summit when the CSCE was renamed the Organisation for Security and Cooperation in Europe (OSCE).

Throughout the years since the end of the Cold War, the German government has been a consistent supporter of the CSCE process, and has encouraged the institutionalisation of the CSCE/OSCE. For Bonn, the OSCE provides a forum for developing new forms of cooperative security, and offers an institutional framework for addressing the legitimate security concerns of Russia. The FRG is unwilling to countenance Russian plans for establishing a collective security regime which would subject NATO and the WEU to OSCE decisions, but it does believe that the OSCE fulfils five key functions. First, it provides a forum for promoting and codifying common standards, values and norms of behaviour, particularly in the sphere of human rights and the peaceful resolution of conflicts; second, it offers a series of mechanisms for the continuous monitoring of human rights, both for individuals and for national minorities (Dalton, 1994 : 99–111; Huber, 1993 : 30–36); third, it acts as a forum for promoting military transparency, arms controls, and confidence- and security-building measures, thereby 'reducing dangers of armed conflict and of misunderstanding or miscalculation of military activities which could give rise to apprehension' (*Helsinki Final Act*, 1975); fourth, it provides a framework for pan-European multilateral diplomacy across a comprehensive range of issues; and finally, it is developing instruments for preventive diplomacy, conflict avoidance and crisis management (Huber, 1994 : 23–30; Höynck, 1994 : 16–22).

Thus the mainstream German view is that the OSCE constitutes an important supplement to NATO and the EU/WEU, within a pluralist, non-hierarchical and multidimensional European security system. There is, however, a minority school of thought, which finds its adherents among radicals on the political left. This minority envisages a much more ambitious role for the OSCE as the institutional basis of a pan-European system of collective security, replacing the Atlantic Alliance and making a European defence and security entity superfluous. Thus, for example, Egon Bahr has called for the transformation of the OSCE into a regional equivalent of the United Nations, with a European 'security council' (capable of taking decisions on the basis of qualified majority voting) and European peace-keeping forces to intervene when necessary (Rotfeld and Stützle, 1991 : 79).

Such a far-reaching transformation of the nature and purpose of the OSCE is unlikely in the foreseeable future, given the vested national interests involved. This leaves the OSCE without the necessary decision-making procedures or enforcement mechanisms that a robust and viable system of collective security would need. The dominant German view is therefore to support the further institutionalisation and development of the OSCE as a forum for cooperative, rather than collective, security, within a multifaceted and non-hierarchical European security architecture. This approach was embodied in the German-Dutch proposal for the agenda of the then CSCE summit in Budapest which called for the further institutionalisation of the CSCE with the aim of creating a 'common CSCE security area' (*Europa-Archiv*, 1994 : D440–D442).

CONCLUSION: GERMAN DILEMMAS AND EUROPEAN SECURITY

The changed nature of late twentieth-century European international relations has left Germany in a uniquely favourable situation. For the first time in its often troubled history, Germany is at peace with its neighbours, and has no clear and identifiable enemies. With the end of the Cold War Germany has also, at long last, become a 'normal' nation-state (Gordon, 1994 : 225–43). Yet Germany still faces a complex foreign and security policy agenda. As the above discussion illustrates, Germany's external relations involve a series of dilemmas: Bonn's special relationship with Paris sometimes conflicts with its special relationship with Washington; its commitment to the European integration process is in tension with its commitment to NATO; 'widening' the EU may well complicate its 'deepening'; and developing close relations with east-central Europe could cause friction in bilateral relations with Russia. The essential point to note when considering these dilemmas is that they are not the same dilemmas as faced by Germany in 1871 or 1918. They are dilemmas arising from the unique historical conjuncture that Germany and Europe find themselves in on the eve of the twenty-first century.

As one surveys the various dilemmas facing contemporary German security policy, a consistent theme emerges. Germany, perhaps more than any other major world power, remains committed to a multilateral approach. Bonn has undoubtedly become more assertive in defending and advancing its national interests in international fora, but it has rarely opted for a unilateralist approach – in stark contrast to Europe's other great powers. There are a number of competing German views on the future external orientation of the FRG, but no mainstream political force has been calling for the 'renationalisation' of Germany's foreign and defence policies. The Bundesrepublik thus remains firmly committed to multilateral diplomacy in the framework of the EU, NATO and the OSCE. This is of tremendous significance, for as Wolfgang Schlör observes,

> Germany has internalized the Cold War era's restrictions on its foreign policy and these limits appear to continue in people's minds, even though they have been formally lifted. The Germany of today contradicts the predictions of many realists – it is as yet both unable and unwilling to follow the pattern of maximising its power and influence in the international system (Schlör, 1993 : 63).

Yet this commitment to multilateralism may also be generating new security policy dilemmas for Bonn. The new Germany has been asked by its allies and partners to accept a greater share of the responsibility for international peace and security. At the same time, organisations like NATO, the WEU and the OSCE are also beginning to play a more interventionist role in international and intercommunal conflicts which were previously regarded as lying outside their geographical ambit or functional responsibility, while the UN itself is developing more robust forms of military peace-keeping and peace-enforcement. Bonn has acknowledged that its economic strength and political influence demand a greater international presence, but it has been unwilling to join America in policing China, Korea, Afghanistan, and other countries, as requested by the US ambassador in 1991. Instead Germany's energies have primarily been focused on the domestic task of reuniting the two halves of Germany. For this reason, along with Germany's amilitary strategic culture and the widespread popular aversion to military force, Bonn has been in no hurry to give up its role as a 'civilian power' and begin projecting its military capabilities overseas (Ropers, 1992 : 217–39). Yet this is generating a new security policy dilemma for Germany, for as Schlör notes,

> multilateral organizations are becoming increasingly associated with military commitments, which Germans are reluctant to undertake. The German public's aversion to military involvement might lead it to reject the multilateralization of German security policy as well. Thus, the feared nationalization of German security policy may take a quite different form from what many observers expect: rather than returning to power politics, Germany may abdicate its ambitions to play a role in international security matters, concentrating instead on solving its domestic problems and avoiding the divisive debate on a greater security role (Schlör, 1993 : 65).

It may well be that the increasing military commitments associated with the multilateral organisations to which Germany belongs will ultimately weaken Germany's commitment to multilateralism in general. On the other hand, it could be that Germany's membership of international organisations might lead to a weakening of the population's amilitary and pacifist impulses. This is certainly the favoured solution of the Kohl government. Over recent years, Bonn has been gradually involving the Bundeswehr in more overseas peacekeeping operations, from Iran to Somalia. The legal constraint on the use of German military power outside the NATO area was finally removed in the landmark decision by the Federal Constitutional Court on 12 July 1994. This ruled that the German armed forces could be used in multilateral actions within the framework of those organisations of collective security or collective defence to which Germany belongs, as long as they were orientated towards maintaining peace. Legally, therefore, the way has been cleared for German troops to contribute to peace-keeping and peace-enforcement actions. Politically, however, the issue remains highly contentious, particularly within the opposition Social-Democratic Party.

Whatever domestic political decisions are taken on the overseas deployment of the Bundeswehr, no one should doubt the generally positive role played by the new Germany in Europe's post-Cold War security. The newly united Germany has certainly begun to demonstrate a new self-confidence, even assertiveness, and Bonn is less willing than in the past to compromise its national interests in order to avoid antagonising its traditionally more nationalistically inclined western partners.[5] Yet this does not presage the birth of a 'Fourth Reich' as some have rather obscenely suggested (Cruise O'Brien, 1989; Scruton, 1989), nor does it indicate an imminent return to traditional balance of power politics in Europe as some neo-realists have argued (Mearsheimer, 1990 : 5–56). Democracy, economic interdependence, robust multilateral institutions and the emergence of a pluralistic security community have provided the historical solution to security dilemmas arising from the 'German problem'. What remains is a 'European problem': namely, the problem of how to overcome Europe's continuing economic, social and political divides, and build a continent at peace with itself and with the outside world. Creating such a *europäische Friedensordnung* (a European peace order) is the historic task facing Germany, in cooperation with its allies and partners, on the eve of the twenty-first century.

NOTES

1. 'The Treaty of Westphalia organised Europe on the basis of particularism. It represented a new diplomatic arrangement – an order created by states, for states – and replaced most of the legal vestiges of hierarchy, at the pinnacle of which were the Pope and the Holy Roman Emperor.' Westphalia thus led to 'the creation of a pan-European diplomatic system based on the new principles of sovereignty and legal equality . . . and a balance of power that would prevent drives for hegemony'. It also 'paved the way for a system of states to replace a hierarchical system under the leadership of the Pope and the Habsburg family, that of the Holy Roman and Spanish Empires' (see Holsti, 1991 : pp. 25–6).
2. This is of tremendous significance for our understanding of the nature of sovereignty in the modern era, for as Chris Brown has suggested, 'if physical violence is no longer a serious option then in practice sovereignty has been seriously weakened, whatever the legal position. In the absence of an effective right to resort to force, sovereignty is, it seems, a very amorphous notion' (Brown, 1995: p. 195).
3. 'The key feature which distinguishes the European Community from an

international organisation and places it within the spectrum of federal bodies may be summed up as follows. The institutions of the Community have the right and power, accorded to them by a treaty concluded for an unlimited period, to make directly applicable law within a broad sphere of competence, law which takes precedence over the law of the member states. There are thus two levels of government, properly so called, in the Community, and this is the very heart of what makes a federal system' (Forsyth, 1994: p. 57).

4. General Klaus Naumann has also argued that '[w]e need a broad political approach and a flexible system of international politics. A suitable security architecture must therefore include both European and the transatlantic institutions in the process' (Naumann, 1994 : 8–13).
5. This can be seen from both the establishment of formal national control over the Bundeswehr and the request that the German language be used more widely in the institutions of the EU.

REFERENCES:

Aggestam, L. (1997), 'The European Union at the Crossroads: Sovereignty and Integration', in Landau A. and Whitman, R., eds, *Rethinking the European Union* (London: Macmillan).

Anderson J. and Goodman, J. (1993), 'Mars or Minerva? A United Germany in a Post-Cold War Europe', in Keohane, R., Nye, J. and Hoffman S., eds, *After the Cold War: International Institutions and State Strategies in Europe, 1989–1991* (London: Harvard University Press).

Atlantic Council (1990), Policy Paper: 'The United States and United Germany: Task Force on German Unification', (Washington DC: Atlantic Council), 31 October.

Blackbourn D. and Eley, G. (1984), *The Peculiarities of German History: Bourgeois Society and Politics in Nineteenth Century Germany* (Oxford: Oxford University Press).

Brewin, C. (1987), 'The European Community: a Union of States Without a Unity of Government', *Journal of Common Market Studies*, vol. 26, no. 1, pp. 1–23.

Brown, C. (1995), 'International Theory and International Society: The Viability of the Middle Way', *Review of International Studies*, vol. 21, no. 2, pp. 183–96.

Bull, H. (1977), *The Anarchical Society: A Study of Order in World Politics* (London: Macmillan).

Buzan, B. (1983), *People, States and Fear: The National Security Problem in International Relations* (Brighton: Wheatsheaf).

Calleo, D. (1978), *The German Problem Reconsidered: Germany and the World Order. 1870 to the Present* (Cambridge: Cambridge University Press).

Coker, C. (1992), 'Post-Modernity and the End of the Cold War: Has War been Disinvented?', in *Review of International Studies*, vol. 18, no. 3, pp. 189–98.

Cruise O'Brien, C. (1989), 'Beware, the Reich is Reviving', *The Times*, 31 October.

Dalton, R. (1994), 'The Role of the CSCE', in Miall, H., ed., *Minority Rights in Europe: The Scope for a Transnational Regime*, (London: Pinter), pp. 99–111.

DePorte, A.W. (2nd edn, 1986), *Europe Between the Superpowers: The Enduring Balance* (New Haven, Conn.: Yale University Press).

Deutsch, K.W., Burrell, S.A., Kahn, R.A. et al. (1957), *Political Community in the North Atlantic Area* (Princeton, NJ: Princeton University Press).

Dinan, D. (1994), *Ever Closer Union? An Introduction to the European Union* (London: Macmillan).

Enzensberger, H.M. (1989), interview in the *New Left Review*, no. 178, November/December, pp. 87–104.

Europa-Archiv (1994), 'Gemeinsame deutsch-niederländische Agenda für den KSZE-Gipfel in Budapest, der KSZE vorgelegt am 17. Mai 1994 in Wien', vol. 46, no. 15, pp. D440–D442.

Forsyth, M. (1994), 'Federalism and Confederalism', in Brown, C.J., ed., *Political Restructuring in Europe: Ethical Perspectives* (London: Routledge), pp. 50–65.

Garton Ash, T. (1993), *In Europe's Name: Germany and the Divided Continent* (London: Jonathan Cape).

Garton Ash, T. (1994), 'Germany's Choice', in *Foreign Affairs*, July/August, pp. 65–81.

Gordon, P.H. (1994), 'Berlin's Difficulties: the Normalization of German Foreign Policy', *Orbis*, spring, pp. 225–43.

Hanson, M. (1993), 'Democratisation and Norm Creation in Europe', *European Security After the Cold War*, Part 1, Adelphi Paper 284 (London: Brassey's), pp. 28–41.

Helsinki Final Act (1975), Document on Confidence-Building Measures (CBMs) and Certain Aspects of Security and Disarmament.

Hobsbawm, E. (1994), *Age of Extremes: The Short Twentieth Century, 1914–1991* (London: Michael Joseph).

Holsti, K. (1991), *Peace and War: Armed Conflicts and International Order 1648–1989* (Cambridge: Cambridge University Press).

Höynck, W. (1994), 'CSCE Works to Develop its Conflict Prevention Potential', *NATO Review*, vol. 42, no. 2, pp. 16–22.

Huber, K.J. (1993), 'The CSCE and Ethnic Conflict in the East', *Radio Free Europe/Radio Liberty (RFE/RL) Research Report*, vol. 2, no. 31, 27 August, pp. 30–6.

Huber, K.J. (1994), 'The CSCE's New Role in the East: Conflict Prevention', *Radio Free Europe/Radio Liberty (RFE/RL) Research Report*, vol. 3, no. 31, 12 August, pp. 23–30.

Joffe, J. (1990), 'The Security Implications of a United Germany', *America's Role in a Changing World*, Adelphi Paper 257/II (London: Brassey's), pp. 84–91.

Jopp, M., Rummel, R. and Schmidt, P., eds (1991), *Integration and Security in Western Europe: Inside the European Pillar* (Boulder, Colo.: Westview).

Juricic, M. (1995), 'Perception, Causation and German Foreign Policy', *Review of International Studies*, vol. 21, no. 1, pp. 105–15.

Kaiser, K. (1991), 'Germany's Unification', *Foreign Affairs*, vol. 70, no. 1, pp. 179–205.

Kohl, H. (1991), *Our Future in Europe* (Edinburgh: Europa Institute/Konrad Adenauer Stiftung.

Kolodziej, E.A. (1992), 'Renaissance in Security Studies? Caveat Lector!', *International Studies Quarterly*, vol. 36, no. 4, pp. 421–38.

Luard, E. (1988), *The Blunted Sword: The Erosion of Power in Modern World Politics* (London: Tauris).

Mearsheimer, J. (1990), 'Back to the Future: Instability in Europe after the Cold War', *International Security*, vol. 15, no. 1, pp. 5–56.

Moreton, E., ed. (1987), *Germany Between East and West* (Cambridge: Cambridge University Press).

NATO Review (1994), vol. 42, no. 1, February.

Naumann, K. (1994), 'German Security Policy and the Future Tasks of the Bundeswehr', *RUSI Journal*, December, pp. 8–13.

Neuer Zürcher Zeitung (1991): 'Anhaltende Unsicherheit über die sicherheitspolitischen Konzepte der EG', 5 May.

Ropers, N. (1992), 'Security Policy in the Federal Republic of Germany', in McInnes, C., ed., *Security and Strategy in the New Europe* (London: Routledge), pp. 217–39.

Rotfeld A.D. and Stützle W., eds, *Germany and Europe in Transition* (Oxford: Oxford University Press).

Rühe, V. (1993), 'Shaping Euro-Atlantic Policies: A Grand Strategy for a New Era', *Survival*, vol. 35, no. 2, pp. 129–37.

Schlör, W. (1993), *German Security Policy: an examination of the trends in German security policy in a new European and global context*, Adelphi Paper 277 (London: Brassey's).

Scruton, R. (1989), 'Don't Trust the Germans', *Sunday Telegraph*, 21 May.

Seiters, R. (1995), 'No Magic Formula for Europe', *German Comments*, vol. 40, October, pp. 6–12.

Stratman, P. (1988), 'Arms Control and the Military Balance: the West German Debate', in Kaiser K. and Roper, J., eds, *British-German Defence Cooperation: Partners Within the Alliance* (London: Jane's), pp. 90–112.

Taylor, A.J.P. (1967), 'German Unity,' in Taylor, A.J.P., *Europe: Grandeur and Decline* (London: Pelican).

Thies, J. (1991), 'Germany: Tests of Credibility', *The World Today*, vol. 47, no. 6, pp. 89–90.

Treaty on European Union (1992), Cm.1934, European Communities no. 3, 7 February: 'Declaration on the Role of the Western European Union and its Relations with the European Union', issued by WEU members and noted by the 'Declaration on Western European Union' adopted by EC members along with the Treaty on European Union and its Protocols.

Wallace, W. (1990), *The Transformation of Western Europe* (London: Pinter).

Wallace, W., ed. (1990), *The Dynamics of European Integration* (London: Pinter).

Weisser, U. (1992), *NATO ohne Feindbild: Konturen einer europäischen Sicherheitspolitik* (Bonn: Bouvier).

Wettig, G. (1991), 'German Unification and European Security', *Aussenpolitik*, vol. 42, no. 1, pp. 13–19.

10 'Present at Disintegration': The United States and German Unification

Michael Cox and Steven Hurst

To this day historians continue to debate the origins of Germany's division after World War II, and whether or not it was the inevitable and logical consequence of the war itself, the product of communist intransigence or, as has recently been argued, the result of an 'American decision' to secure the more important Western part of the country against Soviet influence (Eisenberg, 1996). What they do not seem to question however is that once the country had been divided, there seemed to be little inclination thereafter to undo what had been done in the critical years between 1945 and 1949. Indeed, each time it looked as if the new status quo was under threat – as it certainly appeared to be in 1953 when workers rose up in the East, and then later in 1961 when East Germany began to haemorrhage badly – the Western powers appeared to be far more concerned to shore up the situation than to challenge it. Of course, as John Lewis Gaddis has pointed out, there were a number of reasons why the main powers were unwilling or unable to reunite Germany, one being the logic of the superpower conflict itself (Gaddis, 1997: 113–51). However, there were also historical considerations. While Germany's division could easily be explained and justified in terms of Cold War realities, policy-makers privately agreed that underlying their attachment to the new arrangement was a concern to prevent Germany rising up again and threatening the peace. Some policy-makers did not even bother to hide their true feelings, and at times influential Americans such as Dean Acheson, George Ball and Henry Kissinger openly conceded that Germany's division and West Germany's integration into NATO was the only basis upon which to build a new European order; and those like George Kennan who challenged this essential truth were simply utopian schemers with little understanding of the real world.

Naturally, America's attachment to the status quo was neither unconditional nor principled. After all, the logical corollary of Germany's division was Soviet domination of Eastern Europe – something no US leader could seriously contemplate as a permanent option. Furthermore, whatever American politicians might have thought in private, they had to adhere to the official position of a Europe united and free. To have done otherwise during the Cold War would have been political suicide. That said, the real, as opposed to the ostensible American position towards Germany before 1989 was to secure its loyalty to the West and Western institutions like NATO and the European Community, and if this reinforced its division then it was a price worth paying to keep Europe stable and nervous allies reassured (DePorte, 1979).

In this chapter we shall be looking at the ways in which the Bush administration in particular came to terms with the upheavals caused by the quite unexpected retreat of Soviet power from Eastern Europe during 1989 and the even more unexpected unification of Germany. Based on new memoir material as well as other important primary sources, the argument advanced here is a simple but important one: that in spite of serious reservations at the highest level, the American administration not only came to terms with massive changes in Germany's status but played a critical – some would argue indispensable – role in ensuring that these enhanced European security rather than undermining it. Here we agree with the conclusion arrived at by a former Bush official, Robert Hutchings – director for European affairs at the National Security Council between 1989 and 1992. Though in no way seeking to detract from what he calls Bonn's 'masterful role' (Hutchings, 1997: 91), Hutchings shows, convincingly in our view, that US support for Bonn was absolutely vital, 'not so much for German unification itself, but for ensuring that the process came out right' with all of Europe, including the Soviet Union 'accepting and supporting this outcome' (ibid., 90; Bortfeldt, 1997; Küsters and Hofmann, 1998). What he also demonstrates is the critical part played by diplomacy in the transition. Unification might have happened anyway, but the fact that it happened in the particularly benign way that it did, had a lot to do with the manner in which the American administration in general (and George Bush in particular) dealt with the issue. Large scale changes in the international system and in the character of Soviet power may have determined the direction in which history moved after 1989. But it still required the decisions of certain men and women to ensure that German unification could be managed effectively.

To make good our claim we have divided the chapter in the following way. In the first part we look at the initial caution displayed by the Bush administration towards the Gorbachev phenomenon. In the second part we look at the way in which it began to take the initiative and tried to set its own European agenda, a move undertaken in the spring of 1989 (and importantly some time before the Berlin wall came tumbling down a few months later). In part three we then look at the diplomacy of German unification in some detail. We focus in particular on the delicate three-way negotiations between the US, the USSR and the Kohl government. In the concluding section we reflect on the longer term results of German unification and the US–German relationship during the 1990s. We argue that while both countries clearly do have something close to a new 'special relationship' (some have even suggested that Germany has replaced the UK at the centre of American affections) this should not lead us to the naive conclusion that unification has not caused the United States some concerns, nor that the two nations agree about everything. But one thing both can agree on: that when Germany needed the United States after 1989, the United States was there to give more than just a helping hand. This more than anything else will stand US–German relations in good stead as we move into the twenty-first century.

BEWARE GORBACHEV

When George Bush was inaugurated as President of the United States in January 1989 there were few hints, and even fewer expectations, of the radical changes that were to sweep over Europe in the following two years. The Bush administration's attitude towards the changes under way in superpower relations was one of cautious optimism tempered with scepticism. While Bush himself believed that Soviet leader Mikhail Gorbachev was 'sincere in his desire to change the Soviet Union and superpower relations', others in his administration questioned both Gorbachev's goals and his ability to achieve them (Bush and Scowcroft, 1998: 9, 13; Gates, 1996: 473–4).

The Bush administration's instinctive caution was highlighted by the first major test of relations between the US and West Germany during its term of office. The question of a replacement for NATO's ageing LANCE missile system had been on the table for some time when Bush came to office and had become a source of increasing tension within the alliance. The government and people of West Germany had never evinced great enthusiasm for nuclear weapons that could only be fired far enough to kill other Germans. The thawing of the Cold War only served to reinforce those doubts. When Gorbachev offered first to reduce Soviet armed forces in Eastern Europe by 500 000 and then to remove all Soviet short-range nuclear weapons (SNF) by 1991 if the US would do likewise, West German resistance to the deployment of a follow on to LANCE (FOTL) hardened considerably.

As far as the Bush administration was concerned Gorbachev's proposals contained as many threats as they did promises. NATO's SNF had always been justified by the need to offset the Warsaw Pact's massive advantage in conventional forces. A cut of 500 000 Soviet troops would not remove that imbalance and the elimination of both alliances' SNF would thus weaken NATO's position *vis-à-vis* the Warsaw Pact. Gorbachev's proposals thus looked to Washington to be both self-serving and dangerous.

The FOTL issue threatened to become highly divisive and to drive a wedge between Washington and Bonn (Bush and Scowcroft, 1998: 65–71). Recognising the danger, the Bush administration began to work hard to find a solution to the question and to shore up alliance unity. This was achieved by the development of a two-pronged strategy revealed at the NATO summit in Brussels at the end of May 1989. With regard to FOTL, the administration crafted a proposal that promised negotiations on SNF with the aim of a 'partial' rather than a total removal of those weapons. In addition, a final decision on deployment of FOTL would be postponed until 1992 and taken 'in the light of overall security developments' (Department of State Bulletin, 1989). The proposal thus bridged the gap between those in the Alliance who wished to abandon FOTL and those who desired its deployment by putting off the divisive decision.

In addition, and in order to prevent a recurrence of the arguments of 1989 in 1992, the Bush administration crafted new proposals for the ongoing talks on Conventional Forces in Europe (CFE). In particular, the administration proposed that the US and USSR agree to an equal ceiling on troop levels in Central Europe of 275 000 and do so by 1992 or 1993 rather than 1997 as currently planned (ibid.: Declaration of Heads of State and Government, 20). The great advantage of this proposal was that it helped to neutralise the FOTL question. If the USSR agreed to it there would be no need to deploy FOTL since the crucial conventional imbalance between the two alliances' forces would have been eliminated. If they rejected it then the NATO allies would rally behind deployment in the face of Moscow's intransigence.

SEIZING THE INITIATIVE

Skilful US diplomacy thus served to head off serious divisions within NATO and between Washington and Bonn. Nevertheless, the FOTL issue served as a timely warning of the dangers of inaction in the face of adroit Soviet diplomacy: it also reinforced the growing perception within the Bush administration that it was vital to begin setting the agenda rather than reacting to the initiatives of others.

A key area in which the administration believed that it was possible to seize the initiative was Eastern Europe. Gorbachev had already hinted that the USSR was prepared to acknowledge the right of self-determination for that region in his speech to the UN in December 1988 (*Washington Post*, 8 December 1988, A32; Gorbachev, 1995: 683–6) and the National Security Council staff now suggested that the US should begin putting such promises to the test (Bush and Scowcroft, 1998: 40, 15–16). The appeal of that idea was reinforced by concrete evidence of real reform in Eastern Europe, particularly in Poland and Hungary. When the Polish government and the opposition Solidarity movement agreed terms for elections in April 1989, Bush seized the opportunity to declare his administration's 'vision of the European future'. It was now possible, he declared

> to dream of the day when East European peoples will be free to choose their system of government and vote for their party of choice . . . If we are wise, united and ready to seize the moment, we will be remembered as the generation that helped all of Europe find its destiny in freedom (Public Papers, Bush: 17 April 1989).

The implications of this vision for Germany were not lost on the Bush administration. In the process of formulating the new policy, National Security Adviser Brent Scowcroft told Bush that the administration must now give serious thought to German unification as part of its overall objectives and, moreover, that it should be supportive of that goal. Such a belief was reinforced by considerations arising from the FOTL issue and the need to shore up the Washington–Bonn axis (Zelikow and Rice, 1995: 28–9). Accordingly, on 31 May 1989 in the West German city of Mainz, Bush publicly stated that the unification of Germany was now an explicit goal of his administration. Declaring that 'the Cold War began with the division of Europe. It can only end when Europe is whole', he said that 'we seek self-determination for all of Germany and all of Eastern Europe' (Public Papers, Bush: 31 May 1989).

Thus, for all its initial caution, the Bush administration proved to be bolder and more visionary in its contemplation of the European future than either Gorbachev or its European allies, including the government in Bonn. Bush's readiness to embrace such radical change was, in turn, strongly informed by his implicit confidence in the stability of West German democracy. Unlike many European leaders, Bush was possessed by none of the atavistic fears which characterised their reactions to the idea of German unification. That much was implicit in his remarks in Mainz, but later in 1989 he spelled it out quite explicitly.

> I think there's been a dramatic change in post-World War Two Germany. And so, I don't fear it [unification] . . . I think there is in some quarters a feeling – well, a reunified Germany would be detrimental to the peace of Europe . . . and I don't accept that at all, simply don't (Public Papers, Bush: 18 Sept. 1989).

Both Bush's early acceptance of German unification as a realistic policy objective and his lack of qualms about its implications would prove vital to his administration's successful manipulation of the unification process.

GERMAN UNIFICATION: AMERICAN CALCULATIONS

Thus, by the time Bush's rhetorical call for the freedom of Eastern Europe became a dramatic reality in the second half of 1989, his administration was already psychologically and politically prepared to address the consequences. But one other crucial individual deserves mention here. As the crisis in East Germany had unfolded, Chancellor Helmut Kohl of West Germany had begun to see emerging before him the opportunity to achieve the ultimate political prize for any West German Chancellor. When the Berlin Wall came down on 9 November 1989, Kohl rushed to Berlin to call for the right to self-determination for 'all Germans' and to proclaim that the road ahead now lead to 'unity, right and freedom' (Zelikow and Rice, 1995: 103). He formalized his goal in a speech to the Bundestag on 28 November in which he outlined a ten point plan for gradual unification by means of first establishing a confederation between the two German states (German Information Center, 1989; Diekmann and Reuth, 1996: 157–211; Larres, 2000a: 52–3).

This open call for unification caused consternation, not only in Moscow, which saw the chief prize of its victory in World War II and the keystone of its western security system threatened, but also in most of the capitals of Western Europe – where governments which had always publicly supported unification in the secure knowledge that it was never going to happen – now had to contemplate the uncomfortable prospect of a united Germany dominating Europe once again. Thus, not only was it Gorbachev who claimed that German unification was 'no issue of current policy' (Hutchings, 1997: 95), Prime Minister Margaret Thatcher of the United Kingdom similarly declared that 'the question of borders is not on the agenda. They should stay as they are.' (ibid., 96; Thatcher, 1995, 790–806)

The one exception to the general reluctance to contemplate German unification was the government of the United States, and George Bush in particular – possibly the first in his own administration to back unification unequivocally. More generally, and 'alone among leaders of the Western Alliance and the Soviet Union' according to his Deputy National Security Advisor, he really did believe that the Germans had changed and was 'prepared to gamble a very great deal on that faith'. Hence it was no surprise when the day after Kohl announced his plan for unification to the Bundestag, Bush called him personally to express his support (Gates, 1996: 484).

There were a number of reasons for the Bush administration's swift embrace of Kohl's plan. The first quite clearly was Bush himself who sensed – correctly as it turned out – that after nearly 40 years West German democracy had become so deeply entrenched that any change in Germany's international status could do little to upset Germany's and the German people's attachment to democratic norms and procedures. Bush also had a good deal of faith in NATO and the European Community. Again he calculated that West Germany's political class had everything to gain, and much to lose, if it abandoned the very institutions which had brought it security and prosperity – and so long as the new Germany remained securely integrated into both there was nothing to fear. Indeed, given these realities, unification would represent a clear victory for western policy and would end the division of Europe on western terms.

There was also a more pragmatic consideration. Despite Bush's faith in Kohl, there were still nagging fears that, if necessary, Bonn would do a deal with Moscow in order to attain unification and that the price of such a deal might be German neutralism and the consequent collapse of NATO (Larres, 1996). This fear was exacerbated by the popularity of Mikhail Gorbachev in West Germany in the late 1980s. Within the German government, the Foreign Minister, Hans-Dietrich Genscher in particular, was seen by some in the Bush administration as overly enthusiastic about Gorbachev and his reforms (Pond, 1993: 165–6; Bush and Scowcroft, 1998: 195). The emergence of unification as a real possibility made the fear of 'Genscherism' much more tangible. The nightmare scenario for the US was one in which Gorbachev agreed to German unification but only if a united Germany was neutral (Zelikow and Rice, 1995: 154). In such a scenario, faced with the choice of unity *or* NATO, the German people were bound to choose the former over the latter. Moreover, American insistence on a united Germany's membership of NATO would mean that it, and not the USSR, would be perceived by the German people as the obstacle to unification. The crucial objective of American diplomacy, therefore, was to ensure that Bonn insisted that both unity *and* NATO membership were non-negotiable. Such an insistence would, in turn, make Moscow's demands for German neutrality the perceived obstacle to unification.

Thus, when the administration quickly recognised in November 1989 that unification was becoming inevitable, it became vitally important to be on the inside, shaping the policies that would bring unification, rather than on the outside, opposing it. As State Department Counsellor Robert Zoellick observed, 'our strong support for the process would make it more likely that the German people would voluntarily stay within western structures' (Pond, 1993: 161). In addition, there was also the question of the impact of German unification on Gorbachev's domestic position to consider. Once again, being in a position to influence the process was in the United States' best interests (Baker, 1995: 165; Bush and Scowcroft, 1998: 190).

The administration's desire to shape the process of German unification was evident in the speed and nature of its response to events. By mid November 1989, even before Kohl's speech to the Bundestag, the State Department's Policy Planning Staff had come up with an approach to German unification emphasising four central principles:

1. The United States should support German self-determination without endorsing a specific outcome.
2. Unification must be consistent with German membership of NATO and the European Community.
3. Movement towards unification should be peaceful and gradual.
4. On the question of postwar boundaries, the terms of the Helsinki Final Act should be observed (Zelikow and Rice, 1995: 113; Public Papers, Bush: 4 Dec. 1989).

Of the four the second was obviously the Bush administration's chief concern. By moving this early it clearly hoped to set the terms of the debate.

Besides keeping Germany inside NATO, the other essential role of US diplomacy was to try and persuade both the Soviet Union and the Western Europeans to accept German unification. Because of the unique nature of the US–Soviet relationship and America's central role in NATO, the United States was in the prime position to perform both tasks. Bush accordingly informed President Gorbachev at the December 1989 Malta summit that he would not seek in any way to exploit the German question (Gates, 1996: 484; Gorbachev, 1995: 692–9) and persuaded the NATO summit of the same month to endorse German reunification over British opposition.

THE DIPLOMACY OF GERMAN UNIFICATION: TWO PLUS FOUR

The key questions now for American diplomacy were the pace of unification and the nature of the process. In early 1990 even Chancellor Kohl did not envision unification taking place for four or five years. Within weeks, however, both he and Washington had changed their minds. The reason for this was the accelerating decline of East Germany. The East German regime was bankrupt, its government powerless to act and its people increasingly saw their future in a united Germany. Put crudely, East Germany was falling apart; it was not going to last another four or five years and unification was going to have to come sooner rather than later. In fact, this prospect was far from unattractive to the Bush administration since it calculated that the longer the process took the greater would be the opportunities for Moscow to find ways to obstruct it. At present Moscow was clearly off balance and uncertain as to how to respond to events that threatened to overwhelm it. A rapid unification process might serve to keep things that way and present Moscow with a *fait accompli* (Zelikow and Rice, 1995: 160).

But the administration was not of one mind. The National Security Council staff (like the West German government itself) was in favour of unification being negotiated solely between the two Germanies. The NSC staff in particular saw no reason to allow the USSR a role and believed that unification would occur most quickly if left to the Germans alone (ibid., 167–8). Secretary of State James Baker, however, felt that an attempt to exclude the USSR, not to mention the UK and

France, was 'a recipe for a train wreck' should one of those three attempt to obstruct the process. The State Department, moreover, was looking at the problem in the wider context of US–Soviet relations and believed that the USSR had to be offered some form of face-saving role, both in order to win its acceptance of unification and to protect Gorbachev against his own domestic hardliners (Baker, 1995: 198; Bush and Scowcroft, 1998: 234–5).

The procedure the State Department Policy Planning Staff proposed to achieve this task became known as '2+4'. Under this process the details of German unification would be decided by the two Germanies plus the four occupying powers (US, USSR, UK and France). Thus, '2+4' would be a mechanism *for* unification, not a forum for arguing for or against it, and all matters of substance relating to unification would be decided by the two Germanies alone. The only formal role of the four occupying powers would be to surrender their occupation rights. The NSC staff opposed the idea right up until its formal acceptance at the Ottowa summit in February 1990 but Baker and the State Department eventually won the argument (Baker, 1995: 215; Zelikow and Rice, 1995: 167–8; Pond, 1993: 180).

The NSC staff were not the only people who had to be persuaded of the virtues of '2+4'. Moscow had also to be cajoled into accepting the plan; and the goal of the Bush administration was to give the Russians a role that would prevent their humiliation but which would not allow them to throw a spanner in the proverbial works. The great fear was that, given the crucial importance of East Germany to the USSR, both in strategic terms and as a symbol of the victory over Nazi Germany, its loss could precipitate a hardline backlash against Gorbachev which might even remove him from power. Thus American thinking on Germany was always 'cast in terms of how it would affect the continued process of reform throughout Eastern Europe and the Soviet Union' (Bush and Scowcroft, 1998: 190). Gorbachev and his advisers had come round to the idea of a six-nation process independently before Baker's visit (Boll, 1996–97: 113; Gorbachev, 1995: 714–17). The US sought a means to lessen the pain of the loss of East Germany; '2+4', it was hoped, would serve this purpose. It would give Moscow the dignity of appearing to play a part in the unification process without giving it any real power over the substance of the matter.

In early February 1990 Baker flew to Moscow to try and persuade Gorbachev of the virtues of '2+4'. As part of his effort to woo Gorbachev he suggested that a united Germany inside NATO, denuclearised and tied to the US, would pose less of a threat to the Soviet Union than an independent, non-aligned Germany which might feel the need to acquire nuclear weapons. Gorbachev admitted that he had also been toying with some form of six power structure and agreed that '2+4' was a 'suitable' way forward. Even more significantly, he declared that German unification was 'nothing terrifying' and that while he remained opposed to a unified Germany being inside NATO he could see that the continued presence of US troops 'could have a constructive role' (ibid., 205; Gates, 1996: 490; Zelikow and Rice, 1995: 182–4).

Nor was it only Moscow which had to be persuaded of the merits of '2+4'. On 31 January 1990 Genscher gave a speech at Tutzing in which he spoke out against four power structures and said that unity should be negotiated by the two Germanys alone. Furthermore, according to Genscher, after unification, NATO (and the Warsaw Pact) would only become 'elements' of new Europe-wide security structures and the Conference on Security and Cooperation in Europe (CSCE) would play a strengthened role (Hutchings, 1997: 111). Genscher's remarks, in particular those about future European security structures, were greeted with some anxiety in Washington. The Bush administration was adamantly opposed to any dilution of NATO's role or any absorption of it into the talking-shop of the CSCE (Bush and Scowcroft, 1998: 236–7; Genscher, 1995: 709ff.). Moreover, with Kohl due to fly to Moscow in a few days, it was imperative that Washington and Bonn were as one on the key questions in order to prevent the Russians exploiting divisions between them.

Genscher's concerns about four-power interference were easily laid to rest when he met with Baker in Washington on 2 February. Once Baker assured him that '2+4' was designed to prevent four-power obstruction rather than facilitate it Genscher was amenable to the idea (Baker, 1995: 199–200). Following that, Bush wrote to Kohl in order both to express his absolute support for unification and US readiness to resist Moscow's efforts to obstruct that process in any way. He also used the opportunity to reiterate US preferences concerning the process and above all the imperative need for a united Germany to remain in NATO (Bush and Scowcroft, 1998: 240–1). Kohl later described this letter as 'one of the most important documents in the history of US–German relations' (Hutchings, 1997: 117).

With the Bush administration's views on the unification process thus absolutely clear in his mind, Kohl was able to go to Moscow and present Gorbachev with a united US–West German front. With Kohl also pledging significant economic aid for the USSR and accepting that NATO troops would not be deployed on the territory of the former East Germany, Gorbachev said that he was prepared to accept unification as a matter for the German people to decide (Zelikow and Rice,

1995: 188). The joint Soviet–German communique released after the meeting between the Soviet leader and Chancellor Kohl declared that:

> the Germans themselves must resolve the question of the unity of the German nation and themselves decide in what kind of state system, in what time frame, at what speed and under what conditions they want to bring about this unity (*New York Times*, 11 February 1990: A1, 21; Pond, 1993: 179).

But, importantly, not in which alliances they would be members.

BRINGING IN THE RUSSIANS

It thus seemed clear that by the middle of February 1990 Gorbachev was finally prepared to accept unification (we now know from his own memoirs that at a small meeting with his advisers in January 1990, he had come to the conclusion that unification was almost certainly inevitable). This was then confirmed at the Ottowa conference on 'Open Skies' at which Baker was able to secure the agreement of all six relevant parties to the '2+4' process. The announcement of this agreement clearly stated that the two Germanies would discuss all internal aspects of unification while the four powers would discuss only the external aspects. It was also made clear that while the '2+4' could discuss anything, it could only formally negotiate the ending of four power rights in Berlin. The scope of the talks was thus tightly circumscribed to curb Russian leverage. More interestingly, the announcement also stated that, on unification, Germany would have full sovereignty and no limitations on its choice of alliance (American Foreign Policy: Current Documents, 1990: 348).

The Ottowa announcement thus implied that Moscow was now ready to accept all of the West's terms for unification, including NATO membership. A month later however Gorbachev appeared to reverse course, declaring on 6 March 1990 that 'we cannot agree to [a united Germany being in NATO]. It is absolutely ruled out' (Baker, 1995: 235). This shift was confirmed at the first meeting of '2+4' officials on 14 March when the Soviet delegation denounced moves towards rapid unification and demanded a far broader mandate for the '2+4' process than had been announced at Ottowa, including discussion of the question of NATO membership (Zelikow and Rice, 1995: 225).

This kind of reversal would prove to be characteristic of Moscow's diplomacy on the question of German unification. There would be a series of false dawns, such as Ottowa, when the USSR would appear to concede Western demands only to retract that concession in their next public announcement. This vacillation was a product of two factors. In the first place, it is clear that the speed of the unification process took the Soviet leadership utterly by surprise. Baker realised this in his meeting with Soviet Foreign Minister Eduard Shevardnadze in Ottowa, when the latter at one point said 'we are trying to think things out, to find variants and solutions, I just don't know.' (Baker, 1995: 209)

The other reason for the confusion in the Soviet position was domestic politics. While Mikhail Gorbachev and Eduard Shevardnadze wanted to pursue a policy of interdependence and co-operation with the West, both were aware of the enormous symbolic and strategic importance of East Germany. In the Soviet Union the division of Germany was seen as the great prize of World War II, the tangible reward for the terrible sacrifices of the Soviet people in that conflict and an assurance that the German menace would never arise again. To accept unification – moreover unification within NATO – was bound to be more than many could bear. In fact, Shevardnadze told Baker at Ottowa that at the recent Plenum of the Communist Party of the Soviet Union Politburo member Yegor Ligachev had talked of 'a new Munich', and warned that the conservatives were seeking to use Bush's support for Gorbachev against the reformers (ibid., 208–9).

The Bush administration understood this and responded accordingly. The key issue was NATO. It was German unification inside NATO which was the real problem. The absorption of the keystone of the Warsaw Pact into its main military opponent was a bit much to swallow – even for proponents of the 'new thinking'. Given that German membership of NATO was a non-negotiable issue as far as Washington was concerned, the administration was faced with a very clear but immensely difficult task, namely, to persuade Moscow that German membership of NATO was not a threat to the USSR. The obvious way to do this was to adapt NATO structures and goals in such a way as to make the institution itself appear less of a threat to Soviet security interests.

In early 1990 the Bush administration therefore decided that a major overhaul of NATO strategy was required. In February it put together an interdepartmental group, under the chairmanship of Robert Gates, to analyze the question of NATO's future role (Bush and Scowcroft, 1998: 262). Following this, Bush announced in early May that he would be 'calling for an early summit of all NATO leaders' in order to 'launch a wide-ranging NATO strategy review for the transformed Europe of the 1990s'. The review would focus on four key areas: NATO's political role in Western Europe; conventional defence; nuclear defence and the future role of the CSCE (Public Papers, Bush: 4 May 1990). In making such a declaration Bush was taking a significant risk. He was promising to achieve a major reform of NATO before he had consulted his alliance partners as to whether they were prepared to go along with it. He was clearly driven to take this risk by the importance of finding some form of *quid pro quo* for Russian acceptance of German unification inside NATO.

Another part of this strategy of reassurance was the so-called 'incentives package'. This stemmed from a list of 'seven questions' which Shevardnadze had first raised in a speech to the European parliament on 19 December 1989. These 'questions' included; recognition of existing borders; the future status of the German armed forces and other troops stationed on German soil; the place of a united Germany in Europe's 'military–political' structures, and the national security interests of other states (Hutchings, 1997: 106). The 'questions' effectively constituted a list of concerns which Moscow required to be addressed before German unification could be contemplated. Bush and Kohl consequently agreed to work on a combination of unilateral concessions delivered by Bonn and a number of pledges by NATO that Washington would seek to deliver which would address those concerns. A preliminary version of this package was revealed to the Soviets by Baker when he visited Moscow in mid May. The key points were:

1. A united Germany would not develop or possess nuclear, chemical or biological weapons.
2. German borders must be settled on unification.
3. Soviet troops would be allowed to remain in the former East Germany for a number of years.
4. NATO troops would not be deployed on East German territory for a transitional period.
5. There would be a ceiling on the size of the German armed forces as well as on those of other central European countries, to be formalised in a CFE 2 treaty.
6. NATO would review and revise its strategy.
7. NATO would agree to negotiations on SNF.
8. NATO would agree to an upgrading of the role of the CSCE.
9. Development of Soviet–German economic relations and the fulfilment of all GDR economic obligations to the USSR (Baker, 1995: 250–1; Bush and Scowcroft, 1998: 273–4).

The US and West Germany were thus engaged in a policy of 'trying on two levels to bribe the Soviets out of Germany'. The Germans were offering a range of financial and economic sweeteners while the US sought to make unification inside NATO more palatable (Gates, 1996: 492). There was no indication in the Soviet response, however, of any readiness to give ground in return. They said that any ceiling on the armed forces of a united Germany must be fixed by the '2+4' and not wait for a CFE 2 and, crucially, that NATO membership was not an option. Baker returned from this visit convinced that Gorbachev and Shevardnadze were under severe pressure not to compromise on this issue (ibid.; Baker, 1995: 251).

The first indication of a softening of the Soviet position came at the US–Soviet summit in Washington at the end of May 1990. When the question of German unification was raised for discussion, Bush reiterated the US position that a united Germany must be a member of NATO. He also presented a slightly revised version of the incentives package and told Gorbachev that the US intended to unveil a reformed NATO at a summit now scheduled for early July. In response, Gorbachev initially reiterated the standard Soviet line but then, after further discussion, suddenly declared to the visible consternation of his own advisers that it should be up to the German people to decide what alliances they wished to join (Bush and Scowcroft, 1998: 281–3; Zelikow and Rice, 1995: 278–9; Baker, 1995: 253; Gorbachev, 1995: 721–3, 728–36). When the Soviet delegation accepted the insertion of a similar form of words into the final summit communique, Washington at last had a direct acceptance of German unification inside NATO (Public Papers, Bush: 3 June 1990).

Domestic political pressures, however, continued to shape Gorbachev's attitude to unification. On 12 June Gorbachev told the Supreme Soviet that he would accept a united Germany as a member of NATO providing there was a transitional period during which military forces in the former East Germany retained 'associate membership' of the Warsaw Pact (*New York Times*, 13 June 1990, A1, A18). That was a qualification that Washington was not prepared to accept but nevertheless Moscow appeared to have made the main concession (Zelikow and Rice, 1995: 304–6).

At the 22 June ministerial meeting of the '2+4', however, it appeared that the Washington summit had been yet another false dawn. The Soviet position at this meeting was that the '2+4' settlement should merely be an interim agreement. Four Power rights should remain in place until 1992, when a further convening of the '2+4' would occur to assess German behaviour in the intervening period and to decide whether to relinquish Four Power rights. In addition, all the GDR's international commitments, including its membership of the Warsaw Pact, should be maintained for five years after unification. In effect, the Russians were declaring that if they could not halt unification, then they insisted on major constraints on the sovereignty of a united Germany. This was as hardline a stance as they had taken since their initial refusal to contemplate the possibility of unification at all. In a private meeting after the ministerial meeting James Baker asked Shevardnadze what was going on. The Soviet foreign minister admitted that his statement had been dictated by domestic political concerns and manoeuverings. He told Baker that if the US wanted unification within NATO then the forthcoming London NATO summit must produce an outcome that allowed Gorbachev to declare that NATO was no longer a threat (ibid., 300; Baker, 1995: 257).

The London summit thus became a crucial moment. If Bush could deliver on his promise to initiate a major review of NATO strategy he would provide Gorbachev with the means to accept German unification despite the Soviet hardliners. With this in mind, Bush decided to short-circuit the normal NATO decision-making process of submitting proposals to the NATO bureaucracy and instead circulated his proposed reforms directly to the NATO heads of government for their approval. Despite considerable disquiet about both method and content, Bush was able to get his way with the forceful backing of the Germans and, with minor modifications, the summit approved the Bush proposals (Bush and Scowcroft, 1998: 293–4).

The resulting 'London Declaration on a Transformed Atlantic Alliance' outlined a radical overhaul of NATO strategy and structure. NATO would invite the Warsaw Pact governments to establish diplomatic liaison missions at NATO and to work with NATO on matters of common concern. There would be a move away from the strategy of Forward Defence towards one stressing mobility. Moreover, the strategy of the early first use of nuclear weapons would be abandoned in favour of a policy of 'minimum deterrence'. There was also a commitment to future negotiations on SNF and to seek further deep cuts in conventional forces in a CFE 2 negotiation. Finally, there was a pledge to upgrade the role of the CSCE with the creation of a secretariat and parliament and a crisis management centre (NATO Review, 1990: 32–3). Essentially the message being sent was that NATO was acknowledging the decline of the Soviet threat and moving away from an aggressive military posture. The USSR would be assured of a full role in future debates on European security by its membership of the CSCE and through direct contact with NATO.

The London declaration proved to be a decisive event. Eduard Shevardnadze would later write that 'without the decisions passed by the NATO council in London, membership of Germany in NATO would have been unacceptable to us' (Shevardnadze, 1991: 145). Now they were able finally and decisively to lay the matter to rest. When Chancellor Kohl visited Moscow in mid July he and Gorbachev agreed that a united Germany would be a member of NATO; that once unification was completed Four Power rights would end and Germany would have full sovereignty; that Soviet troops would be allowed to remain in the former GDR for 3–4 years; that for that period NATO troops would not be stationed in the former East Germany, though units of the German armed forces not integrated into NATO could be, and that NATO commitments to common defence would apply to the whole of the united Germany. Germany would also commit itself to a ceiling on its armed forces of 370 000 at the time of the completion of a CFE treaty and would not possess or develop nuclear, chemical or biological weapons (*New York Times*, 18 July 1990, A1, A4; Zelikow and Rice, 1995: 341–2). With these agreements the way was finally clear for unification to go ahead.

CONCLUSION: UNIFICATION AND GERMAN–AMERICAN RELATIONS IN THE 1990S

The American contribution to German reunification was thus enormous. As even Genscher later admitted; 'if America had so much as hesitated, we could have stood on our heads and gotten nowhere' (Pond, 1993: 186; Borinski, 1997). And in every key external aspect of the unification process the role of the Bush administration was crucial. Bush's unequivocal support for Kohl in particular helped drive the process forward and reinforced the latter's vital commitment to membership of NATO. It was that same unswerving US support which forced even reluctant Western European allies such as the UK into line behind unification. Finally, it was the ability of the US to drive through NATO reform which ultimately led to Soviet acceptance of German unification on western terms. Thanks in large part to the diplomacy of the Bush administration, a development with the potential to uproot structures and relationships developed over the previous 40 years occurred with barely a ripple.

The unification of Germany proved to be the high point of US–German relations and for a while at least it seemed that Bush's declaration at Mainz that the two were now 'partners in leadership' would be fulfilled (Public Papers, Bush: 31 May 1989). Certainly, Bush's successor – Bill Clinton (1993–2001) – viewed the new Germany in this way; and indeed many felt that Washington in the 1990s had made a quite conscious decision to abandon the special relationship with London in order to create a new one with Bonn. There was perhaps some truth to this. The new Germany after all (unlike the United Kingdom) did stand at the heart of the new European economic and political order and, moreover, was likely to play a far more central role in Central European and Russian affairs. But to pose the question in this either–or way is far too simple. As Clinton himself revealed over a whole series of issues (from NATO expansion to EMU) in the end the United States did not have any special relationship with one specific country but a series of interests in Europe – which could only be served if it had good relations with all its allies. Furthermore, close relations with the new Germany did not of itself eliminate every single difference between Germany and the United States, as disputes over European agricultural reform, Bosnia, Kosovo, Franco-German defence co-operation and the Middle-East revealed only too clearly. The US was particularly incensed by what it saw as Germany's inept handling of the situation in the former-Yugoslavia in the early 1990s. The Kohl government's almost unilateral action in recognising Croatia in 1991 led to a severe crisis in the western alliance and German–American relations (Libal, 1997). Washington was equally concerned by Germany's blank refusal to adopt a more belligerent stance towards both Iran and Iraq.

It would be wrong, however, to suggest that these various frictions – irritating though they undoubtedly were to both sides – amounted to any kind of significant crisis in bilateral relations. The fact remains that if Germany continued to need the United States, the United States continued to need Germany. This reality is clearly demonstrated in the centrality of Germany to the two institutions, NATO and the EU, which form the core of US interests in Europe. No other country plays such a vital role in both institutions. While France is a driving force in the EU, it remains cautious about NATO and American dominance of that organisation. The UK, in contrast, while ardently committed to NATO, remains outside the core of the EU, even under the more Euro-friendly labour government of Tony Blair (Larres, 2000b).

Germany, in contrast, is equally committed, and vital, to both institutions. Thus, as the Clinton administration seeks to deepen its economic integration with the EU and expand that relationship into a global partnership – as for example demonstrated by the signing of the New Transatlantic Agenda in December 1995 – so the US–German partnership remains as vital as ever. Moreover, the successful eastern expansion of NATO with the inclusion of Poland, Hungary and Czech Republic in April 1999 was a project about which Germany had been noticeably more enthusiastic than either France or the UK and it thus contributed to the further cementing of German–American relations in the post-cold war era. With Germany also central to the third key US goal in Europe, encouraging the development of democracy and free markets in Russia and the CIS, the US–German partnership looks set to remain a vital one in the twenty-first century.

REFERENCES

American Foreign Policy: Current Documents, 1990 (Washington D.C: USGPO, 1991), 'Statement of the Foreign Ministers of the GDR, FRG, France, USSR, UK and the United States, Ottowa,' 13 February 1990, 348.

Baker, J. with T.M. DeFrank (1995), *The Politics of Diplomacy: Revolution, War and Peace, 1989–1992* (New York: G.P. Putnam's Sons).

Boll, M.M. (1996–97), 'Superpower Diplomacy and German Unification: The Insiders' Views,' *Parameters* (Winter).

Borinski, P. (1997), 'Deutschland und die USA in den 1990er Jahren', in K. Larres and T. Oppelland (eds), *Deutschland und die USA im 20. Jahrhundert: Geschichte der politischen Beziehungen* (Darmstadt: Wissenschaftliche Buchgesellschaft), 277–302.

Bortfeldt, H. (1997), 'Die Vereinigten Staaten und die deutsche Einheit', in K. Larres and T. Oppelland (eds), *Deutschland und die USA in 20. Jahrhundert: Geschichte der politischen Beziehungen* (Darmstadt: Wissenschaftliche Buchgesellschaft), 256–76.

Bush, G. and B. Scowcroft, (1998), *A World Transformed* (New York: Alfred A. Knopf).

Department of State Bulletin (DOSB), August 1989: 'The Alliance's Comprehensive Concept of Arms Control and Disarmament,' 30 May 1989.

Department of State Bulletin (DOSB), August 1989: 'Declaration of Heads of State and Government, North Atlantic Council, Brussels,' 30 May 1989.

DePorte, A. (1979), *Europe Between the Superpowers* (New Haven: Yale University Press).

Diekmann, K. and R. G. Reuth, eds (1996), *Helmut Kohl: Ich wollte Deutschlands Einheit*, 3rd edn. (Berlin: Ullstein).

Eisenberg, C. (1996), *Drawing the Line: The American Decision to Divide Germany, 1944–1949* (Cambridge: Cambridge University Press).

Gaddis, J.L. (1997), *We Now Know: Rethinking Cold War History* (New York: Oxford University Press).

Gates, R.M. (1996), *From the Shadows: The Ultimate Insider's Story of Five Presidents and How they Won the Cold War* (New York: Simon and Schuster).

Genscher, H.D. (1995), *Erinnerungen* (Berlin: Siedler).

German Information Center (19 Dec. 1989), *Statements and Speeches*, Vol. XII, No. 25.

Gorbachev, M. (1995), *Erinnerungen* (Berlin: Siedler).

Hutchings, R.L. (1997), *American Policy and the End of the Cold War: An Insider's Account of US Policy in Europe, 1989–1992* (Baltimore: Johns Hopkins University Press).

Küsters, H.J. and Hofmann, D., eds (1998), *Deutsche Einheit: Sonderedition aus den Akten des Bundeskanzleramtes, 1989/90* (Munich: Oldenbourg).

Larres, K. (1996), 'Germany and the West: The "Rapallo Factor" in German Foreign Policy from the 1950s to the 1990s', in K. Larres and P. Panayi (eds), *The Federal Republic of Germany since 1949: Politics, Society and Economy before and after Unification* (London/New York: Longman), 278–326.

Larres, K. (2000a), 'Germany in 1989: the Development of a Revolution' [Chap. 2 of this book].

Larres, K. (2000b), 'Uneasy Allies or Genuine Partners? Britain, Germany, and European Integration', in K. Larres (ed. with E. Meehan), *Uneasy Allies: British-German Relations and European Integration since 1945* (Oxford: Oxford University Press), 1–24.

Libal, M. (1997), *Limits of Persuasion: Germany and the Yugoslav Crisis, 1991–92* (Westport, Conn.: Praeger).

NATO Review (1990): 'The London Declaration on a Transformed Atlantic Alliance,' 6 July 1990, Vol. 38, No. 4, 32–33.

Pond, E. (1993), *Beyond the Wall: Germany's Road to Unification* (Washington D.C: Brooking's Institution).

Public Papers of the Presidents of the United States: George Bush, 1989: 'Remarks to Citizens in Hamtramck, Michigan,' 17 April 1989 [online version at http://www.csdl.tamu.ed/bushlib/papers].

Public Papers of the Presidents of the United States: George Bush, 1989 'Remarks to Citizens in Mainz, Federal Republic of Germany,' 31 May 1989.

'The President's News Conference in Helena, Montana,' 18 September 1989.

Public Papers of the President of the United States: George Bush 1989 'Outline of Remarks at the North Atlantic Treaty Organization Headquarters in Brussels,' 4 December 1989.

Public Papers of the Presidents of the United States: George Bush, 1990: 'Remarks at the Oklahoma State University Commencement Ceremony in Stillwater,' 4 May 1990 [online version at http://www.csdl. tamu.ed/ bushlib/ papers].

Public Papers of the Presidents of the United States: George Bush, 1990 'News Conference of President Bush and President Mikhail Gorbachev of the Soviet Union,' 3 June 1990.

Shevardnadze, E. (1991), *The Future Belongs to Freedom* (London: Sinclair-Stevenson).

Thatcher, M. (1995), *The Downing Street Years*, paperback edn (London: HarperCollins).

Zelikow, P. and C. Rice (1995), *Germany Unified and Europe Transformed: A Study in Statecraft* (Cambridge, Ma: Harvard University Press).

Index

The index excludes such terms as Germany, West and East Germany, FRG, GDR, West and East Berlin, German Question, German Unification as well as scholars mentioned in the text but not actively involved in the activities under consideration. German political parties and some well known institutions/organisations have been listed under their German names.